The Environment in Corporate Management

*To Andrée-Claude,
and Catherine, Clara, Daphne and Ophelia,
who endured our absence during those weekends
when this book took precedence.
May we one day be forgiven.*

*And to all those managers and directors who
under strong pressures
try to do what they believe is right
in an often unforgiving environment.*

The Environment in Corporate Management

New Directions and Economic Insights

Jean-Baptiste Lesourd

Research Professor, Groupe de Recherche en Economie Quantitative d'Aix-Marseille (GREQAM), Ecole des Hautes Etudes en Sciences Sociales, Université de la Méditerranée and Université d'Aix-Marseille III, France

Steven G.M. Schilizzi

Senior Lecturer in Natural Resource and Environmental Economics, Agricultural and Resource Economics, Faculty of Agriculture, The University of Western Australia, Australia

With a foreword by David W. Pearce OBE and preface by Lena Gevert

Edward Elgar
Cheltenham, UK • Northampton, MA, USA

Published by
Edward Elgar Publishing Limited
Glensanda House
Montpellier Parade
Cheltenham
Glos GL50 1UA
UK

Edward Elgar Publishing, Inc.
136 West Street
Suite 202
Northampton
Massachusetts 01060
USA

A catalogue record for this book
is available from the British Library

Library of Congress Cataloguing in Publication Data

Lesourd, Jean-Baptiste.
    The environment in corporate management : new directions and economic
insights / Jean-Baptiste Lesourd, Steven G.M. Schilizzi ; with a foreword by
David Pearce and preface by Lena Gevert.
       p. cm.
    Includes bibliographical references and index.
    1. Social responsibility of business. 2. Green marketing. 3. Business ethics.
    4. Environmental management. I. Schilizzi, Steven. II. Title.

    HD60 . L467 2002
    658.4'08—dc21
                                             2001051070

ISBN 1 85898 916 7 (cased)

Printed and bound in Great Britain by MPG Books Ltd, Bodmin, Cornwall

Contents

Contents	*v*
List of Figures	*x*
List of Tables	*xi*
List of Boxes	*xii*
Foreword	*xiii*
Preface	*xvii*
Acknowledgements	*xix*

1. Introduction — 1

1. Purpose and scope — 2
2. Environmental management: an emerging field — 3
3. Environmental management and the stakeholder approach — 5
4. Outline of the book — 9

2. Environmental management and its benefits to the firm's stakeholders — 15

1. Introduction — 16
2. The firm and the environment: general considerations — 17
3. Directly managing environmental resources, or resources with direct environmental effects — 26
4. Managing environmental risks: its benefits to the firm — 34
5. Indirect costs and benefits of environmental management — 36
6. Conclusion — 39

3. Environment and business ethics — 44

1. Introduction — 45
2. Foundations of environmental ethics for business — 46
   2.1 Overview — 46
   2.2 Environmental ethics — 48
   2.3 Foundations of environmental ethics — 51
   2.4 Changes in social expectations — 55

3. Corporate environmental ethics   56
    3.1 Ethics and economics: two conflicting sources of corporate
        governance?   56
    3.2 Ethical values of different stakeholders   64
    3.3 Globalisation and cross-cultural issues   65
    3.4 Environment and the firm's core values and 'corporate culture'   66
4. Implementing corporate environmental ethics   67
    4.1 Ethical and unethical actions with various stakeholders   68
    4.2 Compliance or proactive initiatives ?   70
    4.3 Ethical values across the firm's structure and hierarchy:
        initiative and implementation   72
5. Are environmental investments ethical investments?   73
6. Conclusion   76

Case study: 'Ethos' (Switzerland).   77

4. **Corporate environmental accounting**   94

1. The foundations of environmental accounting: finance, economics
    and society   95
    1.1 Definition, scope and purpose   95
    1.2 Benefits and costs   96
    1.3 Environmental accounting and the crisis of traditional
         accounting   97
    1.4 The appearance of new accountees   100
2. The practice of environmental accounting   103
    2.1 Overview: the three stages of environmental accounting   103
    2.2 Accounting for environmentally-related financial impacts   106
    2.3 Ecological accounting: towards activity and product
         ecobalances   114
    2.4 Eco-financial integration for assessing environmental
         management performance   123
3. The future of environmental accounting and the issue of contingent
    liabilities   126
    3.1 Valuing environmental liabilities as part of a company's total
         value   126
    3.2 Progress using shareholder and stakeholder value concepts   129
    3.3 Strategic accounting and the bridge to finance and economics   130
4. Conclusions   133
Case studies: A comparative analysis of several corporate accounting
    strategies   134

5. **Corporate environmental reporting**   150

1. Introduction   151
2. Innovative pressures and resistance to change   151
    2.1 Externalities as a source of demand for environmental reporting   152

2.2 The economic rationale of supplying environmental reports 154
2.3 Accountants as instrumental stakeholders in the demand and supply relationship 157
2.4 The appearance of new accountees and their influence on environmental reporting 159
3. The economics of disclosure 160
3.1 Value of information and costs of disclosure 160
3.2 Information entitlements and rights 161
3.3 Determinants of information disclosure 162
3.4 Optimal disclosure 163
3.5 Role of government authorities 164
3.6 Globalisation and disclosure 164
4. The economics of information quality 165
4.1 What is information quality? 165
4.2 Optimal, not maximum quality 167
5. Environmental reports as optimal compromise products 168
5.1 The use of environmental reports 168
5.2 Evaluating environmental reports 170
6. Towards a common accounting framework for corporate environmental reporting 176
7. Corporate benefits of auditing and certification 184
8. Conclusion: higher levels of optimal environmental disclosure? 186

Case studies: Wirralie Gold Mine (Normandy) Ltd., and WMC Ltd. (Australia) 188

6. Environmental management and corporate finance 199

1. Environment in corporate finance: an introduction 200
2. Investment appraisal and project management: some first principles 201
3. The environmental aspects of investment projects 213
3.1 General considerations 213
3.2 The value drivers of environmental investments 217
3.3 Practical assessment of environmental aspects of investments 226
4. The environment, stock markets and financial activities 229
4.1 The environment and financial intermediaries 229
4.2 The environment and banking activities 229
4.3 The environment, financial investments and stock markets 232
5. Conclusion 240

Case studies: Triodos Bank (NL) and Barclays Bank (UK) 241

7. The management of environmental risks 249

1. Introduction 250
2. Environmental risks and insurance 252
2.1 Background 252

2.2 Conditions of insurability 253
2.3 Characteristics of environmental risks 255
2.4 Limitations of insurance as a means of managing environmental risks 259
3. Managing environmental risks: conventional insurance and alternative techniques 262
3.1 A range of instruments for managing environmental risk 262
3.2 Total or almost total risk retention 264
3.3 Captive insurance companies 267
3.4 Conventional insurance and its variants 273
4. Conclusions 277

Case studies: 'Renflex' and Swiss Re (Switzerland) 278

8. Environmental management systems: the ISO 14001 and EMAS international standards 286

1. Introduction 287
2. Emergence of the ISO 14000 and EMAS families of environmental management norms 288
3. The ISO 14001 EMS norms 298
3.1 Overview 298
3.2 Step 1: The firm's environmental policy 302
3.3 Step 2: Planning the environmental policy 307
3.4 Step 3: Implementation and operation 309
3.5 Step 4: Checking and corrective action 312
3.6 Step 5: Management review 313
3.7 The other features of the ISO 14001 standard 313
3.8 The EMAS standards 315
4. The certification of EMSs: ISO 14001 certification and EMAS registration 320
4.1 General considerations 320
4.2 The value and shortfalls of ISO 14001 and EMAS certification 320
4.3 ISO 14001 certification, and globalisation 323
5. Conclusions 326

Case study: ST Microelectronics (France – Italy) 327

9. Eco-marketing and the environmental quality of goods 338

1. Introduction 339
2. Signalling the quality of goods and services 341
2.1 The problem of the environmental quality of goods 341
2.2 Environmental labelling: economic principles 343
3. Environmental marketing techniques 348
3.1 Environmental advertising, self-declared environmental claims, and other environmental declarations 348

Contents

3.2 Third-party certified environmental labelling or ecolabelling
(ISO Type I-labelling)   351
3.3 Organisation marketing and other indirect environmental
marketing techniques   355
4. Life-Cycle Assessment (LCA) and its implications   359
4.1 From cradle to grave   359
4.2 Implications for the environmental aspects of operations
management   363
5. Eco-marketing and the demand for environmental quality   365
5.1 General considerations   365
5.2 Investigating the demand for environmental quality   366
6. Conclusion   367

Case study : Volvo (Sweden)   368

10. Conclusions   376

1. What take-home message?   377
2. What new directions in environmental management?   381
3. What economic insights, and why?   383
4. Environmental management, or sustainable development?   385

Index   389

List of Figures

4.1 Example of a hidden liability (liability for cleaning up polluted property) to be taken into account in the balance sheet of firm B, which is taken over by firm A   111
4.2 The difference between standard accounting and strategic account   132
5.1 Industrial ecology model   176
7.1 Profile for profits and losses against cumulated covered occurrences: the insurer with no reinsurance, and the insurer with reinsurance above some maximum value M for cumulated occurrences   261
7.2 Profile for profits and losses against cumulated occurrences: the case of a self-insured corporation   266
7.3 Profile for profits and losses against cumulated covered occurrences for the operation of a captive, as compared to conventional insurance, with reinsurance above some maximum value M for cumulated occurrences   272
8.1 The ISO 14000 norms: an overview   295
8.2 The continual improvement cycle of the ISO 14001 norms   300

List of Tables

1.1	The logical structure of the book	10
2.1a	The firm's stakeholder relationships	24
2.1b	The firm's stakeholder categories	26
2.2	Examples of firms with EMSs	40
4.1	Typical simplified balance sheet for an industrial company	108
4.2	Environmental items in a typical simplified balance sheet for an industrial company	109
4.3	Environmentally related costs and benefits	113
4.4	Energy accounting for a hotel company	115
4.5	Environmental (atmospheric) impact accounting equivalents	120
5.1	Master Environmental Account	180
6.1	Ratings of bonds by major rating agencies	207
6.2	Practical guideline for environmental or P2-investment calculations (environmental increments for more global projects)	227
6.3	Assessing the environmental risk of a loan: a checklist of questions	231
6.4	Triodos Bank key figures (1997–99)	241
7.1	Techniques available for the management of environmental risks	263
7.2	Environmental performance indicators for the Zürich facilities of Swiss Re	283
8.1	A comparison between ISO 14001 and EMAS	318
8.2	Number of ISO 14001 certifications per country (March 2000)	324
8.3	Dates of ISO 14001 certification and EMAS registration or validation for the sites of ST Microelectronics worldwide	328
9.1	The main signalling techniques for the environmental quality attributes of products according to the ISO 14020 sub-group of norms	347
9.2	National and international ecolabelling schemes	352
9.3	Ecolabels for organic foods and other agricultural, forestry and fish products	354
9.4	LCA technical references, guidelines and standards	361
9.5	Example of an environmental impact evaluation matrix	362
9.6	The evolution of Volvo's financial data (1997–99)	369
9.7	Environmental performance of Volvo's production units worldwide	370

List of Boxes

3.1   Criteria having had an appreciable impact on the rating of companies by Ethos and its subsequent investment decisions   82

8.1   The detail of the ISO 14000 norms   296

8.2   Outline of the ISO 14001 norms   301

8.3   Environmental policy statement of the Sony group (1999)   306

8.4   The environmental policy statement of ST Microelectronics   331

8.5   The environmental decalogue of ST Microelectronics   333

9.1   An example of an environmental charter: the CERES principles   358

Foreword by Professor David W. Pearce

Do firms care about the environment? If they do, why do they care? If they don't, why should they care? On the face of it, the last two decades have seen a sea change in the way that corporations approach environmental issues. Firms now race each other to achieve environmental management standards, more than token sums of money are invested in environmental education, wildlife and habitat conservation, maintaining panels of 'green advisors', ensuring continuing dialogue with conservation groups, assessing the portfolio of investments to minimize environmentally risky liabilities, and so on. Firms seem to care where twenty years ago they seemed not to care. Many resist this environmental concern. They claim they have not seen the evidence for the 'triple bottom line' of sustainable development: environment, social responsibility and profit. In between the committed and the resisters lies a whole range of intermediary positions – some concern, some indifference, some hostility, some uncertainty about what exactly to do. It is against this backdrop that a huge, and some would say unmanageable, literature has emerged on corporate environmental management. It is not too cynical to say that much of this literature has all the characteristics of rent seeking. The consultants and, less frequently, the academics have seen the opportunity to exploit the nervousness within much of industry about environmental issues and, more recently, about social responsibility to vulnerable groups at home and abroad. Rent-seekers aren't always too concerned to get their advice right, or to root it in rigorous analysis. The end result is a mass of really very poor, opportunist and ill-thought-out advice on responsible corporate management. The spin doctors are in there too. Once a firm commits itself to receiving and paying for advice, management has a concern to maximize its own returns from 'being green' or 'being responsible'. I have been to many corporate presentations proclaiming a 'new' way of thinking, a new set of 'green' accounts, or a new way of showing that firm X is well on the way to being a sustainable corporation. Most of them do not stand up to scrutiny.

How has this state of affairs come about? I am convinced that many managers want to be responsible and green. They are nervous because they have to look over their shoulders at what shareholders want, but shareholders are changing too, as is witnessed by the emerging power of green and ethical funds. In other cases, management simply wants to comply with whatever is the relevant social and environmental legislation. They are content to be 'in compliance' and may go as far as achieving a management standard in the belief that this is good publicity and a way of keeping the regulators and the pressure groups off their backs. The reasons that we do not have a wholesale movement towards socially responsible management is (a) because there are still serious tensions between profit and social responsibility, and (b) because the case for being green has been made so superficially that any sensible management would doubt the wisdom of making the change. That superficiality rules is the fault of those who, like me, know it can all be done much better but have failed to make the effort. Visions of the totally socially oriented firm are pipe dreams: ultimately, private corporations are there to make profit and turning the firm into a social service is not going to square with that truth. But it is clear that firms can go a very long way down the road to being social organizations. En route, they will find they can make some more profit by being responsible, as this volume shows. After a point, they will discover that there are real choices to be made – social concerns against the price of their shares.

What is needed, then, is a cool, detached look at environmental and social responsibility in the context of the firm, an analysis unclouded by the rent seekers and one that utilizes the formidable insights that come from the dramatic developments in economics in the last few decades. This is why I welcome Jean-Baptiste Lesourd and Steven Schilizzi's book. It takes the viewpoint of the firm and it brings to bear on the various issues the general findings of the theories of industrial organization and microeconomics, but the authors have done this without being 'academic' in the sense of being obscure. This volume is not littered with maths and formal proofs. Rather, the intuition and results from that thinking have been turned into practical observation and recommendation.

So why are firms interested in the environment? Undoubtedly a major force is the need to comply: environmental and social regulation has advanced independently of corporate concerns, but the incentive not to comply has also been reduced. Monitoring and enforcement of policy are tougher than they ever were. Movements towards citizen information about who pollutes and by how much can do a great deal to ensure compliance. Governments are even now asking regulators to check that utilities serve social and environmental goals as well as complying with their duty to benefit consumers. It simply doesn't pay to under-comply. It also pays to anticipate what is going to happen next, something a few firms are very good at but which most are still not. Some firms will look at the international negotiations on climate change and say 'I told you so: you threatened us with carbon taxes and the need to get into tradable emission permit schemes, and it isn't going to happen.' Maybe not, but it is interesting that most corporations have made no change at all to their environmental plans simply because they suspect climate negotiations will fail. In other words, the motivating forces are elsewhere. Compliance is the least that the workforce now expects. Employees are a strong force for over-compliance because they have a sense of pride in being in a corporation that is leading the way. The story of green consumers is well known. Green investors will be the next big force to push for over-compliance, but there are some green managers too; people who are simply committed to making an environmental and social improvement. Perhaps these are the same people who protested quietly in the 1960s. Perhaps they have swapped the flowers in the hair for a pin-striped suit, without losing all their idealism.

Laggards there will always be. Some of the transport industries have barely started on the environmental and social journey. In the United Kingdom, road hauliers and some farmers demonstrated their lack of environmental credentials by direct action against fuel taxes explicitly introduced to serve environmental ends. They were joined by commuter groups who said they were forced to use their cars because the government did not invest enough in public transport. Ironically, the revenues from the very tax they protested about were to be earmarked for investment in public transport! The story is there to remind us not to oversell the green and responsible corporation or the green citizen. Deep down, many people still have a restricted view of what it means to be a global citizen. I am convinced that it will stay that way until corporate environmentalism is shown to rest on far more secure foundations than so far demonstrated in the popular literature. Jean-Baptiste Lesourd and Steven Schilizzi have done a first-class job of creating those foundations. At last, we have something on which to rest our case.

Professor David W. Pearce

University College London

Preface by Lena Gevert

From the management of environmental issues to environmental management

The work of Jean-Baptiste Lesourd and Steven Schilizzi about the environment in corporate management is topical and timely. I am pleased and honoured to have been able to write a short preface for this book.

In the Volvo group, we have been concerned with the problem of environmental management for a long time. Back in 1972 the CEO of Volvo, Mr. Pehr G. Gyllenhammar, stated that environmental care is also of the highest importance for corporations. He stated that the responsibility for reducing environmental impact from traffic and vehicle production is shared between the industry, the vehicle users and society.

Many studies have been made about the development of environmental management at Volvo. If there are differences between Volvo and other companies, I think that difference lies in the attitudes towards legislation and requirements from authorities. We have always participated in discussions about coming legislation, in order to get agreements of what is achievable. Meeting new requirements, however, usually costs money, at least in the short term. Minimizing cost is one of the most obvious management rules. So, these three approaches have constantly been brushed against each other, and we have found our way to cope with the issues.

Volvo assigned a corporate environmental auditor as early as 1989. The auditor, together with the specially assigned Environmental Task Force, organized the structure for requirements and follow-up of environmental performance, long before any international environmental management systems were discussed.

When the EMAS proposals were published in 1993, we had an obvious opportunity to gain internal acceptance and external publicity by being first in our industry to adopt a formal environmental management system (EMS). So we did.

We have extended the EMS to include all parts of our value chain: from suppliers and product development to marketing and dealers. Hereby we have a framework for distributing requirements, positions and decisions to all parts of the organization. Introducing environmental management systems is not seen as something required from us, but as a tool for structuring cost-effective management of environmental issues.

During our implementation of EMS, we have been in close contact with people who work with Quality Management Systems, and now new systems will be integrated as Business Management Systems. All types of business have a need to structure the different requirements; from customers to authorities, employees, and the owners, and that is what the systems are for: to find the facts, understand the facts, make an inventory of the impact from the business, set goals and improve! The continuous improvement is the most important part.

In their book, Jean-Baptiste Lesourd and Steven Schilizzi develop at length the issues of EMS implementation and of international norms such as ISO 14001 and EMAS. They also mention a number of other relevant issues, such as environmental accounting, the financial and insurance implications of environmental management, and of business-ethics problems related to environmental management. All in all, the book is an excellent guide to the world of business and the environment!

Lena Gevert

Director, Environmental Affairs, AB Volvo, Göteborg, Sweden

Acknowledgements

We would like to thank the following people for reviewing certain chapters and providing us with feedback and useful comments and suggestions:

- Professor Andrew Brennan, Department of Philosophy, University of Western Australia
- Professor Roger Burritt, Australian National University, Canberra
- Professor Ephraim Clark, Middlesex University Business School, UK
- Professor Pierre-André Dumont, HEC, Université de Genève, Switzerland
- Dr Bob Ewin, Department of Philosophy, University of Western Australia
- Dr Miriam Heller, Program Director, National Science Foundation (USA)
- Dr Greg Hertzler, Agricultural and Resource Economics, University of Western Australia
- Professor Jacques Pasquier-Dorthe, Université de Fribourg, Switzerland
- Professor John Quiggin, Australian National University, Canberra
- Professor Michael Shanks, Ecole Supérieure de Commerce Marseille-Provence, Marseille, France
- Professor Stefan Schaltegger, University of Lüneburg, Germany
- Dr David Webb, Faculty of Commerce, University of Western Australia

In addition, we would like to acknowledge and thank the University of Western Australia for having, through the Distinguished Visitors Program of its International Centre, through a Research Award granted to one of the authors, and through its study leave scheme, greatly facilitated the achievement of this work. Thanks are also extended to the Agricultural and Resource Economics group and the Faculty of Agriculture of the

University of Western Australia, as well as to the Université de la Méditerranée, for having funded a Visiting Lectureship, and to the GREQAM (Research Group in Quantitative Economics of Aix-Marseille), for having provided the authors with a favourable working environment. The collaborative agreement between the University of Western Australia and the Université de la Méditerranée, facilitated by Dr Bruce Mackintosh of the UWA International Centre, is also acknowledged. We would also like to thank Ms. Annette Baumann for her help in editing the final version of the manuscript. Finally, we gratefully acknowledge permission given by the British Standards Institute (BSI) to reproduce extracts from BS EN ISO 14001 (1996) under licence number 2001SK/0133.

1. The Environment in Corporate Management: an Introduction

SUMMARY

This chapter introduces the subject of the book and specifies the approach, audience, goals and scope of the work. We start by explaining the precise wording of the title and sub-title, and emphasize the fact that we have adopted the firm's point of view to the exclusion of any other. We also word a basic assumption; that the emergence of environmental concerns corresponds to a gradual revelation of costs and benefits previously hidden to the firm and to its stakeholders. Accordingly, the stakeholder approach is chosen as a framework for analysis, within which we choose to give economic analysis a special role. This is because, in our view, it is lacking from an otherwise luxuriant literature, a point David Pearce already drew academics' and practitioners' attention to. The chapter ends by outlining the purpose and content of each of the following chapters of the book.

1. PURPOSE AND SCOPE

The title of this book was given purposely; inasmuch as it reflects the whole orientation of our work, let us explain why. Although it is now developing as a new branch of business management, corporate environmental management is not, or not yet, an established field or sub-discipline, such as corporate or business accounting. Referring to the latter as to 'accounting in business management', would perhaps be odd, because the question whether accounting is an essential part of business management has already definitely been solved. Not so for environmental management. Although important, it is but an emerging field, rather than an established one. Clearly, *all businesses*, even the smallest ones, are concerned by accounting. Accounting is an essential element of their business practices. This is not true in the case of environment, the introduction of which into management practices is by no means universal in the business world, even if this sounds unfortunate to environmentally conscious persons. Of course, big firms operating in environmentally conscious advanced countries usually do introduce environment into their management practices, especially when their production, or their product, pollutes or damages the environment, or makes intensive use of non-renewable resources.

Our title is thus related to one of the key ideas of our book. In the case where environmental concerns are important and identified as such, environmental management can appear as an autonomous and established management field, and this is reflected in the actual practices of firms. In other cases, the concern is rather diffuse. As will be stressed in many parts of our book, this concern is often related to hitherto *hidden* costs and benefits, or to *hidden* liabilities and assets. It is often by revealing these hidden elements that the environment may be introduced into existing management strategies.

Finally, our title means that we develop environmental management *from the point of view of the firm,* as other branches of management are usually developed. We are conscious, of course, that other attitudes are possible. An extreme point of view would be some kind of 'green' fundamentalism, whereby only zero levels of pollution are acceptable. That would lead us to refuse altogether our industrial societies as they stand. At the other extreme, one could say that these problems do not really matter, and that the market will provide for every adjustment. Neither of these points of view is ours. Our aim is rather to describe how the natural environment may be integrated into business management strategies.

We aim at directing our analysis not only to firms with dedicated environmental management systems, but also to those firms for which the environment is a more diffuse concern. In both categories, one is mostly dealing with large firms that are also public companies quoted on the stock exchange, because disclosure constraints and economic feedback mechanisms are stronger in their case; but private companies, as well as small and medium-sized enterprises (SMEs), are increasingly concerned.

2. ENVIRONMENTAL MANAGEMENT: AN EMERGING FIELD

Environmental management (EM) is an emerging and innovating field. It is characterized by new developments, is moving very fast, and is taking up all the resources of new technologies. Just twenty years ago, at the beginning of the 1980s, the characteristic and new features of EM that we are going to discuss in this book were either completely unknown or still in their infancy. At that time, early discussions about the social responsibilities of firms had already begun, but in the financial community, for instance, the vast majority of investors were not even aware of what corporate ethics could possibly mean. Just after the 'oil shock' of 1973, that is, in the middle of the 1970s, very few ethical investment funds, as we know them today, existed. Even fewer people considered that the environmental aspects of corporate behaviour had ethical implications. At that time, concepts such as ISO 14001 certification, ISO 14000 environmental norms and ecolabels, which are widely used and discussed today, were completely unknown. Talking about them would have been like talking about the social organization of the inhabitants on planet Mars in a science fiction book! Even at the end of the 1980s, a very small number of 'green' investment funds, selecting the stocks of companies according to their environmental behaviour, existed, mainly in the United States, and the ISO 14000 norms were still an unknown concept.

In this book we intend to discuss these very young management concepts that constitute as many *new directions*, specific to the newly established field of environmental management. We shall also attempt to understand the economic rationale commanding the development of these new management tools, so as to develop economic insights into their many aspects. Trying to give a full and exhaustive description of this emerging field as it stands now is a difficult exercise. Clearly, we admit that the description we have attempted is not a complete one. Rather, we try to focus on key *new directions* in our field and on their essential and characteristic features. The review of the literature, and the list of references that we give in the book, are in line with this focus.

As far as *economic insights* are concerned, one of the questions we shall be trying to answer is the following. In a real-world market economy, with democratic institutions, if public opinion (and, therefore, consumers) are concerned with their environment, and if markets are sufficiently competitive and transparent, will firms be compelled by market forces to take steps towards protecting our environment ? The short answer is yes in a number of cases, even if environmental management efforts of environmentally conscious firms are not (or not yet) sufficient to achieve some kind of sustainable growth. Moreover, there have recently been some efforts from national accountants, and from business accountants as well, to define what could be 'sustainable growth'. Simon and Proops' recent book (2000), titled *Greening the Accounts*, provides a timely overview. In Chapter 4, we shall further focus on the corporate aspects of 'green' accounting.

In the presentation of our topic, we wish to be as clear and didactic as possible, presenting analytical developments in such a manner that lay people can understand them. However, our book is also a work of research, trying to explore, if not an altogether new field, at least an emerging field seen under a new angle; namely, that of economic analysis. In this respect, we also made this book advanced, and it should appeal to researchers in an applied discipline – management – that wish to comfort their practices and their techniques by leaning on the scientific approaches of modern microeconomics and industrial organization.

Much work has already been devoted to environmental management and related topics. Yet, we believe – at least to our knowledge – that little work has used the analytical tools of microeconomics and of industrial organization to make an in-depth analysis of management *practices* as far as the environment is concerned. One of the important new facts is that, in a market economy with sufficiently competitive and transparent markets, and with environmentally conscious citizens and consumers, firms will be rewarded for their environmental achievements, and will face penalties if they indulge in environmentally poor practices. In this book, we wish to lean on economic theory to have our readers reach an in-depth understanding of why, or through what mechanisms, managing the environment is, in many cases, in the firms' interests, but we also wish to describe, practically and clearly, the management techniques that are already being used. To this end, case studies and examples will illustrate our discussion. We also believe that it is possible, at the level of this book (aimed as it is at a rather broad audience), to develop economic analyses in an understandable manner, without entering into mathematical developments that might only be useful for academic researchers. Although the topic of our book is *cross-disciplinary*, the economic approach is a most important aspect of the problem of environmental management: firms sell goods on the market place, and environmental concerns influence their markets. Thus, the core question this book addresses is this: to what extent will market mechanisms induce business firms to include the environment *in* their standard management practices, as per the title of the book? We believe economic analysis will also help clarify how managers may optimally respond to these new pressures.

3.   ENVIRONMENTAL MANAGEMENT AND THE STAKEHOLDER APPROACH

In today's discussions regarding the firm, the so-called *stakeholder* approach has become popular. It even tends to dominate many areas of corporate management, including the emerging field of environmental management.

Stakeholder theory presents itself as an attempt to provide new answers to an old question: *in the interest of whom* is the business firm working? At first sight, at least until the 1920s, the dominant idea of both economists and practitioners of management was that, like it or not, the sole objective of the firm was to make profits. When Thorstein Veblen introduced, in a famous book (1923), the concept of *absentee ownership*, it appeared as dissenting with the accepted ideas of the day. Of course, Veblen's path-breaking book lead to the idea of the *managerial firm*, and fuelled a vivid debate among economists. This debate has been recurrent in the economic and management literature, in the USA and elsewhere, at least since the 1920s. The positions in this debate run as follows. On one side, there are people contending that the only objective of the firm is profit maximization, or *shareholders' value*. On the other side, we find other people contending that the firm's objective is some kind of a compromise between the necessarily conflicting interests of various stakeholder groups, shareholders being of course one of them.

Except perhaps in the case of firms which are still owned and controlled by the family of some historical entrepreneur, the idea of the managerial firm implies, especially in the case of public companies, that it is managed in the interest of its appointed directors rather than in the interest of its shareholders. This idea, although it has been under strong criticism at least since the beginning of the 1980s, has been quite popular in the United States since the great depression of the 1930s. It even came to the point of being an accepted theory, at least within the Keynesian stream of economic thought, as it has been expressed by Keynes himself (1936):

> As a result of the gradual increase in the proportion of the equity in the community's aggregate capital investment which is owned by persons who do not manage and have no special knowledge of the circumstances, either actual or prospective, of the business in question, the element of real knowledge in the valuation of investments by those who own them or contemplate purchasing them has seriously declined.

The managerial theory was also made popular by authors such as Galbraith (1967). In truth, it was hardly a new idea even in Veblen's time, since one can trace it back to Adam Smith, who, in his *Wealth of Nations* (1776), already describes the managerial public company as being managed in the interest of its managers rather than in the interest of its shareholders:

> The trade of a joint stock company is always managed by a court of directors. This court, indeed, is frequently subject, in many respects, to the control of a

general court of proprietors. But the greater part of those proprietors seldom pretend to understand anything of the business of the company, and when the spirit of faction happens not to prevail among them, give themselves no trouble about it, but receive contentedly such half-yearly or yearly dividend as the directors think proper to make to them. This total exemption from trouble and from risk, beyond a limited sum, encourages many people to become adventurers in joint stock companies, who would, upon no account, hazard their fortunes in any private copartnery. Such companies, therefore, commonly draw to themselves much greater stocks than any private copartnery can boast of . . . The directors of such [joint stock] companies, however, being the managers rather of other people's money than of their own, it cannot well be expected that they should watch over it with the same anxious vigilance with which the partners in a private copartnery frequently watch over their own. Like the stewards of a rich man, they are apt to consider attention to small matters as not for their master's honour, and very easily give themselves a dispensation from having it. Negligence and profusion, therefore, must always prevail, more or less, in the management of the affairs of such a company.

Here, Smith clearly points out that the modern public corporation conveys some conflicts of interests, one of the most conspicuous being the conflict of interest between its managers and its shareholders. According to Smith, this is a question of inefficient organization due to a lack of suitable incentives, in which we recognize Smith's *utilitarian* standpoint. However, Smith's words 'negligence and profusion', which convey the idea of unethical behaviour of managers (and detrimental to the firm's shareholders), also imply an *ethical* standpoint.[1]

The stakeholder approach can be considered as a generalization of an old debate on the conflicts of interests that are observed in the modern corporation. One of these is the conflict of interests between the managers and the owners of the firm. Another obvious one is the conflict of interests between labour (the firm's employees) and capital (the firm's shareholders or owners), which is also present in the writings of the classics, and is the cornerstone of Marxian economics.

Stakeholder theory is concerned with bridging the gaps between various stakeholders, and finding compromises to solve conflicts of interests in the framework of the corporation viewed as a complex and evolving system. This can be discussed under a utilitarian framework, but also, as implied in

Smith's text, under an ethical framework. The discussions that took place about the managerial firm led to important developments in mainstream economic theory under a utilitarian framework with profit-maximization as the sole objective of the firm. These developments, which follow a seminal work of R. Coase (1937), insist that one of the questions is to provide incentives to managers through efficient contracts. This has been achieved, for instance, in several key papers by H. Demsetz (1967, 1983), among others. Stakeholder theory is a more recent development (Freeman, 1984; Kelly, Kelly and Gamble, 1997). Generalizing an expression that was coined by Veblen (again!) (Veblen, 1919)[2], stakeholders can be defined as all groups of people that have 'vested interests' in the firm.[3] The stakeholder approach views the firm as an interactive system in which all stakeholders have interrelated interests. Starting from an ethical standpoint, it insists on the social responsibilities of business and claims that these responsibilities can be made compatible with profitability. Clearly, protecting the environment is one of those social responsibilities. It creates new obligations toward both existing stakeholders and new groups of stakeholders, as well as new conflicts of interest between them.

Damages to the environment due to acts of production (that is, in market economies, to the very activities of firms) thus recently emerged as creating new conflicts of interests between stakeholders. As will be underlined throughout our book, taking into account the environment in business management acknowledges the existence of new stakeholders who have some more or less diffuse vested interests in the environment: local or 'host' communities, regions, nations and even groups of nations, and public opinion as channelled by various lobbies and the media. Environmental management, however, also increasingly takes into account new demands from traditional stakeholders, such as clients, lenders, insurers, investors and shareholders. Taking into account the new interests of these stakeholders can be done with a utilitarian point of view (looking at the firm's 'bottom line') or with an ethical point of view (examining the firm's behaviour in terms of 'corporate citizenship') (McIntosh et al., 1998). Are these two points of view in conflict? This is one of the big questions that our book wants to tackle (see note 1).

As mentioned previously, it is our belief that, in the real world, and in market economies where environmentally-conscious consumers and democratic institutions prevail, managing the environment is in the interest of shareholders. Environmentally-oriented firms, such as Volvo in Sweden, 3M in the USA, and many others, have been rewarded by the market system for their efforts, while other firms such as Union Carbide (after the Bhopal catastrophe) had to face severe penalties (US$5 billion in the latter case). It is also obvious that some non-market economies, such as the former Soviet Union, and other former Eastern European socialist countries, have had very poor performances in terms of environmental protection.

4. OUTLINE OF THE BOOK

Table 1.1 provides an overview of the book's logical structure. The first two chapters discuss the two basic justifications for corporate environmental concern, homage to Adam Smith's two masterpieces and a balanced view of the economy. The next four chapters examine how environmental management is implemented in practice, the first two focusing on the management of environmental information, and the other two focusing on the financial aspects of environmental management. The last two chapters examine how the firm can communicate the results of its environmental management efforts to its various stakeholders.

The stakeholder approach will reflect from the beginning of our book. In Chapter 2, we discuss the very concept of environmental management, showing that it involves revealing to the firm's stakeholders hitherto *hidden* costs and benefits.

This is a utilitarian starting point that may be completed with an ethical point of view. Thus, corporate ethics will be discussed in Chapter 3 as an important aspect of environmental management. Our approach has been to start with an economic point of view, and to consider the quantitative management tools that may be used to assess the economic objectives of the firm, such as profit, and the quantitative impact of the firm's activity on the environment. We then consider more *qualitative* long-term aspects such as corporate policy towards the environment. Another qualitative aspect, related

Table 1.1 The logical structure of the book

Chapter 2	The two basic justifications for corporate environmental concern		Economics: the profit motive
Chapter 3			Ethics: social responsibilities
Chapter 4	Implementing environmental management in practice	Managing environmental information	Producing the necessary information
Chapter 5			Communicating it internally and externally
Chapter 6		Managing environmental impacts and decisions	Financing environmental management
Chapter 7			Managing environmental risks
Chapter 8	Communicating the firm's environmental efforts to stakeholders		Quality of environmental management
Chapter 9			Quality of environmental products

to features such as environmental quality management, is whether the firm should conform to a code of business ethics. Earlier studies in energy management, a field that is closely related to environmental management, have already considered the role of the environment in business ethics. For instance, the book by J.K. Jacques et al. (1988) included developments on 'Ecology as a system of values'.

Chapter 4 considers the information necessary to achieve effective and efficient environmental management outcomes. To be effective, managers need to be able to measure and integrate the firm's physical, chemical and biological impacts on the environment, so as to know where the main problems are and how they may be corrected. To be efficient, they need to know how they may correct problems to the best of shareholders' satisfaction: by minimizing the costs and maximizing the financial benefits. This is the realm of environmental accounting, which includes both financial and ecological impact aspects. Accountants and managers must face the challenges of identifying and allocating environment-specific financial costs, measuring and integrating many different environmental impacts, and accounting for environmental liabilities, both current and future.

Chapter 5 then examines how a firm's accounts and environmental management efforts may be communicated to its various stakeholders. This is the field of environmental reporting and auditing. A key question is, what information should, and will, a firm disclose to different stakeholders? Here as throughout the book, the two fundamental questions are asked side by side: the ethical, leading to legislation and regulation, and the economic, motivated by market mechanisms. Again, a major emphasis in this book is to combine the two approaches so as to mitigate both 'market failures' and 'government failures'. This chapter logically concludes on the need to provide incentives, so that corporations may wilfully modify their *optimal* level of disclosure regarding their management of the environment. Actually, many firms, even purely private firms[4], are already regularly producing environmental reports. Environmental auditing, and its economic role, is also highlighted in Chapter 5.

Chapter 6 follows with the financial aspects of environmental management. At the level of corporate finance, one of the questions that this chapter will try to answer is: under what conditions can environmentally-oriented and Pollution Prevention (P2) investments be financially of interest? At the level of market finance, we shall discuss the environmental behaviour of firms as one of the criteria of ethical stock-picking, leading to 'green' and 'ethical' investment funds and stock indexes.

Chapter 7 focuses on the management of environmental risks, and the way in which these risks are financed and insured. This includes environmental risk assessment and minimizing the actual probabilities of environmental hazards. Importantly, although environmental risk *assessment* has been amply considered, environmental risk *management* has been dramatically less so. This is mainly due to the technical difficulties of the subject. We believe we can contribute in an innovative way in this emerging field of concern, which also mirrors developments in environmental financial accounting, discussed in Chapter 4.

Chapter 8 discusses the ISO 14000 and the EU EMAS families of norms. They provide a guideline for the implementation of environmental management systems. The discussion of environmental policy is only intended to take place from the point of view of the firm, not as national government policies, which are clearly outside the scope of this book. The focus remains on corporate environmental management throughout. Rather, we shall investigate the implications of the debate concerning regulation versus economic or market incentives on individual business policies. In Chapter 8, corporate environmental policy is discussed within the framework of the ISO 14001 norms.

The ISO 14001 norms may be viewed as an extension of the total quality management (TQM) concept to the environmental qualities of goods, dealt with by the ISO 9000 product quality norms. If we consider quality as anything that may satisfy the consumers' needs, environmental quality is part of quality in general, provided that consumers are concerned with the way the goods they buy are produced with respect to environmental conservation. The ISO 14000 norms indirectly lead to the definition of environmental quality. However, this is only part of the problem regarding the environmental quality of goods, which deserves a full chapter.

Chapter 9 discusses the environmental quality of goods in relation to the various tools that may be used to signal such quality to consumers. This includes the ISO 14000 norms, but also the environmental certification of products and ecolabelling. The concepts of life-cycle assessment and design for the environment, which contribute to the environmental quality of goods, also belong to this chapter. Implementation of the ISO 14001 continual improvement principle results in enhanced environmental quality. The environmental quality of goods, as well as the supply of environmental services are, as several examples will show, a developing and innovating industry. Also, they will in the future most likely be a strong component of sustainable economic growth, or development.

Much work is currently being done in the emerging area of environmental management. Yet, according to David Pearce (1997: p. 122), 'The vast literature on business and the environment is informative but unstructured.' Our approach, rooted in the disciplines of industrial organization and modern microeconomics, will hopefully complement other work, and provide some in-depth understanding of environmental management practices. We hope readers will find this book useful as an original synthesis. This is no small challenge; but at least we shall have put all our heart into it. The stakes are well worth the risk!

NOTES

1. We must remember that Smith appears in his correspondence to have given his second masterpiece, *The Theory of Moral Sentiments*, an equal, if not greater, importance compared to the *Wealth of Nations*. Accordingly, in Chapter 2 we shall espouse the utilitarian view, while in Chapter 3 we shall reflect the ethical view. Throughout, we shall try to highlight by what processes the two can be brought closer.
2. Although in Veblen's original work, that expression was used for large shareholders. It should also be noted that Veblen's work provides an early discussion of damages to the environment that occurred at his time, such as the mass slaughter of the American buffalo, which he showed as leading to huge social losses.
3. R.E. Freeman (1984, p. 46) defines them as 'any group or individual who can affect or is affected by the achievement of an organization's objectives'. In Chapter 4, we provide a narrower but more precise definition: stakeholders are those whose benefits and costs, or welfare, are affected, upwards or downwards, by an organization's decisions or activities.
4. For instance, Cargill, probably the largest trading company worldwide, and one of the largest private companies, has been publishing an annual environmental report.

REFERENCES

Coase, R.H. (1937), 'The nature of the firm', *Economica* (New Series), **IV**: 386–405.

Demsetz, H. (1967), 'Toward a theory of property rights', *American Economic Review*, **57**: 347–59.

Demsetz, H. (1983), 'The structure of ownership and the theory of the firm', *Journal of Law and Economics*, **26**: 375–90.

Freeman, R.E. (1984), *Strategic Management – A Stakeholder Approach*, Boston, MA: Pitman.

Galbraith, J.K. (1967), *The New Industrial State*, New York: Houghton Mifflin.

Jacques, J.K., Lesourd, J.B. and Ruiz, J.M. (1988), *Modern Applied Energy Conservation: New Directions in Energy Conservation Management*. Chichester/New York: Ellis Horwood/Wiley.

Kelly, G., Kelly, D. and Gamble, A. (1997), *Stakeholder Capitalism*, Sheffield: PERC, University of Sheffield.

Keynes, J.M. (1936), *The General Theory of Employment, Interest and Money*, (reprinted 1964), London: Macmillan, p. 153.

McIntosh, M., Leipziger, D., Jones, K. and Coleman, G. (1998), *Corporate Citizenship. Successful Strategies for Responsible Companies*, London: Financial Times: Pitman.

Pearce, D. (1997), 'Corporate behaviour and sustainable development: the view from economics', in P. Bansal and E. Howard, *Business and the Natural Environment*, Oxford: Butterworth & Heinemann.

Simon, S. and Proops, J. (2000), *Greening the Accounts*, Cheltenham, UK: Edward Elgar.

Smith, A. (1759), *The Theory of Moral Sentiments*, London: Printed for A. Millar, A. Kincaid and J. Bell. (A more recent edition by D.D. Raphael and A.L. Macfie (1976), Oxford: Clarendon Press and New York: Oxford University Press).

Smith, A. (1776), *An Inquiry into the Nature and Causes of the Wealth of Nations*, reprinted with an introduction by W. Letwin (1975), London: Dent, Book 5, Chapter 1, pp. 228–9.

Veblen, T. (1919), *The Vested Interests and the Common Man*, New York: B.W. Huebsch Inc.

Veblen, T. (1923), *Absentee Ownership and Business Enterprise in Recent Times: The Case of America*, New York: B.W. Huebsch Inc.

2. Environmental Management and its Benefits to the Firm's Stakeholders

SUMMARY

Chapter 2 examines the basic question of why environmental management (EM) may be of value to the firm. Using stakeholder analysis, and acknowledging value to the firm's direct and indirect stakeholders, it then focuses on how EM may be of value to shareholders. Shareholder value is central to the issue in that it determines the firm's market value and thereby its future. Historically, most of the benefits, but also the costs, of EM, or lack thereof, were hidden or latent. At the end of the twentieth century, they have emerged as significant. Why? Firstly, direct costs or benefits from resource and EM, or lack thereof, appeared following the oil price shock in 1973, which fostered energy but also, as a spin-off, water and other resource-use efficiency. In the 1980s, the development of emission trading permits in the USA and elsewhere further increased direct benefits of EM. Secondly, largely because of highly publicized catastrophes like Union Carbide at Bhopal, but also through new government regulations, environmental risks became a major social, political and, consequently, economic issue. Environmental liabilities soared. Firms had to include environmental risk management, a specific aspect of EM, into their financial and business plans, if they did not want their shareholder value to fall. Thirdly, new indirect costs and benefits of EM appeared through consumer pressure, government licensing, financial markets including so-called ethical investments, and image and reputation effects. Many of the previously hidden costs and benefits have become apparent, warranting various forms of EM.

1. INTRODUCTION

At first sight, there seems to be no reason why a firm should integrate environmental management into its strategies. From an economic point of view, and from that of marketing and business development, there appear to be no incentives for such integration. Environmental management, as defined in the introduction to this study, has been seen as the management of a public good, the responsibility of which should be with the government. Because for the most part the environment is a public good, costs and benefits are not at first sight apparent to the firm. They may be hidden, or at least external to the interests of the firm. Indeed, even when they are apparent, they are often highly uncertain. The opportunity costs of investments in this field may appear too high. However, many firms do practise environmental management, as witnessed by a number of publications, mostly from a practical point of view (Cairncross, 1995; Crognale, 1999; Dallmeyer et al., 1998; Dell, 1995; Harrison, 1993; MacKentum, 1999; Rothery, 1995; Royston, 1989; Sturm, 1998; Welford, 1998 a, b; Wever, 1996).

The purpose of this chapter is to show why and how the integration of environmental management (EM), or the implementation of an environmental management system (EMS) into the firm's strategy can contribute positively to the firm's stakeholders objectives. EM and EMSs may be seen as challenging. This chapter would like to demonstrate that, while being a challenge to the firm's management, an EMS may also be an opportunity towards meeting the interests of the various stakeholders, both in the short and the long run. As a particular case, concerning stockholders, suitable environmental management actions may have a positive effect on shareholder value, depending, of course, on the particular circumstances: every firm, whether large or small, and every production, including the heavy industries as well as some more immaterial services, is in itself a particular case.

This chapter is organized as follows. Following this introduction, the second section presents the general background of the firm's relationship with the environment. How have economists and management scientists approached these problems: what concepts, what methods of analysis have been produced? The three following sections attempt to analyse how the environmental problems that firms face impinge on their management, in particular with respect to their various stakeholders. These three sections discuss the beneficial results of EM actions for firms and their benefits to the various stakeholders. We first examine (Section 3) the possibilities of managing direct environmental costs, and of managing critical resources, such as energy, the use of which is directly related to damages to the environment. More indirect EM concerns are related with the environmental risk, as discussed in Section 4. In Section 5, we shall see that many of these problems stem from indirect, often hidden, interactions, so that the costs that can be reduced, as well as the benefits that can be enhanced through environmental management actions are also, in many cases, indirect and often hidden. We conclude by summarizing the main outcomes of our discussion in terms of environmental management (EM), and environmental management systems (EMS), and highlight the main guiding principles that may be of use in tackling the firm's EM problems. This conclusion is illustrated by some examples of large firms that have successfully integrated the environment into their management practices. We also try briefly to assess how these EM patterns and strategies could ultimately lead to some kind of sustainable development.

2. THE FIRM AND THE ENVIRONMENT: GENERAL CONSIDERATIONS

According to a topical categorization, the firm interacts with its *stakeholders*, that is, people or organizations that have a *stake* or an economic interest in the firm.[1] Most stakeholders interact with the firm through markets. There are stakeholders who sell goods or services to the firm, such as employees (who sell their various labour services), shareholders or bondholders (who sell capital services with various levels of risk), utility companies or various other service companies (who sell energy utilities, or various services such as transportation or telecommunication services), as well as other suppliers (who sell various intermediate goods to the firm, including basic commodities, raw materials or parts, and services such as renting land or real estate for business premises). Other stakeholders, such as public and government agencies, interact with the firm by producing collective or public goods, which are characterized by the fact that they may be consumed simultaneously by several firms or economic agents. In compensation for this, they receive taxes, usually through non-market mechanisms.

Unlike various stakeholders, the environment as such does not interact with the firm through markets, unless it is the object of specific environmental policies that aim at making it interact directly with the economy through suitable payment mechanisms, nor through any direct economic mechanism such as taxes. As will be discussed later, it interacts only indirectly with the firm, as a consequence of so-called external effects to third parties. In the past, as a rule, even these indirect interactions have not been observed, because the firm simply did not care, and did not have to care, about the external effects stemming from its activity, such as nuisances and damages (or sometimes positive effects) to other people's environments. In particular, the environment was absent from earlier discussions of corporate management, such as Taylor's *Scientific Management* (1911), as well as from actual management practices. The services of absorbing and diluting various pollutants and emissions, as supplied by some natural media (the atmosphere, rivers and other freshwater outlets, seawaters, and the soil, were simply considered as free goods), because these media were implicitly considered as infinite. Thus, for a long time, environmental issues have not been on the management agenda of private firms, nor did such firms, or anyone else, care enough to take action. Summarizing, the reasons may be brought under four banners.

Firstly, environmental impacts of industrial activity were not perceived as problems, neither by the firms nor, more importantly perhaps, by the general public or by government authorities. The explanation can come from various fields or disciplines. From a physical and biological point of view, it may be said that depletion, pollution, and various disturbances or nuisances had not reached levels high enough, except perhaps very locally, to be perceived as major problems, or even to be perceived as problems at all. Palaeontologists seem to agree now that the woolly mammoth was driven to extinction by our ancestors who hunted it for meat, tools, fur and basically most of their basic commodities. It is very likely that the relationship of cause to effect of its extinction may never have been perceived given the long expanse of time, in human terms, over which the extinction occurred. It is also very likely that even today, similar processes are at work without anyone having yet perceived them as a problem. Only recently has deforestation, for instance, been designed as a major factor of species extinction. It is well known that in the Middle Ages, whether in Paris or London, or even in ancient Rome, pollution could be an appalling fact, particularly where tanneries were set up. Fish would die, river waters would grow brownish red and emit putrid stenches, downstream effects were not negligible. However, this fact was never conceptualized as a general or social problem, but only as a local technical problem; something akin, perhaps, to an oil leak in one's own garage. One may argue that the lack of general concern was related to the perception and knowledge that these phenomena were very localized and had virtually no impact on the wider environment. The scale of the problem was not large enough.

Secondly, although firms may have known of the impact of their activities on the environment, they did not perceive it to be their responsibility to do anything about it. Such impacts were perceived as necessary by-products of economic activity, the necessity of which dwarfed any other consideration. More importantly, however, and without any contradiction, the environment was perceived as a public good; that is, as will be detailed hereafter, a good the benefits of which cannot be appropriated by anyone in particular. Consequently, it was not the responsibility of the firm to manage it, but the government's. It was a public policy issue, not a business management issue. Accordingly, this assumed that any action would take the form of government regulations. The firm could then, if necessary, enter into negotiations with government administrations in order to mitigate the impact of these regulations.

Thirdly, although firms may know of the impact of their activities and consider themselves as potentially responsible, if they realized that costs associated with these impacts were not borne by them, then why should they bother to do anything about them? They had no incentive for remedial action. If costs were borne by others: local residents, non-local residents, future generations, or plant and animal communities themselves, but the firm itself bore no cost, then, unless it was forced to take action, it would just carry on with business as usual. This aspect of the problem highlights what economists have come to call 'externalities'. If costs are borne by others, then I have no incentive to reduce them.

Another reason why a firm might not wish to reduce external costs was related to the difficulty in measuring these costs and, before doing so, the actual physical impacts on the environment. Many new pollution-measurement apparatus have been built only after the importance of potential impacts on the environment was widely acknowledged. Today, many impacts are still hard to measure with any useful accuracy; for instance, the impact on ecosystem functioning, or the effects of global warming. It is harder for governments to put pressure on firms to reduce negative impacts if there is no way to measure them with a minimum degree of accuracy. This aspect highlights the importance of uncertainty in environmental management decisions.

Finally, benefits arising from actions taken by the firm did not necessarily accrue to the firm. For the same reason that costs associated with environmental disruption were not supported by the firm, benefits from reducing these disruptions would not, or would not all, accrue to it either. The firm would have to support all the abatement costs, but would miss out on the associated benefits. This other manifestation of externalities at work was a further disincentive for private firms to take environmental management on board. Moreover, as with costs, such benefits, even accruing to the firm, could be very uncertain, or hard to measure.

These problems have been discussed through what economists have termed 'externalities'. The concept was first introduced (Kula, 1997) by British economists Alfred Marshall (in his *Principles of Economics*, 1898) and Arthur Pigou (*The Economics of Welfare*, 1920). They first introduced the concept of positive externalities, and second that of negative externalities.

A positive externality is a benefit that an economic agent A bestows on another economic agent B without B compensating A for the benefit thus received. The textbook example is a beekeeper whose bees regularly fly into the neighbouring farmer's fields and help pollinate his or her crops or trees, thus raising yields above what they would have been without bee pollination. Assuming a market value for these crops or tree products, the farmer will earn an extra amount of income that is entirely due to the beekeeper's bees.

Because the beekeeper is not receiving his or her share (potentially 100 per cent) of this extra income, but instead receives no payment at all, the benefit to the farmer is termed an externality. It is a positive externality, also referred to as an 'external benefit', in that it is a benefit that is not paid for. Our beekeeper is therefore not encouraged at all into producing this positive externality, so that, as a rule, he or she will produce it in a less than optimal quantity: we are clearly here not at a Pareto-optimal situation. Marshall used another example, that of the industry as a whole providing benefits to any particular firm, through general scientific and technological developments, infrastructure and network facilities, and possibly economies of scale.

A negative externality is the opposite situation, where an economic agent A imposes costs on another economic agent B and does not compensate B for the damages and costs suffered. Such a situation is typically exemplified by pollution. If a firm pollutes the air of a city or neighbourhood to the point that people fall sick, the rates of asthma and lung disease increase, sunshine and visibility are diminished, and more generally well-being is reduced, and if people do not get compensated in any way for such losses of well-being, health and welfare, a negative externality is said to exist. It is an externality insofar as these costs endured by the local population are not being compensated in any way. It is negative in that it is a cost, rather than a benefit, that is not being compensated. This is why it is also referred to as 'external costs'.

At first glance, only negative externalities may seem to be relevant to the environmental impacts of firms' activities. However, positive externalities may also exist from the pollution-abatement investments and activities a firm may commit itself to and engage in. Although the beneficiaries from these positive externalities may not be the same as the sufferers from the negative externalities, one may think that they do exist. The distribution of uncompensated costs and benefits, that is, who benefits and who suffers, is a different issue from the actual existence of positive and negative externalities.

As the term itself suggests, the environment is something external to the firm. However, suppliers, customers and government, as well as other competing firms, are also, in a sense, external to the firm: they are often called *external* stakeholders. The difference lies in the type of interaction. For the most part, what one might call direct stakeholders, including the firm's employees, the firm's shareholders, its various suppliers and its clients, as well as the government and local authorities interact directly with the firm, through the market and price–quantity relationships, regulatory constraints, or direct feedback behaviour, such as consumer boycotts and government prohibitions. In general, the environment will interact only indirectly with the firm: through modifications in consumers' awareness and product demand patterns, or through government action, often triggered by the action of what one might call indirect stakeholders, such as the general public or the public opinion, environmental pressure groups and the media. These have no direct stake in the firm, except indirectly or through external effects, so that one might call them external stakeholders, to distinguish them from traditional stakeholders who have a direct stake, or 'vested interests'[2] in the firm. This is because the environment is not represented by group pressures having a direct interest in it, since it concerns goods that have no markets and that are characterized by the absence of property rights: the environment cannot speak for itself. There are extreme circumstances, however, when it can 'speak': for instance, when excessive toxic-chemical pollution kills off key resources for the local population, such as fish, or when it causes an immediate threat to human survival; in particular, the firm's own local personnel, as with heavy metal or radioactive pollution. Unless such extremes are reached – and unfortunately they are reached more often than one would wish – the environment will backfire on the firm's agenda only if consumers, neighbours or government themselves react.

Unless such reactions take place, environmental problems and costs will interact indirectly, and may remain hidden to the firm. This can also be true of possible benefits from the firm's efforts to reduce these problems. Pollution reduction, for instance, may, however, go unnoticed by the local population, unless the firm advertises its actions at its own costs, which will add up on top of pollution abatement costs.

The general picture having been set, it is worth specifying in some detail what specific problems the firm may have to face. Tables 2.1a and b attempt to summarize how the environment will enter into the concerns and the interests of the various stakeholders, both 'direct' and 'indirect', 'internal' and 'external'.

To illustrate the above considerations, it is therefore important to answer in some detail the following (closely related) questions. First, how does one introduce the environment into existing management systems? Second, what are the various costs that may be reduced, as well as the various benefits that may be reached, through suitable environmental management efforts?

This means reducing hitherto hidden or latent costs, and increasing hitherto hidden or latent benefits. This also means *a positive impact on most of the various stakeholders' interests*. It is furthermore clear that if the cost of environmental management actions required is proportionate to them, developing an EMS is apt to *increase* the value of the firm to shareholders, that is, *shareholder value*.[3]

Of course, environmental management is not a panacea. It is profitable to the firm only if some necessary conditions are met, whereby its benefits are larger than the costs induced, especially in the long term.

Indeed all categories of costs may be detected and highlighted, and subsequently reduced through suitable EM; this means, more generally, that environmental management concerns all types of resources. Capital costs, the costs of energy and of utilities, and, more generally, the costs of Environment, Health and Safety (EHS) management, labour costs and taxes, are costs that may be reduced, directly or indirectly, at the firm's profit, through adequate environmental management.

To complete the above considerations, it is important to give in some detail the various costs that may be reduced, as well as the various benefits that may be reached through suitable environmental management efforts. What are, from a practical standpoint, the benefits that may be brought about by implementing an EMS system into a firm's strategy? In what way can the costs that have thus been identified be reduced and the benefits also revealed in these preliminary steps be increased? The answers to these questions will be discussed in the next sections, in which three aspects of environmental management will be examined successively. These three aspects consist in the economic impacts and benefits of environmental management for the firm (from the most direct economic impacts to more indirect interactions), taking into account environmental risks, and indirect interactions through the introduction of environmental quality attributes of products.

Table 2.1a : The firm's stakeholder relationships

The firm's relationships concerning the environment		
With whom?	*Through . . .*	*Managed by . . .*
'Direct' stakeholders — Employees	Environmental and security training	Production management, human resources management
Shareholders	Environmental risk	Financial management
Bondholders	Environmental risk	Financial management
Banks	Environmental risk	Financial management
Insurance companies	Environmental risk	Financial management
Various suppliers	Utilities, various materials and Goods	Production management
Clients	'Green' products	Sales management, quality management, marketing management
Government agencies	Environmental regulations, taxes	Public relations management, lobbying
Local authorities	Environmental regulations	Public relations management, lobbying
International bodies (e.g. the EU)	Environmental regulations	Public relations management, lobbying

'Indirect' stakeholders			
	The general public	Indirect or hidden interactions affecting the firm's image	Various channels, direct or indirect
	Environmental pressure groups	Indirect or hidden interactions affecting the firm's image	Various channels, direct or indirect
	The media	Indirect or hidden interactions, through information about the firm	Various channels, direct or indirect

Table 2.1b The firm's stakeholder categories[1]

Stakeholders	Internal	External
Direct	Managers Employees	Shareholders, Investors Lenders, Insurers Suppliers, Customers Tax agency Local community[2]
Indirect	Consultants (employed by the firm) Sub-contractors	Environmental groups, NGOs Environmental Protection Agencies Professional Organizations[3] Media General public

Notes:

1. Definitions used in Table 2.1b are as follows:
Direct stakeholders can be defined as those whose livelihood, in particular whose income, is affected by the firm's activities. *Indirect stakeholders* can be defined as those whose utility, welfare, values, or quality of life is affected by the firm's activities. *Internal stakeholders* are those who are employed by the firm. *External stakeholders* are not employed by the firm. *Internal indirect stakeholders* are those who are occasionally employed by the firm but who have other employers or who are mostly self-employed (e.g. consultants).
2. Local communities are direct stakeholders through income and employment effects and indirect stakeholders through pollution and nuisance effects.
3. For example, the ACCA for British Chartered Accountants.

3. DIRECTLY MANAGING ENVIRONMENTAL RESOURCES, OR RESOURCES WITH DIRECT ENVIRONMENTAL EFFECTS

Direct market costs and benefits resulting from environmental management are the exception rather than the rule, but there may be market interactions for using environmental services whenever environmental services or assets are treated as private goods, especially when environmental policies create market instruments to this effect (about such marketable instruments, see, for instance: Cason and Gangadharan, 1998; Dudek and Palmisano, 1988; Dwyer, 1993; Kulkarni, 1993; Tietenberg, 1994). This is the case for environmental pollution under the US Clean Air Act, which provides for the creation of specific markets for the use of the atmospheric environment. As stated by Tietenberg (1994), this amounts to 'making explicit environmental costs that [hitherto] have been hidden'; these markets are markets for so-called *tradable (or marketable) emission permits.* Under this marketable permit system, industries are ascribed, under a set of regulations concerning air pollution, ceiling emission possibilities for the various pollutants such as SO_2 and NO_x. In the United States, this means that emission permits are issued to firms by environmental protection agencies, generally at the level of the individual states, rather than at the level of the Federal State, through State Implementation Plans (SIPs). These emission permits correspond to a ceiling of emissions for various major air pollutants (sulphur dioxide, nitrogen oxides). However, these permits are tradable, and thus may be sold and rented (by firms who are under their individual ceiling, through anti-pollution investment or through other circumstances) to other firms who either purchase or rent them because they are temporarily above these ceilings. This system aims at encouraging environmental protection investments and discouraging poor environmental performances through direct market incentives. This scheme is clearly based on Ronald Coase's approach to environmental protection. It ascribes externalities to missing markets, because environmental assets such as the atmosphere – while useful to human activities such as production and consumption – are not subject to property rights. They are thus free goods and are used too intensively, thereby encouraging the production of nuisances (negative externalities) (Coase, 1960). However, the efficiency of such a market leads to several requirements, including transparency and information dissemination. This has been one of the objectives of the USA Federal SO_2 Allowance Trading programme, which is managed by the Environmental Protection Agency (EPA). Under this scheme, an allowance authorizes an industrial production unit, or a power plant, to emit one ton[4] of SO_2 during a given year or during some other year afterwards. These allowances were initially (in phase I of the Acid Rain Program, that lasted until the end of 1999), according to the Clean Air Act, as amended in 1990, calculated at an emission rate of 2.5

pounds (lb) of SO_2/million of BTU (British Thermal Units) for existing facilities on the basis of the average fossil fuel consumed by the unit from 1985 to 1987. During phase II of the Acid Rain Program, which started on 1 January 2000, the basis for calculating allowances was toughened and reduced to 1.2 pounds (lb) of SO_2/million of BTU. Allowances are thus allocated on that basis by the EPA. They are freely tradable, and any person, whether an individual, an industrial corporation, a trader or a broker, a public body or an environmental association or group, may either purchase, keep or sell any quantity of allowances. There is an Allowance Tracking System, which is managed by the EPA, whereby it is ensured that any unit complies with the legal requirements, which are that its SO_2 emissions in any given year must be backed by allowances valid for this given year, whether they come from an initial allocation or from purchases or transfers. New units will in principle not be given allowances, but energy-saving or pollution-prevention investments (including renewable energy sources substituting for fossil fuels) will as a rule give rights to allowances on the basis of the nominal power of the source. A further feature of the system is that, in order to foster the liquidity of the market, out of 8.95 million allowances allocated each year, which is a cap for the total SO_2 emissions in the USA after the year 2000, 200 000 allowances will be traded in auctions run by the Chicago Board of Trade (CBOT) for either spot sales (of allowances valid within the auction year) or advance sales (concerning allocations that will become usable for a subsequent period of seven years). Thus, there is an organized market for SO_2 allowances in the USA, on top of the existing over-the-counter market (which previously used not to be very efficient), so that the market overall is gaining in both efficiency and liquidity. The evolution of prices for SO_2 allowances has been recorded since the beginning of the market in 1994; this price was US$145 at the beginning of the recording (August 1994), reached an all-time low at US$69 (March 1996) and peaked at US$212 (May 1999). A recent valuation was US$136 (March 2000).

In California, a state known for its stringent norms on atmospheric pollution, this market-instruments approach has been well developed (Dwyer, 1993). This was achieved through Air Quality Management Districts (AQMD), in charge of validating and certifying marketable permits; in particular, the South Coast Air Quality Management District (in the Los Angeles area) will certify Emission Reduction Credits (ERCs) for firms having carried out pollution-reduction investments such as equipment alteration, new Air Pollution Control (APC) devices, or process change, as well as equipment removal, or putting-out-of-use facilities. ERCs may concern any of the basic pollutants, including sulphur dioxide (SO_2) nitrogen oxides (NO_x), reactive organic gases (ROGs), particulate matters (PMs), carbon dioxide (CO_2), and carbon monoxide (CO); they may be sold on a lb/day basis. Under the Regional Clean Air Incentives Market (RECLAIM), launched at the beginning of 1994, tradable emission permits called RECLAIM Trading Credits (RTCs) have been issued for the two main pollutants, NO_x and SO_2, on the basis of a reducing emission ceiling between 1994 and 2003. These RTCs concern firms that are, or plan to be, below these ceilings. Firms can either sell or transfer their existing allocation of RTCs for any given compliance year. Firms with new facilities or plants in project must buy RTCs covering the additional emissions that stem from their projected operations; existing plants must cover any excess emissions above their ceilings for any given year by buying suitable RTCs. The benefits of RECLAIM, concerning about 400 Los Angeles companies that emit at least four tonnes per year have been estimated at US$60 million per year in terms of savings on compliance costs with respect to a pure command-and-control system. In order to address the problem of market efficiency, the Californian AQMDs have taken several steps, including publishing lists of available credits on the market, as well as keeping certification requirements to a minimum, thus reducing transaction costs. The existence of 'free rider' emissions may also erode the efficiency of an emission trading system, and, as shown by Dudek and Palmisano (1988), this was a common practice in the early days (for example, in the 1980s) of the implementation of 'emission trading' in the USA. This is logical, inasmuch as this system is tantamount to establishing some kind of property rights, as well as markets; these property rights, and the corresponding markets, have to be effective for the system to be efficient. It seems, however, that the market has become more and more efficient throughout the 1990s.

It may be argued that the obligation to purchase new ERCs for firms projecting new facilities is but unfair competition through disguised barriers to entry. However, at heart, this argument does not hold, if one admits that environmental assets such as the atmosphere are subject to some kind of property rights, as it is with land and real-estate assets. Along this line, in opposition to the unfair competition view, one may contend that just as any new industry setting up new facilities – whether in Los Angeles, London, Paris or Tokyo – has to buy or rent real-estate assets and office space, it will also, if emissions permits are considered a tradable asset subject to property rights, have to purchase or rent such emission permits. Indeed, in the USA where the emission trading system is most developed, the prices of ERCs do vary a lot across the various states and locations. This may be thought of as reflecting the scarcity of environmental assets, just as real-estate asset prices and rent prices reflect the scarcity of land and real-estate assets.

Prices and price quotes for all sorts of ERCs across the United States are available from various sources. For instance, the Sacramento Municipal Utility Company (SMUD) paid US\$18 500/ton of NO_x, US\$20 000/ton of ROG, and US\$16 000/ton of PM (Kulkarni, 1993). More recent quotes are supplied by brokers. As an example, in San Diego County, in May 1999, average prices (in US\$/tonnes per year) of NO_x ERCs were reported as US\$24 826, while VOC (Volatile Organic Compounds) traded at US\$13 000. Similar prices may be found for a number of other US states, including Connecticut, Massachusetts, New Jersey, New York State, Pennsylvania and Texas. As an example, figures comparable to the San Diego ones above valid for Massachusetts are (still in May 1999) average prices US\$5950 for NO_x ERCs, and US\$3000 for VOC ERCs. These lower figures may reflect less stringent environmental norms, which probably reflect a less acute atmospheric pollution problem in Massachusetts than in California.

As it stands, the emission trading system as applied in the USA under the Clean Air Act (as amended in 1990) is submitted to a meticulous array of regulations that vary from state to state, with non-negligible trading, administrative, and compliance costs. It might be argued that it is not a universal tool, on the grounds that many other developed countries, as well as emerging and developing economies, do not apply this system, relying rather on more traditional command-and-control systems in their environmental policies. This is true, for instance, of Western European countries such as France and Germany, as well as of Asian countries such as Japan and Korea. However, things are changing very rapidly, and the Kyoto conference (December 1997) has provided for some 'international emission trading' between the European Union countries, the United States, Canada and Russia. Another possibility under the Kyoto agreement is the exchange of emission permits between these countries and other countries. Whatever the official policies, some international bodies, such as the World Bank, as well as large private companies, are already acting in that field, contributing to the development of purely private markets for emission permits. This is a very important point, since the core topic in which we are interested here is firm management, as *purely private applications of the tradable emission permit system between production units of a large corporation* are considered and are actually being implemented. These purely private emission trading systems appear as invaluable tools for the management of pollutant emissions at the level of a large firm, achieving emission targets ahead of the applicable norms, at a lower compliance cost, even under command-and-control environmental policies. The BP-Amoco Group, one of the largest oil companies in the world, provides a significant example of a purely private carbon dioxide emission trading system. The group's target is to reduce its groupwide greenhouse effect gases emissions by 10 per cent by 2010 on the basis of 1990 emissions. The scheme was developed in collaboration with the Environmental Defence Fund (EDF), an American non-governmental organization. Reductions are measured and verified by independent auditors. Initially, the trading was open to 12 production units of the group. The scheme has been extended since that time, and the group is now divided into four entities: exploration/production, refineries, chemistry, and electricity production, which are assumed to be acting independently and are exchanging emission permits under a constraint of achieving emission reduction targets that are part of the policy of the group. However, many other private emission permit trading schemes are developing. For instance, ATOFINA (which used to be ELF Atochem before he merger between ELF and TOTALFINA) a large French corporation with multinational activities, is planning (2000) the introduction of a private marketable emission permit system between all its French production units.

At the moment (2000), carbon dioxide emission permits are trading at about US$10/tonne, but prices of US$30 to US$150 are very likely to prevail when the market gains some momentum.

Other direct market costs that may be reduced through careful environmental management are energy costs, and, in general, the cost of utilities (excluding services such as telecommunications), of raw materials and of other commodities which are responsible for pollution or various damages to the environment. This is of course the case with fuels, such as coal, heating oil, natural gas; savings on other utilities such as water are also apt to reduce pressure on the environment, while at the same time cutting production costs, especially in industry.

Little has ever been published on the management of energy resources at the firm level from a true corporate management point of view, except perhaps for the previous works of Turner (1982) and of Jacques, Lesourd and Ruiz (1988). Consonni and Lesourd (1986) have investigated energy-accounting systems. These early works on energy management were triggered by the 'oil shocks' of 1973 and 1980, which resulted in historically high prices for oil and oil products, such as more than US$30/barrel in 1980. It might thus be argued that, since 1986, energy prices have been very volatile, sometimes reaching quite low values, including, for instance, a very low price of less than US$10/barrel[5] at the end of 1998, and a comparatively higher price of about US$30 on average over the year 2000. But these $30 are less, in real terms, than the $30 that prevailed for some time 20 years ago. For this reason, energy management as such appears at first sight less topical in the early 2000s than it was previously. Furthermore, due to the high volatility of oil prices, energy management as such appears at first sight more risky and hence less rewarding in the early 2000s than it used to be. This is especially true in periods of recession such as the 1997–99 period, that followed economic crises in Asian countries and Russia. Anyway, due to enhanced environmental concerns that have led to the emergence of EM at the level of the corporation, energy management, far from being altogether abandoned, is now rather considered as an aspect of EM. When it concerns fossil energies such as oil products and coal, energy consumption is clearly closely and directly related to some environmental pollutants, such as CO_2 and other gases that are considered to cause greenhouse effects. Energy management is therefore still highly topical in this sense, but it should be extended to all other resources with potentially negative impacts on the environment. It is, therefore, utilities (including all energies and fuels, water, and certain raw materials) that have to be encompassed in the management of resources having a direct bearing on the environment. However, even in the early history of energy management, the very management of energy resources was already linked to the environment, as well as to significant gains in costs. The case of Minnesota Mining and Manufacturing (3M), which has been discussed[6] by Jacques, Lesourd and Ruiz (1988), is an illustration of this early tendency. Actually, 3M introduced and implemented a strategic environmental management programme as early as 1975. A remarkable feature of this programme is that it has always, and still is, concerned, with energy conservation. In the 1980s, as discussed by Jacques, Lesourd and Ruiz (1988), 3M was running a programme called the 3M–3E programme (where 3E stands for Energy Environmental Equation). In this programme, energy savings were integrated with environmental protection, thus improving both the competitiveness of 3M through reduced costs, and its environmental performance through reduced emissions from reduced fuel consumptions. 3M's EM is still concerned with energy and utility management as such; in particular, after a strong effort in improving its energy efficiency in the 1980s, 3M went on to achieve further energy efficiency gains in the 1990s, estimated at 15 per cent over the 1990–97 period, leading to actual cost decreases estimated as US$810 million for 3M's American facilities alone. In the early 2000s, 3M still considers environmental protection as one of its core values. It is clear, however, that concerns other than energy conservation have enriched 3M's EM orientation, including 'developing environmentally improved products and processes' (Minnesota Mining and Manufacturing, Environmental Progress Report, 1999), making use of Life Cycle Analyses. It is 3M's belief that this will lead to greater consumer satisfaction and to strengthening its market position, following more indirect EM patterns that will be discussed later in Section 5.

4. MANAGING ENVIRONMENTAL RISKS: ITS BENEFITS TO THE FIRM

More indirect mechanisms for introducing the environment into management systems appear through taking into account environmental risks in the firm's management. This is because environmental risks constitute a complex problem, inasmuch as they are interrelated to other risks. Damages to the environment are most often linked to other damages, concerning various stakeholders. In the worst case of environmental disasters such as the Union Carbide Bhopal catastrophe (McIntosh et al., 1998) or of some oil refinery explosions such as happened several times at various places, damages to the environment come together with damages to workers, to the fixed capital and, more generally, to the firm's reputation, meaning that the distrust of clients and of the financial community will be harmful to all the firm's stakeholders' interests and, in particular, to the firm's shareholders' interests. It may be argued, however, that risks may be inserted into market patterns through insurance, but this is not completely true of environmental risks, although the insurance and, more generally, the financial community has progressed towards more effectively taking into account environmental risks. As will be seen later, insurance companies are still, in many cases, reluctant to insure environmental risks. This depends crucially, of course, upon the legal environment and the nature of the risk.

Firms are thus led into both reducing the physical risks to the environment pertaining to their activities, as well as taking steps towards making this risk insurable whenever possible. One of these steps is to create a *captive insurance company*, defined as a company that is entirely owned by the insured company, or else by a group of companies. Creating a captive insurance company will reduce transaction costs while transferring the risk to the captive company, while getting easier access to reinsurance. Another step is to pool the risk, meaning diluting the risk between a group of companies and creating an insurance company that insures the risks for the pool. A number of actors of the financial community have, however, become increasingly concerned with offering financial or insurance products aiming at taking into account environmental risks. Good examples of these environmentally conscious actors are Crédit Suisse–First Boston, in the banking and insurance sector, and Swiss Re in the reinsurance sector. All these possibilities and examples will be discussed in Chapter 7 hereafter.

Taking into account environmental risk shows that the environment may influence the firm's competitive position in an indirect, but rather effective manner. It can be said, however, that adequate management of the environmental risk will reduce capital costs. These costs represent *fixed assets, running assets such as inventories, and working capital*. Concerning fixed capital, it is clear that environmental management investments, such as, for instance, all kinds of anti-pollution equipment, and utility-saving equipment (in particular, energy-saving equipment) will generally reduce the environmental risk, and hence the financial risk as perceived by investors, or the utility costs. More generally, an EMS resulting in better environmental protection will reduce the firm's latent liabilities in the form of provisions taking into account corporate environmental risks, and hence increase the firm's equity, thus attracting shareholders and investors as this increase in shareholders' value will sooner or later be reflected in the price of the firm's stocks, especially in the case of large firms quoted on organized stock exchanges. It will also reduce the various components of capital costs. Among the components of capital costs are insurance costs, as well as the costs of debt charged by banks and financial institutions integrating into their credit-scoring patterns environmental risks and liabilities – a practice that is increasingly prevalent in banking practices. Financing through bond loans may also be easier and cheaper if a reduced corporate risk is perceived in the rating of the firm by banks, financial analysts and rating agencies, which will sooner or later be the case. In contrast, a major environmental accident may cause enormous damages, not only to the environment, but also to the firm's reputation and hence to the perception of the risk inherent to either investing in its stocks, or lending to it.

Reducing the environmental risks faced by firms may, clearly, lead to a more efficient use of the firm's capital resources. Assume, for instance, that a firm's environmental risks are not insurable and yet are still significant, both in the case of a major environmental catastrophe and in the case of more diffuse environmental damages. Then, the only way a firm might be able to cope with this risk might be to build up financial cash reserves or provisions that enable it to face financial liabilities occurring as a result of either a major accident or as a result of damages to third parties. This means that significant capital assets will, so to speak, be sterilized towards meeting this risk. Removing a significant part of these risks and/or making them insurable will at least partially free up the firm from that hitherto latent or hidden financial burden, making some capital resources available for profitable ends going towards the firm's objectives, such as investment in new products and in new technologies, improving the quality of the firm's products and generally making a more efficient use of the firm's capital assets.

5. INDIRECT COSTS AND BENEFITS OF ENVIRONMENTAL MANAGEMENT

Indirect costs from not attending to the environmental impacts of its activities may indeed hit the firm from different directions: from consumers and customers, from neighbouring populations, from its own workforce, and from government and local authorities. If a firm is found or believed to be guilty of unattended environmental disruptions, and the fact is publicized by the media or consumer organizations, its reputation will be affected. This in itself might not be a worry, if one of the main consequences was not to induce consumer reactions. In an increasingly environmentally aware society, consumers are likely to decrease their demand for the firm's products. The magnitude of this response will obviously depend on product substitutability. However, even if there are no close substitutes, the firm could underestimate consumer determination to evade its products, if only as a means of pressure. A more extreme response would be an outright boycott of its products, with media coverage unlikely to serve the firm's reputation. With the increased spread of worldwide internet communication, this will be happening not only at the local or national level, but internationally. As a result, at stake are the firm's market share and capacity to make profits. In some extreme cases, the survival of the firm may be at stake.

It may be argued that this is only true where consumers are wealthy enough to care about such matters. In poor countries, environmental concerns are very secondary to more basic needs, such as food, housing and employment. However, wealthier consumers are also those who can pay, and therefore form the bulk of market power on the demand side. An argument relying on the small numbers of wealthy consumers relative to poorer consumers is weak and does not stand up to reality. The firm cannot escape the concerns of the wealthier consumers.

Reactions from local or neighbouring populations tend not to be mediated by the market, but take the avenues of legal and political action. Examples have been many in the recent past. The firm may of course lose such actions, and must then pay all costs. However, even if it wins, the litigation will have cost the firm money, if only in lawyers, and once again its reputation will be tarnished, with the ensuing consequences described above.

The firm's own labour force may turn itself against it. Ideological principles may be involved, but more often direct concerns about health will trigger the response. The workers' own health, within the premises, may be the problem, or that of the workers' families who live in the area or consume the firm's products. This seems to be a frequent case in Russia, and was certainly a major social tragedy in nineteenth-century coal-mining Europe. Today, empirical surveys repeatedly show that worker absenteeism is lower and productivity is higher in firms where employees are proud to work; environmentally responsible management is an important factor in this regard. Whatever the cause, employee resistance of any form may end up costing the firm more than the reduction of the environmental disturbance would have cost.

Last, but not least, government action can affect the firm's objectives in many subtle ways: by refusing future authorizations, by deciding ex-post sanctions, by setting up regulations that are more constraining than self-regulation by the firm would have been, or by imposing new taxes. Such actions are not easy to predict in advance, especially their severity and their timing.

Symmetrically, there are hidden benefits to the firm from tackling these issues head on, and taking the lead on consumers, local populations, employees and government action. It may pay in the end to be proactive. However, there are other possible benefits than the converse of the above costs. Managing environmental impacts has been shown to involve mostly high-tech jobs, requiring not only expensive and sophisticated equipment but also highly trained and competent experts. If the firm is to monitor its environmental impacts on a long-term basis, then it may be uneconomic to hire experts every time. Instead, training its own personnel and hiring experts as permanent employees of the firm, perhaps on a part-time basis, might prove more efficient. The result would involve hidden side-benefits in the form of increased know-how and skills, which could impact on many other aspects of the firm's activity: total quality control, improved product quality, improved customer management, technological and organizational innovations, overall increased creativity.

A more subtle yet no less real benefit to the firm would come from the existence of a correlation between proactive EM and the general perception of the firm's ethics. The idea here is that if the firm is known for its 'duty of care' for the environment, then for many of its partners (consumers, local populations and government) there will be a positive presumption that the firm also cares for other aspects related to its ethical responsibilities in society. The firm can confirm such presumptions by sponsoring or being directly involved in local education programmes, improvement of local amenities and social infrastructures, contributions to national or international nature conservation schemes, health and food relief and aid programmes, and the way it treats its employees, its commercial partners or its shareholders.[7] In a way, the firm can create for itself a positive externality by informing all its partners of the existence and quality of its EM. The positive externality reflects a spillover effect from the realm of EM to other spheres, which are likely to further enhance the firm's reputation and image, which, in turn, are themselves likely to spill over on to the perception of the firm's products. Its sales, market share and profits are likely to be positively affected. Furthermore, carefully managed from a public relations point of view, the firm can ensure a snowball effect. For instance, national or international awards can be granted to the firm for its outstanding achievements in EM and related social responsibilities. A good example is ALCOA Australia, which has been able to win a much-appraised international award for its mine-site rehabilitation achievements south of Perth, Western Australia.

For those firms that have not come round to appreciate and account for the hidden costs and benefits of EM, the question can be raised as to how they can be made explicit to the firm. This is certainly a key question for the future. In order to meaningfully tackle this question, however, some background in the economic principles governing hidden costs and benefits is needed.

This means reducing hitherto hidden or latent costs, and increasing hitherto hidden or latent benefits. Clearly, this also means *a positive impact on most of the various stakeholders*. Furthermore, if the cost of the environmental management actions required is proportionate to them, developing an EMS is apt to *increase the shareholders' value* of the firm. Again, however, the costs related to the implementation of EM actions have to lead to benefits that are higher than these costs. This, of course, applies whether these costs and benefits are hidden or not.

6. CONCLUSION

As this chapter has shown, the benefits of EM may be found in three directions. Firstly, EM can mean reducing direct costs, such as energy and utility costs. Secondly, it may also be concerned with adequate management of the environmental risk. Thirdly, it may be concerned with more indirect interactions of the firm with the environment, such as enhancing the environmental quality of the firm's products and subsequent ecolabelling of these products.

Clearly, all this also means *a positive impact on most of the various stakeholders*. It is, furthermore, clear that if the cost of the environmental management actions required is proportionate to them, developing an EMS is apt to *increase the shareholders' value* of the firm. Table 2.2 gives some examples of successful large companies operating in various sectors and in various regions of the world, if not throughout the world in the case of transnational companies. These examples, and many others, will be discussed as case studies in greater detail in some parts of this book.

Although these examples are concerned with large multinational firms, EM and EMSs are by no means confined to large corporations. Small and medium-sized enterprises (SMEs) may also gain in setting up EMSs, as shown by several previous works, including Welford (1998a and b).

It should of course be emphasized that environmental management is like any other branch of management: it is profitable to the firm only if the costs of such management are smaller than either the cost reductions or the increases in profits due to increased turnover under reasonable costs (for instance, if selling 'green' products is increasing the firm's market share).

Table 2.2: Examples of firms with EMSs

Firm (Country of origin, sector) (Source)	Aspects of EM of interest
WMC Ltd. (Australia, mining) (1)	Materials and environmental risk management; ISO 14001 certification planned
3M (USA, Electronics) (2)	Energy conservation
ST Microelectronics (France, electronics) (3,4)	Energy conservation, environmental performance; ISO 14001 certified
Bridgestone (Japan, tyres, rubber products) (2)	Energy conservation
Volvo (Sweden, automobile) (5-8)	Environmental quality of products; ISO 14001 certified
ATOFINA (France, chemistry) (7)*	Environmental risk management; private emission trading system planned
MIGROS (Switzerland, supermarkets) (9)	Environmental quality of products
Lufthansa (Germany, airline) (10)	Energy conservation; environmental quality of products
Barclays Bank (UK, banking) (11,12)	Environmental risk management
Bank Triodos (Netherlands, banking) (12,13)	Ethical banking services; ISO 14001 certified
Crédit Suisse Group (Switzerland, banking) (14)	Environmental risk management; ISO 14001 certified
Swiss Re (Switzerland, reinsurance) (15,16)	Environmental risk management; ISO 14001 certified

Sources: (1) WMC (2000); (2) Jacques, Lesourd and Ruiz (1988); (3) ST Microelectronics (2000a and b); (4) Chapter 8 of this work; (5) De Sèze in Beaud, Beaud and Bouguerra (1993); (6) Volvo (2000a and b); (7) Lesourd (1996); (8) Chapter 9 of this work; (9) MIGROS (2000); (10) McInerney and White (1997); (11) Barclays Bank (2001); (12) Chapter 6 of this work; (13) Bank Triodos (2000); (14) Crédit Suisse (1998); (15) Swiss Re (1999); (16) Chapter 7 of this work. Note: *ATOFINA used to be ELF ATOCHEM at the time of publication of (7).

Whenever environmental management actions are implemented, whether they come under the form of an EMS complying with international norms such as the ISO 14000 group of norms, or under a scheme that is more specific to the firm's corporate policy, one has to verify that these actions globally end up in the interest of the various stakeholders of the firm. In particular, one has to verify that they are profitable, at least in the long term. In this sense, as noted previously, whatever its intrinsic interest, EM is not a panacea.

NOTES

1. A first definition of stakeholders as groups of people who have 'vested interests' (according to the expression of Veblen, 1919) in the firm was given in Chapter 1. We give here a second definition and a categorization of stakeholders. A final and perhaps more precise definition will be given in Chapter 3.
2. The expression 'vested interests' has been highlighted by Veblen (1919).
3. Note that this concern dates back only to the 1930s. Before that time, and indeed for some time afterwards too, a discrimination existed between major and minor shareholders, whereby the firm catered to the interests of the former to the detriment of the latter.
4. These are short tonnes of 2000 pounds (lb), with 1lb = 453.6 grams.
5. A value which, in real terms, is comparable to the low prices (about US$2/barrel) that prevailed at the end of the 1960s and in the early 1970s, before the 1973 'oil shock'.
6. In the case of its British subsidiary (3M UK).
7. Crédit Suisse may provide a counter-example, in that it has recently been criticized by minority shareholders about its compensation policy toward top management, while maintaining impeccable financial management and environmentally responsible policies.

REFERENCES

Bank Triodos (2000), *Financial and environmental reports for various years*, http://www.triodosbank.com.

Barclays Bank (2001), *Environmental, financial and social reports*, http://www.barclays.com.

Beaumont, J.R., Whitaker, B. and Pedersen, L. (1993), *Managing the Environment: Business Opportunity and Responsibility*, Oxford: Butterworth-Heinemann.

Cairncross, F. (1995), *Green, Inc.: A Guide to Business and the Environment*, London: Island Press.

Cason, T.N. and Gangadharan, L. (1998), 'An experimental study of electronic bulletin board trading for emission permits', *Journal of Regulatory Economics*, **14**: 55–73.

Coase, R. (1960), 'The problem of social cost', *Journal of Law and Economics*, **3**: 1–44.

Consonni, A. and Lesourd, J.B. (1986), 'Industrial Accounting and Control Systems: A Survey', *Energy Conversion and Management*, **26**: 357-61.

Crédit Suisse (1998), *Environmental Report 1997-98*, http://credit-suisse.ch.

Crognale, G. (1999), *Environmental Management Strategies: The 21st Century Perspective*. Prentice-Hall Environmental Management Series, Vol. 5, New York: Prentice Hall.

Dallmeyer, D.G., Ike, A.F. and Young, A. (eds) (1998), *Environmental Ethics and the Global Marketplace*, University of Georgia Press, USA.

De Sèze, A.D. (1993) 'Volvo: Un industriel fier de son bilan', in M. Beaud, C. Beaud and M.L. Bouguerra, *L'état de l'environnement*, Paris: La Découverte, pp 400–401 (in French).

Dell, T. (1995), *Corporate Environmental Leader: Five Steps to a New Ethic*, New York: Crisp Publications.

Dudek, D.J. and Palmisano, J. (1988), 'Emission trading: Why is this thoroughbred hobbled?', *Columbia Journal of Environmental Law*, **13** (2): 218–56.

Dwyer, J.P. (1993), The Use of Market Incentives in Controlling Air Pollution – California Market Permits Program, *Ecology Law Quarterly*, **20** (1), pp. 103–117.

Harrison, E.B. (1993), *Going Green. How to Communicate your Company's Environmental Commitment*, Homewood, IL: Business One Irwin.

Jacques K., Lesourd, J.B. and Ruiz, J.M. (eds) (1988), *Modern Applied Energy Conservation: New Directions in Energy Conservation Management*, Chichester, New York: Ellis Horwood/Wiley.

Kula, E. (1997), *History of Environmental Economic Thought*, London: Routledge.

Kulkarni, P. (1993), 'Impact of Trade in Emission Reduction Credits on Solar Projects', in *Proceedings of the 1993 Annual Conference of the American Solar Energy Society*, Solar '93, Washington DC, 25–28 April, pp. 503–7.

Lesourd, J.B. (1996), *Economie et gestion de l'environnement. Concepts et applications*, Geneva: Droz.

MacKentum, K.M. (1999), *Basic Concepts in Environmental Management*, New York: Lewis Publishers.

Marshall, A. (1898), *Principles of Economics*, 4th edn, London: Macmillan, p. 345.

McInerney F. and White, S. (1997), *The Total Quality Corporation. How 10 Major Companies Added to Profits and Cleaned up Their Environment in the 1990s*, New York: Truman Talley Books.

McIntosh, M., Leipziger, D., Jones, K. and Coleman, G. (1998), *Corporate Citizenship. Successful Strategies for Responsible Companies*, London: Financial Times – Pitman.

MIGROS (2000), *Environmental Reports*, Zürich, http://www.migros.ch.

Minnesota Mining and Manufacturing (3M), *Environmental Progress Report, 1999*.

Pigou, A.C. (1920), *The Economics of Welfare*, London: Macmillan.

Rothery, B. (1995), *ISO 14000 and ISO 9000*, London: Gower.

Royston, M. (1989), *Pollution Prevention Pays*, London: Macmillan.

ST Microelectronics (2000a), *Financial Report 1999*, http://www.st.com.

ST Microelectronics (2000b), *Environmental Report 1999*, http://www.st.com.

Sturm A. (with Suji Upasena) (1998), *ISO 14001. Implementing an Environmental Management System*, Ellipson Management Consultants, Basel, Switzerland.

Swiss Re (1999), *Financial and environmental reports for various years*, http://www.swissre.com.

Taylor, F. (1911), *Scientific Management*, New York: Harper and Row.

Tietenberg, T.H. (1994), *Economics and Environmental Policy*, Cheltenham, UK: Edward Elgar.

Turner, W. (ed.) (1982), *Energy Management Handbook*, New York: Wiley.

Veblen, T. (1919), *The Vested Interests and the Common Man*, New York: B.W. Huebsch Inc.

Volvo (2000a) *Environmental Report 1999*, http://www.volvo.com.

Volvo (2000b) *Financial Report 1999*, http://www.volvo.com.

Wasik, J.F. (1996), *Green Marketing and Management: A Global Perspective*, London: Blackwell.

Welford, R. (1998a), *Corporate Environmental Management, Vol. 1. Systems and Strategies*, London: Earthscan.

Welford, R. (1998b), *Corporate Environmental Management, Vol. 2. Cultures and Organisations*, London: Earthscan.

Wever, G.H. (1996), *Strategic Environmental Management. Using TQEM and ISO 14000 for Competitive Advantage*, New York: Wiley.

WMC Ltd. (Australia) (2000), *Environment Progress Report 1998*, http://www.wmc.com.

3. The Environment and Business Ethics[1]

SUMMARY

Following on from Chapter 2, Chapter 3 shows how corporate culture and core values, in particular those of top management, determine the time horizon over which benefits and costs are considered and how risks are appreciated. The importance given to stewardship towards the environment and specific stakeholders (for example, local communities and employees), including future generations, reflects the firm's 'ethical mix' in terms of utilitarianism and acknowledged duties. The chapter outlines the underpinnings of both environmental and business ethics and their relationships. Implementation confronts firms with the ethical values of different stakeholders, especially cross-cultural values due to globalization. Are some decisions ethical with respect to some but unethical with respect to others? How does the firm promote ethical attitudes and behaviour throughout the hierarchy? Regarding environmental regulations, is compliance sufficient, both from the firm's point of view and from that of its key stakeholders, or are more proactive initiatives needed? Finally, should environmental investments be considered ethical? The chapter shows why ethical motivations by business managers are increasingly redundant for responsible EM. Economics challenges ethics in corporate governance. This is not to say that ethics are unimportant or have disappeared from the scene. Rather, the ethical onus has shifted on to the firm's stakeholders; in particular its employees, consumers, investors, and the citizens and authorities of the host country. The economics of decision making reflect the distance between the firm's ethics and, somehow, that of society at large: the greater the distance, the higher the costs.

1. INTRODUCTION

When, around 1990, the head of Nissan USA decided to completely reorganize car production at the plant with a zero waste objective, and succeeded in doing so (McInerney and White, 1995); when Volvo's president decided to issue an environment report with clearly stated responsibilities for the future (Volvo Environment Report 1998); or when the Swiss 'Ethos' foundation decided to select its investments according to the social and environmental performance of companies[2]; or, again, when members of the British USS superannuation pension scheme fought for a 'more ethical policy for the investments made on our behalf'[3], what exactly was motivating those behind such decisions?

In Chapter 2, we considered the broadening of business concerns to include environmental management in light of what may be termed a utilitarian approach. That is, we tried to highlight the potential benefits, for the firm and its direct stakeholders, of implementing an environmental management, reporting and auditing scheme. It is true, according to many reports, (Donaldson 1992, McInerney and White, 1995, and Donaldson and Gini, 1996 describe several cases), that companies have been able to increase their net benefits by doing so; but often more as a happy by-product than by design. In all the examples cited above, the motivation was not only economic, it was also ethical. This chapter proposes to examine this other dimension of business and the environment.

Actually, the question is twofold. Why are many firms committing themselves to environmental responsibilities, and why are many others not doing so? Is it that there is a conflict between economics and ethics, between environmentally clean business and profitability? Is market competition a serious hindrance? What are the grounds for the exclusion by the Domini 400 Index of 150 companies from the Standard & Poor 500 list? This chapter will show that the answers to these questions strongly depend on how costs and benefits are defined and accounted for (see Chapter 4), and within what framework, time horizon and organizational structure. It will show that environmental concerns of today – not only those of the civil society but also those of the international business community[4] – are changing social values. These, in turn, are changing social expectations from business and thereby business ethics itself. However, environmental concerns are perhaps but the latest force in changing business ethics, which, as the next section shows, have been changing over time anyway.

This chapter is organized as follows. A first section, after a brief historical reminder, highlights the main features of what has recently developed as the field of environmental ethics and provides some key insights into its foundations. A second section examines environmental ethics from the corporation's perspective and how it relates to economic imperatives. A third section considers the implementation of a company's environmental ethics, and how commitments can become reality at least cost. The chapter ends with a case study that illustrates these issues in some depth.

2. FOUNDATIONS OF ENVIRONMENTAL ETHICS FOR BUSINESS

2.1 Historical Overview

Business in its modern sense, and business ethics with it, is a product of the industrial revolution of the eighteenth and nineteenth centuries in Europe and America. The use of the concept for periods before that time is therefore not quite appropriate. Nevertheless, there certainly had been, in practice, a definite business ethics in commercial affairs, where certain values were upheld at least in times of peace. The Egyptians, the Phoenicians, the Greeks and, in the later Middle Ages, the Italian and Dutch merchants, as well as the tradesmen of the Hanseatic League, all followed specific deontologies. Because of the locally integrated and sometimes tribal nature of trade activities, business ethics also included many social concerns, mainly through the distribution of income and support of members throughout the community, the clan, or the family. Environmental concerns seem, however, to have been the exclusive concern of the public authorities. In ancient Rome, and in the Paris and London of the Middle Ages, it was by order of the town councils, or by Imperial or Royal decree, that tanneries had to relocate because of the pollution they created. This may be attributed to the fact that, although pollution could be locally severe, it was not perceived as a general social problem.

One reason for the lack of a general perception of pollution as a social problem was its small scale, compared to the forests and countryside dominating the landscape in those days. Another reason seems to be the partitioning of society into social classes where the distribution of costs due to pollution fell almost entirely on the more destitute classes. This coincided with the wealthier classes holding all the power and the lack of education, indeed of any literacy, of the poorer classes. The conceptualization of pollution as a social problem could therefore only have been voiced by the ruling classes who had no immediate contact with the problem, and so no incentive to give it any further thought.[5] In this context, concern by the public authorities seems to have had two possible origins. The local pollution, like that from tanneries, was such that it affected more people than just the tanners themselves and their families. Another possibility was that the pollution affected the image and prestige of the town and its rulers. Such seems to have been the case for Paris as early as the thirteenth century, and in particular under Louis XI in the fifteenth century.

The impacts of social stratification and discrimination on environmental concerns carried over into businesses as well as out amongst nations. Within firms, the filthier and more unhealthy tasks were left to the socially disadvantaged, whereas management or ownership of the business belonged to the socially privileged. This was particularly marked in the farming and mining enterprises. This is still to a large degree true today, but the relationships between workers and management, as well as between them and the environment, has changed and is highly regulated by law and the public authorities. Amongst nations, colonialism certainly had its own ethics of resource exploitation. Lack of concern by dominating nations for the dominated was even harsher than that between social classes within one nation. Colonialism, to a large extent, represents a long history of resource plundering and environmental disruption, even though there may have been local exceptions. In the economist's terms, environmental and social externalities were, in both domains, totally disregarded.

The Industrial Revolution had an ambiguous effect on business, ethics and the environment. On the one hand, it emphasized profit as a key economic goal and greatly aggravated environmental impacts, especially in a coal-driven economy. On the other hand, far more subtly, it generated the first inklings of environmental ethics in relation to human health and living conditions. According to Max Weber, the nineteenth century German sociologist, modern business ethics as early as the seventeenth century was influenced by the Protestant ethic, mainly from countries around the North Sea. It has been argued that the Biblical heritage – 'Grow and multiply, and submit the creatures of the earth' (Genesis 1:28) – is one of domination of nature by humankind, though this assertion is open to interpretation. The heritage of pre-Christian religions amongst the Celtic and Germanic peoples, strongly revering primitive forces of nature, may have somewhat distorted the biblical heritage, but, if so, in two opposing directions: increased economism and nascent environmentalism.[6] The relationship was heavily blurred by social discrimination, as mentioned earlier, so that the environmentalist potential of the North Sea heritage had to wait for the social and economic progress, as well as excesses, of the twentieth century. This, at least, is one possible interpretation of its voicing in the 1960s and its appearance as a social force in the 1970s.

2.2 Environmental Ethics

Two basic concerns for environmental ethics

One may ask why a business firm should be concerned with the environment if it does not directly affect its profitability? After all, as was mentioned in the previous section, business has in the past mostly considered it to be the government's job to deal with environmental impacts. This attitude does have a rationale in that the environment has largely been considered as a public good.[7] However, the firm's impact on a public good, termed an 'externality' by economists, also backfires on the firm in that the impact reduces social welfare. An externality, negative in this case, appears when a firm causes a reduction in the well-being of others without having to compensate them for this reduction. If there are no mechanisms that will force the firm to deal with the externality, then the firm will make money at the expense of reduced social welfare, unless it mitigates such behaviour by means of an ethical stance.

Concern for the environment includes concern for others through the externality effect, but concern about others today is not all. More important may be the concern for future generations who will inherit the natural resources, the air, the oceans and the ecosystems we bequeath to them. One can quote Saint Exupéry's well known aphorism: 'We do not inherit the earth from our ancestors, we borrow it from our descendants.' For many environmentalists and environmentally sensitive people, the environment itself has value for what it is. Plant and animal species can be seen as having a right to life even if this costs us, and business in particular, money. The natural environment can be seen as an essential part of our basic life-support systems. Without it, our well-being and indeed our very survival are at risk. Accordingly, environmental ethics involves two basic concerns: a social concern in terms of equity or fairness, and an ecological concern in terms of ecosystem integrity or health (Pannell and Schilizzi, 1999).

The equity concern is twofold. With respect to the present-day generation, environmental impacts from economic activity affect the social distribution of welfare. Pollution by an industry, while contributing to the firm's wealth, will decrease neighbouring populations' visibility, sunshine, clean air and water, and will also affect their health and quality of life. Because, however, those affected can, theoretically at least, react to such impingement on their rights, some form of social compensation or remediation can be implemented. The firm can be sued and made to reduce or stop its polluting activity, or pay compensation to the victims, or come to some other arrangement. Alternatively, public action can be taken against the firm, consumers can boycott its products or local constituencies can activate political measures that will reduce the firms' future rights. There are forces tending to 'internalize' the externality created by the firm; that is, make it take its share of the cost imposed by its activity. However, this will only eventuate if the firm is locally not too powerful, either as a monopoly or otherwise.[8]

When future generations are affected, no such arrangements are possible. Unless government steps in and imposes constraints on business (laws and regulations, extra costs), the interests of people in the future will not be catered for. Economists call this a case of intertemporal externalities: making people in the future bear the costs of present decisions. However, business managers can unilaterally decide to deal with the issue, either by restraining their harmful activities, or by investing in a way as to reduce harmful impacts. They can, at a cost, change activity; they can invest in damage-abatement equipment or in environmental expertise; they can even reconsider the whole organization of their production process, as was the case, mentioned earlier, for the US Nissan plant in the early 1990s.

Concern for species' rights to life and for ecosystem integrity or health can be viewed in two ways, not necessarily exclusive of each other: as a form of naturalism or as a form of humanism. The 'deep ecology' movement represents the first case. It basically claims there is absolute intrinsic value in safeguarding our natural environment, irrespective of its economic value to humans.[9] The second case reflects the non-economic values people place on protecting the environment. In the past twenty years or so, environmental economists have put a lot of effort into investigating just how valuable to different people are different natural assets, such as clean air and water, biodiversity, land quality, old-growth forests and wildlife.[10] Although both approaches may end up promoting environmental management and investments, they also represent two conflicting world-views. The conflict arises mainly as a function of the costs, or forgone benefits, incurred in protecting or repairing the environment.

Anthropocentrism and ecocentrism

These two world-views come under the name of ecocentrism and anthropocentrism. The former is nature-centred, while the latter is human-centred.[11] Anthropocentrism reflects the ancient Greek philosophy that 'man is the measure of all things', particularly of what is valuable and what is not. Thus, if nobody cares about the spotted owl in Washington State, or about the blue whale in the Antarctic, then what reason is there to spend money, or forgo production income, to protect their survival? The ecocentrist view is that even if nobody cares or is willing to forgo income for that purpose, it is still our duty as a society, and for everyone of us, to protect life in any form as well as life-support systems: land, water, and air quality. As it happens, the two world-views, which deeply affect both business and public attitudes towards the environment, are unlikely to find grounds for agreement, for they represent two traditionally opposite ethical attitudes: utilitarianism and the ethics of duty or respect. This leads us to the foundations of environmental ethics.

2.3 Foundations of Environmental Ethics

Two main foundations

The brief account given above on nature-centred versus human-centred ethics has its roots in a deeper philosophical divide, which opposes utilitarianism to what is known as deontologism or duty-based ethics. Utilitarianism is based on self-centred interest, whereas deontologism is based on the respect of moral rules, the compliance with which is seen as a social duty. Utilitarianism can be somewhat broader than this, as it does not necessarily centre on an individual's interests but on those of any social organization that functions as a private body, such as a business corporation.[12] It is an 'us first versus them first' kind of opposition, or one between an 'exclusive us' and an 'inclusive us'.[13]

Academics of various disciplines (philosophers, psychologists, sociologists, economists) have extensively debated around this issue, largely because it appears so important in environmental decision making, investment decisions, and business regulation and taxation. It also impacts, as will appear in the next chapter, on the definition of 'cost' for society and for business, and in particular on what is to be considered as an environmental cost and how to measure it. More fundamentally perhaps, the opposition seems to question the very foundations of our economic system, based on a utilitarian world-view, which, for some, has become inadequate to address environmental and, more generally, sustainability issues.[14]

The need and limitations of a utilitarian ethics for the environment

Utilitarian theory has a complex history on which we shall not dwell.[15] The key point of interest for our purpose is that it leads to the principle of consumer sovereignty, based on the free choice of individuals or private organizations, reflecting their own interests and preferences. The important points are, firstly, that each individual and private organization freely decides what it wants as its goal, and everyone else, doing as much, respects this rule; secondly, that this state of affairs is good for society, and, indeed, leads to the best possible outcome. This combination of democratic freedom and free competition lies behind Adam Smith's (1776) invisible hand. It is also at the root of what is known as welfare theory, which underlies cost–benefit analysis. The idea is simple: decision as to what is socially most desirable – for example, to preserve or not a wilderness area – is worked out by finding an expression of individual or private valuations for and against such preservation, then aggregating (summing) them to obtain a social preference ordering. Expressions of valuation can be in the form of free monetary contributions or support of an extra tax levy.

The idea is simple, but its implications are far from simple. First, Kenneth Arrow (a Nobel in economics) showed in 1951 that no social aggregation of individual preferences remains unaffected by the specific procedure used for aggregation.[16] Second, it is unlikely that individuals and private organizations will take into account the interests of future generations, or the impact of wilderness and biodiversity losses on the integrity of ecosystems, even if such lack of interest can backfire on other economic activities or on people's health and welfare. Third, there is evidence that when it comes to ethical issues such as environmental preservation, social equity and moral standing, people's preference structures are not always such that they are willing to make trade-offs. Especially religious-based values (respect for life; earth is God's, not man's) tend to produce what is known as lexicographic preferences. Typically, individuals refuse even to consider receiving monetary compensation (or any sort of compensation) for loss of life or environmental assets. From this 'willingness to accept compensation' perspective, such losses can be viewed as having infinite, absolute value, and must be avoided 'at all costs'. Underlying such an attitude is a duty-based ethics at odds with utilitarianism. However, when the valuation principle is reversed and based on willingness to pay, no such infinite valuation is possible, because people's (and governments') budgets are limited. The 'at all costs' requirement is hard to honour when such costs are very high and someone must pay them. Clearly then, though utilitarian ethics cannot, it seems, be avoided, they are also insufficient to address all aspects of environmental decision making.[17]

The need and limitations of a duty-based ethics for the environment

Deontological or duty-based ethics are closely related to what is known as Kantism (or Kantianism), in reference to the eighteenth century German philosopher Immanuel Kant. Kant elaborated a system of ethics based on the respect of 'generalizable' rules. His method, known as universalism, was to have decision makers ask themselves: if everyone did as I do, would I still support this decision?[18] Presumably, pollution and hazardous waste disposal would not pass Kant's generalization test. Also, presumably, if our decisions today lead to mass extinctions, deforestation, soil erosion and atmospheric pollution, and future generations are poorer by as much, then our decisions would not pass Kant's test either. Insofar as we respect the rights of future generations, then it is our duty to refrain from any decision and action that will impinge on their rights. Kantism, therefore, and any duty-based ethics, is based on a balanced system of rights and duties.[19]

A weak form of deontologism considers propositions of the form: if you value future generations, then respect their rights and refrain from impinging on them. Kant referred to this form as the hypothetical (or conditional) imperative. A strong form of deontologism is: you must value future generations and therefore respect their rights by refraining from impinging on them. This is Kant's categorical imperative. Both forms have problems when it comes to implementation.[20] The weak form comes up against the question: 'What if we do not value future generations?' The strong form will only be listened to by those who are already trying to find an ethical ground for their decisions. It will not affect anyone else. In fact, both forms address the question: how can we make an ethical decision? Neither addresses the issue of how a decision maker can be made to ask that question.[21]

There are other implementation problems. In the case of industrial waste disposal, a duty-based ethic supposes the effects or impacts on the environment, on ecosystems and future generations to be known. Without such knowledge, the rule becomes unwieldy. Instead, risk assessment is involved, and the problem becomes one of knowing when the risks are too great; not necessarily an easier task (see Chapter 7). This leads to the second point: if, under imperfect knowledge, the avoidance of any risk at all is prohibitively costly, we are faced with, like it or not, a utilitarian trade-off. It is very unlikely (and it would be hard to justify) that a government or a corporation refrains from an otherwise highly valuable activity for the sake of a highly uncertain risk to the environment and to future generations. Some might consider the whole issue of global warming to be in this category, because of the uncertainties of the impact of economic activity on climate change. Others might consider the loss of biodiversity to be in this category, because of the uncertainties of the impact of this loss on the well-being of future generations.[22]

This conundrum is well known in studies of environmental policy and has led to the so-called Precautionary Principle. This principle requires decision makers to abstain from any activity that may lead to *irreversible* damage *unless the social costs of doing so are unacceptable*.[23] The relevance of this principle here is that it can be viewed as grounded in a duty-based ethics of the categorical imperative type, with a utilitarian proviso. It can apply equally to private business and public authorities, insofar as they choose to abide by it. Two points need be noted. Firstly, the uncertainty of environmental impacts is not a sufficient condition; the possible irreversibility of the damage is also important. Secondly, the command 'thou shalt abstain' is tempered by a proviso ('unless'). Unfortunately, this proviso can end up making this policy guideline inoperative and unwieldy. In spite of several efforts, there seems to be no way of specifying just how high social costs must be before they are considered 'unacceptable'[24]. More important, this unacceptability is a utilitarian value, grounded in the economics of the situation.

Two-stage value systems

The view of utilitarianism given above is a highly simplified one. It corresponds to what has been called act-utilitarianism, and is based on the 'utility' produced by a particular decision. Another, broader version, called rule-utilitarianism, is more subtle, and has been advocated by some economists (Harsanyi 1976, 1980).[25] It requires that those rules be chosen that consistently yield the outcomes with highest (social) utility. Rule-utilitarianism is thus a two-stage ethics. The first stage consists in choosing a rule, or set of rules, according to utility-based ethics; the second stage consists in abiding to such rules on a duty-based ethics so long as they perform their average social utility-maximizing role. In Kantian terms, such obeisance is a conditional imperative.

In contrast, application of a Precautionary Principle is the sequence in reverse. It consists in first abiding by a general rule, and secondly in tempering its respect by a utility-based rule.

It is not clear at this stage which sequence is to be preferred. Each seems appropriate for different situations, but, to our knowledge, the problem has not been investigated. Game theory is renewing the approach to these questions (Harsanyi, 1992). What does appear clear is that two ethical systems, which in isolation can lead to opposite outcomes, actually need to be combined to overcome the limitations of each. As will be seen in the next section, this is not without implications for corporate environmental ethics.

2.4 Changes in Social Expectations

Fifty years ago, consumer boycotts, aggressive media campaigns, and political pressures would have been unthinkable for issues like Shell's Brent Spar accident or the impact of its oil-extraction activities on Nigerian ecosystems and local populations. The same could be said for the impact of pharmaceutical research and testing on animal welfare, the insufficiency of risk-abatement investments in hazardous activities involving radioactivity or toxic chemicals, or even the failure by a large firm to report on environmental impacts of production processes protected by patents or intellectual property rights. Clearly, social expectations about corporate behaviour have changed, especially since the 1980s. These expectations relate to the environment, but also to bioethics and animal welfare, human health, social inequality and the legacy to future generations.

Such changes in social expectations have not only led to direct consumer and political action but have also had a legal impact. In most countries today, corporate or business law, as well as civil law, include large sections on corporate responsibility and accountability for the environmental, and thereby, social impacts of their activities.[26] The advent of the concept of 'responsibility without fault' can be attributed to environmental legislation and regulation.[27] The same can be said of the concept of 'retroactive responsibility', as implemented in the American CERCLA system for the environmental clean-up of polluted sites. Suddenly, firms may be facing millions of dollars in liabilities for past industrial activity.[28] Worse, if a company cannot meet the costs of its liabilities, its lenders and insurers will be held liable, a chain-reaction effect leading to the controversial 'judgement-proof' issue.[29] These developments reflect a change in social norms and values, and have themselves led to the emergence of new financial and insurance instruments for dealing with environmental risks and liabilities, whether past, present or future (see Chapters 6 and 7). We can also attribute the creation of the ISO 14000 norms to a growing concern in the more industrialized countries over corporate environmental responsibilities around the world (see Chapter 8). How social responsibilities may affect economic efficiency was examined as early as 1973 by the Nobel laureate Kenneth Arrow.[30]

The business implications for environmental management are considerable. It is now in the interest of corporations to integrate environmental management into their overall business strategy, and to be much more forward looking than they have been in the past.[31] Although a matter of judgement, it is probably fair to say that, overall, the change in social expectations have brought about a change in business ethics, and that environmental concerns have been instrumental in the process.

3. CORPORATE ENVIRONMENTAL ETHICS

3.1 Ethics and Economics: Two Conflicting Sources of Corporate Governance?

Conflicts in corporate governance: a role for virtue ethics?
There has been much debate as to what exactly determines the behaviour of a firm. The answer, as one might expect, differs according to viewpoint. Standard economic theory answers: profits; business management answers: keeping shareholders happy; marketing experts answer: increasing market

shares; business organization theorists answer: increasing market power; social scientists answer: customs and institutions. The list could be extended easily. As always, there is an element of truth in each answer, and they are not necessarily incompatible. For our purpose, if we concentrate on the primary motivations of environmental decision making in business, we may ask whether economics is the sole motivation, or whether ethics play, or should play, some role. Whatever the answer, we must remember that all firms operate within a specific, though changing, institutional, legal, political and social context, and this context impacts on their behaviour. By corporate governance is meant, therefore, the determinants of how the firm reacts to, or makes use of, its specific context for achieving its goals.[32]

A view still shared by many business managers is that ethical stances are costly and that ethics and economics do not go well together. This is particularly true with small companies and in developing countries. The argument usually refers to the forces of competition. If competitors do not follow suit in, say, reducing waste emissions and investing in pollution-abatement equipment, then those firms that do will be outcompeted on the market place. Thus, eventually, only the cost-minimizing more-polluting firms will survive, even if ethical considerations were present initially. (Of course, we are considering decisions over and beyond the minimal legal requirements.)

As the example of Nissan USA demonstrates, and many others like it, the above argument may hold only if a number of conditions are held constant: that is, provided that consumer demand for the firm's products and their substitutes does not change; that new technologies do not allow reduced pollution at lower costs; that customers, government and other stakeholders do not care about the firm's environmental management; that technology, choice of products and internal organization are not linked in any way; to name but the more obvious. When any or several of these factors are made to change, the competition argument usually falls, because it is basically a static argument, while the rule of the game in a dynamic world is to change the rules! As Michael Porter, of Harvard Business School, has put it, the conflict between environmental protection and economic competitiveness is a false dichotomy. It stems from a narrow view of the sources of prosperity, and a static view of competition.

Evidence provided by a number of sources[33] shows that many firms have been able to improve their environmental performance while increasing their economic performance, be it increased profits, increased market shares, growth in size, or several of these. The case of Industrial Products Inc. is enlightening.[34] However, it is also true that economic and environmental performances do not necessarily go together. So, what are the ingredients for a successful joint outcome?

There is no magical formula, of course, but several features do seem to stand out from successful businesses: taking a long-term view; initiating a new relationship with business partners; adjusting the business in a structural way by simultaneously changing technological, market and organizational elements; educational investments of both management and the workforce; and a change in mentalities so that new behavioural patterns become internalized and routine.[35] This last aspect is brought about both by education and by a system of incentives within the corporation. In all cases, it seems, strong leadership by top management, or even of one person, appears a necessary ingredient.

Strong leadership and commitment from the CEO and top management are currently regarded as a critical ingredient for success.[36] Why should this be so? A technical answer will be provided in the section on implementation of corporate environmental ethics. There is also, however, the question of the ethical origin of such a need. Is it utilitarian or duty-based? Actually, the question seems to reflect a third kind of ethics: virtue ethics.[37] Virtues were first presented as constituting a consistent ethical system by Aristotle in the fourth century BC. In modern times, this view of ethics was discarded and has only recently regained attention. In our context, it refers to personal qualities of excellence and example. Virtue ethicists see in personal behaviour the source of ethical values in that they create in other people the desire to imitate the virtuous, or, at least, kindle an admiration for their behaviour. In ancient times, such values were courage, self-sacrifice and loyalty to one's king and religion. In today's business world, such values are integrity, honesty, trustworthiness, sense of responsibility, accountability, genuine commitment, and so forth. This view of ethics may have something to offer in situations of moral dilemmas. This is when top executives face conflicting 'external' moral demands, like having to choose between the closing down of an operation for environmental purposes and maintaining jobs. It may happen that existing moral standards, precisely because they lead to such conflicts, are of no help to decision makers.[38] They must then rely on some inner sense of what is the 'right thing to do in these circumstances', in a very context-specific way, and implement their decision in total agreement with their perception and feelings. Virtue then becomes the capacity to solve ethical dilemmas in such a way that, appealing to others, the solutions will acquire the status of moral (that is, general) values. Whilst utilitarianism and Kantism are exogenous value-generating processes, virtues generate values from within specific individuals when faced with moral dilemmas with serious social consequences. Of course, managers may need to learn 'moral skills'.[39] The logic of virtue ethics is controversial, but one can intuitively see the point. CEOs and top mangers need to have enough of this inner 'moral strength' if they are to succeed in harmonizing economics and ethics for improved environmental performances.

To summarize, it is not true, as many still believe, that ethics and economics are mutually exclusive. A firm can live up to its ethical commitments and improve its economic and financial performance. Indeed, more often than not, it is *because of* its ethical commitments, rather than *in spite of* them, that such improvements can be achieved.[40] At the same time, however, such happy results are not automatic. They need careful thinking and planning, a change of mindset and corporate culture, a restructuring of activities, and a redefinition of relationships with business partners and other stakeholders, none of which is easy to achieve. There is yet another point: supposing the will and motivation is there, and both top management and the rest of the firm are committed to improve environmental performance, the question remains: can they afford it? Surely, small enterprises cannot face up to the challenge in the same way as big business? What if the market is very competitive or in decline? What if the costs of acquired equipment are sunk and not recoverable, making a technological rehaul a financially unrealistic prospect? What if the firm is deep into debt? To say that poor environmental performance can only make things worse will not help. The question is, how can it escape the financial trap?

It is worth realizing here how fast the institutional, legal and economic context of the firm is changing. Only ten years ago, the answer to the above questions would have been that small enterprises, or those in difficulty, are unlikely to set themselves ethical commitments and adopt environmental performance standards without strong economic incentives. In the last ten years, many new financial, insurance and investment institutions, not to mention profound legal changes, have appeared on the market that modify the context within which firms must make their decisions. The ISO 14001 norms may also be extended to small and medium-sized enterprises (SMEs) as a new ISO 14002 series. The novelty is that the new context is making it increasingly economic for firms to live up to ethical commitments. The tensions between economics and ethics are being absorbed by social evolution, in turn making it easier for business to carry the flame further. This warrants a closer look at the way ethics and economics may relate to each other.

The ethics of economics and the economics of ethics

Investigating the ethics of economic activity, as well as of economic principles, is a classical theme, and has been looked into since the inception of economics as a distinct field of thought. People sometimes forget about Adam Smith's other great work, *The Theory of Moral Sentiments,* which, to him, could not be dissociated from the better known *An Inquiry into the Nature and Causes of the Wealth of Nations.* John Stuart Mill and Stanley Jevons, also key contributors to modern economic thinking, were sharply aware of the moral dimensions of economics. Karl Marx was morally critical of the very foundations of economics in the Western world. Was maximizing profits morally acceptable? Was the search of economic efficiency at the expense of social equity morally acceptable? Seen from this perspective, the more recent environmental outcry is but the latest manifestation of a 200-year-old trend.[41] Is it morally acceptable to place economic values on natural assets, to figure out whether it is profitable or not to preserve an ecosystem, or worse, to compute under what conditions it is economic to drive a species to extinction, even if the purpose is to avoid creating those conditions? This line of inquiry may be called the ethics of economics.[42] From the firm's perspective, it is an 'internal' issue insofar as its members question the morality of its doings and, in particular, of its management of the environment, or lack thereof. It is an 'external' issue insofar as government questions the morality of the firm's doings and decides whether or not it will sanction unethical behaviour.

The fact that firms try to anticipate government's or society's appraisal of their activity internalizes to a degree their own sense of morality, but, at the same time, blurs the ethical nature of their motivations. Typically, a firm will wish to avoid sanctions and will adapt its strategies accordingly. Mining firms, for example, will do a better job in mine-site rehabilitation than is legally required in order to make sure that in the future, should rehabilitation standards become stricter, they are not held liable to costly ex-post improvements. However, such is not always the case if firms are powerful enough to set the standards and manipulate governmental regulations. This has often happened in developing countries that must deal with powerful multinational firms. In the past, there were no incentives for big firms to act ethically rather than profit from their local power, especially in the case of collusion with corrupt governments. Shell's environmental record regarding its oilfields in Nigeria is a complex mix of bad management, lack of ethical commitment, and collusion with a corrupt government, itself lacking morality. However, Shell's recent about-turn in its ethical commitments and, in particular, its environmental performance standards, as witnessed on its website and by its recruitment of environmental management personnel, shows that the company, like many others, is evolving.[43] What is the source of this evolution?

The answer may be analysed in terms of 'ethical incentives' and thus inaugurate a new line of inquiry: the economics of ethics. Shell and many other companies are making increasingly transparent commitments not only in terms of environmental performance, but also in terms of general business integrity, fair competition, health and safety standards, community involvement and communication.[44] Why? As stated earlier, the evolution of companies may be seen as a response to changes in wider social expectations. Shell companies are concerned with consumers' reactions, and possible political or economic action at home or wherever they have invested heavily. They are concerned with their image and reputation, which will impact on their market share of all direct and indirect products. Because of the increasing social demand in information (through professional media channels and the Internet), the lack of clear and reliable reporting and auditing of the firm's activities and achievements will increasingly receive a negative interpretation and thus damage the firm's interests. As a result, it appears that it is in the firm's best interests to take on some of society's broader interests and, in particular, to anticipate environmental management standards. In short, changes in social expectations and institutional context are internalizing the firm's ethical concerns, merging the 'internal' and 'external' aspects of business ethics; quite a revolution in the history of corporate management.

From the regulator's point of view, the question becomes: what changes must be brought about for firms to internalize the social ethics of the time, for instance best-practice environmental management? This is perhaps the key question in the economics of ethical behaviour. The answer comes mainly in terms of institutional change and the restructuring of business incentives. Thus, implementing a tax on CO_2 emissions is making firms reassess their energy systems throughout, both at the production and consumption end. Special rewards with large media coverage can be offered nationally or internationally that help to foster the environment sensitivity of top managers. In addition, the social processes by which such restructuring of incentives is achieved is becoming instrumental. In Western Australia, the Department of Environmental Protection has actively involved the business community of the Kwinana Industrial Region, south of Perth, in the making of new environmentally oriented incentive mechanisms, with the aim to promote efficient self-regulation of pollution emissions. Negotiations have produced an 'à la carte' menu where firms, depending on their size and finance, can choose anywhere between strict external monitoring and complete self-regulation, with government passing on the costs of monitoring and control to companies.

The New Environmental Business Ethics involves bridging the gap between economics and ethics through the 'economics of ethics', provided that government and the rest of society is willing to do so. Thus, the reduction in tension between economic and ethical imperatives for business can be reduced by appropriate public decision making. This involves changes in legislation, in statutes, in taxation, and in rewarding and sanctioning systems. For instance, this last method can be employed to internalize the effects for the firm so as to allow it to capitalize on any derived benefits. Such is the purpose of environmental excellence awards, which have, for example, strongly motivated Alcoa of Australia in a recent rehaul of its environmental management system. Likewise, in Indonesia, governmental rewards using 'colour tags' to represent companies' environmental achievements have actually 'coloured' each firm and allowed the greener ones to capitalize on the benefits in terms of image building, reputation and competitive edge.

The merging of ethics and economics, once anathema, is being conceptualized by a growing number of game theorists who study strategic interactions between firms, governments, consumers and other stakeholders.[45] The goal is to find institutional mechanisms that reduce, and sometimes do away with, the tensions between a firm's economic and ethical imperatives. As seen above, this process seems to be well under way and constitutes, in our view, a historical breakthrough, the merits of which, we believe, will one day be recognized as attributable to the environmental concerns of our times.

One last point need be made on this issue. If the internalization of ethical standards, as held by the increasingly connected wider national and international community, is to be actively implemented by business firms, they need to have enough manoeuvring space in which to do this. In other words, freedom of choice appears to be an essential ingredient for a successful implementation. There are several reasons for this. One is that firms have the best information regarding the implementation of decisions and can therefore minimize the 'ethical costs', thus raising the chances of actual implementation. Another is that freedom of choice widens the spectrum of available options, which fosters creativeness and innovations, which, in turn, further widens available options.[46] A third reason is that, too constrained in its decision making, a firm will divert its creative potential to countering regulatory constraints, an obviously counterproductive activity.[47] One may ask whether many of the environmental disasters in the former Soviet Union are not attributable to the reduced decision-making latitude that was left to industrial managers, coupled with a lack of any appropriate incentive system.

3.2 Ethical Values of Different Stakeholders

It is all very well to say that the firm should internalize society's ethical, and in particular, environmental expectations, together with the benefits of doing so, but society is not a homogeneous body. Different stakeholders, in different segments of society and in different regions, will hold different values and may have different expectations. A mining town and community will give high priority to safeguarding local jobs and revenues, whereas citizens in cities further away may value higher the environmental impacts of the mine. In western Alberta, Canada, there has been a clash of interests between stakeholders of a local mining industry. Many want the industry to close down because of its environmental impacts, as well as low or negative profitability, while the town and its surroundings, which command political weight, want just the opposite. The issue at stake is the distribution of costs and benefits to different segments of society, arising from closing down the industry or allowing it to continue operating. This is clearly a public choice problem, but unless the Alberta government makes the decision itself, the mining firm must find a way out. Again, it seems that close collaboration between business and government will yield the best outcome. Depending on whether the solution is decommissioning, relocation of activity, or replacement of old equipment with new technology and new production techniques, some accompanying governmental measures may be needed to mitigate the local costs. The firm, however, will most likely rank the interests of its direct stakeholders higher than those of its indirect stakeholders.

The relative weighting by the firm between the interests of direct and indirect stakeholders, or between any subcategory, must depend first on the time-frame and planning horizon and, as a matter of consequence, on the relative impacts of the weighting. In order to carry on mining, firms often have exploitation and exploration licences that are restricted in time, sometimes down to only a few years. This means they have a strong incentive to make a profit during that short time period. This, in turn, heavily impacts on their ability to address long-term issues like environmental impacts, unless, of course, other mechanisms exist, such as retroactive liability. Ultimately, it is unlikely that firms will weight stakeholders' interests in any other way than by how much they affect the firm's financial and economic performance, as defined by its core stakeholders; namely, its shareholders. The subtlety here is that the weighting between stakeholders' interests and value systems will reflect an internal ranking by the key decision makers (top management and board of directors) of stakeholders' value to the firm. That, to say the least, is a difficult and perilous exercise. It will reflect the firm's internal value system and philosophy of business. Here, again, the influence of the CEO and top management appears critical.

One way in which government can influence the internal ranking made by the firm of its stakeholders' interests is by influencing the firm's planning horizon. In principle, the longer the time-frame of decisions, the more inclusive they are of a broader range of interests. The firm's discount rate is an important decision factor that influences its time horizon. The discount rate is strongly influenced by the rate of interest on the market for capital, which influences the firm's valuation of time. Government can to some extent increase or decrease the firm's discount rate relative to the market rate of interest, but only slightly. Its action is more effective through changes in licensing agreements, property rights, entitlements over the access to natural resources, and the time-frame, both past and future, within which legal requirements of liability, accountability, compensation of damage, and disclosure are made to hold.

3.3 Globalization and Cross-cultural Issues

With the globalization of the international economy, in particular through multinational corporations, members of management may have different cultural backgrounds and value systems. Thus, the diversity in stakeholders' values and interests described above carries forward into the firm itself. One possible decision structure is for the CEO to behave dictatorially and impose his or her value system on to the rest of management. This system is becoming increasingly rare in big business, though it is still widespread in smaller businesses. More democratic decision structures, within top management at least, can face ethical dilemmas due to different cultural backgrounds. Firms are solving this problem by monitoring a 'corporate culture' with a definite set of core values. Their elaboration is usually realized through internal discussions leading to compromise; basically, the firm acts as a locus for generating a value consensus amongst its top managers.

Differing cultural backgrounds also put firms from different countries at odds with each other. While one firm may have internalized some key environmental values from its home country, another may have no such incentive. When the two firms transact together, or participate in some joint venture, such differences can create problems and lead to 'eco-dumping' practices – the selling of goods and services at low prices due to liberal environmental regulations. A company's ethics is closely related to a particular culture, even if there does seem to be some general constants worldwide. How is the problem to be tackled in such cases? There seem to be two possibilities. One is compromise, where each firm influences the other to meet somewhere in between. However, in matters of environmental management, such a solution is unlikely. Rather, the more environmentally demanding firm is more likely to impose its conditions on the firm with slacker requirements. This is because, as a matter of experience, the stricter firm is also more likely to be based in a developed country, whereas the other is more likely to be based in a developing country. If the first is economically more powerful than the second, or if its home economy is more powerful, then it will impose its standards of value on the weaker firm and country. This seems increasingly to apply to multinational firms. From the point of view of environmental quality, this may appear to be a good outcome, as it should reduce the risks of eco-dumping. If the so-called environmental Kuznets curve is anything to go by[48], then business corporations engaged in international dealings are instruments for transferring environmental values from wealthier countries to poorer countries. However, the process has its limitations, in that the poorer country is economically constrained in implementing imported values.

3.4 Environment and the Firm's Core Values and 'Corporate Culture'

In order to be able to handle changing social expectations, differing demands from various stakeholders, internal differences in cultural values and international differences in ethical systems, a firm needs to have a set of 'core values'. Whether explicitly worded or implicitly acted upon, the core values define the 'corporate culture' of a firm. They also determine, to a large extent, the firm's vision of the future, its expectations, its aversion to risk, and its goals; the time-frame and planning horizon of its strategic decisions; its passiveness or voluntarist attitude to new environmental values; and its steadfastness in times of turbulence and difficulty.

For instance, a general commitment to sustainable development coupled with a statement of responsibility towards the interests of future generations will lengthen the firm's time frame and foster environmental investments that will not immediately yield any benefits. It will also favour the respect of the precautionary principle with respect to environmental impacts like the extinction of a species, loss of biodiversity or global warming. The firm will abstain from going ahead with a project that does not meet specified standards of environmental safeguards, even at the cost of forgone profits.[49] It will generally adopt a voluntarist, proactive attitude, rather than wait for legislation and public pressures to force it to react. Most importantly, a firm that has committed itself to high environmental and ethical standards, and to sustainable development, will draw on its creative potential when it finds itself in a tight financial fix, declining market trends, or turbulent times, rather than fall back on the easy solution, 'profits first'. As one individual told Shell through the Tell Shell Internet system: 'Will Shell abandon her principles when it fails to make a profit? If so, the Shell Principles are fair-weather principles and everybody knows how bad the weather can get' (Shell web page: Tell Shell). In such cases, the real value of a genuine ethical commitment is to direct the firm's creative energies to imagining new solutions, rather than apply a stereotyped cost–benefit calculus to a stereotyped situation.

Having specified its corporate ethics with regard to the environment, how will a firm implement them in practice?

4. IMPLEMENTING CORPORATE ENVIRONMENTAL ETHICS

In trying to implement its environmental ethics, a firm will face several types of problems. What if an ethical course of action is not at all clear? Is compliance enough for ethicality, or are proactive behaviour and initiative also needed? If ethical commitments must come from top management, how are they to be implemented lower down the line of command? What happens if unethical employees do not implement an otherwise ethical company policy? The next three sections examine these questions.

4.1 Ethical and Unethical Actions with Various Stakeholders

An oil tanker that flushes its engines into the sea close to a coast will undoubtedly attract widespread criticism amongst most stakeholders, not just from coast-dwellers. A paper-producing industry killing all life in a river and nearby estuary will likewise attract widespread criticism. In contrast, a firm reinvesting a portion of its profits in tree plantations, advanced mine-site rehabilitation, and environmental clean-up activities, will attract widespread praise and approval. If there is a large consensus amongst stakeholders, then a decision is likely to appear clearly unethical or clearly ethical. The above examples suggest that a clearly unethical decision is characterized by the availability of affordable, though costly, alternatives that could have been chosen but, for the sake of a quick buck, were ignored. When it was known that Beech Nut Nutrition Corporation had decided to go ahead with selling bogus apple juice to infants, the outcry was unanimous. In the hope of increasing shareholders' satisfaction, the top managers had compromised themselves, and the firm's image with them. By contrast, when AES Corporation unilaterally decided, in the United Kingdom, to offset the carbon dioxide emissions from a new coal-fired plant by investing in reforestation projects, there was unanimous praise, and the company was hailed as an ethical company worth emulating.[50] The tough job is when there is limited consensus amongst stakeholders, and when actions therefore appear ambiguously ethical or unethical.[51]

Such cases typically involve ethical dilemmas, where two or more value systems come into conflict. The example of the Alberta mining community is illustrative. Employment is pitted against environmental preservation, and involves the redistribution of costs and benefits between different stakeholders. Similar examples are found all over the world with communities specialized in fishing, forestry and mining, or deeply involved with heavily polluting industries. As several authors have pointed out, the last thing the firm's management wants is to get caught in ethical dilemmas. The goal is to avoid them altogether.[52] This usually entails a process involving negotiations with and between all stakeholders, the goal being to reframe the issue in a more constructive way. This often means institutional innovation.

Lack of consensus as to what is and what is not ethical should not, however, be considered pathological or abnormal. Henderson (1984) makes a strong point in highlighting what he terms 'a spectrum of ethicality'. According to him, it should be expected, in a free, democratic and multicultural society, that a wide range of values prevail, and that views will therefore differ as to whether a specific policy is ethical or not. The firm must learn to operate with such a spectrum, while the weight of consumer pressure and public opinion increases worldwide. To do so, it must provide a clear statement of its core values that will attract widespread consensus (a point also stressed by Henderson, 1992), and then do its best to live up to them, as many firms are now doing. Some see only propaganda in such statements, and in related documents and websites. Although the firm certainly tries to turn such efforts to its advantage, and elements of propaganda are evident, it also commits itself in a way that is not unlike a process of certification. The game is to build oneself a reputation based on credibility, that can then be harnessed to all other branches of the firm's activities. If the firm fails to live up to its own standards and commitments without providing convincing attenuating circumstances or *raisons de force majeure*, it will lose all its built-up credibility and the cost of rebuilding it will be much higher than previously. The top management of Johnson & Johnson, in the USA, realizing the huge costs needed to rehabilitate the name of one of its pharmaceutical products, Tylenol, a stock of which had been poisoned by a criminal hand, decided to withdraw all stocks from sale and destroy them (Velasquez, 1998). Similarly, Perrier (though not before internal strife) finally decided to undergo the costs of withdrawing all its mineral water bottles from the market, so as to rebuild consumers' confidence. Reputation, credibility and confidence come at a cost, and if the firm fails to even once honour them, this cost must be considered as sunk and lost forever.[53]

In ambiguous situations involving ethical dilemmas, the ethical firm invests the needed effort to resolve the ambiguities and obtain a consensus as to what is the right line of action.

4.2 Compliance, or Proactive Initiatives?

'What is ethical in business?' We may paraphrase Henderson's (1992) book title to further ask: how far do you need to go to be 'ethical'? Is compliance with the law and existing regulations enough, or must the firm be proactive and precede laws and regulations? Henderson distinguishes between what he calls microethics, obeying the standards, and macroethics, changing the standards. The distinction makes sense when the established laws and regulations are seen to be unethical. 'As long as it's legal; even if it's not ethical' has been a much-cited attitude in certain business sectors. Often, this possibility arises as a result of geographical and cultural discrepancies or of some heritage from the past. Waste-management laws and regulations have been much stricter, and their enforcement tighter, in the more industrialized countries than elsewhere. It is thus perfectly legal for a firm to relocate very wasteful activities from one country to another, but such behaviour is increasingly attracting widespread criticism on ethical grounds. Likewise, laws and regulations take time to adjust to new technological and social circumstances, so there is always some lag between the need for new regulation and its supply by public authorities.[54] Firms can legally profit from this time lag, even if doing so is unethical by current standards.

Perhaps the best way, though, to ask the question is to ask it in reverse: when is a firm's behaviour unethical, and what if it is? In section 2, above, we saw there are several ways of considering this question. Philosophers tend to search for universal rules to define what is and what is not ethical, relying on reason and logic. Anthropologists and sociologists, by contrast, tend to view ethics in a relativistic way, and examine what is ethical within a particular culture. In section 3, we suggested yet another angle, that of the economics of ethics. Each view seems to serve a specific purpose. Philosophers tell society what it should value. Anthropologists and sociologists tell society what it values and explain the social consequences of having a specific value system. Economists are more interested in telling business corporations, consumers, and governments what the economic effects of a given behaviour will be. Usually, a firm's behaviour will be seen as unethical if a majority of stakeholders judge it so, and the effects will materialize in the form of governmental pressure, administrative hassle, increased taxation, reduced rights, consumer reactions, loss of market share, and lawsuits – all of which may end up costing the firm millions. The spread of electronic communication systems, in particular the Internet, is changing the speed and intensity of public reaction to corporate behaviour. Times have changed. No firm, no large firm at least, can ignore this new game. Like it or not, it must play it, and play it to its advantage. Many firms have begun doing so.

The choice between simple compliance and proactive initiative in the sphere of corporate environmental management also links, in subtle ways, ethics, attitude to risk and time horizons. Put simply, the more ethical the firm's attitude, the longer the time horizon. This is because an increased time horizon also means a broader scope of concern, since the further one looks into the future, the more private and social impacts tend to mix and interact with each other. Unethical attitudes typically do not care about tomorrow, and heavily discount the future. This is also because feedback effects take time. A firm that dumps its waste in a landfill and thinks no further of it may find itself one day held liable for leaching of toxic substances into the groundwater aquifer; but this may take several years to happen. In reverse, the longer the time horizon in a firm's planning strategy, the more likely it is to adopt an ethical attitude, typically by internalizing the future costs of its environmental impacts. This will create the economic incentive to prevent such impacts by proactive investments, even if they are not presently required by law.

Future impacts are never one hundred per cent sure and are always subject to some uncertainty. There are subtle links between an ethical attitude and attitude towards risk. An environmentally unethical attitude will discount external, social or environmental risks while overemphasizing internal financial risks. Thus, a firm that has committed itself to high environmental standards will tend to adopt the precautionary principle and abstain from projects that may lead to likely irreversible damage to the environment. Firms without such a commitment will emphasize the uncertainty of the irreversibility and oppose the higher certainty of the economic benefits of an industrial project. Economists take attitude to risk as a given parameter, but this parameter is heavily influenced by the underlying ethics of the decision maker.

The links between ethics, attitudes to risk and time horizons (as well as time preference)[55] not only pertain to the relationships between management and its external stakeholders, in particular government, but also to its internal employees, from top to bottom of the firm's organizational hierarchy.

4.3 Ethical Values Across the Firm's Structure and Hierarchy: Initiative and Implementation

Today, most business corporations are complex structures with many nested decision-making systems. It is unlikely that, from top to bottom of the hierarchy and across all branches, the firm's ethical values will be implemented equally or in a similar fashion. The vision of how an organization functions and should function will impact strongly on value implementation. This will, in particular, be true of the positioning between the extremes of Taylorist-like vertical 'command and control' and TQC-like horizontal share of responsibilities (see Chapter 2, section 2). The matrix describing who initiates what and who implements what will have a critical impact. If an environmental ethic based on a specific statement of social responsibilities is implemented from the top, a point highlighted as desirable in the current literature, how is the rest of the organization to follow suit or even do more than pay lip-service to it? How is the worker at the base to feel concerned and internalize the new set of values?

An individual's position within an organization, whether public or private, large or small, will influence his or her time-frame and attitude towards risk, and therefore, as seen earlier, his or her capacity to act ethically; that is, be concerned with others' interests and those of the organization at large. The incentive system will be critical. Is the individual's position stable? Do his/her rewards focus on initiative or implementation, and if both, what are the relative weightings? Is personal achievement emphasized or the impact of the individual's work on others' achievements and that of the firm as a whole? Again, what are the (possibly implicit) weightings? For all these aspects, are the criteria and weightings clearly formulated and part of a transparent corporate policy, or are they only implicit such that they must be deduced by employees, ex-post, from past decisions? In addition, has top management provided clear clues and guidelines on how employees, at various levels of the organization, can implement the firm's values in their specific field, while encouraging initiative and innovation at all levels? How does this tie in with the communication structure within the firm? Is it mainly top-down and vertical, or are multiple horizontal and bottom-up channels also available?

The concept of the 'ethical entrepreneur' has been launched (Einsmann, 1992), and certainly a figure like Emil Hassan of Nissan USA is a typical example. A key characteristic of such figures is the value they place on clarity and certainty (that is, commitment) with respect to their own employees and other direct stakeholders. Ambiguous statements must be avoided, specifically values and principles that will appear ambiguous when viewed from lower levels of the hierarchy or from different branches of activity. That is to say the 'implementability' must be worked into the phrasing of ethical principles from the very outset, if they are to have any impact. Ethical entrepreneurs seem to achieve changes in corporate behaviour because they focus on implementability. This steers them away from inapplicable or inoperative principles; for example, those that will entail excessive reorganization, sudden changes in routine, or simply excessive costs. The style of communication, internal reporting, coordination, spread of responsibilities, incentive system, are all instrumental in the implementability of the firm's environmental ethics.

5. ARE ENVIRONMENTAL INVESTMENTS ETHICAL INVESTMENTS?

One may first ask: what is the point of asking this question? If this chapter has been clear enough, the answer should also be clear. If environmental investments are ethical investments, then profitability, especially short-term profitability, cannot be the sole criterion by which they are to be judged. In terms of financially accountable costs, environmental investments can be unprofitable, at least in the short term, and still be desirable, even from the firm's own point of view.[56] As Chapter 2 stated and Chapter 4 will specify, there are hidden costs and benefits that need to be accounted for. A few examples will clarify the point further.

There are many cases where firms have come to know of negative environmental impacts of their activities and have failed to address the issue, in the hope that it would go unnoticed long enough. The expectation was usually that the time before the problem surfaced would be long enough for the benefits thus reaped to cover the costs of remediation or clean-up, once these were inescapable. The implicit calculation was that remediation, done too early, induced net costs and was not worth it. As it happens, such calculations have mostly proved wrong.[57] This behaviour has helped change the legal setting, causing regulations to evolve in a way that judges such firms to be at fault, and thus imposing fines and compensation on top of remediation costs. However, perhaps the greatest costs in the longer run have been to the firm's reputation. The lesson here is that the decision, based on a cost–benefit calculus, changes the grounds on which these costs and benefits are evaluated, and defeats the original calculation. Chapter 4 (section 3.3) will investigate this issue under the heading of 'strategic accounting'.

We already mentioned proactive mine-site rehabilitation, over and beyond what is required by law. This is increasingly standard practice with large mining companies around the world. When asked why, the answer usually is: 'to stay ahead of the game'.[58] This refers to ensuring future access to new resources, licences to explore for new resources, trust from governmental authorities allowing them some degree of self-regulation, concern about future ISO 14000 norms and their impact on the market of their product, and, of course, good public image. The game means anticipate the future, adopt a long time horizon. This helps reveal otherwise hidden costs and benefits. Small mining companies are lagging behind. For example, in the Kalgoorlie mining district of Western Australia, small gold mining companies do not have a clean environmental reputation. The risk is that they will be prohibited from any mining activity at all, although such a prospect may actually exacerbate their profit-making efforts 'while there's still time' – even if, in fact, profits of small companies are not conspicuous and many are losing money.

Other examples include investments in new, environmentally cleaner equipment, insuring against environmental risks, and directly ethical investments according to environmental criteria. Investments in new cleaner equipment are typically analysed by economists and business accountants in too static a way. The lesson from the deferred remediation cases carries forward here too. Such investments tend to appear least profitable, for a given taxation system, when made before others, because, being new, the market has not taken off yet and prices for the equipment are still high. However, once taken up by one firm and shown to be technically and economically affordable, regulators will have an incentive to change the existing pollution standards and reflect the new possibilities, and this will impose an external cost on firms that have not yet made the new investments. Although price of equipment may come down, the decision will be forced externally, and the timing may not be optimal for the firm, given the age of its existing equipment. With regard to insurance against environmental risks (see Chapter 7), the combination, described above, of ethical attitude, time horizon, and attitude towards risks will make insurance even against unlikely risks, because of potentially irreversible impacts, both ethical and, in a broader sense, economic. Again, doing this will change the economic environment in which the firm is operating, in a way that will help internalize the benefits and costs of its investment. Environmental insurance companies will develop, as indeed they have done in the 1990s, a whole new array of financial and insurance instruments being developed to address these new needs (see Chapters 6 and 7). The particular case of ethical-investment funds highlights how corporate behaviour and social expectations interact to produce new institutions that change the rules of the game and, in particular, the expected costs and benefits. Ethical-investment funds, such as Ethos in Switzerland (see case study below), and ethically-based industrial indexes, like the Domini 400 Social Index, contribute to internalize the benefits firms can reap from ethical decisions, and the costs they must suffer from unethical decisions, thus narrowing the gap between economics and ethics. This is a remarkable evolution not only in the world of business, but in society at large. 'Business as usual' will mean something different from what it meant in the past; that is, before the environmentally sensitive era.

6. CONCLUSION

The clearest and most exciting conclusion that seems to arise from the various points covered in this chapter is that tensions between economics and ethics in the business world are weakening. The evolution in social expectations with regard to corporate environmental management have brought about new mechanisms that tend to merge the economics of ethics and the ethics of economics. New interactions between business firms and their institutional environment, both national and international, provide incentives to look further ahead into the future, and also to broaden the scope of relevant risks. The result is worth reflecting on further. In practice, it will increasingly be less costly for a firm to behave ethically, as it may increasingly be costly to behave unethically. This is because new institutional mechanisms, such as ethical-investment funds and environmentally dependent financial products, are internalizing the costs of unethical behaviour. As witnessed by the ethical statements made by an increasing number of corporations, and published on their websites, a new business ethics is being born. By such action, corporations are giving stakeholders a means of holding them accountable for their decisions, and of checking whether deeds match up to words. This may be seen to reduce firms' freedom to manoeuvre, but they may no longer have the choice. Alternatively, the benefits may end up outweighing the costs.

At bottom, the problem of corporate environmental management is one of the provision of a public good by a private economic agent, because, in general, the environment has properties of a public good. The question then is, why would a private company voluntarily provide a public good? The traditional approach to this question, at least by government and policy makers but also by environmentalists, has been in terms of 'command and control' regulation: laws, legislation, and corresponding sanctions for non-compliance. Economists are increasingly advocating incentive-based systems instead, where, rather than constraining firms to conform to some externally defined demand, the firms' own energies are used to achieve the same purpose. Although still an external initiative, incentives rely on the firms' own inner objectives. A third approach goes even further and completely internalizes the firms' behaviour by relying on its capacity to provide public goods without external stimulus, typically through moral values. Government can foster such behaviour using education, moral suasion, persuasion, and other discourse-based influences. Chapter 2 essentially described the possibility of an incentive-based provision of environmental services by firms. This chapter has described such provision based on appropriate ethical values shared by firms. It has also shown how the distance between the two is a function of the institutional setting, both national and international, within which firms operate, and this distance has been shown to be decreasing with new institutional products. A key consequence of this process is the reduction in incentives for free-riding behaviour, a critical obstacle to voluntary provision of public goods.

From a theoretical point of view, neither pure utilitarianism nor pure duty-based ethics are sufficient for corporate environmental management. Rather, a combination of the two appears more likely to be effective. It is interesting that, in the real world, this is reflected by social and institutional evolutions that lend weight to this conclusion. As will be seen in the next chapters, these changes materialize in new accounting, auditing and reporting systems, new certification procedures, new marketing strategies, new financial instruments and new investment criteria.

Although business as usual will still be the game, business ethics will have changed. The demands of environmental management will have been instrumental in the making.

CASE STUDY: 'ETHOS': CRITERIA AND POLICY FOR ETHICAL INVESTMENTS

'Ethos', Swiss Investment Foundation for Sustainable Development, is an investment fund based in Geneva, Switzerland. It was founded in February 1997 by two pre-existing pension funds, one representing the teachers and public servants of the canton of Geneva, and one representing the building, painting and plastering professions. From the outset, its purpose was defined to be the enhancement of sustainable development in business; that is, of companies demonstrating high financial, environmental and social standards. It achieves its goal by investing in firms that perform best according to its rigorous performance-assessment system. Ethos will buy shares and apportion its investment capability according to a rating of companies that takes into account three aspects of sustainability: financial, environmental, and social. Ethos buys Swiss shares and European shares ex-Switzerland.

Although we are primarily interested in environmental criteria, it is also the case that the three aspects of sustainability of interest to Ethos are closely linked and reflect the common ethics of each company it deals with. Therefore, although we only detail the environmental aspects, we also provide an overview of the financial and social criteria used in Ethos's investment policy.

The first question is how Ethos combines the three sets of criteria to achieve a simple rating. One approach would have been to make use of some multi-criteria method, where each aspect would be weighted according to a set of weights. Instead, Ethos uses a mixed lexicographic and weighting method which gives precedence to long-term financial and economic performance. Firms are first screened according to this criterion, and then those that have passed this first test are screened again according to environmental and social-management standards. These are then used to correct the financial rating either upwards or downwards, with the magnitude of the correction depending on that of the deviation of the company's standards above or below Ethos's own expectations. Thus, a firm performing environmentally and/or socially much below expected standards will find its financial performance downgraded more that a firm performing only slightly below expected standards. This holds of course for the reverse, where firms are performing above expected standards. In all three fields, performance evaluation includes the likely evolution of the firm for the foreseeable future, not just past and present performances.

Finally, a risk assessment is carried out that integrates all three fields: financial, environmental and social risks. This final assessment then determines Ethos's investment decisions.

For a firm to be financially and economically retained, it must meet four sets of criteria, all geared at assessing its long-term potential:

1. Quality of management and strategy (includes management competence of managers and a clear strategy in a growing market).
2. Profitability and growth (market shares, return on investments, visibility of long-term profits, operational cash-flows, geographical diversification).
3. Present-day potential (equity and debt, self-financing, price of growth, competitive position).
4. Risk control (consistency of portfolio management, evaluation of absolute and relative risk levels).

If the firm meets the expected financial standards, it must then meet the following environmental and social standards.

The social standards reflect a concern for all stakeholders, direct and indirect, as well as upholding values of human rights, democracy, social justice, and the particular needs of developing countries. They reflect relationships with:

1. Customers and suppliers, competition (whether products and services reflect real needs; impact of products on human well-being; respect for subcontractors and suppliers; continuity in the relationship; willingness to transfer technology; equitable treatment).
2. Collaborators and employees (working conditions; motivation and satisfaction of personnel; training; participation; attitude towards unions; active policy against gender and racial discrimination; employment enhancement policy).
3. Public authorities and local communities (respect for values of democracy and human rights; taxation; local participation and lobbying activities; respect for local legislation).
4. Shareholders and lenders (provision of adequate information; integration into banking and financial system).

In addition, Ethos has a policy that excludes firms whose turnover in the fields of armaments, nuclear energy, tobacco and gambling exceeds 5 per cent.

The environmental standards reflect:

1. Consistency and effectiveness of strategy and policy (principles and responsibilities, and quality of their implementation; information and publication of firm's environmental policy, standards and performance).
2. Quality and efficiency of management instruments; validity of targets with respect to local legislation and regulations.
3. Production and inputs (quality of production process with respect to energy use, emissions, storage of materials, waste management, risk control; conformity of suppliers to the firm's own environmental standards).
4. Products and use (environmental impact of product use and disposal; innovativeness of products; impacts of products on humans, animals and ecosystems; role of biotechnology).

Box 3.1 provides more detail and organizes the criteria that have had an appreciable impact on the rating of companies by Ethos and its subsequent investment decisions. Note that many criteria could appear in several activity sectors as well as in different stages of activity. Empty cells only mean that, in the sample of firms analysed, no criteria were mentioned; it does not mean that there are none. Ethos thus sets itself strict standards as to where it will invest and where it will not.

Ethos thus sets itself strict standards as to where it will invest and where it will not.

The next question is, how successful is this investment policy? Data published by Ethos show that for Swiss shares, it has performed equally as well as the standard SPI (Swiss Performance Index), while for   European ex-Switzerland shares, a policy only initiated in 1998, results have at this stage (end 1999) been slightly below the other standard, the MSCI index. This is largely due to the long-term perspective adopted by Ethos, whose policy must therefore wait a few more years to be correctly evaluated. Given the constraints Ethos has imposed on itself, results so far seem satisfactory and rather promising.

Where does Ethos stand with respect to the values it upholds and the general field of environmental ethics in business? It is here that, as noted earlier, all three criteria, financial, social and environmental, are closely linked.[59] The first point is the time-frame: companies have to appear sustainable in the long run. One may ask where financial sustainability comes into the picture. The answer is an interesting one. Without financial muscle, companies will not be able to care for the environment, nor for people.[60]

The alternative is for somebody else to pay, as was the case in Holland with Avebe Chemicals[61] (which was bailed out several times by local and national public funds), or for the company to close down and jobs to be lost (the main reason why Avebe was bailed out). Thus, long-term financial sustainability lays the ground for the capacity to produce wealth in an environmentally sustainable way.

The second point is that this justifies a lexicographic ordering, where economics are ranked first and environmental and social performance second. However, such an analysis would be superficial. The vision of Ethos is that firms are an instrument of sustainable wealth production, defined not only by consumable goods and services, but also and perhaps above all by environmental quality and social values, health, equity, freedom, mutual respect, and so on.[62] The economics then appear as the most effective means of achieving such goals. The primary aim of Ethos is to foster environmentally and socially responsible management by business firms. Whether it does so on utilitarian or welfarist grounds, because this is what most people want, or on deontological (Kantian) grounds, because it thinks it is the duty of every business to do so, appears immaterial in this case. What is relevant is that a utilitarian-based criterion, finance, is used as a means to achieve another goal which may not be utilitarian. This illustrates a key point made in this chapter: a combination of utilitarian and non-utilitarian values may best achieve environmental objectives.

Box 3.1: Criteria having had an appreciable impact[63] *on the rating of companies by Ethos and its subsequent investment decisions:*

---

1. Strategy and Policy Aspects

a) Production
- Consolidate environmental policy at whole group level
- Allow external auditor the necessary information for performance evaluation
- Need proactive info efforts
- Good communication from parent company to branches clients, and general public
- After merger, best environmental communication company to transfer to the other
- Clear policy for the future and commitments
- Integrate environmental responsibilities across branches
- Environmental standardization across group
- Hiding behind local laws is a negative point

b) Distribution, Transport and Travel
- Consider environmental aspects of business as opportunity
- Special effort needed when firm is a monopoly (lack of competitive stimulus)
- Mobility needs environmental Management

c) Banking
- Include environmental criteria in investment projects
- Certification ISO 14001
- Environmental performance relative to competitors
- Inform stakeholders of environmental consequences of merger

d) Insurance
- Proportion of capital invested using environmental criteria
Actual investments should reflect environmental declarations
- Environmental policy limited to environmental risks is not good enough

---

2. Management and Control

a) Production
- Environmental report quality
- Be systematic in environmental control and monitoring
- Importance of quantitative measurements & targets and their open disclosure to the public
- EMS must appear and be financially & managerially sustainable for the firm
- Allow for monitoring of progress over time

b) Insurance
- Need for systematic action & management of environmental impacts of activities

3. Production and Inputs

a) Production
- Energy efficiency
- Research effort for substitutes of polluting fuels

b) Distribution, Transport and Travel
- Energy efficiency
- Research effort for substitutes of polluting fuels

c) Banking
- Office ecology: energy efficiency, CO_2 effects, paper use, waste management...

4. Products and Use

a) Production
- Need environmental impact assessment for infrastructure projects (dam in LDC)
- Control shift from better energy efficiency to worse NOx emissions
- Eco-efficiency of products
- Buy-back of old or faulty machines
- Recyclability of product
- Life cycle assessment of products
- For durable equipment, importance of environmental impact during operation

b) Distribution, Transport and Travel
- Monitor environmental impacts of product use & service to customers (energy, etc.)

- Inform customers of environmental impact of product use, transport, waste & disposal
a) Banking
- Activate leverage effect
- Avoid resorting to external environmental expertise
- Have an environmental fund
- Niche market for environmental fund is not enough
d) Insurance
- Create products allowing clients to invest money in accordance with norms
- Explicitly include environmental clauses in LT contracts
- Product ecology

Ethos is just an example of the way ethical investment and ethical asset management can be carried out in the case of a pension fund. More precisely, Ethos is legally a Swiss foundation which is managing a portfolio on behalf of pension funds which represent the interests of various groups of employees. As discussed in this case study, the investment strategy of the foundation consists in selecting the stocks of firms that are profitable according to usual financial criteria. This means, in particular, picking stocks that can meet long-term capital growth requirements which are pertinent from the point of view of a pension fund. Among these, firms that meet some ethical criteria from the standpoint of various stakeholders are further selected. In particular, their behaviour with respect to the environment leads to several fundamental criteria.

Ethos is a stark illustration of how to encourage firms to internalize ethical values by use of a particular institution, the capital market.[64] Hypothetically, one could imagine an anti-ethical organization investing only in unethical and environmentally and socially harmful activities, but it is unlikely there would be any market for its products – all of which tells us something of most people's morality when given the right avenues for its expression. As the new institutional economics would have us believe, morality, like many other aspects of social life, is institutionally determined, not just culturally.[65]

NOTES

1. We gratefully acknowledge the reviewing of this chapter by Andrew Brennan, P.A. Dumont, Bob Ewin, Jacques Pasquier-Dorthe and Michael Shanks. Of course, any errors or omissions are our sole responsibility.
2. Ethos Annual Report 1997: 4, rue des Falaises, Case Postale 179, 1211 Geneva 8, Fax: (022) 708 00 75 (Switzerland).
3. British University Superannuation Scheme
4. For example, through implementation of the ISO 14001 norms (see Chapter 8).
5. Of course, this is a highly simplified account that historians could easily question in many particular cases; nevertheless, it does seem to reflect the general state of affairs of pre-industrial times.
6. See, for example, Jones and Pennick's book, *A History of Pagan Europe*, 1995, and how pagan pre-Christian nature-worship may be one of the roots of deep ecology – a phenomenon of any magnitude only in the Celtic–Germanic influenced cultures. For a broader geographical perspective, see R.S. Gottlieb (1996): *This Sacred Earth: Religion, Nature, Environment.*
7. A public good has been defined as being non-excludable and non-rival. It is non-excludable if there is no practical way to exclude some people and not others, so as to be able to discriminate, typically, between those who pay for it and those who do not. The benefits of atmospheric pollution abatement are non-excludable. A good is non-rival if consumption by any one individual, or group of people, does not reduce availability for other people. Again, cleaner air is non-rival in consumption, since my breathing it will not reduce its availability for you. Biodiversity is non-rival in consumption as long as 'consumption' is not destructive, as with photo safaris; it is rival in consumption if it is destructive, as with hunting safaris. Local biodiversity can be excludable if it lies mostly within national parks for which only those who have paid an entrance fee can enjoy it. Most environmental ethical issues have to do with public goods.
8. Negative externalities are at the heart of environmental economics. See for example T. Tietenberg's very accessible *Environmental and Natural Resource Economics* (4th edn, 1996).
9. Militant ecologists often adopt this view and hold it against our present-day 'economism'. See, for example, M.E. Zimmerman (ed., 1998): *Environmental Philosophy: From Animal Rights to Radical Ecology;* Drengson and Inoue (1995): *The Deep Ecology Movement: an Introductory Anthology;* and A. Witoszek & A. Brennan (1999): *Philosphical Dialogues: Arne Noess and the Progress of Ecophilosophy.* An economic view is given by R. Attfield's Article, 'Intrinsic values in nature, in *Ecological Economics* (1998), **24**: 163–8.
10. This is a huge field in rapid progress. It pertains to non-market values of environmental assets and how they can be identified and measured. Several techniques of non-market environmental valuation have been actively investigated, such as Contingent Valuation, Travel Costs and Hedonic Pricing (see, for example, Hanley & Spash, 1996: *Cost–Benefit Analysis and the Environment*). A key, though controversial, concept is that of 'existence (or non-use) value', which measures the value of a resource to an individual irrespective of the use he or she may derive from it – typically, just from knowing it is being preserved for the future. A wilderness area with dangerous predators may have high existence value but low use value for anyone except hunters.
11. See H. Rolston III (1994): *Conserving Natural Value* for an overview.
12. Reference is made to any social organization that functions 'as a private body' to possibly include government agencies, public utilities or state-owned firms that have in whole or in

part 'forgotten' their public purpose and mostly seek to maximize some sort of positional rent, based on power or information.

13.   Some languages in Asia and Africa, where communitarian values are traditional, clearly distinguish between these two forms of 'us' by using two different words.

14.   See J.P. Maréchal (1991), *The Price of Risk: Economics Challenged by the Environment* (in French), Presses du CNRS, Paris.

15.   Jeremy Bentham, in nineteenth century England, fathered a utilitarian philosophy that today appears as one of its extreme forms. He considered that pleasure maximization was the fundamental social goal and proposed a calculus of pleasure that today appears unworkable. The basic difference with modern utilitarianism as it underlies economics is that 'utility' is left to each individual or organization to define. The only requirement is that it reflects some form of self-interest which, without necessarily being selfish, is nonetheless egocentric. Thus, on top of anthropocentrism, economics adds egocentrism (broadly defined, as it can include ome forms of altruism).

16.   This result, known as Arrow's impossibility theorem (1951), generalized Condorcet's paradox, which showed that if individual A prefers x to y and B prefers y to z and C prefers z to x, you obtain inconsistent social choices. There is no social choice procedure that does not affect the outcome (e.g. electoral system).

17.   On lexicographic preferences and the environment, see, for example, M. Lockwood's article 1996; work done around the idea that people and organizations have double moral standards, as market operators and as citizens (Blamey, Common and Quiggin, 1995, 1996, and comments by Rolfe and Bennett (1996) resting on earlier investigations by Bergson, Tintner and Samuelson – see Kohn, 1993 for a summary). On the insufficiency of utilitarianism with regard to the environment, see A. Brennan (1995), *The Ethics of the Environment.*

18.   For a recent exposition relevant to business, see N. Bowie's book (1999) *Business Ethics: A Kantian Perspective.* For a more general exposition, see, for example, Sullivan's (1994) *An Introduction to Kant's Ethics.*

19.   This version of Kantism is highly simplified and reflects what has been called 'popular Kantism' as opposed to 'authentic Kantism', more faithful to Kant's original writings, where the question is rather 'if everyone did as I do, could I still rationally will my action to be universal?' (Elster, 1989; Wolfelsperger, 1999). The popular version is usually used by economists (see, for example, the study of the voluntary provision of public goods by Laffont, 1975 and Bordignon, 1990), although Sugden (1991) and Mongin & d'Aspremont (1999) achieve better authenticity. However, both interpretations run into problems as soon as practical implementation is considered.

20.   However, John Harsanyi, since 1958, has advocating 'Ethics in Terms of Hypothetical Imperatives'. See J. Harsanyi (1976), pp. 305-16.

21.   As J. Hare (1996) puts it (*The Moral Gap: Kantian Ethics, Human Limits, and God's Assistance*), Kant defines a moral demand (e.g. value the rights of future generations) and then proceeds to investigate the sources of moral supply: where can individuals get what is needed to satisfy the moral demand? Religion is one source, but there are others. Hare argues that none work. Strangely, nobody seems to have asked about the sources of demand, a question we shall ask later.

22.   To be complete, one must put in the balance what was obtained in the process of causing biodiversity loss, and so on, given that, whatever it was, it must have appeared more valuable at the time than biodiversity. For instance, new knowledge and new technologies may have been produced that offset the loss in biodiversity.

23.   Ciriacy-Wantrup in 1952 was the first to formulate this principle.

24. There was a debate in the 1970s between Krutilla, Fisher and Smith, of Resources For the Future, Washington DC, on the one hand, and R.C. Bishop on the other, as to how this indeterminacy was to be resolved. One of the latest attempts is by Randall and Farmer (1995), but they also stop short of a solution.

25. The idea was first put forth by J.O. Urmson in 1967, in 'The Interpretation of the Moral Philosophy of J.S. Mill', published in P. Foot (1967): *Theories of Ethics*, Oxford University Press (pp. 128–36), and later taken up by R.B. Brandt in *A Theory of the Good and the Right*, Oxford University Press, 1979.

26. Enmarch-Williams (1996), *Environmental risks and rewards for business.*

27. See, for example, Anderson (1998), 'Development of environmental liability, risk management and insurance in the United States: lessons and opportunities.' One may also consult the *Journal of Environmental Law.*

28. See Laufer (1993), *Firms Facing Major Risks: on the Uncertainty of Social Norms* (in French), L'Harmattan, Paris; and *Environmental Law: how the Game has Changed*, LAAMS Publications, 1991, Australia.

29. See Shavell (1986), 'The Judgment-proof problem', and Pitchford (1995), 'How liable should a lender be? The case of judgment-proof firms and environmental risks.'

30. Arrow (1973), 'Social responsibility and economic efficiency'.

31. McIntosh et al. (1998), *Corporate Citizenship: Successful Strategies for Responsible Companies.* Dallmeyer et al. (1998), *Environmental Ethics and the Global Marketplace.*

32. Of course, these goals may themselves change as a response to a change of context – the prohibition of some activity or product previously allowed, a technological breakthrough, a change in political regime, and so on.

33. See, for example, D.K. Denton (1994), *Enviro-management: how Smart Companies Turn Environmental Costs into Profits*; Koechlin & Mueller (1992), *Green Business Opportunities:the Profit Potential*; McInerney & White (1995), *The Total Quality Corporation: How 10 Major Companies Added to Profits and Cleaned up the Environment.*

34. R. Wells (1995), *Industrial Products, Inc: Measuring Environmental Performance*, ABT Associates, MEB Publications, World Resources Institute.

35. R. Welford (1998), *Corporate Environmental Management. Vol. 1: Systems and Strategies; Vol. 2: Cultures and Organizations.*

36. See T. Dell (1995), *Corporate Environmental Leader: Five Steps to a New Ethic*, and H. Einsmann (1992), *The Environment: an Entrepreneurial Approach.* Also module 1 of A. Sturm (1998), 'ISO 14001: Implementing an environmental management system', Ellipson Publications, Switzerland (www.ellipson.com).

37. See Baron, Pettit and Slote (1997), *Three Methods of Ethics*, where the authors present and compare the relative merits of consequentialism (of which utilitarianism is a special case), deontologism (of which Kantism or duty-based ethics is a special case), and virtue ethics.

38. See the discussion of moral dilemmas and their meaning and possible sources by H.E. Mason (1996), *Moral Dilemmas and Moral Theory.*

39. E. Schein (1966) had already seen the value of this in 'The problems of moral education for the business manager'. See also D. Murray (1997), *Ethics in Organizations. Values, Codes, Vision, Strategies, Action.*

40. We say 'because of', but not 'thanks to', which would be wrong. As will be made clear later, the 'because of' refers to the many side-benefits a firm can reap from its efforts in trying to live up to a challenging set of ethical commitments, notably with respect to environment and indirect stakeholders. See, for example, B. Pearson et al. (1992), *Using Environmental Management Systems to Improve Profits.*

41. One may also recall that in the Middle Ages, in Europe, earning interest from lending money was considered immoral and banned by the Church; an activity thus left mainly to the Jewish diaspora. That this created scarcity in capital and drove interest rates up to usury levels was not seen as a problem.

42. A recent book by J. Broome (1999) looks at *Ethics out of Economics*; that is, what ethical principles can be generated through the efficient workings of an economic system?

43. Van Engelhoven (1991), in 'Corporate environmental policy in Shell', provides a longer-term perspective.

44. *People, Planet and Profits: an Act of Commitment*. The Shell Report 1999. An increasingly large number of firms are publishing similar reports. However, some reports are better than others (cf. Chapter 3).

45. See, for example, Harsanyi (1992), 'Game and decision theoretic models in ethics.'

46. A. Sen, the recent Nobel laureate in economics, has provided throughout his work a theory of capabilities connecting freedom of choice and social equity. See *Inequality reexamined* (1992).

47. This is one of the drawbacks of command and control (regulatory) policies; namely, that they may involve high enforcement costs. Economists are advocating a greater use of incentives-based policies.

48. This curve seems to show, empirically, a U-shaped relationship between an economy's wealth and environmental care. At first, as wealth increases, so does the demand for economic growth, the value of which is greater than environmental quality. Thus, in this phase, more growth means reduced environmental quality. In a second phase, having reached a certain level of wealth, any further growth translates into increased environmental investments, so that the relationship between growth and environmental quality is reversed. The general validity of this relationship, however, is questioned. See M.P. Vogel (1999), *Environmental Kuznets Curves: a Study on the Economic Theory and Political Economy of Environmental Quality Improvements in the Course of Economic Growth*.

49. To carry on with the example of Shell (because it has inherited such a bad reputation from its past), the company explicitly states its commitment not to go ahead with projects, even though they are profitable, if they do not meet certain environmental standards that are themselves publicly made known.

50. See M. Velasquez (1998), *Business Ethics. Concepts and Cases*, which provides many other examples.

51. By contrast to the (implicit) approach adopted here, which is to investigate *social* procedures for resolving such ambiguities, ethics endeavours to solve them philosophically, using rational reasoning.

52. This point is convincingly argued by V.E. Henderson (1992), *What's Ethical in Business?*

53. Economic analysis shows that sunk costs are at the core of credible and thus efficient certification. Without important sunk costs no certified product or process will have the necessary credibility to give it any value. See, for example, Auriol, Lesourd and Schilizzi (1998).

54. An insightful analysis of the impact of lags between demand and supply of regulations and laws is given by D. North (1990), *Institutions, Institutional Change and Economic Performance*.

55. There is yet another aspect closely linked to these three: attitude towards fairness. Its translation into 'inequity aversion' is an analogue to risk aversion and 'aversion for waiting' (the opposite of time preference). The exact nature of the relationships between all these is as yet unclear and a subject for future research. The discounting of long-term intergenerational benefits from environmental investments is certainly a critical issue in this respect.

56. We are of course primarily concerned here with the firm's point of view, not the rest of society's.

57. For obvious reasons, we avoid naming any specific firm here, but several cases are known widely enough. See, for example, R. Sparkes (1995), *The Ethical Investor*.
58. One of the authors of the present book toured the Pilbara mining region in north-western Australia and specifically investigated this point with several mining companies. The answers were all very similar.
59. See, for example, A. Boyle and M. Anderson (1996) on *Human Rights Approaches to Environmental Protection*.
60. It would be wrong to reason 'no activity, no environmental impact', for then some other firm would be operating which, by assumption, would in the same branch of activity have a worse impact than a financially strong firm. Shell openly acknowledges this as one of its core values.
61. The case is described in Essers et al. (1992) in the context of how to reframe situations in order to avoid falling into moral dilemmas.
62. That is, a rating of at least ++ if positive and – – if negative. Weaker ratings were + and –. Weaker ratings modified the financial rating of the firm by a smaller factor, meaning that Ethos' investment policy was determined primarily by [the sustainability of] their economic performance. For the stronger ratings, economic performance was 'corrected' upwards or downwards accordingly.
63. This is to be taken literally, where in modelling the process of wealth generation, environmental quality and social values would enter the social welfare function, not just consumption of produced goods.
64. See A. Argandoña (1995), *The Ethical Dimension of Financial Institutions and Markets*.
65. See D. North (1990), op. cit.; Brittan and Hamlin (1995), *Market Capitalism and Moral Values*; D. Vickers (1997), *Economics and Ethics: an Introduction to Theory, Institutions, and Policy*; T. Eggertsson (1990), *Economic Behaviour and Institutions*.

REFERENCES

Anderson, D.R. (1998), 'Development of environmental liability, risk management and insurance in the United States: lessons and opportunities', *Risk Management and Insurance Review*, **2**: 1–23.

Arganodoña, A. (1995), *The Ethical Dimensions of Financial Institutions and Markets*, Berlin; New York: Springer.

Arrow, K.J. (1951), *Social Choice and Individual Values*, New York: John Wiley.

Arrow, K. J. (1973), 'Social responsibility and economic efficiency', *Public Policy*, **21**: 303–17.

Attfield, R. (1998), 'Intrinsic values in nature', *Ecological Economics*, **24**: 163–8.

Auriol, E., Lesourd, J.B. and Schilizzi, S. (1998), 'Quality signalling through certification', Paper presented at the AFSE (Association Francaise de Sciences Economiques) Conference, Toulouse, France, 11-12 May.

Baron, M.W., Pettit, P. and Slote, M. (1997), *Three Methods of Ethics*, Cambridge, MA and Oxford, UK: Blackwell.

Blamey, R., Common, M.S. and Quiggin, J. (1995), 'Respondents to contingent valuation surveys: consumers or citizens?', The Australian Journal of Agricultural Economics, 39: 263-88.

Blamey, R., Common, M.S. and Quiggin, J. (1995), 'Respondents to contingent valuation surveys: consumers or citizens? - Reply to Comment by Rolfe and Bennett', The Australian Journal of Agricultural Economics, 40: 135-8.

Bordignon, M. (1990), 'Was Kant right? Voluntary provision of public goods under the principle of unconditional commitment', *Economic Notes*, **3**, 342–72.

Bowie, N.E. (1999), *Business Ethics: A Kantian Perspective*, Malden, MA: Blackwell.

Boyle, A.E. and Anderson, M.R. (eds) (1996), *Human Rights Approaches to Environmental Protection*, Oxford, UK: Clarendon Press and New York: Oxford University Press.

Brandt, R.B. (1979), *A Theory of the Good and the Right*, Oxford University Press.

Brennan, A. (1995), *The Ethics of the Environment*, Aldershot, UK and Brookfield, USA: Dartmouth.

Brittan, S. and Hamlin, A. (eds) (1995), *Market Capitalism and Moral Values*, (Proceedings of Section F (Economics) of the British Association for the Advancement of Science, Keele, 1993), Aldershot, UK and Brookfield, USA: Edward Elgar.

Broome, J. (1999), *Ethics Out of Economics*, Cambridge, UK: Cambridge University Press.

Ciriacy-Wantrup, S. von (1952), *Resource Conservation: Economics and Policy*, Berkeley: University of California Press.

Dallmeyer, D.G., Ike, A.F. and Young, A. (eds) (1998), *Environmental Ethics and the Global Marketplace*, University of Georgia Press.

Dell, T. (1995), *Corporate Environmental Leader: Five Steps to a New Ethic*, New York: Crisp Publications.

Denton, D.K. (1994, *Enviro-management. How Smart Companies Turn Environmental Costs into Profit*, Upper Saddle River, NJ: Prentice Hall.

Donaldson, J. (1992), *Business Ethics: A European Casebook*, Academic Press, UK, Chapter 8: 'European environmental issues', pp. 147–60.

Donaldson, T. and Gini, A. (1996), *Case Studies in Business Ethics*, 4th edn, Upper Saddle River, NJ: Prentice Hall.

Drengson, A. and Inoue, Y. (1995), *The Deep Ecology Movement: An Introductory Anthology*, Berkeley, CA: North Atlantic Books.

Eggertsson, T. (1990), *Economic Behaviour and Institutions*, Cambridge. UK: Cambridge University Press.

Einsmann, H. (1992), 'The environment: an entrepreneurial approach', *Long Range Planning*, **25** (4): 22–4.

Elster, J. (1989), *The Cement of Society*, Cambridge, UK: Cambridge University Press.

Enmarch-Williams, H.E. (ed.) (1996), *Environmental Risks and Rewards for Business*, New York: Wiley.

Essers, J., Huiberts, A. and Wempe, J. (1992), 'National Legislation versus International Competition. The Environmental Clean-Up at Avebe', in B. Harvey, H. van Luijk and H. Steinman (eds), *European Casebook in Business Ethics*, NJ: Prentice Hall.

Foot, P. (1967), *Theories of Ethics*, Oxford University Press

Gottlieb, R.S. (ed.) (1996), *This Sacred Earth: Religion, Nature, Environment*, New York: Routledge.

Hanley, N. and Spash, C. (1996), *Cost–Benefit Analysis and the Environment*, Cheltenham, UK and Brookfield, USA: Edward Elgar.

Hare, J.E. (1996), *The Moral Gap: Kantian Ethics, Human Limits and God's Assistance*, Oxford, UK: Clarendon Press and New York: Oxford University Press.

Harsanyi, J.C. (1976), *Essays on Ethics, Social Behaviour, and Scientific Explanation*, Dordrecht, Holland and Boston, USA: D. Reidel Publishing Co.

Harsanyi, J.C. (1980), 'Rule utilitarianism, rights, obligations and the theory of rational behaviour', *Theory and Decision*, **12**: 115–33.

Harsanyi, J.C. (1992), 'Game and Decision Theoretic Models in Ethics', in R.J. Aumann and S. Hart, *Handbook of Game Theory*, Vol. 1, Elsevier Science Publishers B.V.

Henderson, V.E. (1992), *What's Ethical in Business?*, McGraw-Hill, Inc.

Henderson, V.E. (1984), 'The spectrum of ethicality', *Journal of Business Ethics*, **3** (1): 160–68

Jones, P. and Penninck, N. (1995), *A History of Pagan Europe*, London: Routledge.

Koechlin, D. and Mueller, K. (Eds) (1992), *Green Business Opportunities: The Profit Potential*, London: Pitman Publishing.

Kohn, R.E. (1993), 'Measuring the existence value of wildlife: comment', *Land Economics*, **69** (3), 304–8.

Laffont, J.-J. (1975), 'Macroeconomic constraints, economic efficiency and ethics: an introduction to Kantian economics', *Economica*, (Nov.): 430–37.

Laufer, R. (1993), *L'entreprise face aux risques majeurs. A propos de l'incertitude des normes sociales*, [*The Firm Facing Major Risks. On the Uncertainty of Social Norms*], Paris: L'Harmattan

Lockwood, M. (1996), 'Non-compensatory preference structures in non-market valuation of natural area policy', The Australian Journal of Agricultural Economics, 40: 85-101.

Maréchal, J.-P. (1991), *Le prix du risque: l'économie au défi de l'environnement*, [*The Price of Risk: Economics Challenged by the Environment*], Paris: Presses du CNRS.

Mason, H.E. (1996), *Moral Dilemmas and Moral Theory*, New York: Oxford University Press.

McInerney, F. and White, S. (1995), *The Total Quality Corporation: How 10 Major Companies Added to Profits and Cleaned up the Environment in the 1990s*, New York: Truman Tally Books/Plume; Plume Penguin, UK.

McIntosh, M., Leipziger, D., Jones, K. and Coleman, G. (1998), *Corporate Citizenship: Successful Strategies for Responsible Companies*, London: Financial Times Pitman.

Mongin, P. and d'Aspremont, C. (1999), 'Utility Theory and Ethics', in S. Barbera, P. Hammond, and C. Seidle (eds), *Handbook of Utility Theory*, Dordrecht: Kluwer Academic Press.

Murray, D.J. (1997), *Ethics in Organizations. Values, Codes, Vision, Strategies, Action*, London: Kogan Page Ltd and Coopers & Lybrand.

North, D. (1990), *Institutions, Institutional Change and Economic Performance*, New York: Cambridge University Press.

Pannell, D.J. and Schilizzi, S. (1999), 'Sustainable agriculture: a matter of ecology, equity, economic efficiency or expedience?', *Journal of Sustainable Agriculture*, **13** (4): 57–66.

Pearson, B., Little, B.F.P. and Brierley, M.J. (1992), *Using Environmental Management Systems to Improve Profits*, London: Graham & Trotman.

Pitchford, R. (1995), 'How liable should a lender be? The case of judgement-proof firms and environmental risks', *American Economic Review*, **85**: 1171–86.

Randall A. and Farmer, M.C. (1995), 'Benefits, Costs and the Safe Minimum Standard of Conservation', in D.W. Bromley, *Handbook of Environmental Economics*, Oxford, UK and Cambridge, USA: Blackwell.

Rolfe, J. and Bennett, J. (1996), 'Respondents to contingent valuation surveys: consumers or citizens? – A comment', The Australian Journal of Agricultural Economics, 40: 129-34.

Rolston III, H. (1994), *Conserving Natural Value*, New York: Columbia University Press.

Schein, Edgar H. (1966), 'The problems of moral education for the business manager, *Sloan Management Review*, **8** (1): 1–10.

Sen, A. (1992), *Inequality Re-examined*, Oxford: Clarendon Press.

Shavell, S. (1986), 'The judgment–proof problem', *International Review of Law and Economics*, **6**: 45–58.

Shell (1999), *People, planet and profits. Shell Environmental Report 1999*. London: Shell.

Smith, A. (1776), An Inquiry into the Nature and Causes of the Wealth of Nations, reprinted with an introduction by W. Letwin (1975), London: Dent.

Smith, A. (1759), The theory of moral sentiments, London : Printed for A. Millar, and A. Kincaid and J. Bell. (A more recent edition by D. D. Raphael and A. L. Macfie (1976), Oxford Clarendon Press; New York: Oxford University Press.)

Sparkes, R. (1995). *The Ethical Investor*, London: HarperCollins.

Sturm, A. (1998), 'ISO 14001: Implementing an environmental management system', Ellipson Publications, Switzerland (www.ellipson.com).

Sugden, R. (1991), 'Rational choice: a survey of contributions from economics and philosophy', *Economic Journal*, **101**: 751–85.

Sullivan, R.E. (1994), *An Introduction to Kant's Ethics*, New York: Cambridge University Press.

Tietenberg, T. (1996), *Environmental and Natural Resource Economics* (4th edn), New York: HarperCollins.

Van Engelhoven, J.M.B. (1991), 'Corporate environmental policy in Shell', *Long Range Planning*, **25** (4): 22–4.

Velasquez, M.G. (1998), *Business Ethics. Concepts and Cases* (4th edn), Upper Saddle River, NJ: Prentice Hall.

Vickers, D. (1997), *Economics and Ethics: An Introduction to Theory, Institutions and Policy*, Westport, Conn.: Preager.

Vogel, M.P. (1999), *Environmental Kuznets Curves: A Study on the Economic Theory and Political Economy of Environmental Quality Improvements in the Course of Economic Growth*, Berlin; New York: Springer-Verlag.

Volvo Environment Report, 1998. At www.volvo.com.

Weber, M. (1930), *The Protestant Ethic and the Spirit of Capitalism*, London: Unwin University Books.

Welford, R. (1998), *Corporate Environmental Management: Vol. 1. Systems and Strategies; Vol. 2. Cultures and Organizations,* London: Earthscan.

Wells, R. (1995), *Industrial Products Inc.: Measuring Environmental Performance*, ABT Associates, MEB Publications, World Resources Institute.

Witoszek, N. and Brennan, A. (1999), '*Philosophical Dialogues: Arne Noess and the Progress of Ecophilosophy*', Lanham, Md.: Rowman & Littlefield.

Wolfelsperger, A. (1999), 'Sur l'existence d'une solution kantienne du problème des biens collectifs', *Revue Economique*, 50: 879-902.

Zimmerman, M.E., (ed.) (1998), *Environmental Philosophy: From Animal Rights to Radical Ecology*, Upper Saddle River, NJ: Prentice Hall.

4. Corporate Environmental Accounting[1]

SUMMARY

A key ingredient to efficient EM is environmental accounting (EA). Chapter 4 provides the scope and purpose of EA and clarifies the issues between accounting and economics: though both views are concerned with benefits and costs, these are defined differently. Furthermore, economics can provide insights into the appearance of EA, why it has sprung up, where it is headed. With stakeholder analysis, it clarifies the role of the accountancy profession as environmental concerns face it with new challenges. The first challenge is, whether or not the traditional financial and management accounting framework can accommodate EA. If not, how can the tensions be resolved? Can the financial impacts of environmental decisions be unambiguously identified? The second challenge concerns measurement of ecological impacts. Energy accounting, a response to the 1973 oil-price shock, was relatively simple in that it directly fitted into the costing accounts. With ecological accounting (for example, toxic emissions and global warming), no direct relationship to costs is necessary, and investments can be multifunctional. The chapter discusses the development of corporate eco-balances, life-cycle assessment and full-cost accounting methods. Life-cycle assessment, by looking beyond the firm's traditional boundaries and tallying a product's environmental impacts 'from cradle to grave', questions the limits of the firm's accountability. The third challenge is the integration of financial and ecological aspects for assessing the environmental performance of the firm: eco-efficiency indicators and environmental investment appraisal methods are reviewed. Finally, the strategic nature of corporate EA, which stems from the indirect costs and benefits discussed in Chapter 2, is analyzed. The challenge for the future will be accounting for potential environmental liabilities.

1. FOUNDATIONS OF ENVIRONMENTAL ACCOUNTING: FINANCE, ECONOMICS AND SOCIETY

1.1 Definition, Scope and Purpose

Corporate environmental accounting focuses on recording, analyzing and reporting environmentally induced *financial* impacts, whether current or future, and *ecological* impacts of the firm's activities, whether current or future (see, for example, Schaltegger et al., 1996).

Environmental accounting can also refer to the activities, methods and systems needed or used for recording, analysing and reporting such information. It is a key informational input for both efficient and effective environmental management.[2]

An extensive literature already exists on environmental accounting. This chapter has no intention of duplicating this literature. In particular, one can mention the works of Schaltegger et al. (1996) in Switzerland and Germany and of Gray et al. (1993) in the UK, as well as the publications of the Environmental Accounting Project of the US Environmental Protection Agency (1995a), of the World Resources Institute (Washington DC), of the Centre for Social and Environmental Accounting Research (CSEAR, University of Dundee, Scotland), of KPMG's National Environment Unit, and of Ellipson Ltd (Switzerland).[3] Here, we propose to provide, in line with the general aim of this book, a point of view that seems to be generally lacking (but see Boyd, 1998): the economics of environmental accounting, and, in the next chapter, of reporting and auditing, while providing the reader with an overview of the practice of corporate environmental accounting.

The purpose is to allow our readers, including managers, to determine for any particular firm the value of environmental accounting. In practical terms, this should help decision makers make better sense of the available technical, legal and industrial organizations literature. To quote D. Pearce (1997: p. 122), 'The vast literature on business and the environment is informative but unstructured'. Managers need to decide how much the firm should be willing to spend on such activities and what amount and what quality of information should be produced and communicated to interested parties. Since each case will be different, it is important to understand what underpins the value of environmental accounting and reporting.

This chapter also aims at understanding why and how environmental accounting has surfaced in the practice of an increasing number of business firms. This may be understood partly as a response to the issues highlighted in Chapters 1 and 2: previously hidden costs and benefits have been pushed to the surface by increased government regulation and social expectations about business responsibilities.[4] A second objective is to understand why these developments have been slow to come and are still largely in their infancy. That is to say, environmental accounting, and the correlative practices of reporting and auditing such accounts, present difficulties of their own that increase the costs or prevent the potential benefits from being fully captured. Some of the difficulties are technical, and relate for instance to measurement and compatibility problems, but others are social and institutional, and reflect specific functions and traditions of the accountancy profession.[5]

1.2 Benefits and Costs

Our stated aim calls for a preferred paradigm. Economics, like accounting, is concerned with benefits and costs. It should therefore come as a surprise both to economists and to accountants that the two fields have for so long ignored each other in their respective endeavours. Gray (1990a) speaks of 'psychopathic siblings'. In our view, this has been for two main reasons. One is institutional, in that economists were mainly academics, whereas accountants were mainly practitioners. Hence a language barrier between the two, as exemplified by the recent revival of 'economic value added', alias 'economic rent', as both an accounting and a business management criterion (Grant, 1997). However, both from the practical and academic points of view, accounting is not devoid of institutional and conceptual links with another neighbouring discipline, finance, which owes much to economic theory.

The second reason lies in the definition of benefits and costs, and in the way they underlie the *measurement* of capital assets and liabilities.

Accounting is concerned with money in, money out, and various money balances. If transactions do not translate into some form of monetary transfer, in or out, then they are outside the scope of accounting. To a large extent, this view reflects a stewardship approach (as defined, for example, in Brockington, 1995: Chapter 3), with a focus on a specific stakeholder category: equity providers (Figge and Schaltegger, 2000). This focus is backward-looking and is concerned with how the funds entrusted to the firm have been cared for. By contrast, economics, and in particular financial economics, is concerned with benefits and costs as driving forces for decision making. The focus is forward-looking and is concerned with whether resources are optimally managed. In other words, accounting and economics differ from this point of view in how benefits and costs are defined. When Milton Friedman famously declared: 'The social responsibility of business is to increase its profits', the heat was on, mainly on ethical grounds. In fact, the problem may well be an accounting one. What 'profits' are we talking about, what benefits and what costs? Depending on how we answer this question, we shall agree or disagree with Friedman.

One may conclude that there is no real opposition between the frameworks of economics and accounting, but rather a difference of emphasis and focus; a difference which, as we shall see, is on the decline.[6] Through financial consequences such as market impacts, financial provisions, stock values, and insurance and risk management, as discussed more fully in Chapters 5 and 6, previously non-measurable benefits and costs are coming to light and being, sometimes indirectly, measured or at least accounted for. As we shall see, finance theory seems to be ahead of accounting in providing an in-depth understanding of these phenomena.

Let us now try to make sense of current developments in environmental accounting.

1.3 Environmental Accounting and the Crisis of Traditional Accounting

Accounting was from its very beginnings in ancient Babylon a means of being accountable to owners and lenders.[7] The business community has used traditional double-entry bookkeeping for more than five centuries. Historians of accounting ascribe its invention to Luca Pacioli (1445–1514), an Italian Franciscan monk who was also a mathematician.[8] Pacioli, at that time Professor of Theology at the University of Peruggia, wrote a book entitled *Summa de Arithmetica, Geometria, Proportioni e Proportionalità* (1494), in which the basic principles of double-entry bookkeeping were laid down.[9] It was an important innovation of the early Italian Renaissance,[10] that brought about tremendous efficiency gains to managers and accountants. At that time, and even until comparatively very recently, accounting was still carried out mostly by handwriting, and accounting calculations were still performed by hand, or later with mechanical computers; it is only recently that electronic and personal computers have led to enormous efficiency gains in accounting operations with fast, decentralized and large-scale computing capacity available to both larger and smaller organizations.

Contemporary accounting, however, is in crisis; Christophe (1992), for instance, mentions an 'identity crisis'. This deserves some discussion. One can say that the profession, the standards and actual practice have been in crisis at least since the 1930s, but this crisis is only an aspect of the evolution of the business corporation since the depression of the 1930s. One of its aspects was that, in the USA and elsewhere, before the 1929 crash, disclosure of financial performance by quoted public companies was usually very imperfect, so that capital markets were not efficient in Fama's sense (see Chapter 8). In his book on the crash of 1929, J.K. Galbraith[11] mentions some of the unethical practices of what one might call rogue managers in the 1920s. 'Window dressing' practices, such as omitting negative elements in a balance sheet at the end of the exercise, were common at that time in the USA. These practices contributed to provide false and over-optimistic pictures of the financial performances of companies and investment funds to small shareholders. Combined with attempts at elementary prudential rules such as abuses in margin buying, they were fuelling bullish speculation that was out of proportion with the actual and expected profits of quoted firms. The negative experience of the great crash and of the ensuing depression of the 1930s led the authorities, in the USA and elsewhere, to proclaim both disclosure rules and prudential rules aimed at protecting the economy against systemic risks, and at protecting small and minority shareholders against questionable practices. These disclosure rules enlarged the ethical responsibilities of the accounting profession toward promoting the provision of information to shareholders at large, rather than supplying information only to large shareholders and/or to the managers of the firms. From then on, the ethical demands of stakeholders to the accounting profession gradually increased, with a sharp rise in the 1970s (see, for example, Calhoun et al., 1999). At that time, the 'economic consequences' movement raised its head (Zeff, 1978). Not coincidentally, the 1970s was also the decade when the social accountability of business corporations was questioned (Mintzberg, 1983). Indeed, it was in 1970 that Milton Friedman declared that 'the social responsibility of business is to increase its profits'. To most analysts, the environmental responsibility of business may be seen as an aspect of enlarged social accountability (Bebbington and Gray, 1993).

Most of the debate in the 1970s that followed Friedman's pronouncement, which appeared scandalous to some and inconsistent to others, focused on ethics, as discussed in Chapter 2. However, it is our contention that Friedman's statement belongs to a chapter on accounting as much as, if not more than, one on ethics. One may agree or disagree with Friedman, depending on how one defines and measures profits, benefits and costs. Even to a business corporation, this is not uncontroversial, as the long-standing debates in accounting standards demonstrate. As far as accounting *practices* are concerned, it is clear that under the social pressures of the 1970s they evolved and broadened their scope to the needs of stakeholders other than (large or small) shareholders. This went along with the demand for enlarged disclosure and for better information to shareholders, thus bridging the gap between them and the firm's managers. Environmental accounting is part of the new social demand directed at accountants. It reflects the demands of stakeholders (including shareholders, customers, and communities at large) that are concerned with the environment.

As Gray et al. (1996) repeatedly point out, accounting and accountability always were intimately linked. The question then is: what are the accountability relationships? There are at least three types of players involved: the *accountees*, to whom accounts must be given, the *accountors*, or those held accountable by the accountees, and the *accountants*, who develop and use accounting techniques to ensure that the accountability relationship is achieved to the satisfaction of both parties. These two parties have also been seen, in the light of agency theory, as *principals* (the accountees) and *agents* (the accountors) (Power, 1991). Accountants may then be seen as intermediaries and their honorariums as transaction costs. Finally, there is that which is accounted for: loans, investments, trusts, goods. 'Accountables', a sum of money or some resource in kind, have been entrusted or lent by the accountee to the accountor.

Accounting is in crisis because accountability relationships have changed and because new accountees have appeared on the scene. Environmental accountability is one such novelty, but there are others, related to other social and ethical concerns (gender and racial discrimination, use of child labour in less developed countries, use of 'dirty money' by banks[12], and so on). The existing accounting system is thus at odds with the demands from the new parties. This tension can be felt as a crisis. If so, the crisis we are talking about is but one of the aspects of a crisis of adaptation to a changing world. Since the 1970s, moreover, the accounting profession has been completely upset by changes that occurred at an astounding pace. Firstly, the technological evolution of the information-processing techniques has led to tremendous gains in efficiency: the 'bookkeeper's tally' has been replaced by personal computers, and information can be transferred almost instantly through Internet channels. Secondly, especially as regards large corporations, accounting services are now dominated by very large and global organizations, such as the 'big five' of accounting and audit[13] (Arthur Andersen, KPMG, Deloitte and Touche, Ernst and Young, and Price-Waterhouse-Coopers). Thirdly, the scope of accounting services has extended to a number of new services, including environmental accounting, auditing and reporting. Clearly, global organizations such as the 'big five' are taking fast steps to overcome the crisis we are discussing: as far as environmental accounting and related services are concerned, they all have developed services in this new and still evolving area.

1.4 The Appearance of New Accountees

The foregoing suggests that the rise of public expectations regarding the environmental responsibilities of business, whether emanating from government, consumers or society at large, reflects the appearance of new accountees. In order to find out who they are, we must know who were the old ones to whom the traditional accounting system was tailored. It is to answer this type of question that stakeholder theory has emerged (Kelly et al., 1998). The various parties to an accountability relationship belong to and define a population of stakeholders. *Stakeholders can and should be defined as those individuals or organizations whose benefits and costs are affected, upwards or downwards, by the decisions of any given decision maker.* The surge in environmental concerns may thus be seen as a broadening of the stakeholder population.

At this stage, two issues emerge. One is that stakeholders are now demanding fair and transparent information about many aspects of the firm's activities, including environmental aspects, in order to assess whether their utility or welfare is negatively affected, in which case they may want to claim compensation. The notion of environmental responsibility, however (see note 4), is closely related to a duty or obligation to others, whose corresponding rights are acknowledged and recognized. If a local neighbourhood is being polluted by a chemical firm and the health of the inhabitants is being seriously affected, then environmental responsibility of the firm would make no sense if these inhabitants were not seen by at least third parties (not necessarily the firm) as having a *right* to good health. Thus accounting and accountability are deeply rooted in the existing system of economic, social and political rights, of which property rights and health and safety entitlements are key components.

The other issue is the specific view of reality, and in particular of social and economic reality, that accounting systems claim to reflect but may in fact fail to do. Hines (1988) and Stamp (1993), for example, criticize the views of the American FASB (Financial Accounting Standards Board), as well as of their British, Australian and other counterparts around the world, when trying to elaborate a universal set of standard-setting accounting rules. As Hines and Stamp suggest, accounting and the profession are still struggling with reality 'as it exists'. In one essential area, estimating the value of the firm through pure accounting techniques that traditionally estimate the equity as the difference between the value of assets and the amount of debts, are misleading because of hidden or non tangible liabilities and assets, such as the firm's goodwill. This is especially true in the context of environmental concerns, because there are a number of hidden environmentally related liabilities and assets (Cf. Chapter 1, and later in this chapter). It is quite natural to think that accountants first developed accounting systems for the items easiest to measure: physical, tangible items and sums of money. Items like intangibles and goodwill are difficult to measure, and have not altogether been successfully tackled (Brockington, 1995). In other words, if the easiest items are accounted for first, later items are likely to be increasingly difficult and costly to account for. Financial techniques, such as discounted cash-flow techniques, in which the value of the firm is calculated as the sum of discounted expected cash flows, are relative latecomers on the accounting scene (see Chapter 5). Inasmuch as financial techniques include anticipatory estimates of future benefits and costs, risks and liabilities, they are more appealing than pure accounting methods, which simply reflect *past* benefits and costs, and they have become strong competitors of the more traditional accounting techniques.[14]

The profession is in crisis because: (1) it cannot or does not feel entitled to acknowledge new stakeholders and new accountees, such as local communities, consumers, or even the global community; and (2) it has not yet fully developed the techniques to account for, measure and report to these new stakeholders. It may also be the case that (2) partly induces (1), insofar as it undermines the profession's expertise. A sort of competition between accounting and financial analyses appears as a sign of this crisis.

Our discussion applies entirely to the specific case of environmental accounting. The fact is that environmental monitoring and recording costs have fallen and that, as noticed above, accounting techniques have developed enormously. True, monitoring equipment can be very expensive, as are people qualified enough to make good use of it, but technological improvements have reduced the costs of equipment, and developed adequate hardware and software tools. In addition, firms have gained experience, increasing the efficiency of monitoring staff and organizational structures; in particular, of environmental management systems (Cf. Chapter 7).

With the advent of environmental accounting, there are at least four types of difficulties encountered: a common framework with standard accounting practices; measurement problems; integration problems; and the issue of how far beyond its boundaries a firm is environmentally accountable. The next section examines the practical problems of environmental accounting along these lines.

2. THE PRACTICE OF ENVIRONMENTAL ACCOUNTING

2.1 Overview: the three stages of Environmental Accounting

Corporate environmental accounting may be thought of as a broadening of traditional financial accounting toward environmental concerns. More precisely, environmental accounting may be considered as a three-stage pursuit: (1) introducing into accounting practices hitherto hidden environmental expenses and benefits; (2) measuring the environmental impacts of the firm's activities and products; and (3) integrating the financial and ecological consequences of the firm's activities.

That (1) is a pertinent approach is clear: until quite recently, environmental facts were still either completely missing, hidden, or at best available only through some kind of tedious reprocessing of financial accounts.

This, however, is by no means the end of the story. Financial accounting is composed of, and may be defined as, quantitative information about financial assets, liabilities, inflows and outflows. This information is important and even fundamental within the utilitarian framework. Within this framework, and within the scope of financial accounting, the knowledge of environmentally related financial assets, liabilities, inflows and outflows can of course be of great importance.

From an environmentally-oriented ethical point of view, which, as mentioned in Chapter 3, differs from the utilitarian point of view, quantitative information about the state of the environment, and environmental inflows and outflows due to the activity of the firm, is also very important. This statement of environmental inflows and outflows with respect to the boundaries of the firm's physical production system is usually termed the firm's *ecobalance*.

However, an ecobalance, as has just been defined, is still not a pertinent tool to describe the environmental impacts of a product rather than those due to a firm's production activity. The assessment of the ecological qualities of a given product necessarily rests upon an analysis of its environmental impacts throughout all the stages of its life. This means an analysis '*from cradle to grave*', that is, including the design, the production, the use, and the final disposal of the product. This is what is called the *Life-cycle Assessment* (LCA) of the product, a topic that will be detailed in Chapter 8.

Finally, in order to judge a company's overall environmental performance, and answer questions like: 'Has it been doing enough?' 'Has it done the right things?', the financial and environmental-impact aspects must be related and integrated.

It seems useful to give some details about the practical implementation of these three stages of environmental accounting.

The first stage identifies, in both the balance sheet and the trading and profit and loss account of the company, the accounting increments relating to the environment. Thus, environmental liabilities, which are now being accounted for by most firms, and by all firms in certain countries, find their way into the balance sheet. For example, WMC Ltd (Australia) entered provisions for future mine-site rehabilitation costs in 1999 for $87.7m, up from the 1998 figure of $82.5m. These provisions represent cost accruals cumulatively over the expected lifetime of an operation. WMC also indicated in its (environmental) balance sheet the total current value of its rehabilitation liabilities, should it decide to relinquish all its operations immediately; a value of $264m, again up from the previous year's $250m. A further provision of $167m was down for future contingent liabilities. The increase reflected expanded operations and a net increase in land disturbance, net of past rehabilitation. Capital expenditures for environmental control were also reported; for example, the installation of fume-capture hoods at a nickel smelter.

In the trading and profit and loss account appear operating expenses for ongoing environmental management activities. For example, expenses relating to environmental 'induction', awareness building and training of staff, or to clean-up operations. Conversely, environmentally related income can appear in the form of special subsidies and government aid. The problems specific to the financial aspects of environmental accounting are reviewed hereafter.

The second stage identifies, with respect to the firm's activities, environmental inflows and outflows in a manner that Christophe (1995) finds similar to management costing, where the aim is to be able to cost individual products and services, and thence the profitability of each. Recently, the literature has been suggesting that such accounting information would be much easier to generate by adopting activity-based costing (ABC) or budgeting (ABB) (Brimson and Antos, 1999). Interestingly, whereas ABC includes sensitive technical information that the firm may not wish to disclose to the outer world because of competition, its environmental counterpart, the *eco-balance*, is considered public information. The fact is that the purpose of an eco-balance is different from ABC. Its purpose is to show how much the firm impacts on the environment, what impacts are most important, and how these impacts are distributed. This input–output picture can remain public information to the extent that it is fairly aggregated: external stakeholders are only interested in the final impacts on the environment. More detailed descriptions of which processes generate more impacts can remain private information and guide managers towards process changes. We may note, however, that information on certain specific chemicals can be withheld if they might provide competitors with hints on production processes. WMC Ltd provides eco-balances both of its total Australian operations and on a site-by-site basis. They are described in the case study section at the end of this chapter.

The third stage of environmental accounting goes beyond the boundaries of the firm and identifies environmental impacts of its products. Thus Volvo not only accounts for its production impacts in terms of resource use and air and water pollution but also for the use and disposal of its products, in this case engines and vehicles. Clearly, energy consumption, efficiency, and related gas emissions (CO_2, CO, SO_2, NO_x) from their use is of concern to Volvo. This includes a concern for competitive advantage. Its efforts towards developing alternative fuels, organizing the collection and recycling of used oils and greases, and recycling of used vehicle components is witness to its product life-cycle perspective. Sweden's former welfare policy, from cradle to grave, is mirrored in the Life-Cycle Assessment (LCA) of products. Services can also adopt LCA. Banks like Crédit Suisse and UBS (also Swiss) have clear lending and financial policies for environmentally performing firms, the product then being the loan package (see Chapter 5). Insurance companies, such as Swiss Re, do likewise (see Chapter 6), where the product is the insurance deal struck with the client. Supermarket retailers, such as Migros (Switzerland), will strive to control suppliers; for example by imposing minimum packaging, use of efficient transportation, and so on; and also to control customers by promoting eco-labelling, encouraging recycling of packaging, aluminium cans, efficient home delivery to reduce total fuel use, and such like (see Chapter 8). Accordingly, Volvo reports fuel consumption and efficiency curves of its various products, and Migros of its recycling efficiency (paper, cartons, metals) and proportion of green-labelled sales. Both also report on progress with environmental protection clauses in their contracts with suppliers (part of their EMS, see Chapter 7). The problems specific to LCA accounting are reviewed hereafter.

Because it allows for performance assessment, measurement and integration are crucial to any decision making. Optimal decisions aim at maximizing or minimizing some performance indicator. If environmental performance is at stake, then not only financial but also environmental impact indicators are needed. The latter require monitoring and measurement technologies that can be very expensive, plus highly qualified, high-pay personnel. Producing the information may be very costly, and would need to be justified in terms of its contribution to improved management decisions and, ultimately, to the firm's bottom line Once measurements have been carried out, however, accounting methods are needed to organize, analyse and report this information. Because environmental impacts are so many and must be measured in physical terms, data aggregation becomes a problem. Without appropriate aggregation, its value to decision makers will be limited. Finally, environmental impact information must be able to be coupled with financial information linked to the firm's environmental management efforts. Again, such efforts need to be seen by shareholders and other stakeholders as justified.

2.2 Accounting for Environmentally Related Financial Impacts

As Schaltegger et al. (1996) and Schaltegger and Burritt (2000) discuss at length, there are two kinds of environmentally related accounts. One describes the financial impacts of environmental management (or lack thereof); the other, the ecological impacts. In part, each is of interest to different stakeholders, though overlaps exist, as in the case of employees and the taxation authorities.

Schaltegger calls the first type 'environmental accounts'.[15] Since this appellation usefully avoids confusion with standard costing and financial accounts, let us adopt it. Environmental accounts basically measure the firm's effort in managing the environment and in reducing potential risks. However, such effort may be wasted, poorly engineered, and ineffective. Having spent a million dollars on an environmental management system, possibly certified according to the ISO 14001 norms (see Chapter 7), does not guarantee that sulphur dioxide emissions will have fallen in the following three years. 'Ecological accounts' measure the firm's physical impact on the environment: emissions into the atmosphere and into water bodies, solid wastes and radioactivity. What are the difficulties associated with each?

It may be thought that at least for the 'environmental' (that is, financial) accounts things are fairly simple: surely they reflect traditional accounting systems that use monetary measurement units. This is hardly so. Firstly, allocating environmental costs – that is, costs to the firm from reducing damages or risks to the environment – is far from straightforward. For example, costs can be allocated according to any of the following three criteria: volume of emissions treated, toxicity of emissions treated, and environmental impact added of emissions.[16] Any systematic choice between them appears arbitrary. Schaltegger et al. (1996) conclude (p. 55) that it is a case-by-case decision. Obviously, this does not simplify standard setting.

Secondly, allocating financial costs linked to environmental investments is even less straightforward. There is often an ambiguity as to how much of the investment can really be allocated to the environment. For example, an old and very polluting piece of equipment is scrapped and replaced by a new, less polluting one. If the equipment was becoming economically obsolete and would have been replaced regardless of environmental considerations, can the firm allocate the amount spent for the new equipment to its 'environmental investments' account? Sometimes, it is only a matter of labelling. An in-house training programme aimed at ensuring maximum personnel safety and correct use of technology can be relabelled environmental training and the associated expenses counted as environmental expenses. The reality is that *many investments are multi-functional*: they may partly be aimed at reducing some environmental damage or risk, but that is not their sole purpose, nor perhaps their main purpose. For example, correct use of technology by staff is one way of reducing risks to the environment as well as risks to personal safety. In the case study section, we shall see why, because of this difficulty, WMC Ltd decided in 1999 to abandon environmental cost allocations altogether! They are not the only ones. As a result, standard setting is just as necessary as it is difficult!

The first stage of environmental accounting is thus identifying, in both the balance sheet and the trading and profit and loss account of the company, the accounting increments related to the environment. Some of the elements of a typical balance sheet (Table 4.1) may be directly related to environmental management (Table 4.2).

Table 4.1 Typical simplified balance sheet for an industrial company

Liabilities	Assets
Long-term debts	Land and buildings
	Less: provisions
Medium-term debts	Plant and machinery
	Less: depreciation
Creditors	Stocks (raw materials, products)
Short-term debts	Debtors
Equity	Cash and cash-related assets
	Other financial assets
	Goodwill

Financial accounting has to give a faithful picture of the value of the firm to the stakeholders, and especially to the shareholders and to the management of the firm. However, the financial condition of a firm determines its creditworthiness and its long-term survival, and is thus also of interest to stakeholders such as bankers and employees, among others. However, as mentioned in Chapter 1, there can be hidden liabilities and hidden assets related to the environment that are of interest to a number of stakeholders. If the balance sheet is faithfully to describe the net value of the firm, or its equity, one must take into account hidden liabilities such as being liable for cleaning up some polluted property, even if the firm does not own it. As shown later in Chapter 6, this is now possible under environmental legislation that prevails in many countries, and in particular in the USA. In the USA, under the context of CERCLA, if the firm has used a piece of land for waste disposal while renting it, it becomes liable for cleaning up the polluted property thus created. This liability can be transferred to another company if it takes over the first company, as shown by Figure 4.1.

Table 4.2. Environmental items in a typical simplified balance sheet for an industrial company

Liabilities	Assets
Long-term debts covering environmental and related equipment	Contaminated land less: provisions for rehabilitation
Medium-term debts covering environmental and related equipment	Anti-pollution and related equipment less: special depreciation
Creditors (suppliers of environmental services and so on)	Stocks (raw materials, products) Materials to be recycled Ecological fuels Ecolabelled and other 'green' products
Short-term debts covering environmental expenses	Other financial assets (including: shares of companies with environmental activities)
Increase in equity due to environmental management	Increase of goodwill due to 'greening' of products (Decrease of goodwill due to environmental problems)

We now move on to discussing how to account for environmental costs and benefits. This means that environmental costs, savings and sales (meaning the sales of 'green' products, possibly with ecolabels) have to be extracted from the standard financial accounting of the firm (and especially from the trading and loss and profit accounts).

There are several kinds of environmental costs. Direct costs are costs that are directly available from standard financial accounts, such as pollution-prevention, recycling and rehabilitation costs. There are also direct costs of human resources and of capital, such as pollution prevention equipment and training. Other direct environmental costs include costs of environmental services and costs of insurance policies against environmental risks, costs of environmental certification and costs of environmental audits. However, many of these environmental costs are usually indirect costs, meaning that some cost allocation has to be carried out. In particular, capital costs seldom correspond only to pure pollution prevention or other environmental effects, because the latter are often only one aspect of the investment. The same is true of maintenance costs and of the costs of human resources. Here, some cost allocation has to be carried out by trying to extract environmental costs among all other costs.

There are also direct benefits, such as the sales of 'green' products, products with ecolabels and sales of recycled materials, or by-products that otherwise would have been disposed of as waste. Overheads have to be allocated between the various products as usual in order to single out some overheads and fixed costs related to these 'green' products.

The above costs are simply conventional corporate costs that may be directly or indirectly allocated to the environment. However, as emphasized elsewhere (especially in Chapter 1), there also are hidden costs and benefits that are related to the environment. There are costs that potentially have been overlooked in conventional corporate management and identified as 'image and relationship costs', such as blows to the reputation of a firm due to environmental accidents or incidents and other negative events. Conversely, there are also hidden benefits due to events that positively affect the firm's reputation. We finally end up with accounting for environmental costs and benefits extracted from the firm's trading and loss and profit accounts.

(1) Initially, firms A and B exist; B rents the piece of lan C, using it for waste disposal.

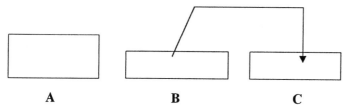

A **B** **C**

(2) A takes over B, without the polluted piece of land C...

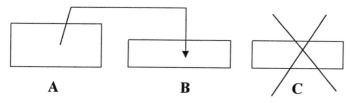

A **B** **C**

(3) A+B is not the owner of C, but may still be liable for the costs of cleaning up C...

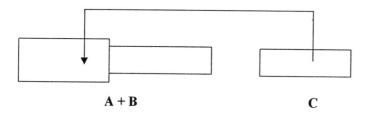

A + B **C**

Figure 4.1: Example of a hidden liability (liability for cleaning up polluted property) to be taken into account in the balance sheet of firm B, which is taken over by firm A

Clearly, the detail of these costs may be used for costing and management accounting. They constitute private information and hence a management tool which aims at assessing the financial impact of the environmental management of the firm.

As noticed by several authors, societal costs, such as the costs of negative externalities, are usually overlooked in this approach, although some authors propose to include them in a more complete practice of accounting (Christophe, 1995). This is *full-cost accounting* (FCA) which has been practised, for instance, by Ontario Hydro in Canada (EPA, 1995b). As the Ontario Hydro experience demonstrates, FCA aims at including and quantifying social costs. Costs imposed on society, through environmental impacts or otherwise, are identified and estimated, although they may not, at least directly, affect the firm's bottom line (Estes, 1972). These include benefits from the environment, such as clean air and water, biodiversity, a pristine ecosystem, or a beautiful landscape, that may be lost through economic activity (Cairncross, 1991). With FCA, the firm is clearly reflecting its responsibility to all of society, but here the measurement problems loom large, as non-market valuation techniques must be relied upon to estimate some of these costs (see O'Connor and Spash, 1999).

One may also ask how far a private firm needs to go down such a path. For a public utility, in which the state is the major shareholder, such accounting appears not only reasonable, but highly desirable (White et al., 1993). For a privately owned firm, or one where private interests are the major shareholders, this is more questionable. As will be examined in more detail later, it is less the social costs themselves that are relevant to a private firm than the consequences on the future value of its business of imposing such costs. This will be the essence of strategic accounting, a weak form of FCA appropriate for the private sector (see section 3.3).

The next stages of environmental accounting deal with 'ecological accounting' in Schaltegger et al.'s (1996) sense. First, we look at ecobalances for the activities of the firm; then for its products (LCA). This means accounting for the various environmental impacts of the firm's activities and products. This was first done in relation to energy use (Jacques, Lesourd and Ruiz, 1988). Energy accounting is a quantitative evaluation of the various energy inputs for the various product lines and production units of the firm. Energy resources are closely linked to the environment given that they give rise to atmospheric emissions. Also, non-renewable energies, or fossil fuels, are exhaustible resources.

Table 4.3:   Environmentally related costs and benefits

Costs	Benefits
Direct environmental costs	Supplementary sales due to "greening" of products
Indirect and allocated environmental costs	Sales of recycled by products
(Savings in raw materials and other intermediary products)	Hidden environmental benefits
(Including: energy savings)	
(Relief in financial and interest costs related to environmentally related investments)	
(Relief in corporate tax related to environmentally related investments)	
Depreciation of pollution prevention and other environmentally related equipment	
Other environmental provisions	
Hidden environmental costs	
Supplementary net after-tax profit due to environmental management	Or: Supplementary net after-tax loss due to environmental management

We thus discuss energy accounting and give a more general description of ecobalances in the next section; first for activities, then for products.

2.3 Ecological Accounting: Towards Activity and Product Ecobalances

The pre-history of ecobalances: energy accounting

The first appearance of 'environmental accounting' depends on how we define it. If *energy accounting* is good enough, then, soon after the first 'oil shock' in October 1973, companies started to monitor their energy-consumption patterns. This was primarily motivated, of course, by cost-reduction incentives brought about by the sudden increase in oil prices. At the same time, however, it was the first time that business started to draw up physical accounts of energy consumption alongside the corresponding monetary accounts. There were two reasons for this.

First, there was the convenient accounting basis provided by the laws of thermodynamics, whereby all energies can be converted into one another in terms of heat or work equivalents (depending on whether the First or the Second Principle is used (see Lesourd and Gousty, 1981; Jacques, Lesourd and Ruiz, 1988). In this respect, energy could be used as a physical numéraire, or accounting unit, for monitoring energy consumption and especially energy efficiency. This provides us with the second reason: that cost reduction implied engineering reassessment of energy systems and energy wastage. Alongside the economics, made visible through monetary-cost accounting (for example, in dollars), the engineering requirements were made visible through physical-energy accounting (for example, in gigajoules or 10^9 Joules). The development potential was made visible through the difference between the thermodynamic limit or Carnot efficiency and the current energy efficiency (Lesourd and Gousty, 1981).

Energy accounting is amenable to easy aggregation because the thermodynamic principle allows all energies to be converted into heat equivalents (measured in BTUs, megajoules, kilowatt-hours, or tonnes of oil equivalent). The common shared property is the generation of heat. Although universally in use, this approach is not correct, on thermodynamic grounds, when work or power rather than heat is of interest. In that case, an exact aggregation principle (the exergy principle), based on the second law of thermodynamics, is usually preferable (Lesourd and Gousty, 1981). However, aggregation is of interest only in the case of interrelated energy consumptions in a complex technical system, and exergy is thus mainly an

Table 4.4: Energy accounting for a hotel company

Hotels	A		B		C	
	Previous year	Base year	Previous year	Base year	Previous year	Base year
Guest nights	14 859	14 061	22 338	36 582	29 374	28 555
Electricity	183 044 kWh	17 4591 kWh	34 7621 kWh	378 502 kWh	144 851 kWh	143 049 kWh
	658958 MJ	628528 MJ	1251436 MJ	1362607 MJ	521 464 MJ	514 976 MJ
LPG (Butane)	610 kg	685 kg	1288 kg	1867 kg	112 kg	109 kg
	28 060 MJ	31 501 MJ	59 248 MJ	85 891 MJ	5152 MJ	5000 MJ
Gas oil	977 982*	765 400*	1 262 996*	1 451 336*	315 792*	306160*
	982 350 MJ	769 500 MJ	1 261 260 MJ	1 450 000 MJ	311 540 MJ	305 620 MJ
Total GJ (rounded)	1665	1425	2574	2900	842	826
MJ / Bed night	112	101	115	79	29	29

Note:
* Imperial gallons (4.54 litre)

Source: Jacques, Lesourd and Ruiz, 1988, pp. 339-40

engineering concept. In the practice of energy accounting from the management point of view, if unrelated sources of energy are used, aggregation may be unnecessary. An example of energy accounting for a hotel company in a Mediterranean country, taken from the work of Jacques, Lesourd and Ruiz (1988) is given in Table 4.4.

This example of energy accounting is only a particular case of environmental accounting, which might encompass such energy figures, whether with aggregation or with no aggregation. Inasmuch as the case study developed in this example was originally aimed at evaluating the impacts of using solar energy in that hotel company, we are indeed very close to environmental concerns.

This example of energy accounting is only a particular case of environmental accounting, which might encompass such energy figures, whether with aggregation or with no aggregation. Inasmuch as the case study developed in this example was originally aimed at evaluating the impacts of using solar energy in that hotel company, we are indeed very close to environmental concerns.

One may object that this energy-accounting example cannot really be classified as environmental accounting, in that, for example, no account was made for greenhouse gas impacts of energy consumption. This, however, would be missing the point, in that energy accounting was just a first step in the business of revealing previously hidden costs (of energy wastage) and benefits (of energy savings). If carbon credits had been introduced as a policy back in the 1970s, it is more than likely that energy and environmental accounting would have developed in closer symbiosis, and much quicker. By contrast, if no oil shocks had happened in 1973 or 1979, and energy had remained very cheap throughout, it is likely that environmental-impact accounting, in terms of atmospheric carbon accumulation, might have preceded energy-cost accounting.[17]

Ecological impacts of activities: towards eco-balance accounting
Be as it may, in the mid-1980s, partly in reaction to the Reagan and Thatcher administrations' 'all business' approach to policy and partly in response to new measurements made by the scientific community, environmental-impact awareness rose sharply in North America, in Western

Europe (particularly in Northern countries), in Australia and in New Zealand. Pollution and pollution abatement became the catchwords of the day. The need for pollution monitoring systems and cost-minimization strategies hit top priority. In a way, pollution abatement played the role that energy saving had played in the 1970s, in that it turned the light beam towards cost reductions, initiating a second wave of accounting needs, at first targeted to management (or costing) accounts.

This time, however, there was no practical equivalent to thermodynamic energy conversions. It was hard to see how an equivalence principle could be drawn between tonnes of carbon emitted into the atmosphere and kilograms of mercury washed out into the ocean at Minamata, Japan.[18] This time, would-be environmental accountants were faced with as many material balance accounts as there were materials being emitted or washed out into the environment. On the one hand, there seemed no practical way of bringing all these accounts together into one consolidated account, and, furthermore, there seemed to be no easy way to correlate existing monetary and financial accounts with these disparate material balance accounts. This explains why energy accounting never attracted much attention outside engineering and cost-management departments, whereas the wider-based environmental accounting issues have hit the whole accounting profession, much of the business world, and even the political sphere.

There is yet another crucial difference between the energy accounting of the 1970s and the environmental accounting of the 1990s and beyond. The former was concentrated around cost reduction, which directly affected the 'bottom line' and profits. The stakeholders were the same as those concerned by 'business as usual': the owners of the firm, investors and shareholders, top management and government, insofar as it wanted to reduce energy imports into the national economy. Because greenhouse gas and other environmental impacts were not yet a concern for the general public, both customers and consumers, no 'value' was placed on carbon and other greenhouse gas emissions. The situation changed in the mid-1980s and became prevalent in the 1990s. This time, new stakeholders appeared in the picture who were not the traditional ones, at least in the eyes of business managers. Concomitantly, environmental pressure groups, NGOs and widespread publicity over industrial environmental disasters like Bhopal and

Exxon Valdez put new pressure on business firms and started to reveal previously hidden costs and liabilities. In the USA, a legal innovation introduced retroactive liability for site contamination and clean-up (the US Superfund scheme), while development of the Internet and information networks around the world facilitated the role of watchdogs over the environmental doings of companies. Shell was a noteworthy example following the Brent Spar and Nigerian events. In short, the new stakeholders created new accountabilities for companies, which in turn created new pressures for environmental accounting.

Meanwhile, some of the equipment installed and know-how acquired for energy monitoring and recording was already in place when the need for a broader accounting framework was felt. To that extent, although we know of no studies that have actually investigated this, energy accounting helped reduce the costs of implementing environmental accounting systems.

Nevertheless, with ecological accounting, technical difficulties loom large. The first is one of consolidation, or aggregation.[19] Accounts in physical units, such as gigajoules of heat, tonnes of carbon dioxide, and kilograms of mercury cannot be added together. It is like adding apples and oranges. Thus, in accounting for the environmental impacts of the firm, accountants (or whoever is given the task) are faced with as many separate accounts as there are impacts. One may ask: so what? Where is the problem? The problem is this. If an investment reduces the emission of greenhouse gases by a certain amount, say 100 tonnes of CO_2 equivalents, but increases the use of clean fresh water by say 5000 m^3, are we to see this change as a net gain or a net loss with respect to environmental impacts? In other words, how do you compare tonnes of atmospheric emissions to water use? The simple answer is: you cannot. Luckily however, this is not always the case.

There is a way of adding apples and oranges, say five apples and three oranges. One can answer: eight pieces of fruit. This answer is much less trivial than one might think. It is based on a trick economists and financial analysts use all the time, that of 'aggregation'. Aggregation is not (or not only) addition. As a first approximation, aggregation consists of bringing together items of different sorts or qualities under the same heading (for example, 'fruit') before adding them up. This implies that they share some common feature that makes them comparable and opposable to other categories (for example, 'vegetables'). Before highlighting the implications, it is useful to notice that any item, be it apples or oranges, is itself a category of disparate things. There are different sorts of apples and oranges, as there are different sorts of 'people', 'birds' and 'trees'. Within any category, one can think of finer categories until one is left with the individual samples. Aggregation can then be understood as the process by which objects of different categories are brought together under a broader category due to some common shared property that makes them comparable. A couple of examples will illustrate this concept.

An exact analogy exists for greenhouse gas accounting with the concept of 'CO$_2$ equivalents'. Methane, nitrogen oxides and carbon monoxide share with carbon dioxide the property of inducing a warming greenhouse effect as they accumulate in the earth's atmosphere. With respect to this specific property, an equivalence can be established on chemical grounds such that one kilogram of nitrogen oxide, say, is equivalent to 310 kilograms of carbon dioxide, because that one kg of NO$_x$ contributes to global warming about 310 times more than one kg of carbon dioxide. Burritt (1995) develops similar lines for the 'ozone regime', in terms of ozone-depletion potential.

This type of aggregation may be called 'functional aggregation' in that it brings together items that share a same function: heat generation for energy equivalents, greenhouse-warming potential for CO$_2$ equivalents. If the environment could be affected in only one way, say through atmospheric temperature, then CO$_2$ equivalents would allow aggregation of all ecological accounts into one master account, and life would be easy – at least, the accountant's life would be. Unfortunately, the environment is itself a very broad category and can be affected in many different ways. There will be many different 'functions' (or contributions to environmental quality), each function demanding a different aggregation principle. Usual patterns of aggregation for atmospheric pollutants are given in Table 4.5. As atmospheric pollutants, global warming, acidification and ozone depletion can each be subject to meaningful aggregation (see Manton and Jasper, 1998).

Given our current knowledge, there is no universal aggregation principle that is not uncontroversial.[20] A system of 'environmental impact points' (EIP), which aggregates all environmental impacts, was developed by

Müller-Wenk (1978) in 1972 and is being experimented in the German-speaking countries: it is described below in section 2.4. For the time being, however, given the diversity of environmental impacts from modern businesses, environmental accounts will remain many and unconsolidated. Environmental managers and other stakeholders will have to contend with an array of curves and graphs that indicate converging or diverging trends in various environmental impacts: sulphur dioxide emissions vs. greenhouse gas emissions vs. energy consumption vs. water consumption vs. lead and mercury emissions, and so on and so on. Presumably, one would wish to see simultaneous improvements in all indicators. As this is unlikely always to be the case, judgmental trade-offs, backed by scientific advice, will have to be made.

Table 4.5:   Environmental (atmospheric) impact accounting equivalents

	Global warming potential	Acidification potential	Ozone depletion potential
Units:	CO_2 equivalents	SO_2 equivalents	CFC11 equivalents
CO_2	1	0	0
CH_4	21	0 ?	0 ?
CFCs (CFC12)	8500	0	0.82
HCFCs (HCFC22)	1700	0	0.04
Halons (halon 1301)	5600	0	12
SO_2	0	1	0
NO_x	310	0.7	0

Overall, ecological accounting means quantitatively determining a set of distinct, and not directly related, impacts on the environment. It ensues that comparison of the environmental impacts of the activity of a company over time, or of the activities of several companies, is essentially a multicriteria pursuit.[21]

Ecological impacts of products: accounting for life-cycle assessment

Environmentally motivated stakeholders in the firm's landscape are increasing the scope of its responsibilities. Increased accountability and liabilities are pushing for an expansion of the accounting framework. Its most tangible expression appears as Life-Cycle Assessment (LCA).[22] LCA considers all resource uses and environmental impacts of a given product from its inception and design through production and distribution to use and disposal. The question LCA asks is how far a firm's accountability extends in what it buys from its suppliers and sells to its customers.

The answer depends to a large extent on the law. The firm's liabilities are at stake. Laws change, however, and they sometimes change unexpectedly. It is often in the firm's interests to be proactive and not to wait to be pressurized by the law. A firm's answer could be: 'the firm is not responsible[23] if it has no knowledge of how inputs are manufactured and outputs consumed'. Does the answer depend on the information available to the firm? The current trend in most countries is that the rule that increasingly applies echoes the old Roman adage: no one is deemed to ignore the law. Likewise, no firm will be deemed to ignore the environmental impact of its products over their life cycle. This is nothing less than a moral obligation to be informed and an incentive to expand the accounting system.

LCA runs counter to most of what traditional accounting systems were designed to do, which is to ignore anything that happens outside the legal boundaries of the firm. A product before it was bought or after it was sold was of no business to the firm. The first difficulty is therefore a psychological and perhaps a cultural one: acknowledging new responsibilities, facing the 'this is none of our business' reaction. The second is that different products have different life cycles, so that the boundary of the firm (or at least of its liabilities) is no longer fixed but may vary with every product. A rigorous conceptual framework is needed, as proposed by Fava et al. (1992). This introduces a new dimension of complexity, which leads to the third, technical difficulty. As Pohl et al. (1996, p. 13) conclude, 'The total error in LCA can easily become larger than the calculated differences of ecological impacts of products and services.' At this level of imprecision, LCA is unlikely to be taken up seriously by decision makers; innovative techniques need to be implemented (Bailey, 1991).

The shortcomings of LCA point to an urgent need for standardization, which the International Standards Organization (ISO) has been answering by developing the ISO 14040 norms, which are discussed in Chapter 8 (section 4). ISO defines three stages in LCA. The second stage, inventory analysis, quantifies the inputs from and the outputs to the environment at every stage of production 'from cradle to grave', from design to final waste disposal. As underscored by Schaltegger (1997) and others, the problem at this stage is that information is not of equal quality across the life cycle: information related to processes happening within the firm, or close to it (the so-called 'foreground data') can be precise and reliable; information related to upstream or downstream processes depend on suppliers' and customers' disclosure policies (see chapter 4), or, alternatively, on industry averages, the so-called 'background data'. These, to quote Johnson and Kaplan (1987: 22-29) in a different context, are 'too late, too aggregated, and too distorted to be relevant'. Some, like Schaltegger (1997), advise against their use altogether, and recommend focusing on site-specific, controllable information (also Schaltegger and Sturm, 1992). Most of the critiques Schaltegger and others formulate (Pohl et al., 1996; Fava et al., 1992; Bailey, 1991) pertain to the implementation of LCA, rather than to its fundamental principles. They intend to facilitate the generation of solutions by practitioners.

Fortunately, a non-negligible part of LCA can be carried out *within* the firm. In an LCA study of the production of the French newspaper *Le Monde*, Rafenberg and Mayer (1998) show the sequence of operations leading to energy and materials wastage and to excessive environmental impacts. Interestingly, this study showed how organizational and institutional factors, here the role of unions, played a major role by inhibiting an environmentally efficient investment, because it would have taxed the working habits of the workforce.

2.4 Eco-financial Integration for Assessing Environmental Management Performance

Eco-efficiency indicators

Given the above difficulties in measuring financial and ecological impacts, it is hardly surprising that it is no easy matter to judge a firm's environmental performance. Is it 'doing enough' for the environment? Is it doing it efficiently? These and other related questions link the firm's efforts to its environmental achievements. At first sight, given that there are many possible cost and financial allocations as well as many different ecological impacts, the number of impact-to-effort performance ratios would be bewildering. This problem has been given careful consideration, especially in the German-speaking countries (Germany, Switzerland, Austria), and a number of synthetic ratios have been developed and are being experimented with by a number of companies, again mostly in German-speaking countries. In Switzerland, the federal OFEFP has helped develop the methodology (OFEFP, 1991).

Müller-Wenk (1978) first conceived of environmental performance indicators for business firms in 1972. The concept may be related to Leibenstein's so-called *X-efficiency* of firms[24], which describes the degree to which a firm's current input–output efficiency approaches the best possible efficiency given current technological knowledge. Schaltegger and Sturm (1992), in Switzerland, developed Müller-Wenk's ideas into an operational set of indicators that have been publicized and put into practice through Bank Sarasin and Co.'s 'Sustainability Research Procedure'® (Schaltegger and Figge, 1998) and Ellipson Ltd, an environmental-management consulting firm based in Bern, Switzerland (Sturm and Müller, 1998). Schaltegger et al. (1996) provide an overview and distinguish between flow-efficiency based indicators and investment-oriented indicators. A commonly used concept is that of EIA, *environmental impact added*, which measures the additional impact on the environment from an activity or set of activities over a period of time, such as a month or a year.

In the category of flow-efficiency indicators, which are operations and cost-management oriented, ecological efficiency is defined as the ratio of an economically desired output to EIA. The output can either be a product (for example, cars) or a function (for example, transport). *Ecological product efficiency* will measure number of product units per EIA (or equivalently, number of EIA units per product-unit produced). For example, number of cars produced per gigajoule of energy consumed and per tonne of CO_2-equivalent emitted (or, average quantity of energy and carbon dioxide per car produced). *Ecological function efficiency* is a broader concept in that it allows for product substitution subject to a given economic demand. The quantity of energy consumed and carbon dioxide emitted will be related; for example, to number of kilometre-persons transported. It is obvious that bicycles will always be more efficient than petrol-based cars, although speed can also be factored into the ratio.[25] Because such efficiency ratios will vary depending on what product or function one chooses, a more general indicator, *eco-efficiency*, was developed, which relates economic value added (EVA) to EIA. Different stakeholders will weight the numerator and denominator differently, so that the indicator appears as

$$\text{Eco-efficiency} = \frac{w_1 \times EVA}{w_2 \times EIA}$$

If $w_1 = w_2$, then economic and ecological aspects of decision making are given equal weights. The ratio can be used as an indicator of sustainable growth, when EVA increases and EIA does not increase or decreases. Depending on the relative weights, either economic growth or environmental protection will rank as a higher priority. Schaltegger and Burritt (2000) discuss the implications. As we shall see in section 3, this view assumes independence between numerator and denominator. Yet, ecological impacts affect economic outcomes, and thus EVA, not only as a function of past decisions but also of current and planned decisions.

Environmental investment appraisal and eco-financial integration

For environmental investments, Schaltegger et al. (1996) propose *ecological payback period* (EPP) (defined as the ratio of the EIA caused with the investment to the annual reduction of EIA expected through the investment) and the *ecological rate of return* (ERR) (defined as the EIA reduced over the total lifespan of the investment to the EIA caused with the investment).

In the first case, the investment is environmentally beneficial if the lifespan of the investment is larger than the EPP, and in the second case if the ratio is greater than one.[26] Müller et al. (1996) then go on to show how eco-efficiency can be interpreted and evaluated from the viewpoint of financial analysis, and why it is correlated with stock-market valuation (see also Cohen et al., 1997).

The previous point sheds some light on the problem of account integration. We saw that there is no simple way to integrate the many different ecological-impact accounts. We specify 'no *simple* way', because there *are* ways. For example, Müller-Wenk, as previously noted, originally developed (in 1972) a system of 'environmental impact points', or EIPs, capable of aggregating all ecological impacts and integrating them with financial accounts, using, for example, EVA/EIA ratios (in \$/EIP units).[27] This point system is based on elaborate ecological-impact science and aims to determine relative 'environmental stress'. The higher the stress, the larger the number of points. Stress is generally defined, locally or globally, in relation to a specific environment's carrying capacity.[28] As Miyazaki (1998) points out, these EIPs play the role of 'ecological prices' in that they measure the relative scarcity of the environmental asset impacted. The problem with this approach is that, to corporate stakeholders and, in particular, to managers, the process underpinning the allocation of EIPs to different impacts is not transparent, nor does it relate easily to what they already know: it is likely to be met with suspicion. Secondly, such a system would need strong backing by government, with widespread standardization and monitoring. Enforcement costs may be too high in relation to uncooperative companies. As a result, a compromise must be struck between transparency and integration. For some time yet to come, environmental managers are stuck with an array of graphs and indicators. Expertise will continue to be needed to integrate ecological and financial performance indicators.

This, however, is also the case with standard financial accounts. In both cases, managers are not entirely free to choose their preferred indicators: the economic and policy context exert a strong influence. The difference lies in the modes of communication. The reading (and, for that matter, the writing) of financial accounts is almost entirely dictated by market and tax considerations, both of which use direct monetary values. In the case of environmental accounting, non-market feedbacks that do not have a readily computable moneta:y value are important. This leads to the concept of strategic accounting, which includes managing the risks of potential non-market feedbacks (see section 3.3).

There are other dimensions of account integration: not only within the firm but also within an industry, a professional organization, a country, and across nations of the world. Numerous accountancy organizations are involved in standard setting: in America, the AICPA; in the UK, the ACCA; in Australia, the ASCPA; and management accountants generally. Concerns with standardization reflect the need for reliability and comparability.

3. THE FUTURE OF ENVIRONMENTAL ACCOUNTING AND THE ISSUE OF CONTINGENT LIABILITIES

3.1 Valuing Environmental Liabilities as Part of a Company's Total Value

Environmental accounting standards and practices have been developed so as to create as little deviation as possible from financial accounting standards and practices. This has been the impetus behind the success in the German-speaking countries, with authors like Figge and Schaltegger, as well as with other developments in the USA and elsewhere, in connection with EPA's Environmental Accounting Programme. Ironically, this is happening as financial accounting standards are themselves in turmoil, and under increasing pressure from financial economists. Environmental accounting is anchoring itself to a moving ship. This may in fact be for the best. In what follows, we summarize the key points at stake and how we believe they will affect the future of environmental accounting.

It is probably safe to say that the current debates in financial accounting revolve around the issue of the valuation of a company. As is well known, there is a 'valuation gap' between valuing a company through the 'book value' of its assets and liabilities and valuing it through its expected market value; a value that is realized, or revealed, when the company is taken over by another company. Standard wisdom interprets the valuation gap as the company's goodwill: intangible assets such as clientele, reputation, corporate image, social and political networks, and so forth. The problem is, the gap can be quite large and not just a minor residual. As a result, valuing a company using the book value of its assets and liabilities makes for a poor predictor of the company's current value on the market, and in particular on the stock market. Furthermore, as Kierkegaard (1997) points out, it makes for a poor predictor of a company's insolvency. One cannot predict if, and when, it may go bankrupt.

This valuation gap may be viewed from two angles. Firstly, it should appear natural that the sum total of a company's net assets, or equity, should not equal its market value. This is because a company is more than just a collection of buildings, machines, patents and real-estate properties: the linear aggregation principle, fundamental to accounting practice, cannot apply to goodwill (Ijiri, 1967). Increasingly, it is the experience, the skills and the know-how of its management and workforce, and how they use the company's tangible assets, that create value. The value of the whole is (often much) larger than the sum total of its parts. This is the classical view from organizations theory: a business is a living organism. This translates in the accounting realm into a conflict between a backward-looking and a forward-looking valuation principle. Many assets are individually valued using their purchase cost, while others are valued using other approaches. This methodological diversity leads to inconsistencies that have traditionally been dealt with through a jungle of conventional rules. Valuing a company as a whole, however, can only consistently be done in a forward-looking manner, by estimating the discounted sum of all future earnings and expenses resulting from the company's expected activities, inclusive of the liquidation value of its net assets (see Chapter 5). If, however, there are no prospects for future activity, valuation is done at book value and the company is valued at its 'break-up value'.

Surely, the two approaches can be subsumed if one considers the likelihood of the 'going concern' hypothesis. This standard hypothesis of traditional accounting assumes that the company will continue operating for an indefinite future. Special and separate accounting standards are used for break-up and liquidation. Realistically, however, the going concern hypothesis is true only to some degree of probability. As it tends towards zero (that is, the company is sure to cease its activities very soon), the break-up valuation method must be chosen; as the probability tends to one (the company is very unlikely to cease its activities in the foreseeable future), the future discounted cash-flow method must be used. Presumably, one can use both methods by weighting them by the relative probabilities of going concern and cessation of activities. Because the weighting would be controversial, special rules carrying liability must be enforced that create disincentives for over- or under-estimation.

Having thus set the stage, accounting for environmental (or ecological) impacts introduces a new twist. It introduces an asymmetry between future assets and future liabilities. Environmental damages may lead to very large liabilities. Many of the benefits expected from environmental management come as a reduction of environmental liabilities, which in turn translate into lower current financial and insurance costs. Chapters 5 and 6 discuss these issues at length; here we are concerned with their implications for accounting. The point is, environmental liabilities can only be valued completely in a forward-looking manner. Given that environmental liabilities put the company's solvency and survival at stake, their build-up is creating mounting pressures to reorganize financial accounting around a forward-looking model. Using Kierkegaard's (1997) concept, a firm's environmental liabilities can determine its financial *solvency*.[29] Point number one.

Point number two: environmental liabilities are not only potentially huge; they may also be uncertain and contingent upon future events. As often as not, environmental liabilities are contingent liabilities. Bailey (1996) identifies compliance liabilities, remediation liabilities, compensation liabilities, and penalties and fines for non-compliance and damages. Just as financial statements in the 1920s underestimated a company's real (financial) liabilities – a lack of transparency that contributed to the 1929 crash – today's practices underestimate a company's real environmental liabilities. When these are uncertain or contingent, current accounting standards and practices do not include them in financial statements other than in the form of qualitative footnotes. If environmental accounting is to make any credible progress, it must find a way to quantify and include environmental liabilities in the main body of financial statements.

3.2 Progress Using Shareholder and Stakeholder Value Concepts

The concept of shareholder value (Rappaport, 1986) seems to open a way forward. In the 1990s, it gained ground among accountants and managers. Shareholder value is usually measured as follows (see further developments in Chapter 6, equations 16 and 19):

Shareholder value = sum of all future discounted cash flows − borrowed capital or:

$$\text{Shareholder Value} = \sum_{t=1}^{\infty} \{FCF_t * [\frac{1}{(1+i)^t}]\} - BC$$

where FCF_t are the free cash flows of future earnings, $[1/(1 + i)^t]$ is the discount factor, and i is the discount rate. Shareholder value measures the market value of the equity owners' share in the company (whether the company is quoted on the stock market or not). As discussed by many authors (for example, Ehrbar, 1998), it is a future-oriented long-term value concept. Thus, it can account for environmental liabilities, *provided they have been translated into financial terms*. Indeed, the concept has gained favour as 'green' or environmental shareholder value, the features of which are studied by Schaltegger and Figge (1998). Although the links between environmental performance and shareholder value have been questioned, they appear on balance to be real (Blumberg et al., 1996; Cohen et al., 1997; Reed, 1998). Environmental performance is considered to contribute to shareholder value in the form of economic value added (EVA) and its incremental translation (see Grant, 1997). Even so, shareholder value, green or otherwise, now appears to some to be too narrow a concept (for example, Hill, 1997).

As early as 1984, Freeman highlighted the stakeholder approach to business strategy. Shareholders or equity owners are not the company's only stakeholders. Also included are other providers of financial services (lenders, insurers, investors), providers of labour (employees, sub-contractors), of goods and services (suppliers), of cash payments (customers and consumers), and of public services (government); each stakeholder demanding in turn some form of payment, in cash or otherwise. A stakeholder is any individual or organization whose costs and benefits are affected, upwards or downwards, by the company's decisions. As discussed in Chapter 1, the company's environmental impacts affect many, if not all, of its stakeholders. Therefore, an extension of the shareholder value concept to that of 'stakeholder value' is an improvement when it comes to the company's environmental liabilities. A further extension is naturally that of 'green' or environmental stakeholder value and its incremental derivative, stakeholder value added. These concepts, their measurement and their implications are presented, in a general setting, by Figge and Schaltegger[30] (2000). To our knowledge, however, the explicit link between stakeholder value and environmental liabilities has not yet been made.

The reason for this is that, although the framework for including environmental liabilities, especially those contingent on future events, now exists, their actual measurement still remains problematic. Quality groundwork is provided by Bailey (1996), of the United States Environmental Accounting Program, and by Figge (1998), in connection with Bank Sarasin and Co. (Switzerland). Bailey describes the tools available for their computation, while Figge clarifies some conceptual issues, albeit from a bank's perspective. The missing ingredient, in our view, is the concept of strategic accounting.

3.3. Strategic Accounting, and the Bridge to Finance and Economics

Strategic accounting is still a new concept. Brouthers and Roozen (1999) argue for such a need in a rapidly changing business environment, but their notion is different from what we have in mind here. Our notion of strategic accounting stems from Estes' (1972) socioeconomic accounting in relation to a firm's external diseconomies, and from stakeholder theory as it impacts on shareholder value (Figge and Schaltegger, 2000). *We define strategic accounting as the quantification of the financial impacts on the company's shareholder value from action taken by its various stakeholders in response to its current or planned decisions.* It is inherently future-oriented, long-term and probabilistic. For example, although large commercial benefits are a major incentive, a company's planned decision is expected negatively to affect employees, so that it should expect increases in absenteeism, strikes, accidents and incidents, theft, internal strife, conflict, and information hoarding, and a corresponding decline in productivity, initiative and internal cooperation. From past experience and a good understanding of current politics, such reactions, as well as their financial impacts on the firm, can be probabilistically estimated. If employees become dissatisfied, future commercial benefits expected from the decision must be reduced by the (contingent) liabilities employees now represent. The same case may be made for consumers, government and host populations if a company fails to avoid environmental damage.

Figure 4.2 outlines the difference between standard (non-strategic) and strategic accounting. The difference is the more important the more irreversible the (expected) outcomes of a decision. For totally reversible decisions (that is, incurring zero reversibility costs), strategic accounting has no *raison d'être*. This combination of uncertainty and (some degree of) irreversibility makes the quantification problem similar in principle to that of valuing a financial option (see Chapter 5). The company must then decide what risks it is willing to take. For so-called 'rare' events that follow a Poisson process, such as nuclear accidents and chemical spills, estimating the parameters necessary for identifying their probability distribution may be difficult. Even in this case, however, the mere reckoning of the possible financial impacts provides an incentive for the company to adopt a precautionary approach.

At present, strategic accounting would appear to be costly, given the level of expertise required by financial analysis techniques. Experience and software development will presumably reduce these costs, but systematic stakeholder consultation may yet be the most efficient strategy. As for its benefits, strategic accounting further consolidates the links between accounting, finance and economics. The requirements of forward-looking environmental accounting, it seems, will have helped build stronger bridges across artificially segregated disciplines, harnessing their synergy. Here too, the environment may have acted as a catalyst.

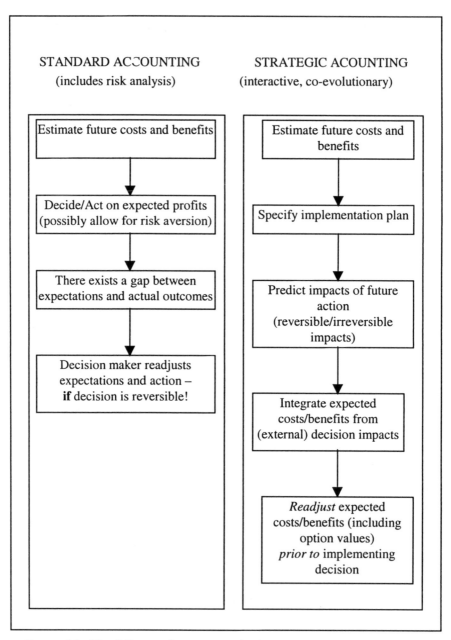

Figure 4.2   The difference between standard accounting and strategic accounting

4. CONCLUSIONS

If the business community wishes to capitalize on the potential benefits of environmental management (EM), it needs to identify where those benefits are, assuming there are any. Firms want to avoid unnecessary costs but also want to avoid missing out on potential benefits that might give them a competitive edge. Environmental accounting produces the information necessary for firms to decide how far they want to get involved in EM, and how.

The evidence from the 1990s is that an increasing number of firms have taken up EM but in an imperfect way, and still only a small number of them, mainly large corporations. This chapter has tried to clarify the role of accounting in this process, while reviewing its technical and institutional challenges.

Technically, environmental accounting has first to contend with measurement issues. Problems of cost allocation blur the financial impacts of EM, or lack thereof. Problems of aggregation and monetary valuation limit the usefulness of accounting for the firm's physical impacts on the environment. Second, in order to be of practical use, environmental accounting needs to mould itself into the framework of standard financial accounting. This is because assessing environmental performance requires the integration of financial and ecological data, so as to answer questions like: is the firm doing enough? Is it spending its money in a way useful to the environment? This chapter has tried to review the solutions being brought to these problems.

Institutionally, business accountants must face these challenges with, until very recently, few guidelines, standards or experience. At the same time, environmental accounting must contend with the strong pressures for change weighing on financial accounting. The tradition of using backward-looking methods and of valuing assets and liabilities 'at book value' is giving way to forward-looking approaches such as shareholder value and economic value added. Slowly but surely, the influence of financial economics is growing in accounting.

This trend is epitomized by the growing importance of environmental liabilities. Not only are they often huge; they may be uncertain and contingent on future events. Environmental accounting will be of definite value to managers when it can include such liabilities. We propose a notion of strategic accounting the purpose of which is precisely to be able to include contingent environmental liabilities. Already, tools from financial economics are being reviewed for this purpose, but perhaps the best way to reduce their cost, and even their need, is for managers to include as a standard business practice systematic consultation with the firm's stakeholders. Rather than a 'triple bottom line', stakeholders are understood to influence explicitly the financial performance of the firm. In this sense, strategic environmental accounting appears as a step towards accounting for sustainable business.

CASE STUDIES: A COMPARATIVE ANALYSIS OF SEVERAL CORPORATE ACCOUNTING STRATEGIES

Introduction

Environmental accounting details in the following companies' environmental reports, for the years 1998 or 1999, were examined: Volvo AB (Sweden), 1999; Royal Dutch/Shell Group (Netherlands), 1999; Swiss Re (Zurich, Switzerland), 1999; Alcoa (USA), 1999; WMC: Western Mining Corporation 1998; Migros (Switzerland), 1999; Dupont (USA), 1999. A specific report by Normandy Mining Ltd, 1998, was examined through its subsidiary Wirralie Gold Mines Pty Ltd (Australia) for its Big Bell Gold Mine, situated in the Murchison District of Western Australia, about 550 km NNE from Perth.

This choice in no way embodies a value judgement relative to other possible companies. Our focus is rather on how the need for normalization, comparability and reliability in environmental accounting can face up to the diversity of economic activities, not only between companies but also within companies. We examine their environmental accounting systems along the following lines:

- energy consumption, types of energy used
- atmospheric emissions
- water use and materials: depletion, waste generation and recycling
- costs, risks and financial aspects of environmental management.

Energy consumption

The focus can be put on total consumption at the company or site level (Wirralie) or on input–output energy efficiencies (WMC, Alcoa). The first highlights the impact on the environment whereas the latter highlight technical efficiency. Of course, both are important, but improvements may be done in one or the other. Big companies like WMC, Alcoa and Shell regularly see their total impact worsen following growth, acquisitions and restructuring of activities. Conversely, Dupont can demonstrate a flat rate of energy consumption from 1990 to 1998, even though its production has grown by 35 per cent. By showing trends over time, these companies show that changes in both overall impact and efficiency involve very different decisions: the operation of existing equipment, replacing old equipment by new equipment, and replacing old activity sectors by new, more (energy) efficient sectors (business restructuring). Accounts must then be adjusted to compare the situation before and after the restructuring (Shell).

Energy consumption can be shown in aggregate (all four companies), or separately by distinguishing electricity, diesel, natural gas and so on (none of the four, though Wirralie specifies the origin of the energy figures: diesel or electricity). This separation is of importance when the greenhouse gas intensity of different fuels differs, such as between petroleum (high intensity) and natural gas (low intensity). By separating fuels, the company shows it is considering fuel substitution for environmental purposes.

WMC specifies the source of electricity production, whether produced on-site or purchased. A MWh of electricity does not have the same energy cost nor the same GHG emission ratio depending on whether it was produced through hydro-power, coal, oil or natural gas. Distinguishing between these sources of production indicates the company has considered possible alternative electricity sources: indeed, it has replaced state-grid-coal- and oil-produced electricity, and on-site diesel-produced electricity, by its own natural gas facilities.[31] This is an extension of the LCA (life-cycle assessment) approach, and of the capacity of the company to choose between suppliers, if possible.[32]

WMC also measures its energy-efficiency trends against its own inner targets, which are dated and quantified. Thus, its 1998 target of 650 MJ of energy per tonne of ore milled was not quite met (700 MJ effective), even though over the previous four years it fell from 750 MJ. This was partly due to an increase in the relative weight of smelting and refining compared to ore milling (activity restructuring), showing that measuring energy use *per tonne of ore milled* may not be the best possible indicator. Total energy use increased, but no inner targets had been set, presumably reflecting expectations of business development and restructuring. Clearly, this accounting strategy can be improved. As suggested by Schaltegger et al. (1996), a more synthetic measure, such as energy use per dollar of economic value added, would have mitigated these problems.

In fact, all four companies stick to technical efficiency ratios rather than develop economic–ecological ratios, such as energy use per dollar value added. This is a scale-related issue. At site or plant level, technical ratios may be preferable given the type of remediating action conceivable – which lies in the field of engineering. At the corporate level, economic–ecological (as well as eco–financial) ratios appear more appropriate, as the type of action is reorganization. However, R&D investments into new, energy-efficient technologies apply throughout.

Volvo distinguishes its on-site operations and the fuel consumption of its products (engines and vehicles). Of course, in the latter case, consumption is monitored with respect to standardized engine regimes; for example, at 90 km/hour steady state. The actual consumption will depend on how Volvo's products are used. This is why Volvo and similar industries provide benchmark fuel consumption charts to clients. In addition, Volvo indicates how developing new products and technologies, such as engines running on natural gas or biofuel compounds, reduces energy consumption and various polluting emissions.

In the service industries, Migros includes transport of goods and Swiss Re includes business travel as items of their energy consumption. In its own choice of products (reinsurance), Swiss Re closely examines the environmental performance of its clients. Although not explicitly stated, Migros presumably maximizes packaging that can be recycled after use by consumers, provided that recycling bins are available to them. Thus, energy consumption and other environmental impacts are inherently tied up with the way these companies do business.

Atmospheric emissions

Regarding greenhouse gas (GHG) and other atmospheric emissions (SO_2, NO_x, and such like), WMC focuses on CO_2 and SO_2 specifically, presumably because these are the only emissions that have been monitored and measured. These are recorded over time and for each operating site (as for energy and water consumption), as well as against preset company targets. The report shows a dramatic fall in SO_2 emissions: from 22 kg per tonne of ore milled and 320 000 tonnes a year in 1994–95 to only 2 kg per tonne and 40 000 tonnes a year in 1998. The reason is given: the commissioning of a new acid plant which captures the SO_2 for conversion to sulphuric acid, an economically valuable product. As for CO_2 emissions, emissions per tonne of ore milled fell from about 100 kg per tonne of ore milled to just under 80 kg, a 21.6 per cent reduction, but total emissions increased from about 1.5 to 1.8 million tonnes, reflecting increased activity levels. In its summary, WMC highlights the efficiency improvements, due to substituting natural gas for oil and coal produced electricity, without mentioning the overall increased CO_2 impact. In all cases, WMC sets itself renewed quantified targets for a specified future date.

By contrast, Volvo aggregates GHG emissions into global warming potential (GWP), CFC and halon emissions into ozone-depletion potential (ODP), and sulphur and nitrogen oxide emissions into acidification potential. GWP is measured in CO_2 equivalents, ODP in CFC-11 equivalents, and AP in SO_2 equivalents. Dupont aggregates into global air toxics and carcinogenic emissions, while Shell aggregates only into GWP. All also provide specific emissions of CO_2, SO_2, NO_x, and so on, and Shell is very specific about a number of gaseous emissions, such as perfluorocarbons (PFCs) (which it reports as being zero emission in 1999), sulphurhexafluorides (SF6) (also reported as zero), and hydrofluorocarbons

(HFCs) (for which data is very punctual: only 1999 emissions are reported, previous years are not, and there are no projections or targets for the future). Dupont also reports PFCs and HFCs, and they are significant. These gases do not appear in Volvo's report, either because they are irrelevant to Volvo's activities, or simply because they have not been monitored (the reader of the report does not know).

Through these examples alone, a wide variety of practices appears, with no clear rationale for the choice of aggregated or detailed emissions. For example, readers of the report do not know (unless they are specialists) what 8.8 tonnes of HFCs mean in terms of GWP or other environmental impact. It might have proved useful for these companies to relate to an equivalence table of the type shown as Table 4.5 in section 2.3 above.

There could be other columns, showing emissions as radioactive, biologically toxic, or otherwise; rows show polluting agents or 'loadings'. Contributions of specific agents to specific impacts might also vary according to atmospheric conditions, such as CFCs with sunlight and SO_2 with ambient humidity. For biological toxicity, finding practical equivalents might be problematic if different environmental impacts are not distinguished: for example, carcinogenic (mostly humans: Dupont), sunlight obstructing (photosynthetic plants), genetic (all life forms), and so on. The focus on columns and rows responds to two different concerns. Columns focus on the firm's impact on the environment; rows focus on the levers it can manipulate to reduce its impacts. Both are important for different reasons. In particular, column aggregates are of interest to external stakeholders, whereas row specifics are of interest primarily to managers.

Swiss Re, in its 1998 and 1999 reports, goes further and defines an overall environmental impact index, measured in environmental impact points (EIPs). The method, described in its 1998 report, is based on an index of relative ecological scarcity. This is an ambitious approach, but its lack of general uptake (it is only implemented in the most advanced firms in the German-speaking countries) makes it difficult to use for comparisons, at least for the present. On the other hand, when Volvo aggregates all atmospheric emissions by simply adding up, in tonnes of emissions, gases with very different environmental impacts, one ends up with a meaningless figure (this would be like having 1's everywhere in Table 4.5).

Water use and materials: depletion, waste generation and recycling

Water use is indicated by all the companies sampled, except Shell. Trends over time and achievements with respect to preset targets are also generally indicated. However, the kind of water used is not. We do not know, for instance, what proportion of water used is fresh or saline; that is, good or not for drinking or irrigation; nor do we know what proportion comes from renewable sources such as rivers and reservoirs or non renewable such as fossil aquifers. Likewise, we do not know in what state the water, once used, is returned to the environment, whether it is first treated, and if so, to what degree, and, furthermore, in what medium it is rejected. Especially for the mining companies, this can be important. Volvo distinguishes only between cooling and processing water use. WMC, although it does not provide explicit figures other than for total water use, provides, in text form, a number of interesting indications. For example, it states that much of the water used in its Australian operations is highly saline and therefore unfit for drinking or irrigation. However, it also states several sources of water, some of which are fresh water: supplies from government-owned utilities and collected storm water, but also bore water and recycled water. WMC states that it tries to maximize water recycling, without however providing, like Migros, recycling ratios. In its figures for industrial water use, it does not include recycled water.

Regarding waste water disposal, WMC again provides verbal indications of reinjection of highly saline waste water back into original fossil aquifers, which were also highly saline. Alternatively, reinjection into nearby salt lakes is also mentioned, but we do not know if this concerns only a small part of the total water used or all of it. In conclusion with respect to WMC, there is potential to develop quantitative accounts of different aspects of water input, throughput and output. Conflict between different environmental impacts do not yet seem to be under focus. WMC, for example, states it was not able to meet its water-use reduction targets because of the new acid plant built to absorb the SO_2 emissions. WMC indicates that, had it planned beforehand, it would have revised its water-consumption targets upward. Implicitly, it is telling us that reducing SO_2

emissions is more important than reducing water consumption; however, the rationale underlying this decision is not made explicit.

In terms of materials, there is wide variation. Migros and Swiss Re provide much detail. Migros specifies throughput of packaging materials (eight categories), while Swiss Re specifies office use of paper, photocopying, amounts recycled, waste. Migros has a clear policy for recycling and is explicit about recycling ratios. The manufacturing and mining companies, on the other hand, are practically silent on materials throughput (except water use). Only Alcoa indicates a clear upward trend in the recycling of aluminium cans, although its optimistic linear trend line is not supported by the significant recycling slowdown after 1988, which tapers off at 62 per cent in 1999, having been at 56 per cent in 1988 and 27 per cent in 1978. Only when materials become waste, particularly toxic waste, are they reported.

Migros provides figures of total waste generated and percentage recycled, Volvo reports hazardous waste and solvents, while Swiss Re, Shell and Dupont distinguish between hazardous and non-hazardous waste. Dupont is quite open about differing regional trends: a decrease in hazardous waste emissions in the United States and Europe is concomitant with increases in Mexico and the Asia/Pacific region; however, from 1997 to 1998 the reductions are about five times greater than the increases. Shell and WMC include hydrocarbon and other spills into the environment, in quantities and number of occurrences for different liability levels.[33] Interestingly, Shell shows more than 60 per cent of spills are due to corrosion, indicating a need for clear but costly maintenance. As is the case for water, none of these companies specify if wastes are treated before rejection into the environment, and if so, to what degree; nor where they are rejected. Nor is the distinction between hazardous and non-hazardous waste made clear[34], nor in what way waste is hazardous, or to whom or what part of the environment. Again, this is not to criticize these companies, but to highlight the challenges that face the future of environmental monitoring, accounting and reporting. WMC shows a clear awareness of these challenges on page 17 of its 1998 environmental report[35], where it highlights the gaps in knowledge by putting question marks on all inflows and outflows of a company-wide materials balance (or eco-balance) scheme.

Costs, risks and financial aspects of environmental management

These aspects are only beginning to be reported in a systematic manner. In many environmental reports, as in Volvo's, they do not figure; instead, they will be in the conventional financial report. Alternatively, as in Alcoa's report, financial data are given in text format. Alcoa focuses on remediation expenses and reserve balances. Shell Group only reports compliance fines, in number and total amounts. Of the reports analysed, only WMC provides a more thorough picture of the financial implications of its environmental management, although it is still rather incomplete. This information appears in both its environmental and (concise) financial reports for 1998: they actually complement each other (in a rather informal way). Regarding rehabilitation provisions, WMC provides three key indicators: an estimated total of rehabilitation costs, rehabilitation provision accrued over the last year, and contingent liabilities. Its nickel refinery spent some of its reserve provisions on local rehabilitation, while others were accrued following upward revisions to closure costs after expansion of one of its operations (Olympic Dam). It also provides figures, both company-wide and for each of its sites, for capital and operating expenditures related to environmental investments and control. For example, it indicates that installation of fume-capture hoods at its nickel smelter increased these costs from 1997 to 1998. Of the reports analysed, WMC's is the most complete. However, especially for contingent liabilities, we do not know how figures were computed nor what the error margins are likely to be.

Conclusion

This wide variety and overall inconsistency between environmental accounting practices is very largely a political effect. Firms respond first and foremost to existing regulations, which vary over time and across countries. The inconsistencies stem perhaps above all from governments, but this form of government failure, like many others, is partly due to the lack of sufficiently developed techniques. The development of a sufficiently general agent-impact matrix, as exemplified in Table 4.5 above, coupled with minimum emission or consumption thresholds below which tracking, accounting and reporting is not legally needed[36], could go a long way in promoting some order in corporate environmental accounting. Note, however, that firms also have their own style. WMC, for example, has clearly decided to focus on only four indicators: total energy consumption, water use, CO_2 and SO_2 emissions, but to collect the information across its many sites and for different operations. This may result from a company-specific cost–benefit cost analysis: by focusing on only four environmental indicators seen as strategic to its business, WMC minimizes its information costs while still being able efficiently to target its main strategies. This leads us to the following conclusion on environmental monitoring and accounting.

Government regulations, types of activity and local conditions vary greatly across industries. Is there any way of providing a common framework to all? Accountants, regulators and managers are working hard on the issue. Perhaps, though, one should not ask too much, and by asking less one may be able to achieve more. Specifically, we believe that one can separate what *needs* to be monitored and accounted for from the general framework within which it can be so done. Flexibility should allow for many empty cells in a reporting matrix while still allowing for comparability across industries and over time. Activity-based analysis appears as a good starting point. An agent-impact matrix, as exemplified in Table 4.5 (but generalized as in section 6 of Chapter 4), would combine two distinct rationales. Columns would reflect stakeholder values, including government regulations. Rows would reflect corporate benefit–cost–risk analysis and available management strategies. Such an approach could combine the power of economics and the dynamics of stakeholder analysis.

NOTES

1. We gratefully acknowledge the reviewing of this chapter by S. Schaltegger and R. Burritt, whose comments greatly contributed to improve earlier drafts. Of course, errors and omissions are solely our responsibility.
2. *Efficiency* links back to financial impacts and aims at least-cost environmental management. This leads to measuring *eco-efficiency* ratios (see infra). *Effectiveness* links back to ecological impacts and aims at successfully avoiding or repairing environmental damages. Costs can be kept low but at the expense of ecological damage (ineffective efficiency). Conversely, damage may be avoided but only at a very high cost, higher than the costs induced by the damage

(inefficient effectiveness). Environmental accounting aims at finding ways to be 'efficiently effective'. The time span allowed for doing so is crucial.

3. www.gla.ac.uk/departments/accounting/csear; www.wir.org; www.ellipson.com

4. The terms 'responsibilities', 'liabilities' and 'accountability' will be used here with very precise meanings. *Responsibility* is taken as a moral or ethical term: one may feel responsible or not according to certain moral standards. *Liability* is taken as a legal term: one is liable or not according to existing law. *Accountability* is taken as a socioeconomic term: one is accountable or not depending on what stakeholders expect and on how they are empowered to affect the firm's business. Here, liability is *de jure*, accountability is *de facto*. This view is meant to tie in with policy instruments, respectively: education, regulation and economic instruments. We focus here on accountability, noting that *potential future liabilities extend the firm's current accountability*.

5. See Antheaume, N. (1996), (in French) 'Accounting and environment: what future for accountancy and chartered accountants?' Revue Française de Comptabilité, 284 (December): 55–61; Christophe, B. (1992), (in French) 'The accountant faced with environmental accounting', Revue Française de Comptabilité, 235 (June): 51–7; Gray, R.H. (1990b), The Greening of Accountancy: the Profession After Pearce, Certified Accountants Publications Ltd, London; Hopwood, A.G. and Miller, P. (eds) (1994), Accounting as a Social and Institutional Practice, Cambridge, UK: Cambridge University Press; Perks, R.W. (1993), Accounting and Society, London: Chapman and Hall. More on this in Chapter 5.

6. Authors such as Edwards and Bell (1961), and, much earlier, J. Canning in 1929 and J. Stamp in 1921, long advocated cooperation between the two disciplines.

7. An amazing example is how most of the Linear B inscriptions of Minoean Crete, in the 2nd millennium BC, relate to accounting records and how, from these, a picture emerges of the social structure of ancient Cretan civilization.

8. See R. Emmett Taylor, *No Royal Road: Luca Pacioli and His Times*, London: Ayer, 1981; and Conference on Accounting and Economics, *Proceedings of the Conference on Accounting and Economics: In Honour of the 500th Anniversary of Luca Pacioli's Summa de Arithmetica (Siena, Italy, 1992)*, Garland.

9. See D.P. Ellerman (1985), 'The Mathematics of double entry bookkeeping', *Mathematical Magazine*, **58**, 226–33. Notice it was only two years after Columbus, another Italian, 'discovered' America (1492).

10. The Italian Renaissance was quite prolific in financial and banking innovations.

11. J.K. Galbraith (1972), *The Great Crash, 1929*, (3rd edn), Boston: Houghton Mifflin.

12. For a number of years, Swiss banks have faced widespread criticism regarding ethics, even with impeccable financial management. In the case of Crédit Suisse, it is interesting to note, according to social ratings used by the ethical pension fund Ethos (see, for example, Chapters 2 and 5), an exemplary attitude toward the environment, which is perhaps not mirrored by other social aspects of ethical behaviour.

13. Which were the 'big six' previous to the merger of Price Waterhouse and Coopers and Lybrand (2000).

14. See, for example, H. Kierkegaard (1997), who makes a strong case oriented towards measuring beforehand the potential insolvency of a firm. His ideas may be directly extended to account for environmental liabilities (see further).

15. More precisely, the authors distinguish between 'environmentally differentiated' management (or cost) accounts and 'environmentally differentiated' financial accounts. For our purpose here, we can lump these two together.

16. That is, volume times impact per unit of volume (Schaltegger (1997), op. cit. p. 54).

17. Environmental accounting began indeed to be a concern at the end of the 1980s, when energy was comparatively cheap.
18. Some ecologists, in the wake of Howard T. Odum (see *Environmental Accounting*, 1996), would dissent from this view. They claim to have found such a universal principle, based on *solar energy equivalents* and on the maintenance of biological life on earth. Though worthy of study, their view appears inappropriate for the corporate world, at least for the present. See, however, applications in Hall, C.A.S., Cleveland, C.J. and Kaufman, R. (1992), *Energy and Resource Quality: the Ecology of the Economic Process*. New York: Wiley.
19. See Schaltegger and Burritt (2000) for further details on this.
20. We must again mention Howard T. Odum's claim to the contrary. See note 18.
21. The idea is to reveal the otherwise implicit weights that decision makers place on different environmental impacts. See Chapter 8, section 4.1 and, for further developments, Dale et al. (1999).
22. For other (similar) expressions and their definitions, see Schaltegger et al. (1996), Box 4.4, p. 51. 'Product eco-balance' has also been used, particularly in France and Germany.
23. Following our initial definitions, responsibility here provides an argument meant to change existing law. Liabilities, on the other hand, reflect current law.
24. Leibenstein, H. (1966), 'Allocative efficiency versus X-efficiency'. *American Economic Review*, **56**: 392–415.
25. By relating EIA to number of km-persons transported per hour. Note, however, that other economic characteristics, such as comfort and protection from the weather, are excluded from this measure.
26. Schaltegger et al. (1996), p. 182, point out that end-of-pipe investments not only produce ERRs that are less than one, but, more often than not, less than zero, indicating a net damage to the environment (a worsening of the environmental indicator). Blanket regulatory policies are often to blame for this. From the firm's point of view, end-of-pipe investments may still make sense in terms of *marginal compliance costs*. That is, if the standard is a maximum daily emission of 100 units, and, in site A, emissions increase from 30 to 80, while in site B they decrease from 120 to 90, the overall EIA is an increase of 20 units, but financial liabilities will have decreased by 20 units times their unit compliance cost. This means policy design was sub-optimal.
27. Note the parallel between 'economic value added' and 'environmental impact added'. The relationship can be traced back at least to Georgescu-Roegen's 1971 book: *The Entropy Law and the Economic Process* (published a year before Müller-Wenk's 1972 work) where, on thermodynamic grounds, he placed much importance on the notion of EVA.
28. 'Carrying capacity' is a rather involved ecological concept. Basically, it measures the level of stress beyond which the system (for example, forest, wetland, population) looses its resilience and breaks down: the forest does not regenerate, the wetland disappears, the species (locally or globally) goes extinct. 'Resilience' measures the capacity of an ecosystem to survive some shock and recover its previous functions.
29. Solvency, as opposed to liquidity, describes the capacity to honour all long-term debts and liabilities.
30. It must be said here that thinking and practice in German-speaking countries are ahead of their English-speaking counterparts in environmental accounting. Key authors include Stefan Schaltegger and Frank Figge (University of Lüneburg), Andreas Sturm and Kaspar Müller (Ellipson Ltd), among others.
31. Itself permitted, it must be said, by Western Australia's development of natural gas production off its north-west shore and the building of a gas pipeline across the state to where mining operations are located.

32. From this it is clear that disaggregating energy data relates to considerations of resource substitution. It is a sign of the firm's degree of awareness regarding its resource use alternatives and also of its willingness to consider structural changes in its resource use patterns.
33. WMC, for example, distinguishes between five levels, from minor compliance to major accident levels. This information is important in that it links directly to financial costs and liabilities.
34. Although Shell, for example, reminds us that the definition depends upon local legislation.
35. See WMC 1998 Environmental Report at www.wmc.com
36. As shown by the proponents (in Germany) of the so-called ABC analysis, a small proportion of operations generate a large proportion of pollution. One can thus reduce most pollution with low administrative costs. Schaltegger et al. (1996: p. 161) illustrate the concept and provide references.

REFERENCES

Antheaume, N. (1996), 'Accounting and environment: what future for accountancy and chartered accountants'? *Revue Française de Comptabilité*, 284 (Dec.) : 55-61, (in French).

Bailey, P.E. (1991), 'Full cost accounting for life cycle costs – A guide for engineers and financial analysts', *Environmental Finance*, (Spring): 13–29.

Bailey, P.E. (1996), *Valuing Potential Environmental Liabilities for Managerial Decision-making: A Review of Available Techniques*, US EPA, Environmental Accounting Project.

Bebbington, J. and Gray, R.H. (1993), 'Corporate accountability and the physical environment: social responsibility and accounting beyond profit', *Business Strategy and the Environment*, **2** (2): 1–11.

Blumberg, J., Blum, G. and Korsvold, Å. (1996), *Environmental Performance and Shareholder Value*, World Business Council for Sustainable Development (WBCSD).

Boyd, J. (1998), 'The Benefits of Improved Environmental Accounting: An Economic Framework to Identify Priorities'. Resources For the Future, Discussion Paper 98-49, Washington DC.

Brimson J.A. and Antos, J (1999), *Driving Value Using Activity-based Budgeting*, New York: John Wiley & Sons, Inc.

Brockington, R. (1995), *Accounting for Intangible Assets. A New Perspective on the True and Fair View*, Economist Intelligence Unit Series, Wokingham, UK: Addison-Wesley.

Brouthers, K.D. and Roozen, F.A. (1999), 'Is it time to start thinking about strategic accounting'? *Long Range Planning*, **32** (3): 311–22.

Burritt, R.L. (1995), 'Accountants, accountability and the 'Ozone Regime'', *Accounting Forum*, 19: 219-43.

Cairncross, F. (1991), *Costing the Earth*, The Economist Books Ltd.

Calhoun, C.H., Oliveiro, M.E. and Wolitzer, P. (1999), *Ethics and the CPA: Building Trust and Value-added Services*, New York: John Wiley & Sons, (CPA: Certified Public Accountants, USA).

Canning, J.B. (1929), 'Some divergences of accounting theory from economic theory', *The Accounting Review*, 4 (March): 1–8.

Christophe, B. (1992), 'The accountant faced with environmental accounting', Revue Francaise de Comptabilité, 284: 55-61, (in French).

Christophe, B. (1995), *La Comptabilité Verte. De la Politique Environnementale à l'Ecobilan*, De Boeck Université (Belgium): Entreprise.

Cohen, M.A., Fenn, S.C. and Konar, S. (1997), *Environmental and Financial Performance: Are They Related?*, Washington DC: World Bank Environment Department.

Dale, V.H. and English, M.R. (eds) (1999), *Tools to Aid Environmental Decision Making*, New York: Springer.

Edwards, E.O. and Bell, P.W. (1961), *The Theory and Measurement of Business Income*, Berkeley, CA: University of California Press.

Ehrbar, A. (1998), *EVA: The Real Key to Creating Wealth*, New York: John Wiley & Sons.

Ellerman, D.P., (1985), 'The Mathematics of Double Entry Bookkeeping', *Mathematical Magazine*, 58: 226-233.

Environmental Protection Agency (1995a), *An Introduction to Environmental Accounting as a Business Management Tool: Key Concepts and Terms*, EPA 742-R-95-001, June 1995.

Environmental Protection Agency (1995b), *Incorporating Environmental Costs and Considerations into Decision-making: Review of Available Tools and Software*, EPA 742-R-95-OXX.

Estes, R.W. (1972), 'Socio-economic accounting and external diseconomies', *The Accounting Review*, April: 284–90.

Fava, J., Jensen, A., Pomper, S., DeSmet, B., Warren, J. and Vignon, B. (eds) (1992), *Life-cycle Assessment Data Quality: A Conceptual Framework*, Wintergreen: SETAC.

Figge, F. (1998), 'Systematisation of economic risks through global environmental problems', Bank Sarasin & Co., Switzerland, at www.sustainablevalue.com/ - Published in German as 'Systematisierung ökonomischer Risiken durch globale Umweltprobleme', Zeitschrift für Angewandte Umweltforschung, 2.

Figge, F. and Schaltegger, S. (2000), *What is Stakeholder Value? Developing a Catchphrase into a Benchmarking Tool*, Lüneburg/Geneva/Paris: University of Lüneburg/Pictet/UNEP.

Galbraith, J.K. (1972), *The Great Crash, 1929*, Boston: Houghton Mifflin (3rd ed.).

Georgescu-Roegen, N. (1971), *The Entropy Law And The Economic Process*, Cambridge, MA: Harvard University Press.

Grant, J.L. (1997), *Foundations of Economic Value-added*, USA: F.J. Fabozzi Associates.

Gray, R.H. (1990a), 'Accounting and economics: the psychopathic siblings – A review essay', *British Accounting Review*, **22** (4): 373–88.

Gray, R.H. (1990b), *The Greening of Accountancy: The Profession after Pearce*, London: Certified Accountants Publications Ltd.

Gray, R.H., Bebbington, J. and Walters, D. (1993), *Accounting for the Environment*, UK: Paul Chapman Publishing.

Gray, R.H., Owen, D. and Adams, C. (eds) (1996), *Accounting and Accountability: Changes and Challenges in Corporate Social and Environmental Reporting*, London and New York: Prentice Hall.

Hall, C.A.S., Cleveland, C.J. and Kaufman, R. (1992), *Energy and Resource Quality: the Ecology of the Economic Process*, New York: John Wiley.

Hill, W. (1997), 'Stakeholder versus Shareholder Value', in Basler Bankiervereinigung (ed.), *Shareholder Value-Konzepte in Banken*, Bern (Switzerland): Haupt.

Hines, R.D. (1988), 'Financial accounting: in communicating reality, we construct reality'. *Accounting, Organisations and Society*, **13** (3): 251–61.

Hopwood, A.G. and Miller, P. (eds.) (1994), *Accounting as a Social and Institutional Practice*. London: Cambridge University Press.

Ijiri, Y. (1967), *The Foundations of Accounting Measurement*, Englewood Cliffs, NJ: Prentice Hall (reprinted 1978 in Accounting Classics Series, Houston, TX: Scholars Book Co.).

Jacques K., Lesourd, J.B. and Ruiz, J.M. (eds) (1988), *Modern Applied Energy Conservation: New Directions in Energy Conservation Management*, Chichester and New York: Ellis Horwood /Wiley.

Johnson H.T and Kaplan R.S. (1987), 'The rise and fall of management accounting. Management accounting is too late, too aggregated, and too distorted to be relevant', *Management Accounting*, January: 22–9.

Kelly, G., Kelly, D. and Gamble, A. (1998), *Stakeholder Capitalism*, Political Economy Research Centre, University of Sheffield, UK.

Kierkegaard, H. (1997), *Improving Accounting Reliability: Solvency, Insolvency, and Future Cash Flows*, (Original title, translated from Danish: *Dynamical Accounting*), Westport, London: Quorum Books.

Leibenstein, H., (1966), 'Allocative efficiency versus X-efficiency'. *American Economic Review*, 56: 392-415.

Lesourd, J.B. and Gousty, Y. (1981), 'Bases économiques et thermodynamiques des techniques de comptabilité de l'énergie' [Economic and thermodynamic bases of energy accounting techniques], *Revue d'Economie Industrielle*, **15** (1): 44–59.

Manton, M.J. and Jasper, J.D. (1998), 'Environmental Indicators for National State of the Environment Reporting: The Atmosphere', State of the Environment 1998, Environment Australia, Canberra.

Mintzberg, H. (1983), 'The case for corporate social responsibility', *The Journal of Business Strategy*, **4** (2): 3–15.

Miyazaki, N. (1998), 'Applying Eco-balance to Management Control: Combining Economic and Ecological Accounting, APIRA 98 Conference in Osaka, Japan: paper #63 (5th August), 10p, www3.bus.osaka-cu.ac.jp/apira98/archives/paper63.htm.

Müller, K., de Frutos, J., Schüssler, K.-U., Haarbosch, H. and Randel, M. (1996), *Eco-Efficiency and Financial Analysis*, EFFAS Commission on Accounting, Sept. 1996 (available from Ellipson Ltd at http://www.ellipson.ch).

Müller-Wenk (1978), *Ökologische Buchhaltung* [Ecological Bookkeeping], Frankfurt: Campus (the original 1972 text is a mimeo from St Gallen, Switzerland).

O'Connor, M. and Spash, C. (eds) (1999). *Valuation and the Environment: Theory, Method, and Practice*, Cheltenham, UK and Brookfield, US: Edward Elgar.

Odum, H.T. (1996), *Environmental Accounting: 'Emergy' and Environmental Decision Making*, New York: Wiley.

OFEFP (1991), 'Eco-balance methodology based on ecological optimization' (in French), *Cahiers de l'Environnement*, no. 133 (October), Bern, Switzerland.

Pearce, D. (1997), 'Corporate behaviour and sustainable development: the view from economics', in P. Bansal and E. Howard, *Business and the Natural Environment*, Oxford: Butterworth & Heinemann.

Perks, R.W. (1993), *Accounting and Society*, London: Chapman and Hall.

Pohl, C., Ros., M., Waldeck, B. and Dinkel, F. (1996), 'Imprecision and Uncertainty in LCA', in: S. Schaltegger, *Life Cycle Assessment (LCA) – Quo Vadis?*, Basel/Boston: Birkhauser.

Power, M. (1991), 'Auditing and environmental expertise: between protest and professionalisation', *Accounting, Auditing and Accountability*, **4** (3): 30–42.

Rafenberg, C. and Mayer, E. (1998), 'Life Cycle Analysis of the Newspaper "Le Monde" ', *The International Journal of LCA*, **3** (3): 131–44.

Rappaport, A. (1986), *Creating Shareholder Value: The New Standard for Business Performance*, New York: The Free Press (Macmillan Inc.) and London: Collier Macmillan Publishers.

Reed, D.J. (1998), *Green Shareholder Value: Hype or Hit?*, Sustainable Enterprise Perspectives, Washington DC: World Resources Institute (www.wri.org)

Schaltegger, S. (1997), 'Economics of life-cycle assessment (LCA). Inefficiency of the present approach', *Business Strategy and the Environment*, **6** (1): 1–8.

Schaltegger, S. and Burritt, R. (2000), *Contemporary Environmental Accounting. Issues, Concepts and Practice*, London: Greenleaf.

Schaltegger, S. and Figge, F. (1998), 'Environmental Shareholder Value', WWZ Study no. 54, Center for Economics & Business Administration (WWZ), University of Basel, and Bank Sarasin & Co., Basel, Switzerland.

Schaltegger, S. and Müller, K. (1997), 'Calculating the true profitability of pollution prevention', in *Greener Management International* (GM), **17** (Spring): 53-68.

Schaltegger S. and Sturm, A. (1992), *Environmentally Oriented Decisions in Firms: Ecological Accounting Instead of LCA: Necessity, Criteria, Concepts*, (in German), Bern/Stuttgart: Haupt.

Schaltegger S., Müller K. and Hindrichsen H. (1996), *Corporate Environmental Accounting*, Chichester; New York: John Wiley & Sons.

Stamp, J. (1921), 'The relation of accountancy to economics', *The Accountant*, October: 501–13 (reprinted in R.A. Parker and S.A. Zeff (eds) (1996), *Milestones in the British Accounting Literature*, New York and London: Garland Publishing, pp. 91–106.

Stamp, P. (1993), 'In Search of Reality', in M. Mumford and K. Peasnell, *Philosophical Perspectives on Accounting. Essays in Honour of Edward Stamp*, London: Routledge, pp. 255–314.

Sturm, A. and Müller, K. (1998), 'Eco-Controlling: A Tool to Implement a Value-Based Environmental Management', Paper presented at the European Brewery Congress in Maastricht, NL., 1997. Re-edited 1998, www.ellipson.com

Taylor, R. Emmett (1981), *No Royal Road: Luca Pacioli and his Times*, Ayer, London; and: Conference on Accounting and Economics, *Proceedings of the Conference on Accounting and Economics: In Honour of the 500th Anniversary of Luca Pacioli's Summa de Arithmetica (Siena, Italy, 1992)*, Garland.

White, A.T., Becker, M. and Savage, D.E. (1993), 'Environmentally smart accounting: using total cost assessment to advance pollution prevention', *Pollution Prevention Review*, (Summer), 247–59.

World Resources Institute (1999), 'The new millennium and the next bottom line. Can business meet new social, environmental and financial expectations and still win?', *Business Week*, 3 May 1999. Available through http://www.wri.org.

Zeff, S.A. (1978), 'The rise of "economic consequences"', *Journal of Accountancy*, 146 (6: December): 56–63 (reprinted in S. Jones, C. Romano and J. Ratnatunga (1995), *Accounting Theory: A Contemporary Review*, Sydney, NSW: Harcourt Brace.

5. Corporate Environmental Reporting and Auditing[1]

SUMMARY

A firm's EM performance needs to be communicated to its stakeholders if it is to carry any benefits. Hence the importance of environmental reporting (ER), in particular to external stakeholders. This chapter starts by examining what determines stakeholders' demand for ER – environmental externalities are seen as a key factor – then explores the rationale for supplying ERs. The role of asymmetric information and the principal–agent relationship have led to increasing government regulation. Accountants are then seen as instrumental stakeholders in the demand and supply relationship. The appearance of new accountees is seen strongly to have influenced the orientation and development of ER. Several sections follow on what may constitute the value of disclosing initially private information, and the problem of choosing to provide adequate information quality. ERs are seen as optimal compromise products, targeted to specific stakeholders, not all equally important for the firm. Professional bodies can then evaluate these reports, and evaluation criteria are reviewed. Given the diversity and relative anarchy in reporting practices, a section examines the possibility of a common framework for corporate ER, based on a matrix representing environmental impacts and related liabilities, and resource uses and related costs. A last section examines environmental auditing and certification by accredited authorities, and its value to the firm and its stakeholders. The chapter concludes by asking how, if needed, higher levels of privately *optimal* disclosure can be achieved.

1. INTRODUCTION

In Chapter 4, we examined the economics of environmental accounting; that is, the *production* of environmentally sensitive information. We considered both its production costs and its expected benefits, both visible and hidden as explained in Chapter 2. We now turn to the question of how much of the information produced will be *communicated* to different stakeholders. One group has special status: top management. Top managers decide what and in how much detail information will be produced. They then need to decide how much of it they will communicate to different parties.

Obviously, part of the information produced will not be communicated outside the firm, and, even within the firm, outside key decision makers (Mathews 1987). Highly sensitive information on special physical, chemical or biological processes will remain sealed, whether for competition, military or political reasons. With regard to environmental information, the temptation may exist not to let certain details fall within earshot of environmental groups. More often, though, it is the overlap of environmental and economically sensitive information that will keep managers from disclosing it. A toxic chemical pollutant can, if disclosed, reveal a production secret with intellectual property benefits. Both the content and the style of environmental reporting will reflect this fundamental tension between the benefits and the costs of disclosure.

2. INNOVATIVE PRESSURES AND RESISTANCE TO CHANGE

The fundamental tension between the benefits and costs of corporate environmental disclosure can be approached, from an economic perspective, in terms of demand and supply of environmental reports. Accordingly, we examine the determinants of such demand and supply and use this framework to analyse the role of the accountancy profession. Of course, a special role is held by government in its capacity to impose on companies certain disclosure obligations, as certain countries (for example, Holland and Germany) have started to experience.

2.1 Externalities as a Source of Demand for Environmental Reporting

Positive and negative externalities, or external benefits and costs

Economics provides a framework for understanding the emergence of environmental accounting and reporting. One key concept is externalities. Simply put, a decision maker will generate an externality if by his or her decision or activity s/he increases or reduces the benefits of a stakeholder without any compensation one way or another. If stakeholders benefit and do not 'pay' the decision maker for their gains, a *positive externality* is said to exist. Implementing a new environmentally friendly technology is an example. If, instead, stakeholders suffer from his or her decision or activity and are not compensated for their losses, a *negative externality* is said to exist. Pollution is a typical example of a negative externality, until all affected stakeholders are fully compensated; for example, for medical and relocation costs.

Externalities as a source of demand for compensation

Thus, externalities generate *claims for compensation* in various ways. First, with every major environmental disaster, responsible firms have had to face millions of dollars in compensation. Exxon faced a $2 billion compensation bill (plus an extra billion in clean-up costs) following the *Exxon Valdez* oil spill. Naturally, this raises the issue of the amount of compensation to be paid. Who is to tell? How? This is the story for disaster-type events. Second, ongoing recurrent externalities also exist, as with greenhouse gas emissions, toxic gases, smoke and fluids, deforestation and natural resource degradation. In such cases, too, there may be claims for damage compensation. These are trickier issues because of corresponding positive externalities in the form of increased products (cars, plastics, computers, and so on) and new technologies. Firms will want to emphasize the positive aspects of their activities. The question boils down to how we should value and compare, say, a new technology to the depletion of a ressource. A third concern is that firms will need to keep track of what their potential liabilities might be in case damage compensation was held against them. This generates a further need for keeping track of things and setting up appropriate accounts. Firms need background information to show the courts and argue their case.

Offsetting externalities through compensation payments is a reactive approach. A proactive approach is possible, for state-owned companies, through full-cost accounting and, for private companies, through strategic accounting, as discussed in Chapter 4.

Difficulties created by public and intertemporal externalities
As outlined in the introduction to this chapter, there is yet another novelty. Externalities such as greenhouse gas emissions, resource depletion and extinction of life species have 'everyone' as potential stakeholders: all the citizens of a nation and, increasingly, humankind at the global scale. Such externalities affect what economists call *public goods* and what can be called *public externalities* as opposed to private externalities. The atmosphere, the oceans, plant and animal genetic resources are all public goods, in that it is difficult, if not impossible, to assign private property rights to them.[2] It is either technically impossible, as with the atmosphere, or much too costly, as with rare species. Externalities affecting public goods thus generate an almost *universal constituency* of stakeholders and, at the same time, one that no longer has a known face: everyone is no-one in particular. The accountees have become indeterminate.

A further aspect is that we are concerned with people in the future as well as the present, creating so-called *intertemporal externalities*. In this case, it may be difficult to identify who are the stakeholders likely to demand compensation when the time comes. Victims of radiation from nuclear wastes or of slow-release toxic chemicals are likely to turn against all those who were, in one way or another, implicated in the release of such nuisances. The firm's liabilities will depend on the legal system, but this system is likely to evolve as a consequence of these effects. In a dynamic world, firms often contribute in bringing about the changes they would like to avoid. In this case, they help create the stakeholders to whom they are accountable. Accountees become, to some extent, a product of the firms' decisions.

The above points show that there emerges a *demand* for environmental accounting from within the firm, in particular as a tool for use in potential disputes over the firm's past activities. If, for example, it can prove it spent important sums on environmental risk management but was unsuccessful in its efforts, its liabilities may be reduced. Other motivations are tax and publicity related, where tax exemptions and reputation benefits can be expected. There is, however, a second source of demand for environmental reporting: the firm's employees and external stakeholders.

2.2 The Economic Rationale of Supplying Environmental Reports

Because of the firm's technological expertise, much of its information on the environmental impacts of its activities remains private. This is true not only of management with respect to employees and external stakeholders, but also between different levels of management within the company: each level holds some private information. Often, the firm is alone in knowing the extent of the physical, chemical and biological consequences of the substances it sells or emits. This is particularly true when obtaining this information is very costly, as is the case with emissions of highly specialized chemicals into complex ecosystems (for example, wetlands). In such cases of *asymmetric information*, stakeholders like local communities and government will demand detailed and certified reports of the firm's environmental impacts.

Firms have responded to these internal and external demands by increasing their *supply* of environmental accounting information. Decreasing supply costs have facilitated the process: experience gained, new monitoring technologies, more efficient software for data analysis have reduced the costs of gathering, analysing and reporting information. With regard to managers, local communities, environmental pressure groups, the information of interest has been ecological. With regard to shareholders, creditors, insurers and taxation authorities, the relevant information has been of an economic and financial nature. Accordingly, two types of environmental accounting systems have developed, as discussed in Chapter 4: ecological-impact accounts and environmentally related financial accounts.

In this demand and supply relationship, the question arises: how can we understand the amount and the quality of the information supplied?

Demand and supply have different cost and benefit curves

Schaltegger et al. (1996: p. 10) succinctly summarize the economic rationale of supplying environmental accounting information in terms of costs and benefits to the firm. This rationale reflects the basic rule that marginal costs of environmental accounting must equal their marginal benefits (the avoided costs from environmental impacts). The *strategic dimension* of information provision, absent in this book, appears in Schaltegger and Burritt (2000). The role of external stakeholders (in particular, of government) cannot be taken as given. In reality, because of asymmetric information, the supply of accounting information mirrors not only the costs and benefits of the supplying firm but also those of the demanding party. As a rule, a higher quality of information, reflecting higher accuracy and reliability, will cost more. Of course, the benefits derived will also be higher. The question then is: which increases faster as quality rises; costs or benefits?

The answer is that it depends, firstly, on what kind of information is needed (say, ecological or financial) and on whether one considers the firm's or the government's costs and benefits (as one of the other stakeholders). The relative shapes of the benefit and cost curves are of importance here. As a rule, increasing quality becomes increasingly costly (in economic parlance, marginal costs increase). On the other hand, marginal benefits tend to decrease with quality: the value of extra accuracy and reliability decreases. The second point is that the firm and government are likely to have different benefit and cost curves. The government's costs correspond to the verification of the quality of information. The existence of private information means that to increase the reliability of what the firm discloses, government must invest in verification and control processes. As the quality demanded increases, information becomes increasingly specialized and, as noted earlier, obtaining and verifying it becomes increasingly costly (for example, through employment of highly qualified and highly paid specialists).

The economic rationale recalled by Schaltegger applies: in all cases, quality, just like quantity, will be increased up to the point where marginal costs equal marginal benefits. At this point, the provision of information is at optimum quality (and quantity). The problem here is this: different stakeholders have different benefit and cost curves, so that each will have different *optimal* quality demands. In particular, the firm and the government will demand differing optimal quality levels. Strong tensions in accounting standards will appear. Differences will also vary with financial and ecological accounts. It is very likely that for ecological accounts, government and other environmentally concerned stakeholders will have a higher optimal quality demand than those that are financially interested; the relationship will be reversed for financial accounts. When the quality demanded by external stakeholders is higher, one is faced with a principal–agent problem (Power, 1991).

The impacts of private and asymmetric information

It is this principal-agent problem, based on asymmetric information between stakeholders inside and outside the firm's private information system, that motivates the increasingly complex legislation relating to environmental disclosure and reporting (see section 5). There results, for a given structure of costs and benefits across stakeholders, an optimal level of disclosure as well as an optimal level of information quality in environmental reporting. To increase these levels, the demanding party must incur higher costs in monitoring, control and enforcement of standards and regulations; for example, expenses that will be accepted only insofar as they are justified by the extra benefits expected; such as extra votes in an election campaign, more supporting funds for an environmental group, and direct benefits in terms of health and quality of life for local communities.

What function for environmental accounting and reporting?

The amount and quality of information provided by environmental reports also reflects the *services* expected from them. As highlighted by Perks (1993) and, in particular, by Brockington (1995, Chapter 3), the original function of accounting was stewardship to creditors and investors. A lender wished to know whether the funds were properly entrusted. In modern times preceding the Industrial Revolution, providers of financial capital were the first accountees. Since then, accounting history seems to have come full circle. The nineteenth century developed accounting systems so that they may serve beyond the stewardship function (Parker and Zeff, 1996). Caring for one's funds did not imply they were used in an optimal manner.

Accounting systems were developed to aid managers in optimizing their decision making. Cost accounting and analytical (ratio) accounts can be seen as products of this aid to decision making. Since then, it seems that most of the technical difficulties encountered by the accounting profession stem from this unresolved tension between the two functions of stewardship and aid to decision making (Mattessich, 1995). Today, because new stakeholders have appeared on the scene with environmental rights, the *stewardship function seems to be back on stage with a revenge*, but with a new twist. This time, the accountees are faceless and are even, in the future, undefined. As a result, although morally justified, the stewardship function is hardly operational. This may put increased weight on contractual relationships in the future. Those who bear the brunt of these new technical challenges are the accountants. Because they have to invest in new learning, their own cost–benefit structure is modified: they are another key stakeholder in environmental accounting.

2.3 Accountants as Instrumental Stakeholders in the Demand and Supply Relationship

Gray (1990) and Gray et al. (1993) deplored that in the United Kingdom and elsewhere the accounting profession has been slow to endorse the development of environmental accounting. From the above discussion, one would presume that, perceived by the accounting profession, the costs of change outweigh the benefits of change. The fact is that any cost–benefit structure is largely determined by the prevailing institutional system. This includes the sanction and reward system, whether through inner promotion and payrises or through increased labour-market opportunities. The economics of the innovation and adoption by accountants of environmental accounting systems obeys the same general principles as the adoption of any innovation.[3]

One way to understand the role of accountants, whether negative or positive, is in terms of returns on capital investment.[4] As section 4 will describe, environmental accounts introduce new and challenging technical issues for which the accounting profession has not traditionally been well prepared. Firstly, they have been taught to only account for items of financial relevance, measurable in monetary terms: physical (ecological) accounts appear beyond the scope of their acquired competence. Secondly, they have been taught to format information for specific stakeholders: cost accounts to company managers, financial accounts to shareholders and creditors, and special tax-related accounts to government agencies. These types of reporting have, over time, been very strictly encoded – largely in response to principal–agent issues, as described above – to the point that it has become an accountant's virtue and pride to know how to apply with utmost rigour the jungle of existing rules. In other words, practising accountants have been trained to apply the rules rather than to change them, and because the system has become so complex, this has meant a significant investment. When changing the rules is costly, change is likely to be resisted. When the rules change, the profession is in crisis: it can no longer extract the full benefit of its initial investment. This makes perfect economic sense.

Nevertheless, accounting boards at national levels (for example, the FASB in the USA) have been active in exploring changes to current accounting systems and setting new standards in order to face up to the new challenges. The problem then is uptake by the accounting profession. Accounting Standards boards in several countries, for example, have produced innovations regarding intangible assets and goodwill, not without controversy amongst practitioners or resistance by firms.[5] One of the issues is how accountants must accommodate the innovations into the rest of the existing system, a challenge discussed by Macve and Carey (1992) and Antheaume (1996). Problems of compatibility and consistency arise, as in any rules-based system, which, until they are amended, create loopholes for the less scrupulous to use; for example, creative accounting (Neal, 1996). The increase in irregularities may put at stake the responsibility of accountants and jeopardize their reputation.

The role of accountants raises the notion of '*instrumental*' stakeholders. Their role is in providing a service between two other parties, the accountor and the accountee. This service, as we have seen, is at least twofold: accountability and stewardship on the one hand; aid to decision making on the other (Perks, 1993; Brockington, 1995). Remuneration of this service, because of its instrumental and intermediate nature, appears as a '*transaction cost*' between the two parties.[6] If the goal of a reform is to reduce transaction costs, leading to a reduction in the role of instrumental stakeholders, the latter are likely to oppose change, even if from society's point of view this appears inefficient.

2.4 The Appearance of New Accountees and their Influence on Environmental Reporting

The novelty with environmental concerns is that many of the *new accountees* are undefined or absent. One party in the relationship is either missing or inactive in some way (future generations, the public 'at large'). The transaction cannot happen naturally and the firm does not have the incentive to pay for accounts to such accountees. Accountants then are not likely to be rewarded or paid more to provide such accounts. Of course, the regulator (government) steps in at this stage and requires a minimum amount of information on environmental impacts. Other external stakeholders do the same, though without coercive power. However, unless the firm perceives direct benefits, such as through increased reputation and market share, it will minimize the costs and thereby the rewards for accountants. The incentive for innovation remains minimal. Furthermore, as discussed above, the incentives for quality are limited. This introduces the rationale for environmental auditing processes.

The need, or rather the demand, for environmental auditing is not fundamentally different from financial auditing (IAPC, 1995). Audits belong to the certification process and are destined to guarantee a minimum level of credibility to disclosed accounts and reports (Owen, 1992). To internal stakeholders like management and employees, audits convey the message that the accounting information provides a reliable picture of the firm's current situation, and can thus correctly guide them in their decision making. To external stakeholders like shareholders, government, consumers and local communities, audits are a way to deal with asymmetric information and possible irregularities. In both cases, firms increasingly anticipate the issue of credibility and have their accounts and reports audited and certified. Those who do not, may simply fail to gain the benefits from having produced the accounts and reports in the first place. If they are not believed by anyone, of what use are they? The time and effort in producing them could have been invested more usefully elsewhere.

3. THE ECONOMICS OF DISCLOSURE

3.1 Value of Information and Costs of Disclosure

If accounting is production of information, disclosure is supply of information. In both cases, the information must be of sufficient value *to the firm* to warrant the costs of producing it. However, once produced, information may not be disclosed. Information is a very particular commodity in that it changes the distribution of power amongst stakeholders. Disclosing information may increase future costs to the 'discloser', notably in terms of 'comparative disadvantage': competitors can use the information to their own advantage (Elliott and Jacobson, 1994). It is unlikely that total disclosure will be the rule; rather, there is bound to be an optimal degree of disclosure, the degree of which will depend on the relative costs and benefits to the discloser. Exceptions to this rule will lie with mandatory disclosure imposed by government, particularly with hazardous emissions (Campbell, 1994).

We saw in Chapter 4 that accounting information is primarily of value to the firm for management and decision making. Environmental monetary accounts inform on the costs of meeting targets and regulatory requirements while ecological accounts allow management to assess the effectiveness of their action. By combining both types of information, the firm can assess its efficiency in environmental management.[7] To external stakeholders, environmental accounts, both financial and ecological, will hold different values. The regulator wants to know if standards and regulations have been met; environmental groups and environmental protection agencies are primarily interested in how effective the firm is in its environmental management; investors are interested to know how efficiently their funds are used but also, increasingly, how well the firm is doing on the EHS side (Environment, Health and Safety), if this impacts on stock values. Obviously, if standards and regulations are not met, if investors' funds could have been used more efficiently and if environmental impacts have been worsening, disclosing such information is bound to carry high costs for the firm. It therefore has an incentive not to disclose all the information, and to sin, so to speak, by omission.

3.2 Information Entitlements and Rights

Different stakeholders may value the firm's environmentally related information, but do they have a right to access it? Are they entitled to be recipients of it? Does the firm have any obligation, once it has produced information for internal use, to disclose it? A toxic chemical pollutant can, if disclosed, reveal a production secret with intellectual property benefits. This is a key issue that pre-empts all other questions of disclosure. The answer varies across countries and over time. We are in murky waters here, but the general tendency has been for increasing empowerment of stakeholders, as shown in Table 2.1 of Chapter 2. This increase must be viewed, however, in the light of very modest beginnings (UN-ESC, 1992; Mathews and Davey, 1996). An example: consumer rights to food-quality information is rather recent. In the USA, it followed a presidential address to the US Congress by John F. Kennedy in 1962.[8] Today, the debate is on between corporations, government and the general public as to just how much information consumers are entitled to regarding genetically modified foods. The same question may be asked of environmental impacts.

In the case of strategic information, when economic, military or political stakes are high, it is a matter of balancing different stakeholders' rights. Consider a firm that patented a production process using a toxic chemical before that chemical was listed on the list of hazardous substances (the so-called black list). Suppose revealing use of the chemical provides key information to competitors about the production process. Suppose, also, that its disposal is environmentally harmful. If the firm has a right to its intellectual property and other stakeholders have a right to a clean environment, there is a case of conflicting rights, with direct implications for environmental reporting.

Conflicts of rights are seldom directly resolved, except by superior authority or by force, where one right is proclaimed to supersede the other.

Indirect methods are more likely to succeed. In particular, one may assess how changing the status quo will affect the economic costs and benefits for the different parties. Furthermore, these costs and benefits can be made a function of time, since gradually phasing out a polluting process will, in general, cost less than immediate cessation. The question then becomes, how long can the firm be given before it must make the use of its chemical publicly known? As it phases out its use, the costs of disclosing it to competitors will fall. Also, it will have time to develop substitute products or processes.

3.3 Determinants of Information Disclosure

What are the implications for private information disclosure? The answer depends on whether there has been an explicit demand by a stakeholder group for a particular kind of information; for example, polluting emissions into a water body or into the atmosphere. If there has, then non-disclosure will raise suspicions and distrust, which will in turn put increased pressure on disclosure. The outcome will most often be independent of whether the stakeholders have explicit rights to be informed or not. Rather, it will depend on what means of action they have. As consumers, they can change their purchasing patterns or boycott a company's products. As citizens, they can change their voting preferences if their concerns are not listened to by government, which will increase government pressure on the firm to disclose. Through the media, they can tarnish the firm's reputation by highlighting non-disclosure of environmentally sensitive information. To some extent therefore, consumer empowerment is immaterial if the market is sufficiently competitive or if there are close enough substitutes for the incriminated products. Note, however, that the higher the environmental risks to consumers, the less competition and substitution will matter. In the extreme, consumers might decide to forgo the utility derived from an imperfectly substitutable product in a bid to avoid further losses in utility from environmental impacts.

In the case where an explicit demand for information has not been made, either by government, consumers or environmental organizations, should the firm disclose? Again, the economics weigh in. If non-disclosure by the firm is motivated by a lack of perception of benefits to external stakeholders compared with costs of disclosure (for example, length of environmental report), then the risks of not disclosing are small. After all, if external stakeholders suspect any dangers, they will demand information. If, on the other hand, the motivation is one of concealing environmental damage and hoping to go unnoticed for as long as possible, while cashing in on the benefits, then the firm must take a gamble.[9] This leads us into the issue of the relative value of withholding versus disclosing environmentally (and financially) sensitive information, ESI.[10]

3.4 Optimal Disclosure

The economics literature has investigated both the economics of information and that of fraud; in particular, tax evasion. The economics of disclosure builds on both. Elliott and Jacobson (1994) provide a good overview of the approach. Put simply, one may consider the relative costs and benefits of withholding versus disclosing ESI. Withholding ESI when damage has been or is being done will avoid all the consumer, citizen and government backlashes listed above, at least in the short term. These forgone costs contribute towards the benefits of non-disclosure. In parallel, the potential liabilities build up, as well as the risks of being discovered if the damage is ongoing. The longer the withholding period, the larger the stakes, until it becomes a matter of player lose all. The dynamics are such that the longer the firm waits, the riskier it is to disclose, and so the stronger the incentive not to disclose. It is a vicious downward spiral. It is clear that public authorities have a role to play in modifying the *expected* benefits and costs and the *perceived* risks from withholding ESI, and thus tilting the balance in favour of disclosure.

From the firm's point of view, *optimal* disclosure includes a kind of informational insurance. It will hedge its bets over the likelihood of being caught withholding ESI. Such an insurance scheme takes on the form of . . . information disclosure! In other words, to avoid risking too much, a firm will disclose more than under perfectly known costs and risks. However, this by no means equates to total disclosure. Unless the costs of disclosing to all relevant stakeholders – in practice, to everyone – are zero, there will optimally remain a residual quantity of privately held information. For instance, information that is commercially sensitive in terms of competitiveness.

3.5 Role of Government Authorities

Government authorities, but also consumers and the general public, can change the firm's optimal disclosure rate. By *disclosure rate* is meant the ratio of information already produced and held to that which is disclosed to external stakeholders. This is a different issue from that of the optimal *level* of information production discussed in the previous section. There are three basic strategies by which optimal disclosure may be modified (in this case, increased): exhortation, incentives, and regulation. Exhortation is talk, persuade, convince, moralize. It is unlikely to be very effective overall. Regulation is effective provided it is enforceable; that is, if enforcement costs are low enough to outweigh the benefits expected from disclosure. Finally, incentives minimize enforcement costs but their effectiveness depends on the firm's expected costs of disclosure; that is, ultimately, on the costs of avoiding the environmental damage the firm wishes others to be informed about. In that case, alternative strategies, such as reducing costs of R&D investments into new technologies, may be more effective.

3.6 Globalization and Disclosure

Globalization seems to exacerbate the impacts of firms' decisions. Benefits are amplified given the scale at which they apply, but so are costs. Outcomes become more sensitive to firms' attitudes towards risk, ranging from cautious and risk averse to gambling attitudes. Also, the international community is less effective at enforcing penalties than local and national authorities. Although consumer action can still backfire, action by local and national authorities is likely to be less effective. Still, current evidence shows that most multinational firms adopt higher standards than requested by their home countries, and this includes EHS information disclosure.[11] This may be an indication that, all things considered, consumer power has become greater than government power when it comes to environmental management. At the global scale, there are more substitutes and more competitors, and markets are more flexible. For better or for worse, globalization seems to increase the power of market feedbacks.[12]

4. THE ECONOMICS OF INFORMATION QUALITY

Much of what has been said in the previous section holds for informational quality, albeit with some differences. While investigating the economics of disclosure, we paid no attention to the quality of the information disclosed. It was a matter of whether a piece of information, like the amount of sulphur dioxide emitted into the atmosphere last year, was released or not, and how many such pieces of information were released. The firm may decide to highlight its progress with sulphur dioxide and greenhouse gas emissions but remain silent on water consumption and amounts of heavy metals released into water bodies – a way of diverting the attention of stakeholders. We saw why this is increasingly a losing strategy, but there are other, more subtle, ways of 'withholding' information: namely, through playing with information quality.

4.1 What is Information Quality?

Information quality is an umbrella term that covers several aspects. In the context of environmental reporting, these include: scope, completeness, precision, transparency, reliability and comparability (over time and across activities, firms or sectors). One might add: 'assessability'; a function of both transparency and reliability. That is, information quality includes in itself what is necessary for the recipient to assess this quality. Information is a very special commodity indeed! Let us first be a bit more specific about the above terms.

Scope refers to the range of impacts from the firm's activities, now and in the future. If there are several sites across different countries, covering a range of activities, is the whole range of environmental impacts covered over the whole territorial range? Does the recipient of the report get the big picture, such as conveyed by overall worldwide impacts? Are possible impacts into the long-term future, such as radioactive wastes, covered?

Completeness refers to how exhaustively, within the scope of impacts, every impact is accounted for. While scope focuses on the big picture, completeness focuses on the specifics of every site and every activity, so that variations across sites, countries, activities and over time are visible.

Precision, an aspect on which Schaltegger and Burritt (2000) place much emphasis, covers both level of disaggregation and accuracy of measurements and indicators. For example, progress in sulphur dioxide emissions may be reported in percentage terms relative to a base year, without indication of the initial level of emissions. One can hear statements like 'we have reduced our emissions over the last three years by 50 per cent, the greatest reduction in the industry', while initial levels were three times higher than anywhere else.

Transparency refers to the specification of the methods and assumptions used to measure and compute emissions and resource use. Transparency is perhaps the key quality of an environmental report, as it affects both its reliability and its comparability. It ideally includes the specification of the measuring equipment and data-processing techniques. As for the financial aspects, allocation rules, for example, must be clearly specified and, where appropriate, justified.

Reliability covers aspects of *continuity* (Have measurements been carried out often enough to be meaningful?), *competence* (Were those entrusted with the task sufficiently qualified to do a good job?), and *honesty* (Is the firm to be trusted? Is the information to be believed?). In the next section, we shall see that reliability can be enhanced through the audit and certification process.

Comparability over time ensures either that methods and assumptions have remained the same or that, where they have changed, appropriate recalculations have been made using the initial or the final year as a base. Comparability over time suffers from tension between the need for continuity and the need for methodological improvements. High transparency of method, assumptions and limitations maximizes comparability. Across sites, firms and sectors, comparability is more problematic, but less so at aggregate levels than in the specifics, which vary structurally across industries. Finally, '*assessability*' is a combined product of transparency, reliability and comparability. The report is transparent enough for the recipient to assess the reliability of the information relative to other sources. This is the crowning attribute of information quality. It is similar to a company specifying values and goals that can be used as criteria for assessing its achievements. 'Have you matched deed to word?' can be reread 'What deeds have you matched to your numbers?'

4.2 Optimal, Not Maximum Quality

Obviously, maximum scope, completeness, precision, transparency, reliability, and comparability would be excessively costly and unnecessary. Some quality attributes are more necessary than others: namely, transparency, reliability and comparability over time. The others obey a principle of optimization rather than one of maximization. Furthermore, as discussed by Schaltegger (1997), demand for quality varies across stakeholders. No-one needs maximum quality in every aspect. Overall, the quality of information provided by the firm may be such that, in principle, the marginal costs to itself just balance the marginal benefits to targeted external stakeholders. In practice, by a trial-and-error adjustment process, firms try to meet all those quality requirements, the absence of which would generate greater costs to them than providing that quality.

Again, market structure and degree of competition influences the quality of environmental reports. State monopolies of weakly substitutable goods and services have little incentive to provide quality reports. A study by Chabredier et al. (2000) showed, for instance, that the French state-owned railroad monopoly SNCF produced environmental reports of relatively poor quality. State-owned industries in many former communist countries and in many developing countries suffer from the same lack of incentive. Not only are consumers unempowered; government itself is part of the problem.

Information quality lends itself to subtle manipulations for hiding otherwise valuable information. A firm that wishes to maximize the positive picture and turn an environmental report into a PR tool has several strategies at its disposal. First, it can zoom in on positive achievements, providing details and quality attributes, while providing more aggregate information on less positive outcomes. This presupposes a two-stage process. On the one hand, such achievements will themselves have been subject to a previous cost–benefit analysis. That they were achieved is an indication that the expected benefits outweighed the expected costs. In this calculus, however, their communication to interested parties would presumably have been included. It should therefore, ex-post, be optimal for the firm to communicate its achievements. A second-stage optimization then communicates more emphatically the highest levels of achievements, while obliterating, more or less, the lower levels. More subtly, it can highlight one or two failings in order to better hide others, while showing its willingness to communicate all outcomes, whether good or bad.

Second, it can use the information-overload strategy so as to hide the forest behind the trees, by drowning the negative outcomes in excessive or less relevant information. Manipulating information quality in this way allows firms to remain on the safe side if they come under criticism. They can always argue that the information was present in the report. Increasingly, however, such tricks do not escape the vigilance of expert watchdog organizations, whether environment or consumer oriented. With help from the media, their careful analyses are then communicated to government agencies and to the general public, to the detriment of the firm. As a result, playing with information quality in environmental reports is becoming a risky exercise.

5. ENVIRONMENTAL REPORTS AS OPTIMAL COMPROMISE PRODUCTS

5.1 The Use of Environmental Reports

The combined outcome of information disclosure and quality provision results in a key communication tool, the annual environmental report – sometimes called the EHS report when it also encompasses health and safety aspects. Accordingly, the theoretical issue of optimal disclosure and information quality translates into practical questions like: how big, how detailed, how exhaustive should the report be with respect to the ecological and financial aspects of environmental-impact management? In particular, should there be separate reports to different stakeholders, or only one report with different sections? Should all stakeholders have access to every section, or should there be selective access? Increasingly, environmental reports on company Internet websites is rendering such questions irrelevant. On inspection of reports available on the Internet, it seems that wide accessibility is the rule. If companies cannot avoid producing quality reports, they might as well try to use them as PR and image-building instruments.

Given the previous observations on disclosure and information quality, poor company results, if any, are cast into a mitigating context; for instance, against the backdrop of improvements with respect to the past. Worsening performance, as communicated through performance indicators (emissions, emission-abatement investments) can be explained by the purchase of an old and heavily polluting company, which the purchasing firm will gradually restructure and retool with low pollution equipment.[13] If no such explanation is available, then the rate at which pollution has increased may be shown to have decreased, a form of improvement that governments, when it comes to inflation and unemployment, know how to use. Be as it may, in all such cases pressure exists to improve performance. The mere existence of an environmental report, subject to the disclosure and quality constraints discussed above, is a driver for on-the-ground improvements. If firms turn environmental reports into effective PR tools, all the better: the reporting benefits from real environmental improvements will constitute incentives for further improvements. One is reminded of the 'continuous improvement' required by the ISO 14001 certification of environmental management systems (see Chapter 8).

Improvements also refer to the content and presentation of the report itself. As noted earlier, these improvements may run against continuity and comparability over time. Good reports provide recalculations using the improved method to allow for comparisons over time. Strictly speaking, the firm is only expected to cater for internal comparability. Comparability across firms and activity sectors is the concern of the accounting profession, through standards and normalization.

The accounting profession is just one of the regulating bodies behind environmental reporting. Environmental protection agencies, tax agencies, and government determine minimum requirements for environmental reports. Firms have the choice between just meeting these minimal requirements and overcomplying, by going beyond them. As shown through a recent study by INFORMS®[14], firms in the more developed countries increasingly overcomply and try to capitalize on the benefits of high-quality reports: image-building, reputation, customer loyalty, trust, competitive edge. Environmental reports are increasingly being used as marketing and value-adding tools. Globalization and the Internet only amplify the potential benefits; in particular, spillovers across different activity branches or subsidiaries within the same firm.

Environmental reports are also subject to national and international awards. Prizes for the best environmental reports specify quality attributes and enhance public visibility of company performance. Such, for example, are the Environmental Reporting Award Schemes (ERAS), delivered by the British Association of Certified Chartered Accountants (the ACCA).[15] These awards end up having a pulling-up effect, as even the Indonesian experience shows. The best performing firms set the standards and gradually an increasing number follow.

Environmental reports also contain the standards by which they may be judged. Statements of vision and mission, of responsibilities and commitments, of values and goals, provide external stakeholders with the standards needed to assess the firm's environmental performance. Visions and statements vary in their language from caring for and stewardship of the environment to statements about sustainable development and 'be profitable to allow for environmental investments' (Shell; General Motors). Beyond the rhetoric, however, specific quantified targets over specified periods of time are needed to carry the reader's adhesion, while the firm's financial results will continue to be of primary importance to many stakeholders.

5.2 Evaluating Environmental Reports

Standards are still largely lacking when it comes to environmental reports. As a result, quality criteria, including, as reviewed above, transparency, comparability and reliability, are also lacking. At the same time, it is very hard for standard-makers to legislate in this field, given the extraordinary diversity of industries. The solution seems to be one where accounting bodies try to reward and promote systems already implemented by companies and which seem to be better than others. This is somewhat like depending on jurisprudence, rather than codification, for developing new law. A key instrument in the process are environmental-report award schemes.

The ACCA, the Association of Certified Chartered Accountants of the United Kingdom, is well known internationally for its Environmental Reporting Awards Scheme (ERAS), in line with the European Management and Audit Scheme (EMAS). Every year the ACCA jury analyses an increasing number of submissions, shortlists a sub-sample, and rewards the three best reports. They also have a first-time reporter award. All submitted reports, including those not rewarded or shortlisted, are then in due course summarized, studied and evaluated, in particular in the *Certified Accountant*, a journal of the ACCA, but also in other journals, such as the *Revue Française de Comptabilité* in France. In the USA, *The Accountant* has done likewise with the Investor Relations Magazine Prize, which awarded the *Exxon* report in 1996.

Award Schemes produce very useful material in terms of evaluation criteria, namely: what constitutes a 'good' environmental report? On what bases are the winners selected? What recommendations are made for improvements? As a matter of 'jurisprudence', certain norms and standards are emerging strongly enough to be adopted as evaluation criteria for class exercises at University and in Business Schools (see, for example, Chabredier et al., 2000). In the case of ACCA, these come under nine headings, each with their own sub-headings:

1. Company profile
2. Scope of report
3. Environmental management system
4. Relations with stakeholders
5. Communication format
6. Environmental impact details
7. Financial impacts of environmental management
8. Sustainable development and eco-efficiency
9. External certification and accreditation.

Each of these headings includes a list of sub-headings, as shown below:

1. *Company profile*
- Socioeconomic context
- Environmental policy
- Management commitment (both top and lower management)
- Key environmental achievements
- Key challenges, both environmental and otherwise.

2. *Scope of report*
- Number of business units included
- Reporting principles (stakeholders, disclosure, audience)
- Accounting principles (methodology)
- Inclusion of all aspects of direct relevance
- Inclusion of all aspects of indirect relevance
- Topics included: environment, health, safety, ethics, sustainable development.

3. *Environmental management system*
- Existence of an EMS
- Certification/accreditation goals
- Integration of environmental management into everyday business
- Risk management
- Internal audit
- External audit
- Environmental performance goals
- Compliance with environmental regulations.

4. *Relations with stakeholders*
- Environmental policy regarding dialogue with stakeholders
- Organization of dialogue – with employees, consumers, clients, suppliers and sub-contractors, administrations and NGOs
- Voluntary initiatives.

5. *Communication format*
- Justification of environmental indicators chosen for the report
- Graphical presentation
- Ease of reading; user-friendliness

- Feedback system (prepaid envelopes, Internet site)
- Diversity of approaches used.

6. *Environmental-impact details*

- Inputs by category of materials
- Outputs into the environment
- Waste outflows
- Packaging
- Transport
- Land contamination or disturbance and rehabilitation
- Presentation by activity sector
- Presentation by site
- Presentation by production stage (segment)
- Explanation of results with respect to past years and pre-defined targets.

7. *Financial impacts of environmental management*

- Environmental costs
- Provisions for risks and charges
- Environmental investments
- Fines related to environmental mismanagement or non-compliance
- Financial impacts of government regulations
- Financial quantification of benefits
- Mixed eco-financial indicators (also comes under sustainability and eco-efficiency)
- Future opportunities and risks; contingent liabilities.

8. *Sustainable development and eco-efficiency*

- Environmental design of products
- Eco-efficiency indicators
- Eco-financial indicators
- Sustainability indicators
- Sector-specific discussion on sustainable development
- Opinion of employees and managers
- Concern for social and ethical factors and impacts.

9. *External certification and accreditation*

- Verification by one or more external auditors

- Transparency of methods utilized and their limitations
- Report of critiques made to the company (and how it intends to meet the challenge)
- Credibility (to the evaluator of the report).

Certain organizations also issue internal criteria. For example, Crédit Suisse (a Swiss Bank) has produced a normalized format for environmental reports by banking institutions, which, slightly adapted, also fit insurance and other service companies. These are categorized into several sections as follows (the text in brackets is ours for further clarification):

1. *General information, environmental policy*
- Foreword (company's aims, challenges, stakeholders, targeted audience of report)
- General information on bank (general policy, size, scale of activities, recent trends and so on)
- Environmental policy of company (principles, commitment, strategies and so on)
- Summary/Assessment (bird's eye view on key goals/achievements in recent years).
2. *Environmental management system*
- Organization and responsibilities (EMS diagram and staff, who does what, accountability)
- Controlling (monitoring, intervention, urgencies, insurance, resources and so on)
- Commitment of employees (means of training, continuous improvement, assessment)
- Environmental goals and measures/goal attainment (quantitative and qualitative).
3. *Corporate ecology*
- Methodology for obtaining data; systems boundaries (for example, any FCA?)
- Inflows/Outflows of relevant materials and energy: corporate eco-balance (justification for degree of aggregation – competition, patented processes and so on)

- Environmental goals and measures/goal attainment (recycling, waste management and so on)
- Corporate ecology over the years (past trends, future projections).

4. *Product ecology*

- Aspects of lending/insuring and their environmental impacts (client discrimination)
- Aspects of capital investment and their environmental impacts
- Environmental goals and measures/goal attainment (eco-efficiency of clients and so on).

5. *Communication and dialogue to stakeholders*

- Environmental communication with stakeholders (which stakeholders? ease of communication?)
- Feedback offers (Internet, media, how is/was feedback used and so on).

6. *Summary*

- Goals achieved during report term (compliance and internal targets)
- Milestones in environmental protection (new targets and the future) .

As is clearly evident, there are numerous overlaps between the two reporting formats and criteria presented above. Yet both seem still to lack some overarching logic. What could such logic be predicated upon? Surely, it should allow for flexibility. It should be able to adapt to the diversity of stakeholders, of environmental impacts, of industrial and service activities, and, to some degree, of reporting styles. These, as will be illustrated in the case-study section, cannot, and presumably should not, be standardized out of existence. A report, environmental or otherwise, contributes in creating a company's image and differentiates it from competitors. In a world of *imperfect competition*, creating niche markets and captive clienteles has become crucial: competition is less through price than through product differentiation. Nevertheless, for reporting purposes of transparency and comparability, a common framework would be highly desirable. Is it achievable?

6.   TOWARDS A COMMON ACCOUNTING FRAMEWORK FOR
     CORPORATE ENVIRONMENTAL REPORTING

A satisfactory framework for environmental and eco-financial accounting
and reporting does not seem to exist as yet, although Schaltegger and others
have been making valuable suggestions in this direction. What is lacking is
a comprehensive model of eco-financial relationships between a business
corporation and its natural environment.

Our view is that the foundations of such a framework lie with a sound
understanding, in biophysical terms, of what may be called *industrial
ecology*. Such a view is not new, but it has not been capitalized upon. At its
simplest, it may be represented as in Figure 5.1 hereafter.

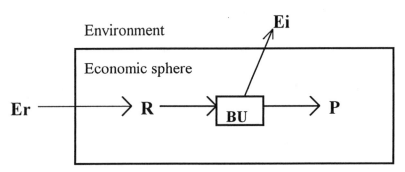

Notes:

Er = environmental input or resource.
Ei = environmental impact (air, water, land, or life).
BU = business unit (economic decision making unit).
R = resource use or input.
P = production or output.
(Note: all resource flows are per unit time).

Figure 5.1: Industrial ecology model

When such a view is held, it immediately appears that most, if not all, environmental business reports are prone to much confusion. For example, some companies report total emissions per year (Ei), others emission ratios per unit output (Ei/P), measured either in physical units (such as tonnes produced) or in dollars (sales). Some report total energy consumption (R); others energy use per unit output (R/P); others, still, energy use per employee or per dollar of business turnover. In general, there is no clear principle as to what flow must be reported or if absolute values or efficiency ratios must be reported, and, in the latter case, which efficiency ratios, and whether these should be in physical or monetary terms. As a result, comparability and benchmarking are next to impossible. For example, in Müller and Sturm's *Standardized Eco-efficiency Indicators* (Ellipson Ltd, August 2000), we see in Table 4 on page 27 a focus on non-renewable energy consumption, on water use, on atmospheric emissions, and on solid and liquid waste disposal. These indicators appear, however, as one dimensional, so that resource use by the business unit and environmental impacts cannot be clearly distinguished. An example will make this clear.

Suppose a mining company regularly (over the years) discovers new resources, that it rehabilitates its mine sites, that it uses woody residues from nearby sawmills for its energy needs, as well as hydroelectricity; that it carries out reforestation; that it treats its waste water before rejecting it into the environment; that this water is from a renewable resource (such as a large river or lake); and that it recycles a proportion of its waste, treats another proportion, and stores a residual amount under high security and very costly conditions (for example, radioactive waste). In such a case, it would be essential, both for the firm's internal management needs and from external stakeholders' point of view, clearly to distinguish between resource use and environmental impacts, as well as between resource-use efficiency and eco-efficiency.

Because the primary motivation of environmental accounting and reporting is impact on the environment, it is total absolute values, not relative ratios, that must be the final focus of accounting. Relative ratios have an instrumental role in that they indicate to managers and other stakeholders where and by what means undesirable impacts may be reduced. If this very basic principle is not adhered to, there will be confusion.

In the table referred to above, and recalling the above example, burning woody residues for heat generation or electricity production would apparently not be recorded if only referred to in terms of primary energy input, and so the corresponding greenhouse gas emissions would not be accounted for. If trees were planted in sufficient numbers, the tally for GHG gas emissions would be reduced. Thus, not only *net* resource use needs to be recorded, but also *net* environmental impact. Another example is when the recycling of a waste product, which apparently reduces environmental stress, actually makes it more damaging. The recycling ('retreatment') of waste uranium into plutonium produces nuclear waste of far higher radioactivity and risk than the original product. Such a case cannot be accounted for in a one-dimensional framework as shown in the table referred to above.

A special case is that of energy 'producers', like oil companies and electricity-generating plants. A better name for them would be energy 'converters'. Even hydroelectric plants only convert kinetic energy, of little economic value, into electric energy, of high economic value. In Table 2, p. 23 of Müller and Sturm (2000), primary non-renewable energy inputs of secondary energy consumption are reported, but it is not stated whether these should be used in energy accounting by a business unit. Our view is that they should not. The values rely on processes outside the boundary of the firm; that is, outside its field of direct control, and have therefore less decision-making relevance than has the recording of direct consumption quantities and their costs. Rather, energy 'producers' will need to record their direct extraction of primary (non-renewable) energy, to which they must add the energy needed to extract that energy. Economically, it sometimes makes sense for an energy producer to indulge in negative net energy production! This happens when, for instance, a locally cheap form of energy can be liberally used to extract another very valuable form – for example, if liquid fuels become very scarce, Quebec Hydro could conceivably use its abundant hydro-power locally to extract rare oil-producing minerals. Thus, from 'production' to final use, all primary energies will have been accounted for. Accounting for indirect primary energy use produces risks of double counting.

Accordingly, we propose in Table 5.1 a 'Master Environmental Account' (MEA) format that is a two-dimensional matrix and clearly distinguishes resource use   in   its rows, which relates to instrumental efficiency parameters, and environmental impacts in its columns, which relates to both specific and aggregate objectives. Its strength and generality lie in three facts. First, levels of aggregation can be freely specified, both for rows and for columns. Second, the matrix can be sparse without loss of generality (many cells can be empty). Third, sub-matrices can be derived (as illustrated) that provide 'zoom' detail while remaining coherent with the master account. With such a structure, companies with very different activity structures and operating in different ecological and legal environments can all use this same framework, though they may use it very differently; for example, by leaving different cells empty or specifying different sub-matrices.

Within the Master Environmental Account, several sub-matrices can be embedded. For example, section SM1 provides the energy sub-matrix, SM2 the atmospheric-emissions sub-matrix, and SM3 the waste water and material waste sub-matrix. This last account is still subject to research, given that the number of different waste items is very large and their environmental impact varies widely. However, the rationale is likely to be similar to that for atmospheric emissions. One needs to categorize the types of damage done through waste water and material waste; one needs to devise an impact indicator or measure for each impact type, and finally one needs to work out impact ratios, where each unit of a particular waste item converts to so much impact for each relevant impact type. The difficulty here is that material waste items can interact, amongst themselves and with different parts of the environment, to produce very different impacts. Often, the level of such impacts is unpredictable *a priori*. Nevertheless, just as in our auxiliary energy-use conversion sub-matrix (SM1), waste to impact conversion coefficients can very well be site specific and account for the particular interactions at that site. For example, two chemicals may interact very differently in the humid tropics and in a dry polar environment like Antarctica. The specification of this site-specific conversion matrix can very well be part of the environmental information a firm needs to produce, just as it measures and monitors atmospheric emissions and pollutants.

Table 5.1 : The Master Environmental Account (in absolute units per common unit time)

ENVIRONMENTAL IMPACT AGENTS: RESOURCE USE (See notes below)	DEPLETION OF NATURAL RESOURCES (land & water)					IMPACT ACCOUNTING — ATMOSPHERIC DISRUPTION (EMISSIONS) (The starred X* reflect conversion coefficients when emissions are not directly measured).				WASTE EMISSIONS (solids / liquids)	
Categories	Fossil fuels	Non Renewable Waters	Minerals (net)	Forests (net)	Natural habitat	Global Warming	Ozone Depletion	Acidic potential	Toxic/ Carcinogenic Potential	Water pollution	Land pollution
Units	GJ or Specs	m3	tonnes	ha, m3	ha	CO2-e	CFC11-e	SO2-e	several (+radioact)	m3	ha, vol
TOTALS =>	Total FF / SM1	TNRW	TNM (Types)	TF							
Energy use	X					(X)*	(X)*	(X)*	(X)*		
Water use		X		X	X						
- recycled water											
= net water use				X	X						
Waste Water reject				X	X					X	X
Materials used			X								X
- recyled materials											
= net materials used			X	X	X						
Waste materials reject				X	X		SM2 below	below		SM3	X
Gas emissions				X	X	X	X	X	X		
Resource investment	-(X)	-(X)	-X	-X	-X					-X	-X

180

Notes:

Energy, gas emission and other **sub-matrices** can be derived (e.g. thick rectangles labeled SM1, SM2, SM3). Cells contain absolute values per unit time for a given level of company structure (group, subsidiary, local plant).

Types of energy use: Coal, petroleum products, natural gas, electricity, wood, solar power (MWh)

Types of fossil fuels: Coal, crude petroleum, natural gas, uranium

Types of water: Fresh water, brackish, saline, highly saline; ocean, lake, river, aquifer

Types of materials: Appropriate categorization: focus on environmental impacts, but also on substitutability

Types of gases: CO_2, CO, CH_4, SO_2, NO_x, VOCs, CFCs, HCFCs, halons, fluorides....

Waste categories: Can be categorized as non-, moderately, or highly hazardous

Resource categories: Can be categorized as globally / locally abundant, scarce, and threatened. Habitat includes forests, grasslands, wetlands, deserts, tundra, etc.

Forests and habitat: Forests and habitat are impacted through energy use (resource depletion) and through waste and gas emissions (poisoning, degradation, etc.)

Resource investmen Mineral discoveries, reforestation, habitat restoration, waterbody and land decontamination. Matrices showing environmental impacts per unit resource use or per unit output, and resource use per unit output, are to be considered as derivatives of this master matrix.

181

To account for the above uncertainties, each impact factor can be associated with a risk factor, ranging from close to zero (low risk) to one (certain impact). The totals of each impact in each column can be weighted by the respective risk factors (probabilities) to achieve an expected environmental impact (EEI). This concept and the related data can provide a firm foundation for associating expected insurance costs and contingent liabilities. To date (2000), we have seen no environmental report do this in any systematic manner.

So far, no costing or financial considerations have been included. Is there an excessive environmental impact, or one with a potential for profitable impact reduction? Obviously, such information is derived from the columns of the MEA, but the firm focuses on the rows. What *environmental impact agent* (EIA) is most responsible and why has it increased? Typically, technical efficiency ratios are computed. They may be per unit of output, measured in physical terms (as CO_2 emissions per tonne of ore milled) or in monetary terms (as per thousand dollars of sales). Alternatively, some companies, especially the service companies, measure resource use per employee, while farmers may measure per hectare of land farmed. A third alternative consists in relating EIAs to input use, such as quantity of waste generated per unit of resource used (rather than per unit of output produced).[16] Visibly, there is as much inconsistency as there is variety.

Schaltegger, Müller, Sturm and colleagues suggest a way to integrate all these possibilities, which we strongly support. It is to refer EIAs to economic value added (EVA), as defined in Chapter 4. Given that EVA can be defined as sales minus purchases of goods and services, or, equivalently, as the sum of wages, interests, taxes, and net income, it combines all the three alternatives listed above. It appears reasonable to conclude that companies should abandon their current practices and adopt, as a starting point for their eco-financial analysis and reporting, the EIA/EVA ratios. Thus, each row item, at the appropriate level of (dis)aggregation, of Table 5.1 can be related to an EVA figure. This accounting approach is the only one to accommodate technological change and business growth or restructuring, including acquisitions and takeovers, in a meaningful way. It furthermore relates directly to shareholder value, and through it, to financial stock market valuations. EVA is the meeting point between the environmental and the financial worlds.

No unique EIA indicator, or measure, can easily summarize all environmental impacts, with the exception perhaps of the environmental-impact-point (EIP) system imagined by Müller-Wenk (Chapter 4, section 2.4.). Most of the time, however, this may not be as necessary as it might seem. Only in the particular situations where different impacts are to be traded off against each other is such a lack of universal measure an issue. For example, significant increases in water use may be necessary to achieve a drastic reduction in SO_2 emissions, through their capture and conversion to economically valuable sulphuric acid (see Case Study 5.2). In this case, however, trade-offs are local, and specific trade-off rates can be estimated in terms of local relative scarcity, with already well established methods.

On the other hand, next to every resource-use item, a running cost can generally be associated. Energy use, water use and materials use all carry costs, as well as waste disposal. Some of them are expenses, others are investments, like the use of solar panels. If tradable emission permits become the rule, then direct costs will correspond to emissions too. At the same time, many environmental impacts carry present or future liabilities, including contingent liabilities, and these must be entered in the capital account in the form of reserves and provisions that accrue as impacts accumulate. Such practice does not cover, generally speaking, the depletion of natural resources, which the calculation of the resource rent, or marginal user cost, would provide, but certainly any waste generation that is not recycled but disposed of carries a potential future liability, the estimation of which, by probabilistic methods, reduces the firm's shareholder value. Thus, both running costs and financial liabilities are, through resource use or waste production, to a large extent correlated with environmental impacts. It makes sense for the firm to consider reducing these impacts, and in particular, to investigate if it can do so profitably.

A particular line in Table 5.1 is that of resource investments, or investments in resource amelioration, restoration, rehabilitation, or simply conservation. This line affects environmental impacts with a negative sign, since standard industrial impacts are damaging and have been, quite arbitrarily, allotted the positive sign. (One could have chosen the reverse, it does not really matter.) For each firm, at each level, from the group to a specific site, a reduction in environmental impact may mean a reduction in cost associated with resource use, a reduction in financial liabilities and insurance costs, or nothing at all (pure externality). It can also mean direct benefits in terms of higher stock values because of investors' recognition. These benefits and cost reductions must be set against the cost of achieving the impact reduction – a standard case of investment appraisal, subject to the usual uncertainties. If the investment goes ahead, it will appear on the eco-financial balance sheet. If it turns out that the prospect is not profitable, the firm can stop there. However, in practice, this is usually not the end of the story. There may be community and government pressure which, although not immediately quantifiable, may nevertheless lead to loss of market share and ultimately to loss of profits. The firm has an incentive to investigate whether it could not achieve the reduction more cheaply. This usually involves some form of technological and/or organizational innovation. This itself carries a cost, the benefit being a cost reduction in achieving cheaper environmental amelioration. If achieved, the investment and its result will appear on the eco-financial balance sheet, but investments in innovations have become part of standard business. Thus, investors and other stakeholders are provided with a framework that allows consistent comparisons between firms, across industries and across different ecological and legal environments.

The Master Environmental Account proposed here seems to be the previously missing link that allows the ecological and the financial worlds to communicate and the eco-financial chain to hold firm.[17]

7. CORPORATE BENEFITS OF ENVIRONMENTAL AUDITING AND CERTIFICATION

Environmental audits and certification obey the same rationale as financial audits. The key issues are well summarized in a discussion paper by the International Auditing Practices Committee (IAPC, 1995). Perusal of corporate auditing theory, as for example per Lee (1993), suggests that the general principles of financial auditing can apply to environmental auditing.

However, financial analysts generally have no expertise in environmental impact assessment: it must be complemented with the help of environmental specialists. As Ledgerwood et al. (1992) discuss in their book, an environmental audit forms part of a total quality approach to business management.

Once the report has been produced, the firm may as well capitalize on its benefits. These benefits will only materialize, however, if recipients of the report grant it full credibility. Otherwise, benefits are likely to be nil, or even negative, if distrust and hostility develop. The economics of credibility are such that a small loss in credibility may be sufficient to jeopardize the value of a product. Current legislation in Australia regarding the labelling of GM (genetically modified) foods may illustrate the point. As in the United Kingdom, a majority of Australian consumers are still wary of GM foods. The government is debating whether to accept labels that provide only a probabilistic statement of 'not genetically modified', given that highly processed foods have GM components that are very difficult to trace. Furthermore, firms want to limit their potential liabilities and to future consumer attacks. On the other hand, consumers may treat a less than complete assurance with respect to GM components as worthless information, and classify the food item as GM, along with the non-labelled items. Transposed to environmental reports, this is like saying that without a proper certified audit by an accredited certification authority the value of an environmental report may be close to zero. Auditing and certification appear like an insurance scheme for preserving the economic value of the report. From the addressees' point of view, they reduce the risk that key pieces of information have been omitted or distorted. They know more confidently whether their interests have been catered for or not. This holds for external audits carried out for the sake of external stakeholders.

Firms also carry out internal audits. In this case, managers want to be sure that they will make decisions based on reliable information. Internal audits play a technical assurance role. Have any errors been committed? Has anything important been left out? Internal audits are more like a counter-expertise than a real credibility test. However, the difference is one of degree rather than kind. At bottom, both internal and external audits provide assurance that no important omissions or distortions have been perpetrated.

The goal of the firm is then to ensure that recipients of the report will value it to its full. Auditing regulations and standards assist in this task by providing quality guidelines. The International Standards Organization (ISO) is extending this service globally.

More specifically, the ISO 14010, 14011, 14012 and 14015 norms specify norms and standards for the auditing of environmental management systems (EMSs) (see Box 8.2 in Chapter 8).

- the ISO 14010 norms provide general principles and definitions
- the ISO 14011 norms specify audit procedures and how to audit EMSs
- the ISO 14012 norms specify the qualification criteria for auditors
- the ISO 14015 norms, a later addition (1999, the others date to 1996), discuss how to carry out environmental assessments of sites and organizations.

The purpose of these norms is to provide guidelines for producing a high-quality service that will carry credibility. Of particular interest is the specification in ISO 14011 of the roles and responsibilities of the requesting party (who has asked for an audit), of the auditor and the audit team, and of the audited. Regarding qualifications of the auditor, ISO 14012 emphasizes training, experience and competence in the following areas: environmental science and technology; environmental engineering and maintenance aspects; environmental law and regulations; norms of best practice in environmental management systems; and knowledge of auditing procedures and techniques.

8. CONCLUSION: HIGHER LEVELS OF *OPTIMAL* ENVIRONMENTAL DISCLOSURE?

One fact is clear from the last decade of the twentieth century: environmental reporting increased both in quantity and in quality. Of course, mainly the large corporations have been active, especially those quoted on the stock exchange, but it must be remembered that in many activity sectors, the largest companies, though smallest in number, are responsible for the largest proportion of environmental impacts.[18] That they should have done so, but smaller companies not, is witness to the relative costs and benefits of environmental reporting for different types of firms. Two questions seem worth asking in relation to taking stock. First, what are the key factors explaining this recent trend? Second, if desirable, what processes could further promote environmental reporting in the future?

The answer to the first question is complex, but may perhaps be summarized as follows: because of a general increase in social awareness of the environmental impacts of economic activity (though more so in some countries than others), several industry 'feedback channels' have been increasingly activated. These include government regulation, consumer pressure, and capital-market influence. More specifically, it seems that publicly owned companies – that is, owned by shareholders and quoted on the stock market – have been leading the dance. Paradoxically, the large wave of smallholder investors in the 1980s and early 1990s may have facilitated democratic pressures through capital markets, which directly impact on a firms' market value. Simultaneously, the increased frequency in the 1980s of company takeovers has struck home the message that shareholder-value matters and, through it, environmental liabilities even if contingent on future unknown events (Chapter 4). If these trends are to be taken at face value (a subject open to further research), it would appear that smaller businesses are not open to as many influences as large corporations. This observation paves the way for the second question.

It is to be expected that the smallest businesses will always find the costs of environmental reporting higher than the benefits. The exception is when they use or produce hazardous substances that are officially listed. In that case, as argued by Campbell (1994), they will submit to a duty of disclosure. Also, stakeholders of smaller businesses are more dispersed and less organized, reducing their potential influence. From society's perspective, or perhaps from government's, the question becomes: how many firms in a given country should report the environmental impacts of their activities? Or, what needs to be done to increase the proportion? Certainly, further reducing the costs of environmental monitoring and reporting will help. Special conditions for protecting intellectual property rights will be a key aspect. Alternatively, there could be regulations ranking the importance of reporting according to criteria like toxicity and irreversibility of impacts. The ranking could reflect fines paid if caught, and policing authorities could apportion enforcement efforts accordingly. If strict enforcement is preferred to gradual incentives, the choice will end up being whether to preserve polluting and marginally profitable activities or not, and, if not, facing the costs of local unemployment and social unrest. In this sense, provided capital markets are sufficiently efficient and democratic, industry concentration may be beneficial for environmental reporting and for greater knowledge of environmental impacts by business!

CASE STUDIES

Case 5.1 Wirralie Gold Mine Pty Ltd, Subsidiary of Normandy Ltd

It is interesting to examine Wirralie's 1998 Action Plans for the Greenhouse Challenge Programme at its Big Bell Gold Mine in Western Australia, because it is exclusively focused on reducing energy consumption and GHG emissions. It does not report SO_2 or ozone-depleting emissions, nor does it provide details on waste production, mine tailings and slurry management, or toxic waste. The report is obviously targeted at a very specific audience, government regulators, including the Department of Environmental Protection of Western Australia, shareholders and local environmental organizations. The local (human) community other than the company's employees is virtually non-existent, the operation being in outback Australia.

In an introductory section, the report informs the reader of its goal (to 'reduce greenhouse gas emissions by implementation of *financially viable* action plans'), lists the variables it has monitored and at what frequency (monthly), specifies what its baseline year is, and documents the fact it uses a computer spreadsheet to allow for quick monthly calculations of GHG emissions. Unlike what would have happened in the 1970s, the focus is not on reducing energy use *per se*, but only insofar as it is highly correlated with GHG emissions. However, as the company clearly points out, this (positive) correlation allows for the possibility of *financially viable* emission reductions. Although not stated as such, the company highlights the importance of eco-financial aspects and its readiness to capitalize on their potential. In this respect, it is exemplary. Secondly, it indicates the historical trend and the distribution of energy use and GHG emissions as a backdrop to setting future reduction targets. Clearly, this is to justify these targets in the eyes of shareholders as well as of government and environmental watchdogs (though obviously for different reasons). The third section then proceeds to detail its actions, but not before having separated quantitative from qualitative actions into two different sub-sections. This is most interesting, as the company shows firstly, its commitment to quantitative targets, monitoring and assessment, wherever possible; and secondly, the importance of unquantifiable benefits, the alternative being, either that they would not be reported, or, more radically, that they would not be undertaken.

By covering both types of actions, the company signals its seriousness about GHG abatement. Accordingly, as recommended in particular by the ACCA jury for the ERAS awards (see introduction of case studies in the previous chapter), it specifies the nature of each action and, in the quantitative section, how much GHG abatement is expected (in CO_2 equivalents) and at what cost to the company. It shows that several projects can be achieved at zero (marginal) cost, while others show a return on investment (ROI) of three (automatic/manual control of secondary ventilation fans) or four (improving high-pressure air consumption in process plant). ROIs can be calculated by the reader by noting the cost savings generated by the GHG-abatement project (mainly through reduced energy consumption). A final table summarizes both quantitative and qualitative projects and provides a final GHG-abatement expectation of 5.1 per cent from 1996 to 2002 (about 5000 tonnes of CO_2 a year out of some 100 000). Although this figure might appear small, the detailed plans show how much work is needed to achieve such a result, given, of course, the constraint of financial viability. At the same time, it is encouraging for the reader to see that even under such a constraint, progress is possible. In addition, no major technology shift is envisaged, but rather short-term technical adjustments. This is an indication that a larger potential for GHG abatement is possible once medium to long-term technology shifts are considered.

Case 5.2 Western Mining Corporation: WMC Ltd

We shall now investigate the reporting strategy of WMC Ltd (Western Mining Corporation, Australia). Because environmental reporting is not yet fully standardized, even in countries like Holland that require compulsory reporting, we need to use the comparative method to get a sense of such a strategy. We shall compare its first and most recently available reports (that is, the 1995 and 1999 reports), knowing that, in the meantime, its 1997 report received a best-practice award. We shall also compare WMC's and Volvo's reporting strategies, taking Volvo's first and most recently available reports (also 1995 and 1999). Contrary to Wirralie's (Normandy) report, WMC and Volvo aim at a diversified international audience.

WMC Ltd is a Western-Australian-based mining and processing company which has several offshore operations around the world and also has non-mining operations, such as fertilizer production. Mining and processing include nickel, copper, zinc, gold, and uranium. Its first report, covering the financial year 1994–95, provides a clear statement of commitment, 'A Journey to Excellence', with a number of specific quantified targets. It specifies its environmental policy and commits itself to establishing an environmental-management system, first at the company level, then at its different operations, to be fully effective by end 2000. Throughout its first report, WMC highlights its key environmental problems and challenges, in the four fields that it will stick to in its later reports: water, land, air and energy. Interestingly, graphs show that WMC had been monitoring various environmental impacts five years before its first report.

In terms of water, the challenges involve efficiency in use and recycling, use of water valuable for other, non-industrial uses (drinking, irrigation), and use of groundwater aquifers, plus storage of used water and dam tailings. The report is mostly qualitative, but clear and specific, with diagrams to present the issues. A bar diagram highlights the degree of salinity in water used at different operations. Tapping into the artesian basin and its effects on local springs are acknowledged; plans are defined to mitigate these effects. The improvement objective is clearly stated: improve water-use efficiency per tonne of ore milled, and a target of 15 per cent reduction over three years is set. Details are given for each operation site.

Land disturbance and rehabilitation is reported, quantitatively for all Australian-based operations and qualitatively for each site separately, both in Australia and overseas. Rehabilitation details and degree of effectiveness are reported. This section includes management of surplus rock and tailings and sponsorship for biodiversity preservation projects in Australia.

Atmospheric emissions, particularly of CO_2, are closely tied in with energy use. In a coloured box, the report explains the greenhouse effect and how the company plans to meet the challenge. WMC reports investments in natural-gas pipelines to its mining operations that should considerably reduce GHG emissions. For SO_2 emissions, it reports planning to capture them by building sulphuric acid plants, leading to a 75 per cent reduction in three years. Both total per annum and quantity per tonne of ore milled are reported for the last five years (1990–95). Finally, radiation from its uranium operation is acknowledged and commitment is made to high national and international safety standards.

The environment management system (EMS) includes commitment to 100 per cent compliance with laws and regulations, internal environmental audits, internal environment compliance; setting targets, monitoring progress, and correcting mistakes (plus specification of the system needed to correct mistakes); definition of five different incident levels and reporting of frequency of each; site-specific details given for the more important ones, including fines paid. Corporate environmental governance is specified.

The 1995 report announces improvements in data coverage in the near future. The 1999 report is indeed far more detailed and comes in two separate documents: one for the company as a whole and one that details each on-site operation. The title wants to convey a clear message: 'The company is committed to compatibility between economic development and maintenance of the environment'. It starts with an interview with the CEO, who states what he sees as the key achievement for 1999; namely, establishing internal standards for clear guidance. There are 14 of these. As of 2000, all operating units are to be audited against these standards. The report notes improved tracking and measurement systems, but also acknowledges that the company will not be able fully to implement its EMS by the end of 2000, as initially planned, except in one or two major operations. A graph shows percentage implementation for different stages of the EMS. The report also voices concern over fully implementing the Kyoto greenhouse gas abatement agreements and their implications for the company's international competitiveness, given the high energy intensity of its operations. It reports progress against the plan and specifies areas of underachievement; for example, determining the effect of environmental performance on market share. It provides a diagram of environmental responsibilities. These are all improvements on the 1995 report.

Reporting of performance has stuck to the four main indicators of 1995 (energy, water, air, and land, including biodiversity), but is more systematic, now including (qualitative) risk assessments, an input–output eco-balance diagram that highlights gaps in knowledge (for example, waste sent to landfill, scrap metal sent for recycling) for each operation and company-wide, specification of chemical elements used (some potentially hazardous), and *some* (not all) financial impacts of environmental management, absent from the 1995 report.

Here, the report is interesting in that, although it highlights rehabilitation costs, it clearly informs the reader that previous efforts towards environmental cost allocation and expenditure estimates have been abandoned. The reasons given are, first, reporting of these costs is not consistent between business units; and, second, there is insufficient agreement as to what constitutes an environmental cost compared to production or maintenance costs, and, within industry, there are no agreed standards for allocating expenditure on environmental protection. As a result, 'the numbers have little meaning and will not be reported'. The motivation is made clear: 'until there are clearer guidelines . . . and there are more obvious benefits to our business in doing so, we will not change our practices.'

A clarifying example is given: in one case the construction of an acid plant was considered an environmental cost because its main purpose was to capture SO_2 emissions, while in another case it was not, because its main purpose was to supply processing needs. Yet, in both cases, emissions were likewise reduced. 'Purpose' appears too fickle a base on which to make cost allocations. WMC goes on to turn this information reduction into a sign of success: 'Cost allocation will become increasingly difficult as we more fully integrate environmental issues into our routine business.' Environmental cost allocation seems to have no future until proper standards have been defined.[19]

We also note that graphs showing SO_2 emissions (shown profusely in the 1998 and previous reports) no longer appear in the 1999 report. This presumably is due, at least partly, to WMC judging it has 'solved' its SO_2 emission problem through recycling into production of sulphuric acid. In the 1998 report, emissions were shown to have fallen dramatically, from 312 115 tonnes in 1995–96 to 37 866 tonnes in 1998 (or 12 per cent of the original value). Emissions per ton of ore milled fell from 16 951 to 1 667 (or 10 per cent). In 1999, total emissions further fell to 33 780 tonnes (or 11 per cent), and unit emissions to 1 374 (or 8 per cent). However, these values were not reported other than in a final summary table.

Risk assessment is reported to be carried out for new projects: scale, severity, duration and probability of impacts are estimated. However, the report remains only allusive to this activity. Potential investors and insurers would need more details.

Eco-balances categorize, around the core activities of mining and processing:

- inputs: ore milled, energy use, explosives, chemicals, water and land disturbed
- products: nickel, gold, uranium, fertilizer, talc and so on
- by-products: sulphuric acid, ammonium sulphate, copper sulphides and such like
- air emissions: SO_2, CO_2, particulates, radiation (in milli-Sieverts)
- recycling of air emissions: SO_2, sulphuric acid, heat
- waste materials: water, oil, metals, slag; tailings, refinery and smelter residues, landfill wastes
- recycling of waste materials; newly rehabilitated land.

Some flows are reportedly not yet measured, for example, particulates, oils and greases into landfill, waste materials and amount recycled. Interestingly, question marks beside the unknown quantities, shown in 1998, disappeared in the 1999 report.

Details on non-compliance incidents and trends in auditing are reported. External audits now complement internal audits, an improvement over 1995. However, a lingering deficiency is in specifying environmental standards with contractors, who can make up 70 per cent of the workforce at certain sites. As the comparison with Volvo will show, this reflects an overall inward-looking approach to environmental management by WMC.

Over five years, WMC has remained both faithful to its initial reporting commitments and improved the scope and quality of the information provided. A particularly auspicious commitment is the provision of an eco-balance that highlights the gaps in knowledge, and the reduction of those gaps from one annual environmental report to the next.

Comparison Between WMC Ltd and Volvo AB Reporting

By comparison, Volvo's reporting philosophy, clearly visible in its first (1995) report, is more outward looking than WMC's, partially because of the nature of its business: Volvo produces engines and vehicles for the world market, and has operations around the world. This translates into life-cycle assessment of its products (instead of an eco-balance of its operations) and into a leadership role with suppliers, contractors and customers, a point that WMC felt should be developed in its 1999 report. Like WMC, Volvo occasionally refuses to disclose some information, but justifies it in this case because of 'competitive reasons'.

The 1995 characteristics are confirmed in Volvo's 1999 report where, like WMC's, greater detail and coverage is provided. However, Volvo has stuck far less to its initial format and content, clearly preferring to capitalize on improvements in data and method rather than maintain continuity – one of the key tensions discussed in the main text of the chapter. Note that both approaches carry positive messages: WMC's continuity evokes commitment to promises made, while Volvo's changes evoke state-of-the-art innovations. Clearly reporting is also a matter of personal style. This is perfectly consistent with optimal rather than complete disclosure.

We cannot end this case study, however, without pointing out that both companies, although environmental impact information appears reliable and of high quality, do not provide information which would be demanded by investors, and particularly by environmentally sensitive investors. WMC's decision not to estimate environmental costs highlights a major methodological challenge, and a need for urgent standard-setting. This need extends to the issue of expensing vs. capitalizing environmental costs and to providing a clear and complete picture of the company's environmental liabilities, both current and contingent.[20]

NOTES

1. We gratefully acknowledge helpful comments made by S. Schaltegger and R. Burritt. Of course, all remaining errors and omissions are our sole responsibility.
2. Economists have a technical definition of how to recognize a 'public good' as opposed to private goods. It is one where nobody can be excluded from using it (non-excludability) and the use of which by any person A will not diminish the ability of any person B to use it (non-rivalry in consumption). However, we need not worry about these technicalities here.
3. An overview of the economics of innovation and adoption is given by Lindner (1987).
4. The specific form of capital here is known as 'human capital'. It mostly refers to an individual's education, experience and expertise, but more generally to any characteristic of value to the community that might earn him or her an income. To a professional pianist, for example, it includes the nimbleness of the fingers.
5. See Dunstan, 1991 for an Australian study of corporate reaction to accounting regulations.
6. The notion of a transaction cost was first introduced by the Nobel Prize-winning economist R. Coase in 1937, in a seminal paper titled 'The nature of the firm' (*Economica*, 4: 386-405), and later developed by O.E. Williamson (1985), *The Economic Institutions of Capitalism: Firms, Market and Relational Contracting*, New York and London: Free Press. They opposed the standard assumption in economics that such costs are zero. This is particularly relevant to the costs of accounting viewed as information gathering and processing costs. The inclusion of non-zero transaction costs modifies the standard implications for optimal decision making.
7. This remains true even if cost accounting, environmental-impact assessment and efficiency performance are far from perfect. We are concerned here with whatever information is seen as valuable.
8. See Trevino, K.L. and Nelson, K.A. (1999), *Managing Business Ethics*, New York: John Wiley & Sons, p. 181, and Hay R.D., Gary E.R., and Smith P.H. (1989), *Business & Society: Perspectives on Ethics and Social Responsibility*, Cincinnati: Southwestern Publishing Co., p. 288.
9. Experience has shown in the past decade that such gambles are very risky and carry high costs to the company: loss of reputation, loss of markets, severe regulation, close scrutiny by watchdog organizations and the media. However, such losses are not necessarily irreversible if the company then cleans up its act. Royal Dutch-Shell, for example, has put much effort into reversing its tarnished image following the Brent Spar incident and its activities in Nigeria.

10. ESI includes both ecological and financial aspects of environmental management, or lack thereof.
11. See, for example, web based publications by KPMG, KLD (Kinder, Lyndenberg and Domini), the World Bank Group and Bank Sarasin in Switzerland.
12. Given the weakness of international government, a sufficiently regulated and competitive market may still generate the most efficient form of corporate governance.
13. Alternatively, the firm can highlight to public authorities the loss in jobs brought about by newer and more efficient technology, whether it does so in earnest or strategically.
14. Institute For Operations Research and Management Sciences, USA. Forthcoming by G. Dowell, S. Hart and B. Yeung in *Management Science* (2000).
15. One will find information on the environmental reports submitted in the *Certified Accountant*, annually.
16. For 'competitive reasons', some firms use indirect units. Volvo, in its first 1995 environmental report, relates energy, water consumption and air emissions to production in number of labour hours, rather than units produced (p. 17).
17. Not coincidentally, financial and environmental economics are also merging in their use of the option value concept, which originated in the latter (see Fisher, 1997, cited in Chapter 3).
18. A rule of thumb cites a 20–80 rule: 20 per cent of firms create 80 per cent of environmental impacts. This is mostly true of industrial pollution.
19. This should not be surprising. Even in fundamental physical measurements, like length, mass and time, standards are crucial to their widespread use. This should be even truer of economic and ecological measurements.
20. Note that it may be that shareholders do receive such information but that it is not otherwise made public. However, as the importance of environmental performance increases, pressure from investors, and also from insurers, will push for further accounting for and disclosure of such information.

REFERENCES

Antheaume, N. (1996), (in French), 'Accounting and environment: what future for accountancy and chartered accountants?', *Revue Française de Comptabilité*, **284** (December): 55–61.

Brockington, R. (1995), *Accounting for Intangible Assets. A New Perspective on the True and Fair View*, Economist Intelligence Unit Series, Wokingham, UK: Addison-Wesley.

Campbell, D. (ed.) (1994), *Environmental Hazards and Duties of Disclosure*, London: Graham & Trotman/M. Nijhoff and Boston: Dordrecht.

Chabredier, V., Dalegre, K., Decker, M., V. Dupont, and Durin, O. (2000), 'L'Evaluation des Rapports Environnementaux', DESS Economie et Environnement, Faculté des Sciences Economiques, Université de la Méditerrannée, Aix-Marseille, France.

Coase, R. (1937), 'The nature of the firm', *Economica*, **4**: 386-405.

Dowell, G., Hart, S. and Yeung B., in *Management Science* (2000), forthcoming.

Dunstan, K.L. (1991), *Corporate Reaction to the Regulation of Accounting for Goodwill*, CEDA Prize 1991, Committee for Economic Development of Australia, CEDA Monograph No. M99, ISBN No. 0-85801-203-1.

Elliott, R.K. and Jacobson, P.D. (1994), 'Costs and benefits of business information disclosure', *Accounting Horizons*, (December): 80–96, (also in A. Riahi-Belkaoui (1997), *The Nature and Determinants of Disclosure Adequacy. An International Perspective*, Westport, Conn. and London: Quorum Books. Appendix 1A: pp. 60–76).

Fisher, A.C. (1997), '*Investment under Uncertainty and Option Value in Environmental Economics*', University of California, Dept. of Agricultural Economics, Working Paper No. 813, February 1997.

Gray, R.H. (1990), *The Greening of Accountancy: the Profession after Pearce*, London: Certified Accountants Publications Ltd.

Gray, R.H., Bebbington, J. and Walters, D. (1993), *Accounting for the Environment*, London, UK: Paul Chapman.

Hay R.D., Gary E.R., and Smith P.H. (1989): *Business & Society: Perspectives on Ethics and Social Responsibility*, Cincinnati: Southwestern Publishing Co.

International Auditing Practices Committee (IAPC) (1995), 'The Audit Profession and the Environment', Discussion Paper, International Federation of Accountants, Australian Accounting Research Foundation. Victoria, Australia.

Ledgerwood, G., Street, E. and Riki, T. (1992), *The Environmental Audit and Business Strategy. A Total Quality Approach*, London: Financial Times, Pitman.

Lee, T. (1993), *Corporate Audit Theory*, London: Chapman and Hall.

Lindner, R.K. (1987), 'Adoption and Diffusion of Technology: an Overview', in B.R. Champ, E. Highly and J.V. Remenyi (eds), *Technological Change in Postharvest Handling and Transportation of Grains in the Humid Tropics*, No. 19, Australian Centre for International Agricultural Research, Bangkok, Thailand, pp. 144–51.

Macve, R. and Carey A. (1992), *Business, Accountancy and the Environment: A Policy and Research Agenda*, The Report of The Environmental Research Group of The Institute of Chartered Accountants in England and Wales, London.

Mathews, T. (1987), 'Social responsibility, accounting, disclosure, and information content for shareholders', *British Accounting Review*, **19** (2): 161–8.

Mathews, C. and Davey, B. (1996), 'The Collection and Analysis of Environmental Information in the Top 150 Australian Companies', Working Paper No. 96/3 (June), Royal Melbourne Institute of Technology, Faculty of Business, Melbourne, Australia.

Mattessich, R. (1995), *Critique of Accounting. Examination of the Foundations and Normative Structure of an Applied Discipline*, Westport, Conn: Quorum Books.

Müller, K. and Sturm, A. (2000), 'Standardized Eco-Efficiency Indicators', Ellipson Ltd., Switzerland, www.ellipson.com/ (August 2000).

Neal, D. (1996), 'Creative Accounting', in J. Wilson, *Current Issues in Accounting and Auditing*, UK: Tudor Business Publishing Ltd.

Owen, D. (1992), *Green Reporting: Accountancy and the Challenge of the Nineties*, London: Chapman and Hall.

Parker, R.H. and Zeff, S.A. (eds) (1996), *Milestones in the British Accounting Literature*, New York, and London: Garland Publishing.

Perks, R.W. (1993), *Accounting & Society*, London: Chapman and Hall.

Power, M. (1991), 'Auditing and environmental expertise: between protest and professionalisation', *Accounting, Auditing and Accountability*, **4** (3): 30–42.

Schaltegger, S. (1997), 'Information costs, quality of information and stakeholder involvement', *Eco-Management and Auditing*, (November): 87–97.

Schaltegger, S. and Burritt, R. (2000), *Contemporary Environmental Accounting. Issues, Concepts and Practice*, London: Greenleaf.

Schaltegger S., with Müller K. and Hindrichsen H. (1996), *Corporate Environmental Accounting*, New York: John Wiley & Sons.

Trevino, K.L. and Nelson, K.A. (1999), *Managing Business Ethics*, New York: John Wiley & Sons.

United Nations, Economic and Social Council (1992), *Environmental Disclosures: International Survey of Corporate Reporting Practices*, 30 January 1992.

Williamson, O.E. (1985), *The Economic Institutions of Capitalism: Firms, Market and Relational Contracting*, New York and London: Free Press.

6. Environmental Management and Corporate Finance[1]

SUMMARY

Chapter 6 examines the financial aspects of EM. Chapter 4 only examined them from the point of view of providing information for decision making. Here decision strategies are dealt with: first environmental investment and pollution-prevention (P2) projects, then the use of financial markets and intermediaries. To start with, the basic principles of financial management and investment appraisal are reviewed. These apply directly to EM, although there are difficulties in identifying the specific costs and benefits attributable to environmental investments, so that some remain hidden, as discussed in Chapter 2. For both P2 and whole-site projects, it is worth identifying the 'value drivers' that increase shareholder value. These include green product differentiation, direct and indirect cost reduction, and risk reduction, whether through environmental damages and liabilities or through reputation effects, which often constitute hidden risks. The implication for EM is to reduce environmental hazards and the probability of accidents, so as to lower risk and insurance premiums and the cost of capital. These are further influenced by tax-deductible provisions, and other fiscal effects of capital depreciation. Implications for the practical assessment of the environmental aspects of investments are given. The focus then shifts to investments in companies, and the role of the environment in bank loans, investment funds and environment-related financial instruments, with special emphasis on risk. Environmental liabilities, possibly hidden in real-estate contamination, affect the risk premiums and hence the cost of bank loans. The rapid emergence of 'green' or 'ethical' funds influences company share values, as witnessed by special stock indices.

1. ENVIRONMENT IN CORPORATE FINANCE: AN INTRODUCTION

An essential feature of environmental management is taking into account environmental expenses and benefits, as well as environmental risk, in financial decisions. In Chapters 4 and 5, we already discussed how some of the hidden liabilities and assets, as well as the hidden expenses and revenues, resulting from taking into account environmental facts, may be taken into account in corporate accounting. However, the bookkeeper's tally is not everything; it is merely a quantitative tool for management, which may be oriented towards environmental management. Taking into account environmental protection and the existence of environmental risks are also concerns from the point of view of financial management, as well as from the point of view of risk management and insurance. This chapter thus aims at discussing the financial aspects of corporate environmental management.

More precisely, *finance* is concerned with transferring value in time, as occurs in investments and through using financial services such as loans. It is also concerned with transferring economic risks to agents such as bankers, insurers and other members of the financial community. *Financial management* therefore deals with managing *investment, financial services and risks.*

The financial aspects of environmental management as such are thus concerned with several questions. How can one take into account environmental protection and environmental risks in investment and project appraisal through the usual financial techniques, such as discounted cash flow and internal rate of return calculations? For more global investments at the firm level, such as mergers, takeovers, or simply investment in a firm's stocks, what are the implications of environmental risk? What are the implications of environmental risk management on cash management? The financial management of physical risks, which may take place either through insurance, when there are adequate insurance products on the market, or through self-insurance, meaning the constitution of suitable financial reserves, is another question. This question of environmental risk insurance, or more generally, of environmental risk management, although closely related to the financial topics of this chapter, will therefore be discussed separately in Chapter 7.

The following sections intend to discuss these financial aspects of environmental management from all the aforementioned angles. We start with a survey of the various methods used for investment appraisal.

2. INVESTMENT APPRAISAL AND PROJECT MANAGEMENT: SOME FIRST PRINCIPLES

Investment appraisal and capital budgeting are generally carried out through discounted cash-flow techniques, which lead to the so-called *net present value* (NPV) method, or through the *internal rate of return* (IRR) method, which is derived from the NPV method. Both these methods have strong theoretical foundations, whether for certain or uncertain future cash flows. Simpler methods, with less theoretical background, are, however, often used, such as *payout time* (POT) techniques (or payback time techniques), among others. Thus, the financial techniques that are pertinent for the appraisal of environmental projects are well known (Brealey and Myers, 1988), just as the accounting techniques described in the previous chapter.

Economists distinguish between *consumption goods*, which are immediately consumed (meaning that they are readily and irreversibly destroyed when used), and investment goods, or *capital goods*, which are lasting goods, the consumption of which is lasting or taking some significant time. Investing is defined as acquiring investment goods, aiming at receiving net income or profits in the future, or at least throughout the investment lifetime. More precisely, any investment may be characterized by: the initial investment I_0, and the sequence of successive investments I_1, $I_2, \ldots I_t, I_{t+1}, \ldots I_T$ carried out during successive periods of time 1, 2, ...t, $t + 1, \ldots$ T; the sequence of net incomes, or profits, derived from the investment $CF_1, CF_2, \ldots CF_t, CF_{t+1}, \ldots CF_T$.

There are several ways of expressing these profits. These may either be after-tax accounting profits, but these take into account the depreciation of equipment, which depends upon the corporate tax laws, thus describing somewhat arbitrarily the true economic depreciation of equipment, and perhaps giving an inadequate picture of the cost of capital.

After-tax cash flows, or *free cash flows*, may be considered as a pertinent description of profit, because they correspond to the actual increase in liquid assets available to the firm for either paying dividends to shareholders, or to carry out investments. However, the CF_t's are *expected* free cash flows available in the future, so that they are almost always estimated only up to the forecasting error, because of course the future cash flows related to the investment are usually uncertain. Thus, calculations pertaining to investment appraisal and to capital budgeting are very often conducted in terms of free cash flows, which may be either reinvested or be used to pay for the shareholders' dividends.

Let τ be the rate of corporate tax applicable, and let A_t be the depreciation of capital at time t, as allowed for corporate tax calculations. These free cash flows at periods 1, 2 . . . t, t + 1, . . . T may be expressed as follows:

$$CF_t = (R_t - C_t)(1 - \tau) + A_t \tau \qquad (6.1)$$

In this equation, R_t stands for the revenues related to the investment (in terms of sales, and other incomes such as financial incomes), during period of time t, while C_t stands for all the costs related to the investment during period of time t. Of course, revenues and costs related to environmental protection and environmental management have to be singled out for the purpose of environmental management as such. This is of course one of the key issues in this chapter; it will accordingly be discussed in detail hereafter. Before this, however, let us discuss the implications of the various investment appraisal methods, as well as their specific aspects in terms of environmental management, beginning with the NPV method, which, as mentioned above, is the method that has the most complete theoretical foundations. In order to discuss these theoretical foundations, we assume the existence of markets for financial services and, in particular, markets for loans. Banks, in particular, offer loan services. Banks are actually intermediaries between capital suppliers that are investing in fixed-interest instruments such as bonds or deposits carrying an interest, and borrowers. What is the economic rationality underlying the market for loans? A loan is a financial service in which the lender will accept being deprived of some sum of money for some specified time, in return for interest, which is charged to the borrower. This price can be paid at the end of the specified time period. It can also be prepaid, or deducted from the amount of the loan at the beginning of this time period. The present value of some cash flow, or amount of money received at some future time, stems from the rationale of the markets for financial services. This may be shown through a simple example. Assume, for instance, that on the market for loans, an investor or capital supplier is lending some amount of money, such as $ 1000 (or £ 1000, or € 1000) at an interest rate of 3 per cent for a time period which is one year. This means that the borrower will, if the interest is to be post-paid, or paid at the end of the contract (after a year), receive a sum of $1000 (or £ 1000, or € 1000) at the beginning of the contract. This sum has to be returned to the lender, with the interest which is $30, (or £ 30, or € 30) at the end of the contract; thus, after one year, the borrower has to pay back to the lender $ 1030 = 1 000 × (1 + 0.03) (or £ 1030, or € 1030). By definition, the *net present value* of $1030 (or £ 1030, or € 1030) after one year, with a discount rate of 3 per cent, is $ 1000 = 1030/(1 + 0.03) (or £ 1000, or € 1000). Similarly, if the interest is to be prepaid, or paid at the beginning of the contract, the borrower will return $ 1000 (or £ 1000, or € 1000) at the end of the contract, and receive the net present value of these $1000 (or £ 1000, or € 1000) upon signing the contract, which is 1000 / (1 + 0.03); that is, approximately $ 970.87 (or £ 970.87, or € 970.87).

More generally, the NPV of a riskless loan (which is, from the lender's point of view, an investment) of the sum V_t for t years, and with a rate of interest i over t years, is:

$$V_0 = \frac{V_t}{(1+i)^t} \tag{6.2}$$

In this case, the lender is certain to be redeemed, so that the investment is riskless. Otherwise, as will be discussed later, a risk premium will have to be added to the riskless rate of interest. A further generalization is the definition of the NPV of a sequence of certain future free cash flows, or cash payments CF_1, CF_2 ... CF_t, CF_T at times 1, 2 ...t ...T. More precisely, the NPV generated by an investment of lifetime T is defined as :

$$NPV = \sum_{t=1}^{T} \frac{CF_t}{(1+i)^t} \qquad (6.3)$$

In equations (6.2) and (6.3), V_t and CF_t are expected net cash flows (that is, after deduction of taxes and all costs); i is the interest rate prevailing over the lifetime of the investment. In general, the interest rate over a period of t years is varying with t. Therefore, strictly speaking, one would have to discount CF_t with the interest rate i_t for an investment with lifetime t. However, we assume here that i is the interest rate over the total lifetime T of the investment.

Among the various methods for investment appraisal, the NPV method (which rests upon calculating the NPV of a forecast of the sequence of future cash flows related to the investment), is one of the most important; it also rests on strong theoretical foundations. These theoretical foundations are outside of the scope of this book. Let us just say that this method rests on intertemporal preferences of economic agents, which are such that a net revenue X, received today, will be preferred to the same net revenue X at time t (usually, after t years). It also rests upon the existence of markets for financial services, on which loans are exchanged against interests, which is related to these preferences. This existence implies that receiving the sum X $(1 + i)^t$ within t years (if i is the compound-interest rate for fixed-interest loan over t years) is equivalent to receiving the sum X today.

We say that X is the NPV of the net cash flow X $(1 + i)^t$ at time t. Whence, dividing by X $(1 + i)^t$, one may also express the NPV λ_t of cash flow X at time t, if i is the investor's discount rate over the lifetime of the investment. This leads to:

$$\lambda_t = \frac{1}{(1+i)^t} \qquad (6.4)$$

Finally, if the investment (I > 0) is entirely carried out at time 0, the *net present value* (NPV) is defined as:

$$NPV = -I + \sum_{t=1}^{T} \frac{CF_t}{(1+i)^t} \qquad (6.5)$$

T is the lifetime of the investment, also called the investor's time horizon. CF_t is the expected net cash flow, as defined by equation (6.3). T may be infinite but, in practice, the NPV will always be finite. While in (6.5) time is described as a discrete sequence of (generally annual) periods, one might describe it as a continuous interval. R(t) stands for a cash-flow forecast at future time t. Again, there is no uncertainty at this stage, although suitable generalizations are possible. The NPV method is thus derived from the above considerations, and rests on estimating NPV values through equations such as (6.5). Inasmuch as some uncertainty does occur in any real project, the problems of uncertainty and risk have to be addressed. Uncertainty leads to risk, inasmuch as the actual profit outcomes may be either smaller, or larger, than the forecasts. This point may be theoretically discussed and proved under the so-called expected utility theory, but this is outside the scope of this work. Let us just say that there are two equivalent methods which take risk into account in NPV calculations. The first method is to calculate the so-called *certainty equivalent* of some uncertain future cash flow, which is always smaller than the expected cash flow for a risk-averse investor. The certainty equivalent is defined as the certain cash flow which, compared to the given uncertain cash flow, is indifferent to the risk-averse investor. A second method, which is equivalent, is through an adequate choice of the discount rate i, allowing for a *positive risk premium with respect to the riskless asset.* The riskless interest rate is usually chosen, as the rate on short-term treasury bonds issued by well-rated governments, such as the United States, the United Kingdom and other countries, is a good proxy to such a riskless investment. If we use this second method, the discount rate applicable to previous equations may be expressed as:

$$i = i^o + \rho \qquad (6.6)$$

where $i° > 0$ stands for the return of the riskless asset, while $\rho \geq 0$ is the so-called risk premium, with $\rho = 0$ corresponding to the particular case of the riskless asset. Otherwise and in general, the discount rate used in (6.6) is the discount rate which is pertinent to the firm's situation: it must correspond to the actual cost of capital available to the firm. A first way of evaluating i is to evaluate the *shareholders' opportunity cost of capital* (SOCC) applying to the firm. This is the cost that would apply to the firm for raising external capital in the form of raising new stock, rather than in the form of financing the investment through cash or liquid assets already available to the firm, and part of its equity. This opportunity cost of capital can also be defined as the rate of return that is required by the firm's shareholders for investing in the firm, rather than investing in other available investments with the same level of risk.

Cost of capital estimates can be derived through calculations of rates of returns for firms of the same sector and facing similar risks. This is a comparatively easy task for large firms with their stocks quoted on financial markets. In other cases, rates of returns may also be estimated, although this is a more difficult exercise. In this exercise, much will rely on the analyst's judgement and experience in an assessment of the cost of capital. The riskless rate of interest, $i°$, is well known. For instance, for 10-year investments in treasury bonds, at the end of year 2000, it used to be about 5.1 per cent in the euro area and in the UK, about 5.8 per cent in the United States, 5.7 per cent in Canada, 6.0 per cent in Australia, but only 1.8 per cent in Japan and about 3.7 per cent in Switzerland. The problem is the evaluation of the *risk premium* rather than the cost of capital itself: knowing the risk premium, since the riskless rate is well known, calculating the WOCC from equation (6.6) is a trivial matter.

In order to calculate the risk premium corresponding to an investment or a firm, one may try to assess its creditworthiness or its ability to reimburse a loan; an ability that clearly is related to the probability of default of the firm. This means marking the creditworthiness of a firm. This task is done routinely by financial analysts in the loan and capital-market activities of banks. It is performed through examining some financial ratios such as the total debt/equity; of course, the equity should more than cover the debt, so that this ratio should ideally be smaller than one. Grading the creditworthiness of firms is also done by so-called rating agencies, such as Moody's, Standard and Poor's, Fitch and DCR. For instance, there are ten grades for the rating of bonds as carried out by Moody's and Standard and Poor's (Table 6.1).

Table 6.1: Ratings of bonds by major rating agencies

Moody's	Standard and Poor's	Corresponding creditworthiness
Aaa	AAA	Practically riskless
Aa	AA	Very fine quality
A	A	Strong ability to pay
Baa	BBB	Adequate ability to pay (last grade for banks)
Ba	BB	Risk exposure
B	B	Significant risk exposure
Caa	CCC	Major risk exposure
Ca	CC	Important risk exposure
C	C	Default on interest
D	D	Default on interest and principal
NR	NR	Rating not requested

In the United States, there are so-called 'junk bonds' which are high-yield but high-risk bonds issued by corporations with a significant risk of failure. The rates of interest on junk bonds do give an idea of the risk premium for some high-risk investments with respect to US treasury bonds. For premium corporate bonds with an A rating, the risk premium might be of the order of 1 per cent. For BBB-rated bonds with a comparatively low but significant risk of default, the risk premium might be something like 3 per cent, but for CC or CCC-rated bonds with a large rate of default, it might be of the order of 10 per cent. This last figure may be compared, as an order of magnitude, to the rate of default on the junk-bond market in the United States. This rate of default reached a peak of about 18 per cent during the recession period of 1990–91, but has been much smaller (perhaps 5 to 10 per cent) during the rest of the 1990s, a more prosperous period. These premiums are, as has been discussed earlier in the case of environmental investments, of the order of magnitude of the probability of failure of the firm. Otherwise, calculations of accounting rates of return, as well as forecasts of future returns might be useful, and the risk might be identified with an estimate of the *probability of failure* of the firm as a first approximation.

The weighted average cost of capital (WACC), defined as a weighted mean of the costs of equity capital and of borrowed capital, may also be used for that purpose:

$$i = w_{BC}\, i_{BC}\, (1 - \tau) + w_{EC}\, i_{EC} \tag{6.7}$$

In this equation, w_{BC} stands for the fraction of the investment, which corresponds to borrowed capital, while $w_{EC} = 1 - w_{BC}$ corresponds to equity capital. i_{BC} and i_{EC} stand, respectively, for the corresponding costs of borrowed capital and of equity capital. If τ is the rate of corporate tax applicable either to the project, or to the whole firm, the factor $(1 - \tau)$ should be applied to the borrowed cost of capital i_{BC} , because, in most countries, the interests paid on borrowed capital are deductible expenses for the calculation of taxable corporate income.

Besides the NPV method, another investment appraisal method, which is very often used in investment appraisal, and is derived from the NPV method, is the so-called *internal rate of return* (IRR) method. This method rests on the fact that, in (6.5), the NPV may be considered as a function B(i) of i. This function is a decreasing function whenever the R(t)'s are positive. It is thus such that, under rather reasonable conditions, one, and only one, positive root i*, interpretable as an interest rate, exists for :

$$B(i) = 0 \tag{6.8}$$

The calculation of the IRR therefore rests on determining the feasible root of equation (6.8) (such that i* > 0).

The IRR i* depends on the characteristics of the investment alone; that is, on the RN_t or $RN(t)$; hence its name of *internal* rate of return. i* may readily be given a clear interpretation. Assume, for instance, an investment V_0 in fixed-interest instruments such as bonds, which are redeemed *in fine*, such that the capital V_0 is completely reimbursed after T years.

Let r be the nominal interest rate of the loan; at the end of every year, the investor will receive the sum rV_0; and let i (with, in general, i ≠ r) be the investor's discount rate. Under these conditions, the investor's NPV will be:

$$NPV = b(i) = -V_0 + V_0\, r\, f(i,T) + V_0 /(1+i)^T \qquad (6.9)$$

In this expression, $f(i,T) = \displaystyle\sum_{t=1}^{T} \frac{1}{(1+i)^t}$ may be expressed as:

$$f(i,T) = [(1 + i)^T - 1]/ [i\,(1 + i)^T] \qquad (6.10)$$

Assume now that i = r; r is the interest rate observed on capital markets for a loan T. One can see that, taking (6.9) into account, in (6.8), B(r) = 0. This means that the IRR of our investment in bonds with *in fine* redeeming is just the interest rate i prevailing on capital markets. This result may be generalized and an interpretation of the IRR of any investment may be provided.

Under this interpretation, *the IRR is the interest-rate equivalent to the one that would be offered by investing in a loan with the same characteristics as the investment actually contemplated, in terms of cash flows, duration, redeeming characteristics and risk.*

This rate of return may therefore be compared directly to the rate r (often called the *hurdle rate*) which would prevail on capital markets for a loan with equivalent duration and risk.

At least from the purely financial point of view, the investment will not be carried out if i < r. This would imply a return on the investment lower than the return of an investment corresponding to same level of risk and available on capital markets. On the other hand, the investment may be carried out if i ≥ r.

There are some obvious problems with the IRR method, which is consistent only if the IRR is well defined. For this purpose, equation B(i) = 0 must have only one acceptable root (i > 0). Inasmuch as B(i) = 0 is an equation of degree T of the unknown variable $\xi = 1/(1 + i)$, it may have no acceptable roots or several acceptable roots. One can find a sufficient condition for the existence of a unique acceptable root; if I > 0, and if CF_t > 0 for any t, with $-I + \Sigma\, RN_t$ > 0. Since B(i) is a continuous and strictly decreasing function of i for any i ≥ 0, with B(i) > 0 and B(∞) < 0, there exists one unique and finite i > 0 such that B(i) = 0. Under more general conditions, which we will not discuss here, there is a unique root of the equation B(i) = 0. In plain terms, these mathematical conditions mean *that the investment has the characteristics of a loan,* as pointed out by several authors, including, recently, Promislow and Spring (1996). Most practical investments are expected, up to some random variations, to have such characteristics. We will assume here that the above conditions are fulfilled, or, more generally, that there is only one acceptable root. If so, the only difficulty encountered in calculating the IRR is solving equation B(i) = 0, but this is just a practical problem, which is easily tackled with adequate computer facilities.

Another problem associated with the use of the IRR method is that, in some cases, it does not lead to the same conclusion than the NPV method (Lorie and Savage, 1955) in the comparison of two projects. This may happen for a discount rate that is much lower than the IRRs found for the two projects. This anomaly, however, disappears if the cash flows are reinvested, because reinvestment of all cash flows is a hypothesis underlying the IRR method.

In the particular case in which the following simplifying assumptions are made: (1) T goes to infinity; and (2) CF_t can be considered as a constant CF (so that CF_t = CF), one has:

$$B(i) = - I + (CF/\, i) = 0 \qquad\qquad (6.11)$$

Therefore:

$$\lim_{T \to \infty} (1/i) = I\, /\, CF = POT \qquad\qquad (6.12)$$

This means that the limit of the reciprocal of the IRR for $CF_t = CF$, where CF is a constant, and for $T \to \infty$ is equal to the so-called *payout time* (POT), or payback time. The payout-time method is one of the simplest methods for investment appraisal. It may be defined as follows: let I (considered as a positive constant) be the amount of the investment, and CF be the free cash flow (also considered as a constant); in this case, the payout time, at least under its simplest definition, may be defined as follows:

$$POT = I / CF \qquad (6.13)$$

This quantity, which represents the time after which the cumulated free cash flows related to the investment (which, as mentioned above, have been assumed to be constant, at least as a first approximation, constants) become equal to this investment. It is, in general, expressed in years. According to (6.11), the reciprocal of the payout time 1/POT may be considered as a first approximation of the IRR. Thus, this reciprocal has to be compared directly to the rate of return pertinent for the investment, knowing the level of risk (and hence the risk premium associated to it).

The POT method is a simple method, but, as discussed above, it is only a first approximation method, inasmuch as 1/POT is a first approximation to the IRR.

How the investment is financed is also an important issue. We assume that a fraction EC (equity capital) of the investment I is financed through the firm's own capital, while the rest of the investment BC (borrowed capital) is financed through one or several loans. Thus, we are left with several variants of the above investment-appraisal methods and, in particular, of the NPV and IRR methods.

If we use the free cash flow concept as an indicator of profit, we are left with a version of the NPV method in which we discount all future cash flows, using the rate of discount corresponding to the class of risk of the investment:

$$EC = I - BC \qquad (6.14)$$

The final net present value thus obtained is said to be calculated under the *equity residual* method:

$$NPV = \sum_{t=1}^{T} \frac{CF_t}{(1+i)^t} - EC \qquad (6.15)$$

A variant of the method is to calculate the so-called *shareholders' value* SV, defined as:

$$SV = \sum_{t=1}^{T} \frac{CF_t}{(1+i)^t} - BC \qquad (6.16)$$

Whereas in (6.15) one has to check whether the NPV is positive or at least non-negative, in its variant (6.16) one verifies that the net initial investment I - BC is smaller than SV, which is clearly strictly equivalent.

SV is therefore equal to the discounted value of all future free cash flows, less the outstanding debt. It may be calculated for a whole firm, or, on an incremental basis, for an investment project. The discount rate used in (6.14) is the discount rate, which is pertinent to the firm's situation: it must correspond to the actual cost of capital available to the firm. The pertinent rate of discount is either the shareholders' opportunity cost of capital, as defined above, or, to take into account the effect of external borrowing, the weighted average cost of capital (WACC), as defined by equation (6.7). Theoretically, in a so-called perfect capital market characterized by one rate of interest, the SOCC should be equal to the WACC. For instance, in the absence of any corporate tax, the two concepts of discount rates will be equal, so that $i = i_{BC} = i_{EC}$, but this is not true in general. If so, it may be considered as somewhat logical to take into account the WACC as the discount rate rather than the shareholders' opportunity cost in any NPV calculation if there is a non-zero corporate tax rate applying to the firm. However, under these conditions, the SOCC is usually higher than the WACC. It may therefore be argued, in favour of the former, that it gives a conservative or pessimistic estimate of the NPV. But both estimates of NPV are obtained with different cash flow terms. It is not clear, finally, that the estimate reached by using the SOCC is any smaller than the estimate reached by using the WACC as the pertinent discount rate.

All the above methods of course apply to environmentally directed investments, such as pollution-prevention (P2) investments, as well as to the environmental aspects of any investments. This means that environmental-specific expenses or revenue stemming from any investment have to be taken into account. There are, however, several scales at which these considerations are pertinent: the investment may, in particular, be either a whole-firm investment, or a more particular or local project. The problems raised by local or particular projects are somewhat different from those raised by whole-firm investments. The latter are generally carried out on specific capital markets, or stock exchanges, while the former are financed through a combination of borrowed capital, direct reinvestment of the firm's free cash flow, and, in some cases, emission of new stock. We therefore propose to discuss first the environmental aspects of investment projects.

3. THE ENVIRONMENTAL ASPECTS OF INVESTMENT PROJECTS

3.1 General Considerations

Before discussing our subject in detail, some important general considerations must be made, given the specificity of environmental concerns and environmental variables in complex investment projects. It is indeed often difficult to isolate the specific effects of environmental aspects of an investment in terms that are readily interpretable for investment appraisal. In other words, what is the incremental capital expenditure of a project related to environmental protection, and what are the incremental free cash flows generated by this incremental investment, if known? The answers to these questions are often difficult, and, in this way, the costs and benefits of environmental management are, to some extent, hidden, as highlighted in Chapter 2. This first point corresponds to a difficulty often encountered in management accounting. For instance, calculating an average cost is quite easy in principle if there is just one product, but this is a particular case which is very seldom encountered in corporate management

practice. In general, calculating an average cost in the most general case of
several products is difficult or meaningless. In general, only marginal costs
may, at least in theory, be defined and calculated without ambiguity.
However, in the most common case in which several distinct products are
offered, accountants are generally able to do some costing under some
simplifying assumptions concerning the inputs or resources which are jointly
used. The most common simplification consists in a repartition of the costs
of such joint inputs between products, proportional to some accounting
index, such as the market value of the products. Similar devices may be used
when trying to estimate the environment-related costs and benefits of an
investment proposal.

A second aspect of the previous point is the following. Even if one is able
to assess the incremental benefits and the incremental costs due to
environmental variables in a given investment, there is some added
complexity. One must keep in mind the fact that we are, in general, dealing
with complex systems which interact in all their parts. We assume,
therefore, that one has been able to assess at least approximately (1) an
environmental investment or a P2 investment within a given production unit
or (2) the environmental aspects of a whole-site investment. Even if that
should be the case, it may not be taken for granted that there is no effect on
seemingly unrelated parts of the production unit or seemingly unrelated
production units, products or aspects of the management of the firm as a
whole. This hints at strategic concerns, or at all-embracing concerns for the
firm, especially when several management actions, whether related or not to
the environment, are conducted at the same time. In that case, care must be
taken to optimize these management actions under what might be called
synergic strategic planning (see, for example, Jacques, Lesourd and Ruiz,
1988).

Often, environmental protection investments do not improve the firm's
shareholder value by themselves; this is especially true of 'end-of-pipe' P2
investments, which may not, actually, be considered as pollution-*prevention*
investments, because they simply remove emissions that already occurred
elsewhere, usually at quite a large capital cost. More effective, but often
more costly, are P2 investments that really modify the process, leading to
upstream reductions on emissions, and/or to recycling of potential

pollutants. If the investment is to be considered, these direct environmental effects of what one might call *process retrofitting investments* are likely to be only one of a number of positive effects, including better-quality attributes for the product, including its environmental-quality attributes. As a rule, however, retrofitting of existing processes leads to much higher costs of pollution reduction than whole-site projects involving complete rebuilding of an existing plant, or building a new production unit altogether.

Some other issues should be mentioned in the environmental aspects of either retrofitting existing technologies, or whole-site projects. A first issue is that it may be valuable, in many cases, to wait for some time in order to have some technical and/or regulatory problems solved. In other terms, and as noted by several authors (Boyd, 1998) there may be some *option value* in differentiating a project until these questions are answered: the costs of deferring such a project are tantamount to buying a call option. In a similar manner, let us take into account the fact that the incremental cost and effectiveness of P2 investments are much higher in retrofitting some existing facilities than in a new whole-plant project. If so, it may be worthwhile to defer a P2-retrofitting project on an old plant, which is to be renewed anyway, until an altogether new plant is rebuilt.

In principle, and notwithstanding the difficulties that we just discussed, it is an easy task to evaluate any environmental investment, and/or the incremental effects of any other investment such as a new whole-site investment. In those contexts, both the IRR and the NPV methods may be used; as discussed previously, the IRR method is more complex and may lead to several difficulties, but the IRR obtained may be directly compared to a hurdle rate that usually is the SOCC. Knowing that the IRR is making use of the discounted cash flow as well, one may start with the NPV method as an investment-appraisal method, and express the incremental NPV as:

$$NPV^E = -I^E + \sum_{t=1}^{T} \frac{CF_t^E}{(1+i)^t} \qquad (6.17)$$

In this equation, NPV^E stands for the incremental NPV due to the incremental investment I^E that is related to environmental protection; CF_t^E tands for the incremental free cash flow related to environmental protection.

If R_t^E, C_t^E and A_t^E respectively stand for the incremental revenue (or benefit) related to environmental protection, the incremental costs related to environmental protection, and the incremental tax-deductible asset depreciation and provisions related to environmental protection, then CF_t^E may be defined as follows:

$$CF_t^E = (R_t^E - C_t^E)(1 - \tau) + A_t^E \tau \qquad (6.18)$$

More generally, we may express the shareholder value SV as the sum of a term SV^E that is related according to (6.17) and (6.18) to previous and current environmental investments, and of a term SV^o which is unrelated to these environmental investments:

$$SV = SV^o + SV^E - BC \qquad (6.19)$$

Whenever the IRR method is applied, it may either be applied to the total $B(i)$, or to the increment of $B(i)$. These quantities are calculated through (6.17) and (6.18), with a varying discount rate as usual. However, this is done assuming that $B(i)$ may be considered as a sum of a term $B^o(i)$ (which is unrelated to the environmental or P2 part of the investment) and of a term $B^E(i)$ (related to the environment):

$$B(i) = B^o(i) + B^E(i) \qquad (6.20)$$

The IRR is a quantity that might be thought of as being defined for a whole investment only. However, one may show that, under some reasonable conditions, it is meaningful to calculate the IRR of the incremental part of the investment related to the environment, which is the root of the incremental equation $B^E(i) = 0$. If this root is larger, or at least equal, to the hurdle rate, it may be shown that carrying out the incremental environmental investment will increase, or at least not decrease, the overall IRR of the whole investment. Thus, calculating the IRR of the incremental investment may be carried out, and will lead to meaningful conclusions.

Therefore, both the NPV and the IRR methods may be applied on an incremental basis to any incremental investment that is related to environmental protection. Let us assume that the terms of (6.18), or the variables that constitute the NPV, or B(i) in the case of the IRR method, can be considered as the sum of additive incremental components. Then, the idea underlying the application of both the NPV and the IRR method to incremental environmentally related investments appears quite straightforward. The practical implementation of these methods is a less trivial matter, and, in general, taking into account environmental effects or increments in investment and project appraisal is a somewhat difficult task. Such a task can nonetheless be performed through attempting to estimate the forecasted environmental costs and benefits related to the project, which may be, so to speak, a by-product of adequate accounting systems, as shown in Chapter 4. It is to this point that we now turn.

3.2 The Value Drivers of Environmental Investments

Investments should, of course, contribute to increasing the firm's shareholder value, but they may do so in several ways. Firstly, investments may aim at increasing the turnover, or the sales, through either so-called capacity investments, which are directed at increasing the production and hence the sales at profitable conditions. Secondly, investments may be aimed at improving the *quality* of some products, and hence the corresponding sales or the market shares for these products in offering better quality than the firm's competitors. Thirdly, investments may contribute to cut costs, or to decrease risks. As shown by Schaltegger and Figge (1998), all this applies to environmental investments or to P2 investments, or, in more global investments such as whole-site investments, to their environmental components. We are thus led to the following question: what are the determinants of increasing shareholder value through environmental or P2 investments? Or, in short: what are the 'value drivers' of environmental investments?

A first value driver corresponds to the direct benefits provided by environmental or P2 investments. One may say that these investments may improve the environmental quality of some products (as discussed in Chapter 9). Thus, environmental investments may contribute to enhance the sales or market shares for some products through product differentiation.

One may therefore mention 'green' product differentiation as the first of the value drivers provided by environmental or P2 investments.

A second value driver related to environmental or P2 investments is that they may lead to some significant decreases in various costs. This is of course true of direct environmental costs, such as the costs of emission permits and/or the costs of emission or pollution taxes or fines (whenever applicable). It is true also of costs that are related to emissions of pollutants, or to the depletion of exhaustible resources or of environmentally related resources. Non-renewable fuels, such as coals, oil fuels or natural gas, fall into this category. Costs concerning other utilities, such as water, are also concerned as costs of environment-related resources or as costs of non-renewable resources. The same may be true of the costs concerning other raw materials, when non-renewable materials are either saved or recycled. The costs of waste treatment, including waste water treatment, or the costs of scrapping solid waste, may be reduced through either saving or recycling some raw materials or utilities. Finally, many other costs, including the costs of services such as insurance services and financial costs, may, in some cases, be reduced with suitable environmental or P2 investments. Of course, a number of costs may increase as a result of carrying out the investment, and these costs have to be taken into account. These may be direct costs, such as labour costs required for the maintenance of the new environmentally related equipment and any other extra running costs related thereto.

There may, in some cases, be cost increases rather than decreases; for example, in costs of waste treatment; and, more generally, regulatory over-compliance may be costly. There are also extra fixed costs that may occur as a result of the investment. The conclusion is that this second 'value driver' of environmental or P2 investments is the net decrease in all running and fixed costs, if any. This shows that environmental or P2 investments are likely to add to the firm's shareholder value through decreasing costs only if this net decrease is positive. This means that, again, 'end-of-pipe' technologies, which usually lead to net cost increases, are to be avoided in favour of some more 'upstream' technologies. Among these technologies, one can mention economies in energy, utilities and raw materials, or recycling of used or spent utilities (such as water) or raw materials or waste recycling leading to savings in raw materials and/or to savings in waste or scrap treatment. Other direct costs that might be cut through environmental-protection investments are capital costs as well as insurance costs, if these investments lead to significant reduction in physical risks.

A third value driver is indirect, being related to risk reduction even in the absence of direct or immediate reduction in interest or insurance payments. This means that the cost of capital, or the shareholders' opportunity cost of capital can be reduced as a result of important physical risk reduction through environmental or P2 investments. The evaluation of this reduction in the cost of capital is not, however, a very easy task. Estimations conducted from information disclosed by banks interested in the environmental aspects of financial risk in their corporate loan activities, lead to an estimated decrease of anything between a few basis points (0.01 per cent) to something like 0.25 per cent in interest rates. For instance, Kvaerner, a Norwegian environmentally conscious company, was able to secure preferential conditions (a few basis points cheaper than the normally applicable interest rate) for a revolving loan facility of several hundred millions of US dollars 'because of its environmental performance' (Blumberg, Blum and Korsvold, 1998). This estimate of 0.25 per cent is an order of magnitude for the decrease of risk premium effect due to reduction in environmental risks in a loan, but its outright calculation is somewhat difficult. There are, however, some techniques, which rest on a probabilistic approach, as described by Jacques, Lesourd and Ruiz (1988). The technique involves first defining, for each period of time, a distribution of possible returns under the form of free cash flows, and a distribution concerning environmental accidents or incidents. This being done, the method consists in simulating the results by a so-called Monte-Carlo technique, in which quasi-random numbers are generated, conforming to a distribution defined beforehand. This method, as applied to the selection of projects, requires selecting beforehand some distributions for the incomes and the costs, so that the values of CF_t are subject to a random distribution.

Its implementation is simple, at least in principle: a number of tests in which quasi-random numbers are generated for the variables composing CF_t through suitable random-number-generating programmes are carried out, so that one is left with values of the NPV for each test. One is thus able to estimate numerically the distribution of the NPVs, so that a suitable assessment of the risk is possible through an analysis of the worst possible results. A number of trials, at least 100, should be carried out.

The latter approach merely rests on introducing probabilities, including probabilities of environmental disasters, in the terms of equations (6.16) to (6.18); it may be combined with both the NPV and the IRR methods, but this does not lead to any direct estimation of the risk premium due to environmental hazards for a firm. Although the application of the IRR method will lead to some estimate of the reduction of the cost of capital due to some environmental or P2 investment, a more direct but quite crude approach to such an estimate may be described. This approach is interesting in highlighting the fact that environmental and P2 investments may be *risky*. In particular, the effect of some environmental investment, resulting in increased sales and hence increased profits and increased shareholder value, may be ruined by any serious environmental accident or incident. Of course, one must beware of superficial environmental claims that just hide a poor or average environmental performance through publicity: this may prove a very risky exercise if public opinion discovers the actual performance of the firm, for instance, after some environmental disaster. Even if the environmental performance of the firm is genuine, and leads, for instance, to significant reductions in pollutant emissions and to recycling of some materials, there may be some residual risk in environmental investments. This is the case if a significant probability of an environmental disaster, or even of less important environmental accidents or incidents, remains.

Thus, the probability of environmental accidents must be reduced as part of any corporate environmental management. It is only through a significant reduction in the probability of environmental hazards, together with an in-depth environmental management, that the robustness of shareholder value creation through environmental investments may be achieved. Otherwise, incomplete environmental policies may lead to devastating upturns in public opinion, and hence in sales, if, for instance, some environmental catastrophe does occur in spite of the company's efforts. Environmental management is more than a mere reduction in emissions, and more than managing the company's exposure to environmental risks. It is a *whole-system concern*, and any gross deficiencies might be devastating to the firm's image and even to its financial performance, so that environmental investments that fail to conform to this whole-system philosophy may be somewhat risky. Although this indirect effect of the environmental risk might be difficult to estimate, one may at least obtain a rough idea of the risk premium associated to it. For this purpose, let us assume that the firm is either insured against environmental disasters or is self-insured through a captive insurance company (see, for example, Chapter 7) or through the constitution of some retention fund. Whatever the precise way in which the firm manages its environmental risks, all these steps correspond to significant additional costs of capital that should be taken into account through additional risk premiums. Even a rough estimate of these risk premiums is not an easy task, but it may be useful to try to give at least some guidelines as to the actual costs of risk that may be incurred. There are at least two kinds of such risks. The first is the risk of *physical damages* to the environment, but there is a second kind of risk, that might well be overlooked, and hence may be considered as a hidden risk. This might be called the *reputation risk*; in other words the risk that, following some environmental incident or accident, the environmental increment to the value of the firm NPV^E might be partly destroyed as a result of a blow to the reputation of the firm to its clients. Obviously, such a situation can severely hit its sales and its market share. The first kind of risk can, in some cases, be insured against. This means that having an idea of the insurance premium or, more generally, of the expected losses due to physical damages to the environment will give a rough idea of the risk premium that should be applied. As far as the second kind of risk is concerned, it may also be estimated, at least in principle, if one can estimate the expected decrease in sales due to the fact that the reputation of a firm would be hit in the event of an environmental disaster.

These are indirect effects of the environmental risk, but they are not the only effects. There is a direct effect on the firm's cash flows, since the firm will usually (as discussed in Chapter 7) take some steps to manage its environmental risk. This means that our company will either purchase insurance through an external insurer or through a captive insurance company (as discussed in Chapter 7, a captive insurance company is an insurance company that is controlled by a firm for the purpose of insuring the risks of its parent company). The firm can also maintain a fund that should be able to meet the cost of an environmental disaster. Clearly, the insurance premium, if any, should be integrated into the cost of capital because it is paid as a counterpart of the direct risk on capital that is transferred to the insurer at a price, which is the insurance premium. Let IP be this insurance premium. If the insurer may benefit from the law of great numbers, IP may usually be expressed as the sum of expected loss, of a risk premium that expresses the insurer's risk aversion, and of the insurer's management costs. Whenever this premium is tax-deductible, if τ is the constant corporate tax rate, the actual cash flow corresponding to IP will be $-$ IP $(1 - \tau)$. For risks that cannot be insured, as discussed in Chapter 7, the firm may be obliged to maintain either a captive insurance company or a retention fund.

This means that the firm will need some additional assets in addition to its industrial assets, usually in the form of liquid assets that earn an interest close to the riskless rate of interest. However, these assets are faced with a significant risk of being used up in the event of an environmental emergency. Hence, the firm will either have to pay an insurance premium CIP to its captive or take an annual provision RF to its retention fund. This could be acknowledged by an appropriate accounting provision, but the assets constituting the retention fund should actually exist and be clearly identified. Neither CIP nor RF is usually tax deductible. Under tax deductibility of the insurance premium IP, the cost of environmental risk will be the sum of the insurance premium IP of the captive insurance premium and of the provision to the retention fund, if any. Therefore, the total cash flows corresponding to the cost of risk will be:

$$CR = -\ IP\ (1 - \tau) - (CIP + RF) \qquad (6.21)$$

We assume that this sum is some fraction q of the shareholders' value SV of the firm, which may be expressed as:

$$q = \frac{IP(1 - \tau) + CIP + RF}{SV} \qquad (6.22)$$

Therefore, if T → ∞ (a good approximation if the investor's time horizon is long enough), we obtain, taking into account previous equations:

$$SV (1 + \frac{q}{i}) = \frac{CF}{i} \qquad (6.23)$$

Thus, the true cost of capital, which takes into account the impact of the risk on the firm's value, is:

$$\frac{CF}{SV} = i + q \qquad (6.24)$$

Finally, discounting the cash flows related to environmental investments with the risk of losses due to environmental damages would increase the cost of capital above i; the apparent environmental risk premium will be q.

The effect of a significant risk of losses due to environmental incidents, or even disasters, is therefore clearly interpreted as being twofold. The first effect is a direct effect through the costs of physical environmental damages. A second effect is an apparent increase in the cost of capital due to the fact that the firm's reputation could be damaged, ruining previous environmental efforts and investments and leading to some negative effect on cash flows, finally destroying part of the firm's shareholder value (SV).

Conversely, if one carries out an additional investment that reduces the probability of occurrence of a major environmental accident to a negligibly small value of, say, 10^{-4} per year, the effect of such an investment will be twofold. It will (1) reduce capital costs through reducing the physical risks due to damages to the environment, and hence the insurance costs; and (2) reduce the cost of capital, through decreasing the effect on the firm's reputation if an environmental incident accident or disaster occurs.

Finally, in the appraisal of environmental investments, one should take into account the fiscal effects of capital depreciation, or of depletion in the case of an exhaustible resource, in cash flow and discounted cash flow analyses. Accounting for capital depreciation or resource depletion is not, strictly speaking, a fourth value driver on top of the three possible value drivers that we already discussed. It merely represents the more or less favourable fiscal effect, in terms of cash flow, of the fiscal deductions or write-offs corresponding to part of the capital costs. Furthermore, accounting depreciation rules vary a lot across various countries, and in time, according to the variations of fiscal legislation. They should, of course, nevertheless be taken into account. In the context of environmentally oriented investments, or of the environmental aspects of more global investments, there are several possibilities of fiscal deductions corresponding to capital depreciation, in a broad sense, that are more or less common to most jurisdictions. They may therefore be discussed in terms of simple effects and economic principles that are broadly valid. In the United States, for instance, the Internal Revenue Service (IRS) defines depreciation rules.

In this respect, it should be noted that most categories of equipment are subject to accounting and fiscal depreciation, including, of course, environmental protection and P2 equipment. It is well known that there are several methods for accounting depreciation. The most simple method is the straight-line method, in which the annual depreciation of the asset is a constant. This means that the asset is completely depreciated after a certain number of years N that is usually imposed by current fiscal rules. This time constitutes, so to speak, the accounting lifetime of the asset. In this case, the annual depreciation is a constant A, expressed as a constant fraction of the initial accounting value V_0 of the asset:

$$A_t = A = \frac{V_0}{N} \qquad (6.25)$$

The accounting lifetime of the asset N is usually defined by current fiscal legislation. Clearly, under this scheme, the current accounting value of the asset, defined as:

$$V_t = V_0 - \text{previous cumulated depreciation} \qquad (6.26)$$

is a *straight line*, such that the initial accounting value be equal to V_0, and that the final value after N years be zero, so that the method is called 'straight-line depreciation'. It is widely used internationally, with different values for N for various types of equipment, as well as for various jurisdictions. A more sophisticated method, also widely used internationally, is the so-called *declining-balance (or reducing-balance) method*. In this method, the depreciation is a constant fraction, usually a multiple of the straight-line depreciation, of the current accounting value of the asset, so that (the multiple in question being defined as $1 + \rho$ with $\rho > 0$), the depreciation may be expressed as:

$$A_t = \frac{1+\rho}{N} V_t \qquad (6.27)$$

Under a number of fiscal jurisdictions, a choice is left between the two methods, and the choice of the declining-balance method is popular as it allows for more depreciation of the asset initially. A value such as $\rho = 1$ is common, so that, for an equipment with an accounting lifetime of five years, the depreciation is 200 per cent of the straight line depreciation, with a fiscal advantage thus doubled. Here, the variation of V_t is exponential rather than linear, so that V_t should reach zero only after an infinite time. However, many fiscal jurisdictions allow, or impose, the choice of the straight line depreciation whenever, after some time, the straight-line method gives a larger value than the declining-balance method. Following this rule, V_t under the declining-balance method reaches zero after N years.

There are a number of other methods of depreciation, such as the 'sum-of-the-years' digits' method, which is a variant of the declining-balance method used in the United States. The discussion of these methods is outside of the scope of our book.

As far as environmentally oriented investments are concerned, a more important point is that in some countries and jurisdictions there may be some preferential or accelerated declining-balance depreciation for environmental protection equipment, allowing for a larger fiscal benefit than is normally permissible. For instance, in Germany, where declining-balance depreciation is commonly carried out with N = 5 years and $\rho = 1$, thus allowing for a 40 per cent depreciation during the three first years, environmental laws provide instead for an initial allowable depreciation of 60 per cent for some environmental equipment.

Other allowable provisions and write-offs that are directly related to the environment or to the depletion of exhaustible resources also exist in a number of situations and in a number of countries. The first example concerns quarries and mines, for which many jurisdictions provide for the obligation of restoring the site in its initial environmental condition after the mine has been exhausted and is thus closed down. For this purpose, corporate tax-deductible provisions may be written off every fiscal year, corresponding to the constitution of a suitable fund aimed at covering the restoration expenses after closing down the site. Other provisions that may be constituted, and are fiscally deductible, correspond to the depletion of exhaustible resources such as oil wells, mineral or ore deposits, or mines. All these should be taken into account in assessing the environmental aspects, in a broad sense, of any investment, whether a whole-site investment or a more specific, environmentally oriented, investment.

Having discussed at some length the value drivers encountered in the environmental aspects of investment appraisal, we are now going to discuss some practical implications.

3.3 Practical Assessment of Environmental Aspects of Investments

The practical assessment of the environmental aspects of investments requires a number of steps and conditions (Moilanen and Martin, 1996). These mean, identifying the components of cash flows that may be value drivers, as discussed in the previous section. This means, in turn, identifying other variables that may influence the cash flows, such as the fiscal effects of capital depreciation and of various other authorized provisions and fiscal deductions. An important value driver is the cost of capital. Further, investing in order to lower the environmental risks faced by the firm might be an effective value driver, since it will cut the risk premium components of the cost of capital. This effect of environmental investments is, however, somewhat difficult to assess, but some estimate of the cost of capital has to be used, especially in NPV or SV calculations. Such an estimate may be derived through calculations of rates of returns for firms of the same sector and facing similar risks. Table 6.2 gives the detail of the main large categories of benefits and costs related to either an environmentally related investment or the environmental aspects of some more global investment.

We have so far discussed how to integrate environmental concerns into investment appraisal at the level of a project, which may be a partial project (especially a P2 project) concerning a site or whole-site or whole-production -unit project. We now move on, in the next paragraph, to discuss the same issue at the level of a whole firm, especially when its stocks are quoted on a stock exchange, or at the level of financial or capital markets.

Table 6.2 Practical guideline for environmental or P2 investment calculations (environmental increments for more global projects)

Items to be taken into consideration (related to the project)
Increase in gross benefits (+)
Gross extra sales due to 'greening' or ecolabelling of product(s)
Gross extra sales generated by price gains related to the project
Other gross extra sales (of recycled materials, of engineering and consulting services and so on)
Other gross extra revenue (grants, subsidies, patents and licences and so on)
Decrease in gross costs (+)
Gross savings in energy
Gross savings in other utilities (water and so on)
Gross savings in other raw materials
Gross savings in waste treatment (due to recycling, improvements in the process and so on)
Gross savings on insurance premiums
Gross savings on other costs
Decrease in gross sales (-)
Gross decrease in sales due to higher pricing of the product(s)
Other decreases in gross revenues

Gross extra running costs (-)
Gross decrease in sales due to higher pricing of the product(s)
Gross extra costs of regulatory extra compliance
Other extra running costs
Engineering and study costs
Other extra fixed costs
If τ = corporate tax rate:
Apply factor $1 - \tau$ to:
Sum of all previous positive items,
minus: sum of all previous negative items,
unless non-deductible (beware of non-deductible items; beware of double counting!!)
Tax effects of depreciation and of other deductible provisions
Depreciation of equipment (including extra allowances for environmental protection equipment, if applicable)
Other deductible provisions
Apply factor τ to the sum of depreciation and provisions
Calculation of the cost of capital
Estimate riskless interest rate (rate on treasury bonds for the investor's time horizon)
Add: risk premium as calculated through:
(1)   Rate of return calculation for similar quoted firms;
(2)   Rate of interest on quoted (e.g. 'junk') bonds, or on banking loans f similar firms or projects;
(3)   Statistical estimate of risk from past data for similar firms or projects;
(4)   Estimate of probability of failure for similar firms or projects.
Add: Environmental risk premium

4. THE ENVIRONMENT, STOCK MARKETS, AND FINANCIAL ACTIVITIES

4.1 The Environment and Financial Intermediaries

We are now concerned with several questions concerning the implications of environmental concerns on corporate and market finance. We are thus focusing here on capital- and stock-market activities and on investments in existing firms, rather than in comparatively smaller-scale investments on a site. These topics mainly concern financial intermediaries, such as banks and investment funds. Some of the problems concerning other financial intermediaries, such as insurance companies, will be discussed in Chapter 7, which is concerned with the direct management and/or insurance of environmental risks. However, the investment and portfolio management of insurance companies is still in the scope of this section. Our discussion will be organized as follows: it will first discuss the implications and the assessment of environmental risks in the loan activities of banks, including corporate loans, and their real-estate aspects in which the problem of contaminated land may occur. A related problem is the rating of environmental risks from the point of view of an investor; this problem is closely related to stock picking for the management of environmentally oriented investment funds. A third topic is the emergence of environmental risk-related financial instruments.

4.2 The Environment and Banking Activities

We are here concerned with corporate banking, rather than with personal banking. Clearly, corporate banking is one of the segments of banking services in which banks might have to appreciate the environmental management of client firms. In this field of activities, one of the main services rendered by banks is financing firms through loans.

Corporate loans may be direct loans, but loans for larger corporations may be arranged through bond issues, for which banks, or groups of banks called syndicates for large (or syndicated) loans, act as underwriters, by issuing bonds to the general public. Investment banking, or corporate financing through issuing shares is also one of the businesses of banks, which, here again, may either buy shares for themselves or underwrite some share issues before selling the shares in the general public. The ultimate objective of bond or stock issues might be either financing the growth of a company, or financing a takeover; that is, buying another company. In both these cases, the environmental performance should be of interest to the investor. Thus, the environmental performance of either the company being financed, or, in the case of a takeover, the environmental performance of the target company, might have to be appreciated as part of banking practice.

In the lending business, banks have to address two problems. The first of these problems is the environmental aspects of the risk of failure. This risk is defined as the risk that the company to which a loan is granted is unable to repay its debt, as far as the interest is concerned, or even in terms of both interest and principal. There are general possibilities of assessing the creditworthiness of companies, which have been briefly discussed previously; a more detailed discussion is outside the scope of this work. A second problem, which is especially of concern in the case of loans guaranteed by real-estate assets, is whether these assets have not been overvalued, and whether they will not give rise to hidden liabilities. This last point of hidden liabilities has special environmental implications, because in the case of polluted land, the bank granting a loan might be responsible, in some jurisdictions such as US jurisdictions, for cleaning up the land if the borrower defaults.

We first discuss the environmental aspects of the assessment of risks in the loan business from the point of view of banks.

As mentioned above, there are methods that enable one to calculate risk premiums, at least approximately, and hence pertinent rates of interest that could eventually be applied to loan granting. We have seen in particular that a rough approximation of the environmental risk premium would be the probability of an environmental disaster, with a suitable coefficient reflecting the part of the value of the firm that is at risk. This, however, is a rather crude technique, which it is not always possible to implement. A more effective technique might be checking for a number of features of the investment, leading to a multicriteria assessment of the risk, that may be applied to its rating (Jacques, Lesourd and Ruiz, 1988; Crédit Suisse, 1998).

Table 6.3 thus gives a 'checklist' of problems that might serve as a guideline for an assessment of the environmental risks of some investment.

Table 6.3   Assessing the environmental risk of a loan: a checklist of questions

---

In technical and accounting terms ...

• Have environmental health and safety problems been the object of audits? How do the firm's facilities comply with existing environmental regulations? If the firm has multinational facilities, do they differ in terms of environmental standards according to differing national environmental norms?

• What is the cost share of energy, utilities, raw materials, and of environmentally related expenses?

• What are the greenhouse gas emissions of the firm's facilities (carbon dioxide, CFCs, halons and so on) as global figures and per unit of output? Are the figures improving?

• Does the firm participate in an emission permit scheme, whether public or private?

• How are emissions into the atmosphere and into water dealt with?

• How are solid wastes dealt with?

• Are there any hidden or contingent liabilities of the firm in terms of polluted land, or in terms of ongoing or possible legal disputes related to the environment?

In terms of management ...

• What is the general financial background of the firm, as described by the usual financial analysts' ratios and/or creditworthiness ratings?

• Has the firm implemented an operational environmental management system (whether certified or not)?

• If so, has the firm's EMS been certified (under the ISO 14001 norms and/or, for its production sites, and if applicable, under the EMAS norms)?

- If so, is the firm insured against environmental risks? Or does it maintain an environmental retention fund? Or has it a captive insurance company taking care of environmental risks?
- Did the firm take adequate steps, including, in particular, adequate investments, towards significantly reduced physical environmental hazards?

In terms of products ...

- Is the industrial or activity sector of the firm a risky sector in terms of environmental hazards? Are the technologies implemented by the firm subject to environmental problems?
- What is the firm's record in terms of environmental incidents, accidents, or even environmental disasters?
- What is the environmental quality of the firm's products, in terms of reputation?
- Does the firm include the environmental impacts of its products in its relationships with its clients?
Do suitable LCA analyses confirm this reputation?
- Does the firm include the environmental impacts of their products in its relationships with suppliers and subcontractors?
- Have the environmental qualities of the firm's products been certified, in terms of ecolabels, or in terms of other environmentally related attributes, such as biological products?

4.3 The Environment, Investments and Stock Markets

Investment funds are also financial intermediaries for which the environment is becoming a significant issue.

This concerns, in particular, regulated investment funds throughout the world. These regulated funds are investment vehicles that are either companies, or trusts, the only activity of which is to manage a portfolio of either listed securities (bonds and shares), or money-market positions, so that these investments are available to comparatively small investors. They are submitted to prudential rules; in particular, some minimal diversification of assets is imposed on them, they may not borrow and have any uncovered liabilities, and they may not invest in uncovered futures and option instruments. In the USA and Canada, these regulated funds are known as mutual funds. In other English-speaking countries (UK, Republic of Ireland, Australia and New Zealand), they are known as unit trusts. In the European Union member countries, they are known as UCITS (Undertakings for Collective Investments in Transferable Securities), submitted to a European directive of 1985 providing for the aforementioned prudential rules. These include most unit trusts available in the UK and Ireland. Switzerland, although not an EU member country, has similar regulations for its funds. There also exist pension funds (including, in the UK and Australia, superannuating funds). The investments of pension funds are financed by compulsory contributions from employers, self-employed people and employees, by personal contributions from employees and self-employed people in some cases, as well as by supplementary employers' contributions as part of employees' fringe benefits. These funds cover the pensions of employees and of self-employed persons.

There are many orientations of investments within investment funds. There are money-market funds, which manage short-term liquid assets through almost riskless money-market instruments. There are also funds investing mostly in bonds, or in stocks, and funds that specialize in some industry, or in some country or geographical area. Some whole funds also have a particular orientation. Among these, there are, as mentioned in Chapter 3, so-called ethical funds. Ethical funds are funds in which the allocation of assets obeys certain ethical rules. These include funds managed according to various ethical codes, including the ethics of particular religious groups, or ethics defined by labour unions (usually in the case of pension funds), individual employers, self-employed persons, or employees. There are also ethical funds directed at a broad public of ethical investors. Historically, ethical funds started in the early years of the twentieth century, especially as denominational funds. Thus, in the 1920s, the Methodist Church in North America, while it decided to invest in quoted shares, avoided companies involved in the production and the sale of alcoholic drinks and in gambling. In a similar manner, the Quakers' investment ethics avoided companies oriented towards weapon and ammunition manufacturing. More recently, most ethical funds decided to include environmental criteria within their ethical criteria, and there are environmental funds that constitute a particular case of ethical funds. They are usually equity funds oriented towards companies that positively contribute to the environment. Conversely, environmental funds tend to exclude the shares of companies that cause damage to the environment, or to invest less in the stocks of such companies than in the stocks of environmentally 'smart' companies. In both the United States and the UK, ethical funds appeared in the 1970s, but environmentally oriented funds developed later, perhaps in the late 1980s. In the United States, the first socially responsible mutual fund, the Pax World Fund, was founded in 1971. Environmentally oriented funds, such as the Dreyfus Premier Third Century Fund were introduced later, in the late 1980s. In addition, one of the leading American ethical funds is the Domini Social Equity Fund, which is replicating the Domini 400 social index. This index and fund, together with their performance, will be discussed shortly.

In the UK, the first ethical unit trust, the Friends Provident Stewardship, which was also an environmental fund, was launched in 1984. In the UK, the first 'green' unit trust was launched in 1988 by Jupiter-Tyndall, a prominent fund-management company. At present (2000), the amount of assets managed by ethical and environmental investment funds is comparatively small. By the end of 1999, it was estimated to be about £2.2 billion (US$3.3 billion) in the UK, US$3 billion in the United States, and A$100 million (US$70 million) in Australia. However, it is expected to grow at a very fast pace, perhaps doubling every two years, with a forecast of £10 billion in assets by 2003 in the UK. Other countries in which 'green' funds are growing steadily are European countries such as Switzerland, Germany and Scandinavian countries, among others. The actual practice of ethical funds is therefore to select stocks of companies according to various ethical criteria that reflect various concerns or groups of stakeholders, which might be: community concerns at large, environmental concerns, relationships with various stakeholders such as employees, clients, suppliers, subcontractors, and shareholders.

How do ethical and environmental investments and, in particular, environmental funds perform? This is indeed an important question that has already been studied in a number of previous works (Butz and Plattner, 2000; Cochran and Wood, 1984; Cohen, Fenn and Naimon, 1995; Cormier, Magnan and Morard, 1993; Davidson and Worrell, 1990; Schaltegger and Figge, 1998; Schaltegger and Müller, 1997). We have shown that, under some conditions, environmentally related investments may be value drivers, but this is only a possibility and there is no theoretical rule whereby environmentally oriented investments necessarily outperform other diversified investments. However, it is possible to verify whether, in practice, existing 'green' funds outperform other diversified portfolios. In this respect, a reference or *benchmark* that is very often used would be a suitable stock index. Suitable indexes can be the Dow-Jones or the Standard and Poor's 500 (S&P 500) indexes in the United States, the FTSE 500 index in the UK, the CAC 40 index in France, or the DAX 100 in Germany.

In the United States, several ethical indexes have been proposed. One of these indexes, as mentioned earlier, is the Domini 400 Social index, introduced in 1990 by Kinder, Lyndenberg and Domini & Co. (KLD), and especially by Amy L. Domini, chairperson of KLD's board, as well as chairperson of the Domini Social Equity Fund. This fund is an index-tracking mutual fund replicating the Domini 400 index. KLD is an organization that is involved in the assessment of socially responsible investments, including, in particular, environmentally oriented investments. Supplying the values of the Domini 400 index, and, more generally, performing ethical ratings of companies and portfolios are among the most important activities of KLD. The Domini 400 index was composed out of an ethical screening of the 500 companies composing the S&P 500 index, giving 250 companies. The stocks of 150 other large quoted companies considered as ethical were added, so that the index is composed of 400 companies. It is market-capitalization-weighted; a fairly common practice in the calculation of stock indexes. The screening of stocks in the Domini 400 index is submitted to several groups of criteria. Pertinent groups of criteria are the relationships with the community (generous giving, support for education and for housing and so forth), and relationships with minorities (absence of discrimination against minorities and women in hiring and promoting employees, and other related issues). Other groups of criteria include the relationships with employees (compensation practices, relationships with labour unions, work safety issues, workforce reductions), practices in non-US operations (at its beginning, the Domini 400 index excluded company operations with South Africa), and miscellaneous concerns such as tax disputes, ownership concerns. Other important criteria are related to the environmental management of the company. Finally, exclusion criteria concern companies that are substantially involved in non-ethical or controversial products, such as alcohol, tobacco, gambling, military equipment, and nuclear power.

The Domini 400 index (which may be considered as representative of the performance of large 'ethical' companies in the United States) has existed since 1990, so it is possible now to assess its performance. The result is that the Domini 400 index frankly outperforms the S&P 500 index. Since its beginning in May 1990 until the middle of 1999; that is, after about ten years, a significant period of time; the final value of an investment of US$1 in a portfolio representing the Domini 400 index was approximately US$6. This can be compared to a final value of US$5 for each US$1 invested in a portfolio representing the S&P 500 index. This means an annual compound return of 17.4 per cent for the S&P 500 portfolio, to be compared with a return of 19.6 per cent for the Domini 400 portfolio. Consequently, it appears that the Domini 400 index outperforms the S&P 500 index by about 2 per cent per year.

Of course, the performance of the Domini Social Equity Fund, already mentioned as an index-tracking equity fund that replicates the Domini 400 index, matches the performance of the Domini 400 index. This performance represents a growth of 18.25 per cent since its launch (1991), to be compared with a performance of 18.21 per cent for the S&P 500. It slightly differs from the above performance of the Domini 400 index because the period on which it is calculated is not the same and also because of management costs. The gross performance, allowing for management costs of about 0.25 per cent, as reported by MorningStar (1998) should therefore be of about 18.50 per cent, again outperforming the S&P 500 index by 0.3 per cent per year. This performance is quite good; the fund received a four-star risk-adjusted rating (the best rating being a five-star rating) by

MorningStar, a leader in the evaluation of American mutual fund performance. Another ethical and environmental fund (the largest American ethical fund) is Dreyfus Premier Third Century, which over the last ten years had a performance of 17.09 per cent, to be compared with a performance of the Standard and Poor's 500 index over the same period of time of 17.25 per cent. This is also a quite good performance, and the Dreyfus Premier Third Century Fund is also given a four-star rating by MorningStar.

The Dow Jones Sustainability Group Index (DJSGI) is a family of stock indexes for socially responsible companies worldwide. Its interest is that, whereas the Domini 400 index concerns only US companies, there are several versions of the DJSGI with one global index, three regional indexes for Europe, North America and the Pacific, and one country index for the USA. There are five sub-versions of each index (one with no exclusion, one excluding tobacco producers, one excluding producers of alcoholic drinks, one excluding companies involved in gambling, and one excluding suppliers of tobacco, alcoholic drinks and gambling services altogether). Companies involved for more than 50 per cent of turnover in arms and armaments are excluded from all DJSGI indexes, and companies involved for more than 5 per cent and less than 50 per cent in arms and armaments have their weights reduced. This means that there are 125 indexes of the DJSGI family altogether. The companies, which constitute the index, are screened by calculating a sustainability performance score as a function of a number of environmental and social criteria. Among the criteria taken into consideration are illegal commercial practices, human-rights violations, conflicts with the labour force, environmental care, corporate governance, development of intellectual capital, quality management, but no financial criteria. In each industry, companies having a score of less than one third of the best score are excluded from the DJSGI indexes. If a company previously included in one of the indexes reaches such a low score, it is excluded from the index. Other reasons for exclusion are takeovers and mergers. The DJSGI indexes are all market-capitalization-weighted, except for the fact that the weight of companies involved in arms and armaments for between 5 per cent and 50 per cent of their sales is reduced.

Regarding the performance of the DJSGI indexes, the situation is similar to that which has been discussed for the Domini 400 index. The comparison of the global DJSGI index with the DJGI indicates a significant but small over-performance between the beginning of 1994 and July 2000.

In the UK, the oldest ethical fund is Friends Provident Stewardship, an environmentally oriented fund that had a performance of 10.2 per cent over ten years, to be compared with a performance of the FTSE 100 index of 11.9 per cent, also a quite good performance. This quite significant performance of leading ethical and environmental funds and of the Domini 400 index requires some discussion.

A first remark is that the Domini 400 index and Domini Social Equity Fund reflect a number of different social responsibility or 'ethical' criteria, environmental management criteria being merely one group of criteria. This means that the actual contribution of environmentally responsible practices of companies composing the Domini 400 index may not be assessed as such. However, inasmuch as other ethical funds that are more directly oriented toward the stocks of environmentally responsible firms also perform well, it may be assumed that environmental management criteria also positively influence the overall performance of related portfolios.

A second remark is that the beta of the Domini Social Equity Fund and of the Domini 400 index, as calculated by MorningStar with respect to the S&P 500 index, is 1.05. The same is true of the global DJSGI index, which has a beta of 1.06. This means that both the Domini 400 index and the global DJSGI index are composed of stocks that are a little more risky than the average company composing the benchmark index with respect to which the beta factors are estimated. Their performance should therefore be slightly higher than the performance of these benchmark indexes.

Among the shares included in the Domini 400 index and in the Domini Social Equity Fund are the shares of many 'high technology' firms, especially in the computer, software and telecommunication sectors. Among these are companies such as Intel, IBM, Hewlett-Packard, Bell Atlantic, and many others, known to be more risky than average market stocks. Furthermore, these are large corporations with production technologies that are less likely to endanger the environment than the technologies of other profitable companies, such as companies involved in the oil industries and other heavy industries. The same is true of the companies that are components of the global DJSGI index. These also include a number of high technology companies such as Compaq, Dell Computers, Intel, Pfizer in the United States; British Telecom, Glaxo Wellcome, and Johnson Matthey in the UK; Deutsche Telekom and Siemens in Germany; ST Microelectronics in France; Novartis in Switzerland; Canon and Toshiba in Japan, and many others. Global banks and financial-services companies that are noted for their significant environmental management concerns, such as Deutsche Bank, Crédit Suisse and Swiss Re, are also components of the global DJSGI index.

Knowing this, one may ask oneself if there are any causality links between the ethical practices of these companies and their increased performance. The causality link may indeed be that the high performance of these companies may stem at least partly from their ethical practices. One can, for instance, expect, all other things being equal, that treating the labour force well will result in higher labour productivity, higher motivation and a smaller turnover, reflecting positively on the company's performance. We have seen that sound environmental management practices may serve as a value driver, which is, of course, beneficial to the company's performance. However, it may also be that these companies may afford ethical practices *because* their financial performance is high. Concerning environmental management practices, we have seen that many companies composing the Domini 400 index are 'high-technology' companies with both a higher profitability and a smaller environmental impact from their activities. The causality links may very well run two ways, thus creating some kind of a virtuous circle: these companies may afford to be ethical, this reflects on their reputation, hence on their market shares and on their financial performance. The virtuous circle may, however, be closed in that this increased profitability enables them to carry out socially and environmentally responsible investments, leading to increased profits again.

Finally, it may also be argued that the 1990–2000 period has been a strongly bullish period. Whether similar findings regarding the performance of socially responsible enterprises would be observed during a bearish or depression period remains to be proved.

5. CONCLUSION

In this chapter, we have dealt with the financial dimension of environmental management, discussing the specific properties of environmentally responsible investments. We have seen that environmental investments may be value drivers for firms, provided they are suitably oriented. Environmental and P2 investments may indeed create value through the promotion of sales of 'green' products, through savings on a number of environmentally related costs, and through reduction of the costs of capital due to reduction of environmental risks. However, value creation through environmentally oriented investments is a possibility, not a panacea, because there are additional costs that must be taken into consideration. Anyway, it is useful to reach an assessment of the environmental component of the risk in any investment, including investments that are specifically oriented towards environmental purposes. Direct investments, loans in the practice of banking, and investments in the stocks of various companies in the practice of asset management for investment funds, may be concerned by the assessment of environmental risks as well as by the assessment of environmental performances. There are, in particular, 'green' funds, which are a particular case of ethical funds, a more general class of funds. There is some evidence (such as, for instance, the performance of the Domini 400 American stock index) that the financial performance of these funds might be higher than the performance of all-share indexes such as the S&P 500. However, this evidence is only partial and has to be confirmed. We may conclude that the environment is an issue in financial management, and may be introduced into the services rendered by financial intermediaries such as banks and investment funds. Insurance companies constitute another kind of financial actor, to which the financial consequences of risks are transferred, at a price; namely, the insurance premium. We have not discussed so far the management of physical environmental risks as such, which may be formulated as an insurance problem. However, traditional insurance is just a tool, among others, for the direct management of environmental risks, which will be discussed in the next chapter.

CASE STUDIES

6.1 Triodos Bank: Environmentally-oriented and Socially Responsible Banking Services

Introduction

Triodos Bank, a European leader in ethical financial services, was founded in 1980 in the Netherlands. It is now also operating in Belgium and the UK. It is a comparatively small bank in terms both of liability capital (which was € 38.8 million at the end of 1999) and balance-sheet total (which was € 462 million at the end of 1999) (Table 6.4).

Table 6.4: Triodos Bank key figures (1997–99)

Years	1999	1998	1997
Liability capital	38.804	32.444	30.633
Balance sheet total	461.647	350.510	284.754
Loans	233.814	152.838	128.604
Total income	11.703	9.948	8.249
Operating expenses	8.500	7.108	5.670
Operating result before taxation	2.474	1.892	1.716
Corporate tax	0.920	0.952	0.623
Net Profit	1.554	1.240	1.093

Source: Triodos Bank (2000). Amounts are in € million.

However, it has grown at a very fast pace over recent years. As shown by Table 6.4, the liability capital has grown by 19.6 per cent. The balance sheet total has grown by 32 per cent in 1999 and by 23 per cent in 1998. After a recent successful share issue, the liability capital went up to € 58.356 million in July 2000. Savings and investments in the UK grew by 68 per cent in 1999; the UK loan portfolio went up by 89 per cent in 1999. Since 1985, it has always served a dividend to its shareholders and significant capital growth was recorded.

Triodos Bank is specialized in profitable lending and banking activities directed toward enterprises with social and environmental objectives. It is also undertaking asset management oriented toward socially responsible investments for investment funds and for other partners. In particular, it operates several ethical and 'green' investment funds in the Netherlands.

Products

Triodos Bank finances several kinds of socially responsible enterprises and organizations. In particular, its lending activities are oriented toward social economy, environmental activities, healthcare, non-profit and art activities, and toward developing countries through microcredit, together with several institutions specialized in microfinance in countries such as Bolivia, Peru, Kenya, Uganda and the Philippines.

As far as the environment is concerned, Triodos Bank is involved in developing renewable-energy investments (solar energy and wind energy). It is also involved in organic agriculture and organic food production. It thus finances the Organic Milk Suppliers Cooperative in Somerset, which supplies 85 per cent of all organic milk and dairy production in England and Wales. It also supports the Shipdrove Organic Farm, an 809-hectare farm based in Berkshire and involved in raising sheep, beef, turkeys, pigs and chicken using environmentally friendly breeding techniques. It is also involved in financing environmental innovations and environmental technology. Triodos Bank is also providing loans oriented toward improvements in the urban, rural and housing environment. For instance, it is supporting Bail Dulra Teoranta, an Irish company which has built and is managing a model eco-village near Cork, Republic of Ireland.

Triodos Bank also offers traditional account service to its clients, including individuals, corporations, charities and public organizations, including checking accounts and various savings and interest-bearing accounts. Triodos Bank's clients, who may be sure that their money is directed toward socially responsible investments, are supplied information about all the investments of the bank.

Triodos Bank is also involved in asset management directed at socially responsible and environmentally oriented equities. It thus manages several 'green' investment funds and also portfolios for third parties such as charities, donor organizations and some public bodies.

In particular, Triodos Bank is managing the Triodos Greenfund, which is a closed-ended fund listed on the Amsterdam Stock Exchange, with assets of about $60 million. According to Dutch fiscal legislation, the dividends of this fund are tax-free in the Netherlands. The Triodos Greenfund invests in organic farming, wind energy and in other environmentally oriented businesses and investments. Furthermore, it manages the Added Value Investment Fund, also a closed-ended fund quoted on the Amsterdam Stock Exchange, with assets of about $20 million. This fund is oriented toward firms and investments creating environmental and social added value. It also manages the Wind Fund, a British investment fund investing in wind-energy technology and windfarms.

Triodos Bank selects its loan activities as well as its investments in stocks of socially responsible firms through a combination of financial, environmental and social criteria.

Environmental management
Triodos Bank has obtained ISO 14001 certification in all three countries in which it is operating. It was the first bank to be ISO 14001-certified in the Netherlands, Belgium and the UK. Its head office in Zeist (the Netherlands) has been especially designed as environmentally friendly, with, in particular, 46 per cent energy savings and 50 per cent savings in water consumption with respect to current standard office buildings.

Conclusion
Triodos Bank is an example of a profitable financial institution with activities oriented toward all traditional banking products (loans to corporations, to charities and to public bodies) and asset management for public investment funds, charities and public bodies. Its loan and investment portfolios give a number of examples of profitable investments that are at the same time socially responsible investments and, especially, environmentally oriented investments.

**6.2   Barclays Bank plc: Introducing the Environment into Banking
Products and into the Social Responsibility Policy of a Large
Banking Group**

Introduction

Barclays Bank plc is one of the largest British banks, as well as a global
bank. It has subsidiaries throughout the world; in Europe (France, Spain and
Switzerland, in particular), the United Sates, Japan, and a number of
African countries. Its total assets amounted to £254.793 billion, with
shareholders' funds of £8.483 billion, a before-tax profit of £2.460 billion
and an after-tax profit of £1.811 billion (on 31 December 1999).

Barclays Bank Group is involved in most banking and financial activities:
corporate and retail lending, investment banking, asset management and
fund management, and insurance through special subsidiaries.

While the environmental management of Barclays Bank plc appears less
comprehensive than for some other banks, it appears to be more integrated
into a complete pattern of socially responsible practices, including
relationships with its clients, with its employees and with communities.
Although Barclays Bank plc is currently not fully ISO 14001 certified,
unlike other large banks such as Deutsche Bank together with some Swiss
banks such as Crédit Suisse Group and the UBS (Union Bank of
Switzerland) group, it nonetheless has introduced environmental care into
its operations. However, the group has, since 1999, decided to gradually
introduce worldwide an Environmental Management System (EMS) in line
with ISO 14001 specifications. It has issued a environmental report for year
2000, which was certified by PricewaterhouseCoopers. This means, in
particular, improved and comparatively satisfactory environmental impacts
of all of its operations. It has also introduced the environment into its
products, and in particular into its lending activities. We are especially
interested here in Barclays Bank plc's introduction of the environment into
its banking products.

The environment in Barclays Bank plc's products and socially responsible attitude

In addition to managing the environmental impacts of its facilities and its activities as such, Barclays Bank plc has integrated the environment into its banking practices and its financial services, and especially into its lending products. This concerns mainly its corporate clients. The environmental risks attached to any project under consideration for granting a credit are carefully studied by Barclays' Environmental Risk Management Unit (established in 1992), which is a small team of environmental specialists whose expertise is made available to Barclays' credit managers worldwide. This unit has written a comprehensive guide to environmental risk. Among its main concerns is the use of clean technologies and cleaning up contaminated land property; a very important aspect of environmental management, as discussed several times in this work.

The integration of the environmental risk into Barclays' lending practice mainly concerns medium and large companies. For small business customers, Barclays has elaborated, with the European Investment Bank of Luxembourg and with the European Investment Fund (which is an organ of the EU supporting, in particular, environmental projects) a preferential loan scheme aimed at environmental projects as such. This includes regeneration of contaminated property or of derelict land, environmentally oriented investments, and also investments that produce indirect environmental benefits. Loans are granted with a reduced rate of interest (by about 1 per cent), a lower fixed fee and some cashback facilities.

Supporting and sponsoring non-profit environmentally friendly achievements by non-profit and community groups is also part of Barclays' practice.

Barclays Bank plc's environmental practices also concern its very operations. In particular, since 1979, Barclays' facilities in the UK (about 2500 buildings) are carefully managed in terms of energy and water consumption, and other environmental aspects such as getting rid of toxic and dangerous substances. For instance, by 1997, the energy consumption of Barclays' facilities had first been reduced by 33 per cent with respect to what it would have been without any energy management. In 1997, a new three-year plan for energy savings was carried out, on the basis of an initial consumption estimated at £ 8493212. This plan first included no-cost 'good housekeeping' (the first level of energy management according to Jacques, Lesourd and Ruiz, 1988) leading to savings of £ 581782 per year. The plan also involved low-cost capital investment of £ 411497 (the second level of energy management according to Jacques, Lesourd and Ruiz, 1988) leading to energy savings of £ 479452 per year, a payout time of less than one year, or an apparent rate of return of about 100 per cent, certainly more than in many of the financial investments carried out by Barclays in its asset management activities. Barclays also reports significant results in the management of water and of ozone-depleting chemicals. This concerns refrigerants, which have been reduced and substituted by zero ozone-depleting potential (zero ODP) refrigerants.

We can also point out that the environmental policy of Barclays Bank plc is part of a whole corporate culture oriented toward social responsibility with respect to various stakeholders, including employees, clients and local communities. In particular, Barclays' employees enjoy extensive social and healthcare benefits (extended maternity break and parental leave, career breaks, pension benefits and equal opportunity for employees from all sorts of origins and so on). In the UK, especially, Barclays' individual and small-business clients also benefit from its code of conduct toward responsible lending.

Finally, Barclays Bank PLC publishes each year an environment review and a social review, which, in addition to its yearly financial report, disclose the detailed results of its activities from the environmental, financial and social points of view, for the information of all stakeholders.

Conclusion

Is the introduction of environmental concerns into its products and management, Barclays ranked 11th out of 26 other major European banks, according to Oekom Research AG in Germany. Its environmental management achievements compare favourably with other major European banks, such as Crédit Suisse Group, which has introduced the environment into almost all of its products, including not only lending but also asset and fund management, as well as in insurance products through its insurance subsidiary Winterthur. Banks that significantly and explicitly introduce the environment into their products, such as lending in the case of Barclays, are currently few worldwide. A number of large global banks have an explicit environmental management system, which is ISO 14001 certified. This is the case, for instance, with major continental European banks such as Deutsche Bank, UBS and Crédit Suisse. Although Barclays is currently not formally ISO 14001 certified, it has built up an EMS which is in line with most ISO 14001 requirements (2001) and could be certified soon. This shows that, as will be discussed in Chapter 7, having an ISO 14001-certified EMS is neither a sufficient, nor even a necessary, condition for sound environmental practices. There remains that Barclays Bank PLC has significantly reduced the environmental impacts of its operations and introduced the environment into its banking products. Furthermore, Barclays Bank PLC's environmental practices have been established for already some time (its energy management system dates back from 1979, its introduction of environmental risks into lending practices dates back from 1992). This environmentally responsible management of the Barclays group is also in line with more comprehensive socially responsible and ethical practices than some of its competitors.

NOTES

1. We gratefully acknowledge the reviewing of this chapter by Ephraim Clark and Greg Hertzler. Any remaining errors or omissions are of course our sole responsibility.

REFERENCES

Barclays Bank (2001), *Environmental, financial and social reports*, http://www.barclays.com.

Blumberg, J., Blum, G. and Korsvold, A. (1996), *Environmental Performance and Shareholder Value*, World Business Council for Sustainable Development.

Boyd, J. (1998), *Searching for the Profit in Pollution Prevention: Case Studies in the Corporate Evaluation of Environmental Opportunity*, Washington DC: Resources for the Future.

Brealey, Richard A. and Myers, S.C. (1988), *Principles of Corporate Finance* (3rd edn.), New York: McGraw-Hill.

Butz C. and Plattner, A. (2000), *Socially Responsible Investment. A Statistical Analysis of Returns*, Sarasin Basic Report, Basel: Bank Sarasin.

Coase, R. (1960), 'The problem of social cost', *Journal of Law and Economics*, 3: 1-44.

Cochran P.L. and Wood, R.A. (1984), 'Corporate social responsibility and financial performance, *Academy of Management Journal*, **27**: 42–56.

Cohen, M.A., Fenn, S.A. and Naimon, J.S. (1995), *Environmental and Financial Performance. Are They Related?* Nashville, TN: Owen Graduate School of Management, Vanderbilt University.

Cormier D., Magnan, M. and Morard, B. (1993), 'The impact of corporate pollution on market valuation: some empirical evidence', *Ecological Economics*, **8**: 135–55.

Crédit Suisse Group (1998), *Environmental Report 1997–98*, http://credit-suisse.ch.

Davidson, W.N. and Worrell, D.L. (1990), 'A comparison and test of the use of accounting and stock market data in relating corporate social responsibility and financial performance', *Akron Business and Economic Review*, **21**: 7-19.

Jacques, J.K., Lesourd, J.B. and Ruiz, J.M. (1988), *Modern Applied Energy Conservation: New Directions in Energy Conservation Management*, Chichester/New York: Ellis Horwood/Wiley.

Lorie, J.H. and Savage, L.J. (1955) 'Three problems in rationing capital', *Journal of Business*, **28**: 229–39.

McIntosh, M., Leipziger, D., Jones, K. and Coleman, G. (1998) *Corporate Citizenship. Successful Strategies for Responsible Companies*, London: Financial Times Pitman.

Moilanen, T. and Martin, C. (1996), *Financial Evaluation of Environmental Investments*, Houston: Gulf Publishing Company.

MorningStar (1998), *Mutual Funds 500*, Chicago: MorningStar.

Promislow, S.D. and Spring, D. (1996), 'Postulates for the internal rate of return of an investment project', *Journal of Mathematical Economics*, **26**: 325–61.

Schaltegger, S. and Figge, F. (1998), *Environmental Shareholder Value*, WWZ Study No. 54, Basel, Switzerland: University of Basel.

Schaltegger, S. and Müller, K. (1997), 'Calculating the true profitability of pollution prevention', *Greener Management International*, **17**: 53–68.

Triodos Bank (2000), *Financial and Environmental Reports*, http://www.triodosbank.com.

7. The Management of Environmental Risks[1]

SUMMARY

Whereas Chapter 6 examined environmentally-induced financial risks, Chapter 7 looks at the direct management of environmental risks. These are complex and range from very diffuse, slow-release impacts, but with potentially huge damages, to major disasters with immediate impact. These large but also uncertain liabilities lead to insurance and indeed reinsurance problems. However, insurance is not the only, or even the best, means for managing environmental risks. Not all risks are insurable, because no insurance market may exist. Conditions for insurability are therefore examined (risk pooling; large number of little correlated occurrences; no moral hazard; no adverse selection; sufficient causality and responsibility) and related to the characteristics of environmental risks (few occurrences but large damages; unknown probability laws; hidden damages). This has created incentives for designing several novel risk-management instruments, ranging from purely financial to purely insurance treatment, the former leaning on the company's own (or borrowed) capital reserves. The range of options corresponds to full, partial and nil risk retention by the company. In order to gain insight as to how each company may identify its optimal degree of risk retention, the range of instruments are analysed and, using a simple model, their relative merits compared. Particular attention is given to captive insurance companies, which provide partial and flexible risk transfer. Overall, recent instruments blend risk retention and risk transfer, while insuring a wide range of ideally uncorrelated risks that improve their efficiency. The trend in higher risk retention by companies may reflect these options. All these developments are triggered and driven by public concern for the environment.

1. INTRODUCTION

In the previous chapter, we analysed the financial aspects of environmental management. Of course, these financial aspects are closely related to risk, for there is indeed some financial risk. In our above discussions, risk was taken into account from the point of view of financial theory; for instance, through a risk premium on discount rates. The direct management of physical environmental risks, which is a different problem, was not discussed.

The remaining questions concerning environmental risk management that have to be solved are, however, manifold, and all of them stem from the following question. How does the risk manager of a firm take care of environmental risks, with all their characteristics? This question leads to the following one: how can one transfer the risk to other parties, at a price? Taking care of this problem is the job of insurance companies, so one of the main questions we need to ask is: how can one insure against environmental risks? As we shall see, traditional insurance is by no means the only answer to that question, because of the specific characteristics of environmental risks. Environmental risks are complex; as discussed previously, they may to some extent be hidden, and they may be huge. In terms of their intensity, risks may vary between two extreme cases. One extreme is diffuse environmental damages, with little or no short-term apparent damages, but, in the long run, very large damages. The other extreme is the risk of a major environmental disaster that causes immediate and enormous damages. Features of the first case are to be found in all instances of diffuse pollution, such as land, water and air pollution. Regarding the second case, there are several examples, such as the *Torrey Canyon* oil spill in Brittany, the Bhopal catastrophe in India, or the Seveso disaster in Italy, among others.

Whether we count natural catastrophes such as earthquakes as environmental disasters can be debated. Are the damages inflicted by earthquakes on persons, properties and human activities acts of God, or human-made disasters? This has been the object of debate for a long time. In 1755, just after the earthquake that ruined most of the centre of Lisbon in Portugal, the French-speaking philosopher Jean-Jacques Rousseau contended, against the dominant opinion of his time, that this was a man-made catastrophe in the sense that Lisbon had been built on this particular site as the result of human decisions (David and Barnaud, 1999). The adverse view was held after the San Francisco earthquake in 1906, when some fundamentalist preachers considered this catastrophe as a punishment inflicted by God for the supposed wickedness of its inhabitants. In terms of economic analysis, we would tend to include such natural disasters into environmental disasters resulting from human decisions. Making use of the Marshallian concept of externalities, we would say that choosing the site of economic activities in a large city is a decision that is taken considering the beneficial externalities (such as being close to an estuary and to a large harbour in the case of Lisbon) as well as the detrimental externalities (such as being in a seismic area). These externalities are indirectly internalized, through market effects, because they are reflected in the prices of real estate, positively for beneficial location externalities and only partially negatively in the case of negative externalities. Thus, we would tend to include natural disasters into other environmental disasters: in both cases, we have negative externalities that reflect only partially in market prices but that may be more completely internalized through insurance systems and through suitable investments, such as anti-seismic buildings.

In all cases, and for both gradual environmental damages and environmental disasters, the risk and the financial liabilities may be huge, so that the company's insurer may be obliged to propose a policy with a maximum guarantee, unless reinsured for any additional guarantees that its client company might seek. Thus, we are dealing with a *reinsurance* problem for the company's insurer, which is addressed by some reinsurance company, which is, so to speak, the insurer's insurance company. These insurance and reinsurance problems stem from both the potentially large liabilities that may be encountered, but also from the fact that little is known about the probability distribution of environmental disasters. Thus, insuring a company may be one of the solutions to the problems of environmental risk management, although one may choose not to insure at all, or to make use of non-conventional insurance systems. There are indeed several ways to take care of environmental risks other than using conventional insurance services. As will appear throughout this chapter, a company may well choose either to retain the risk in some cases, or to use financial services in order to address the capital or cash-management problems that are encountered if environmental liabilities do occur as a result of environmental hazard.

The steps taken by large corporations to manage their corporate risks and, in particular, their environmental risks have been discussed by several authors (Calow, 1998; David and Barnaud, 1999; Ritchie and Marshall, 1993; Zagalski, 1991; Zeckhauser, 1996). Of course, these steps are largely triggered or fostered by environmental regulations. As will be discussed below, the regulations concerning polluted land, in the USA and elsewhere, have been at the origin of concern over the risk of being held liable for cleaning up some piece of property, with insurance products eventually taking care of this risk at a price.

2. ENVIRONMENTAL RISKS, AND INSURANCE

2.1 Background

In the previous chapter, we have discussed risk from a financial point of view, which takes care mainly of *economic risk*. By economic risk, we mean the risk that the firm does not reach its economic objectives, such as being profitable. This kind of risk is, at least in simple financial models, measured by the variance of the profit. For the purpose of investment appraisal, it should reflect either in a higher discount rate, if the NPV method is being used as an investment-appraisal method, or in a higher IRR rate, if the IRR technique is being used. Of course, environmental risk may be a component of economic risk, and this was one of the main objects of the previous chapter.

Clearly, economic risk is inherent to the entrepreneur's activity and is not usually subject to risk transfer to another party. Usually, the entrepreneur, who is personified by the firm's management, will endeavour to make this economic risk as low as possible for a given return on the firm's equity. However, the firm's managers will also usually do their best to concentrate on producing and supplying the firm's products at the best possible quality, and at the lowest possible cost, to as large a number of clients as possible.

This might lead them to transfer some risks to other parties at a price. These are risks beyond their control that might potentially threaten the very survival of the firm. Such risks, under certain conditions that will be discussed later, are potentially insurable, at least from an economic point of view. Economic rationality indeed requires, from the division of labour point of view, that some risks be transferred to firms, such as insurance companies, that are specialized in accepting risks, at a price. We are thus concerned with potentially insurable risks that concern unexpected – and unwanted – adverse events beyond the control of the firm's management. However, this does not mean, as will appear from suitable examples, that such a risk is actually insurable. This is because insurance is a service produced by insurance companies for which there must be a market in terms of both supply and demand. For instance, a risk might not be insurable because the liabilities of the insurance company would be very high with too high a probability, and the insurance company would consequently have to charge a risk premium too high for the potential demand. Insurance, however, is nonetheless one of the ways one might manage environmental risks. Its marketability in terms of both supply and demand is submitted to a number of conditions, to which we now turn.

2.2 Conditions of Insurability

The conditions for a risk to be insurable from the insurers' point of view (that is, from the point of view of supply) have been defined precisely by a number of authors (Freeman and Kunreuther, 1997). The business of insurance companies usually rests on the following conditions:

1. There is some *pooling of the risks* over a large number of occurrences (*risk spreading*).
2. The probability of the occurrences follows a quantitatively known probability law approached empirically, due to *the law of large numbers*. Thus, *variance reduction* occurs, making the business of insurance financially acceptable in terms of risk-return patterns. Another feature of financial risk reduction is that the risks should be *uncorrelated*, meaning that the covariance between two risks insured must not be positive. Positive covariance would increase the insurer's

financial risk, but zero or even negative covariance would reduce the
financial risk.

3.   There must be no *moral hazard*. By moral hazard, we mean the fact that
the insured party behaves in a less cautious way because of the
protection granted to it by the insurance policy, thus increasing the risk.
In extreme cases, this might lead to criminal behaviours, such as falsely
reporting an accident, or purposely setting a building on fire to get some
indemnity from the insurer. Even short of such extreme cases, the
insured party may be consciously, or even unconsciously, less careful or
less oriented towards risk prevention, because of the protection that
results from the insurance contract.

4.   Finally, there must be no *adverse selection*, meaning that the insurer
must be able to *segregate risks*, or distinguish between good and bad
risks, and as a result charge a higher premium to insured parties
presenting a higher risk profile, or even refusing to insure such parties
if it appears that the risk is too high for the expected return.
Furthermore, some legal conditions must usually be encountered for a
risk to be insurable under third-party liability (and a large segment of
the market for insurance against environmental accidents or damages to
the environment falls into this category). This is because of some
fundamental principles of law regarding liability towards a third party
who has been the victim of damage due to an accident or unforeseen
adverse event that might potentially be insured. In English common
law, under so-called *tort liability*, a party (called the defendant in legal
language) responsible for some kind of damage to either properties or to
people, is liable to compensate the victims (also called the plaintiffs in
legal language). These parties might be individuals or companies.
Similar legal provisions exist in many other countries, including
continental European countries as well as Asian countries such as
Japan. All these legal systems, however different they might be, have a
fundamental principle in common. In most, if not all, legal systems in
advanced market economies, liabilities for damages rest on a fifth
condition, which applies to insurance coverage for environmental
damage liability; a particular category of environmental risk, but an
important one.

5. The fifth condition, which is not related to previous conditions, including absence of moral hazard, may be expressed as follows: there must be some kind of responsibility for the damage, and some kind of causality must clearly be established between the defendant's actions and the damages invoked by the plaintiff. There must be some wilful action, or some negligence on the defendant's side. In the case of damage to property[2] as well as in the case of damage to the environment, such damage must clearly concern the plaintiff's property.

These principles, as well as being important from a legal point of view, are also important from an economic point of view. Their economic significance has been at the basis of a number of analyses concerning the economics of environment. In particular, they have been analysed by Nobel Laureate R. Coase (1961) in a paper which is well known to economists. In this paper, Coase shows that, if there are some well-defined property rights, and a legal system under which liability for damages caused to other people's property exists, economic agents have an incentive to avoid being responsible for externalities leading to damage to other people's property.

Conventional liability insurance therefore rests on all these legal principles, as well as on the economic principles discussed above. Whether societal risks such as risks of damage to the environment obey these principles is an important problem that we are going to discuss now. This will lead us to a discussion of the various tools that answer the problems of the management of environmental risks: as we shall see, conventional liability insurance is only one of these tools, and (perhaps unfortunately) it does not apply in many situations. Clearly, environmental risks have specific characteristics that make them quite peculiar, especially in terms of insurability and, more generally, in terms of risk management. Let us examine these characteristics in the light of the above conditions of insurability.

2.3 Characteristics of Environmental Risks

Conditions (1) and (2) are fulfilled, in principle, if there is a large number of occurrences, so that the insurer may have a significant number of independent clients, making it possible to pool the risks, as well as to have some idea of the probability distribution of occurrences, and to take advantage of the law of large numbers; all these features allow the insurer to price its services. In plain terms, this means that the insurance company is able to calculate the insurance premiums in such a manner that its activity is profitable with a reasonably low risk. However, these conditions are not met in many instances of environmental risks. As far as conditions (1) and (2) are concerned (the possibility of pooling risks and the possibility that the law of large numbers applies), it is clear that the number of occurrences of large environmental disasters is rather small but leads to damages that might be enormous, beyond the means of ordinary insurance companies and even beyond those of reinsurance companies. The *Exxon Valdez* catastrophe, for instance, led to damages estimated at US$ 3 billion, a colossal amount for any insurance or reinsurance company to guarantee. Such disasters leave little or no possibility of pooling the risk, but fortunately, the number of occurrences of major disasters has been comparatively very small. Even if we consider disasters of the magnitude of the RENFLEX disaster reported in Case Study 7.1, which gave rise to much smaller damages (€ 15.56 million), one must say that, fortunately again, the incidence of such disasters is still quite small, numbered in tens rather than hundreds. In comparison, the number of automobile accidents is a matter of millions.

In other instances of environmental risk, pollution is gradual and might lead to damage that is either undetectable at first, or detectable only after a considerable time-lag. Such risks due to gradual pollution, are probably more important, overall, than risks that manifest themselves through disasters and catastrophes. For instance, the total liabilities for environmental damage in real-estate properties in the United States was estimated at a staggering US$ 2000 billion; this was about 20 per cent of the value of all real estate in the United States (Wilson, 1987). Finally, little is known about the probability laws that apply to much environmental risk, as these may result from only a limited number of observations or correspond to data that are either hidden or unknown.

Simulations, however, can be carried out in a number of cases. In the nuclear industry, several probabilistic studies have been undertaken. In France, Electricité de France estimated the probability of the worst possible accident as 5.10^{-5} per year for one nuclear plant. Similar quantitative tools also exist for the chemical and oil industries, and it is clear that insurers will increasingly have to rely on engineering simulations in order to quantify some risks. Insurance and reinsurance companies are usually very reluctant to guarantee against environmental disasters, because they lack sufficient information on the probability distributions of such accidents and also because the risks are potentially very large. This is especially true when a comparatively small number of companies can eventually be insured and when risk pooling is not possible.

Another problem is that companies are using technologies that are either patented by them or used under licence, usually held by engineering companies that sell or license technologies on a highly competitive basis. Companies such as chemical, oil and engineering companies do not typically disclose the particulars and environmental characteristics of the processes they own, even to their insurers. They may also be over-optimistic about their environmental risks. There are existing insurance policies that include environmental risks, but insurers and reinsurers that sell such policies will, as a rule, ask their clients to provide some comprehensive technical information through a detailed questionnaire, followed by some technical audit conducted by an expert appointed by the insurer or reinsurer. The purpose of such an audit, of course, is to gain some quantitative idea about the level of risk.

In relation to condition (3) (that is, to *moral hazard*), the insurance policy must include incentives for the insured party to take steps to decrease the risks for which they are insured. These may be investments such as environmental protection investments and, more generally, security investments, and/or giving an adequate security training to its employees. To achieve this, the insurance policy might provide for positive incentives, in the form of participation in the insurer's profits should the claim record be small, as well as penalties under various forms if, on the contrary, the claim record appears to be poor after some time.

Condition (4), which is related to the possibility of segregating risks, is addressed by incentives that are quite similar to those used in tackling condition (3). Companies will usually charge comparatively low premiums to clients whose risks appear to be comparatively small. Clients presenting comparatively higher risks will, on the other hand, be charged higher insurance premiums, and the insurance company might even refuse to insure them altogether if the risk is so high that no realistic premium can be charged.

Condition (5) is pertinent only in the particular case of insurance covering liability when the legal preconditions for such liability are met. This is not the case in many instances of environmental hazards, although the legal conditions for liability have recently been extended in the United States, especially for soil pollution under the Comprehensive Environmental Response, Compensation, and Liability Act (CERCLA) (1980), that has been amended several times, notably in 1986. Under CERCLA, as interpreted under the jurisprudence of US courts, liability for polluted property has been considerably extended. This broadening of liability involves several features.

First, there is *joint and several liability*, which means that if several parties share liability for land pollution, one of them may be found liable for the whole costs of decontamination, irrespective of its own share of responsibility in the pollution.

Second, *retroactive liability* means that any current owner of a property may be liable for its pollution, even if it is due to actions by previous owners who, when they were in charge of the property, acted legally.

Third, *strict liability* means that a landowner may be liable for the costs of clean-up even in the absence of any criminal behaviour or violation of any law or regulation, whether past or present.

Clearly, this extends the possible liability for owners of real-estate property, but it does so also for other parties, such as previous owners or tenants. Banks or financial institutions that arrange a loan for buying real property may also be found liable for clean-up, since it is in their power to make any loan they issue subject to environmental conditions, which might oblige the new owner to decontaminate the land. All these extensions of liability lend themselves to insurance coverage for polluted property. Since about 20 per cent of real estate in the USA appears to be polluted, the risks are considerable, but insurance policies are nonetheless offered by a number of American insurers. Of course, insurers in that case will, as a rule, try to assess the risk beforehand through an environmental audit. Many other countries followed the USA in introducing similar extensions of liability into their environmental regulations for environmental risks concerning soil pollution. In particular, this is true of a number of European countries.

However, in the USA as well as in Europe, the demand for insurance coverage for liabilities resulting from land pollution did not follow. This is because many owners do not feel the need for such a coverage, unless some third party (such as a bank financing a project) requests it. In addition, in the case of abandoned property, when there is no known party that is able to support its liability for cleaning up a polluted site, CERCLA provides for a public fund (called the 'Superfund'), which is able to support depollution costs. Such a superfund system has also been introduced in most European countries.

Another risk related to land pollution is the risk of leakages into the soil from Underground Storage Tanks (USTs) in which petroleum products, particularly petrol, are stored. This is a risk that has lent itself to specific regulations and also to specific liabilities and thus to specific third-party liability insurance coverage.

2.4 Limitations of Insurance as a Tool for the Management of Environmental Risks

One may conclude that there are possible ways of insuring against environmental risk liability, whether it stems from environmental accidents or disasters or from gradual pollution such as land pollution. However, the use of insurance as a tool to manage environmental risks is by no means universal, because of problems that are encountered on both the supply and demand side.

On the supply side, the insurer that does not buy reinsurance coverage is very much in the same position as a put option seller on the insured firm's capital. A put option is a contract that works very much in the same way as an insurance policy against losses that may occur on the price on some asset, called the underlying asset. It gives the right, but not the obligation, to sell the underlying asset at some fixed price, called the exercise price. This right, of course, is bought on a market, at a price called the premium, just in the case of insurance coverage. If the price of the asset has fallen against the exercise price, the party that bought the option may sell it at the exercise price, and then buy it back at the prevailing price, therefore obtaining a profit equal to the loss on the asset price. Conversely, the other party that sold (or underwrote) the option, is committed by the option contract to cover the option buyer against adverse losses on the asset. The option writer will, of course, receive the price of the option, and is thus very much in the same situation as our insurer, risking a loss which, however, is limited to the exercise price (less the premium) in the hypothetical case when the price of the asset falls to zero. Here, the insurer is committed through the insurance policy to cover all the cumulated losses due to events mentioned in the contract; the loss is theoretically unlimited, at least if the insurance policy provides for no upper limit to the coverage.

Again, akin to a put option seller, the liability of a limited liability insurance company is limited to its equity.[3] The put option writer is selling a contingent asset that is in effect an insurance against downward variation of an underlying asset. He or she faces the possibility of unlimited losses up to the exercise price. A reinsurer faces the same possibility of losses.

Clearly, as shown in Figure 7.1, it appears that the insurer providing unlimited coverage is faced with possibly unlimited losses (up to its equity) with an intercept for the case of zero occurrence at P minus C, where P is the price of the premium, and C represents the insurer's costs (for instance, in terms of labour and capital).

If, as is the case for environmental risks, the number of occurrences is small, our insurer is unable to spread the risks, so that the risk of very large losses may be much too high and thus unacceptable. The insurer may, however, *reinsure* part of his or her risk; for instance, above some value M for cumulated occurrences. M is the maximum cumulated losses that the insurer accepts to support. The reinsured insurer is thus obtaining full coverage for any guaranteed costs corresponding to cumulated occurrences above M. The insurer's loss is thus limited to a maximum value L_0 (Figure 7.1).

This means that the reinsurer bears an unlimited risk of loss[4] for any cumulated occurrences over M; but this risk is pooled over several insurers, so that the reinsurer finally supports a smaller risk than the insurer does. A point that matters very much in estimating the risk for an insurance company as well as the risk for financial derivatives such as options is *to what extent the liabilities are covered.* Of course, a portfolio of insurance or reinsurance policies, as well as a portfolio of positions on options or derivative markets, represents risky financial assets, which must be pooled with some other uncorrelated portfolio assets in the form of liquid financial instruments, such as bonds, money-market deposits, other riskless or low-risk liquid assets, and equity investments. As far as the liabilities are concerned, the policies have their counterparts in terms of reserves for

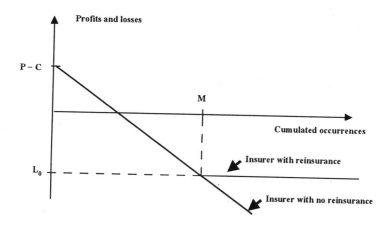

Figure 7.1 Profile for profits and losses against cumulated covered occurrences: the insurer with no reinsurance, and the insurer with reinsurance above some maximum value M for cumulated occurrences.

for claims, which must be balanced by suitable assets, among which a significant amount of liquid assets such as money-market positions and other low-risk assets such as bonds are present, to face payments to the policy holders in the event of guaranteed occurrences. It is clear that the larger these assets and the balance between assets and liabilities (the equity of the insurance or reinsurance company), the lower the risk. Whatever the form of management of environmental risks, one fact prevails: environmental risks mean costs and liabilities that are uncertain and potentially huge but that must be covered somewhere by available capital, in particular under the form of liquid assets and other fixed-revenue instruments such as bonds. This does not apply to some environmental and natural catastrophe risks, which are larger than the firm's equity. In that case, the firm cannot cover the risk by even large financial reserves. If the risk is not insurable, the firm is potentially bankrupt.

On the demand side, this means that insurance covering environmental risks, when it exists, may be unacceptably expensive for several reasons. Firstly, the insurer, and the reinsurer above the maximum cost that the insurer accepts to cover, will charge a high premium reflecting the fact that the losses incurred due to an occurrence under coverage may be extremely high. Secondly, both the insurer and the reinsurer will charge a high risk premium reflecting the lack of risk pooling. A further increase on the premium will reflect the additional costs due to moral hazard, which are costs of ensuring that the insured party will take steps to decrease the insured risk. Therefore, a firm may contemplate other methods for managing its environmental risks than conventional insurance. The next section explores these various methods.

3. MANAGING ENVIRONMENTAL RISKS: CONVENTIONAL INSURANCE AND ALTERNATIVE INSTRUMENTS

3.1 A Range of Instruments for Managing Environmental Risks

As we shall see, purchasing conventional insurance products is just one method among several others to manage environmental risks. Environmental risks have their specific characteristics: particularly, high occurrence costs, lack of pooling of the risks, and moral hazard. This means that, in a number of cases, insurance products covering against environmental risks are not available, simply because no insurance company can market them at a profitable price. The risk manager, or the person in charge of environmental risks whatever his or her title in the organization, is therefore not merely a purchaser of insurance coverage: in many cases, there are other solutions that are either cheaper or more effective in controlling environmental risks. In some cases, there might even be no insurance services available at all. No insurance at all might be a perfectly rational choice, either because there are no insurance products or because it represents a better choice in terms of the cost–risk equilibrium. Moreover, the management of environmental risks consists in determining the optimal balance between not insuring, or *risk retention*, and making use of some kind of insurance products. There are many solutions, some of them being quite complex, ranging from total risk retention to some sort of total insurance coverage. The implementation of any of these solutions is a matter of particular cases.

Rather than standardized solutions, there are, so to speak, *à la carte* solutions adapted to each particular case in terms of the nature of the industry, the size of the firm, the legal and fiscal environment, and many other parameters. Between total risk retention and total insurance coverage, there are many intermediary solutions that are given in Table 7.1.

Table 7.1 Techniques available for the management of environmental risks

Risk-management technique	Risk retention or risk transfer?
- No insurance, self-insurance, financial provisions - Financial reinsurance	Total or almost total risk retention
- Captive insurance companies (with or without reinsurance, or financial reinsurance) - Conventional insurance, with partial coverage ('finite' insurance products)	Partial risk retention
- Industrial insurance pools or mutual insurance companies, coinsurance - Conventional insurance (with or without reinsurance)	Total or almost total risk transfer

From Table 7.1, it appears that a number of techniques are available for the management of environmental risks, depending on the optimal balance between risk retention or risk transfer that applies in each particular case. The nature of the industry and of production, the size and specific characteristics of each firm, as well as the fiscal and environmental regulations and constraints, and the cost of capital, are factors that have to be taken into account to find this optimal balance in each case. It should be emphasized that the choice between total retention of risks, meaning no insurance, and total risk transfer, meaning total insurance coverage, when available, is a choice between a financial treatment of the risk and an insurance treatment. The question may also be formulated as follows. Where are the assets that balance the uncertain (and sometimes hidden) liabilities represented by environmental risks? Of course, it is important and even fundamental to reduce the physical risks as much as possible, so that assets may take the form of physical assets such as environmental protection investments and anti-pollution facilities; we have discussed this sort of investment in the previous chapter. For the residual risk, which, again, should be as low as possible, assets might be available in the form of some readily available capital, perhaps in the form of liquid assets but available either within the firm's assets or outside the firm's assets; for instance, in the reserves of insurance and reinsurance companies. If we are talking about assets held by the firm, the firm practises *risk retention*, and we may talk about *financial treatment* of the risk; if, on the other hand, we are talking about assets held by an insurance or reinsurance company, the firm relies rather on risk transfer, and we may talk then about *insurance treatment* of the risk. Let us now examine the different possibilities of environmental management, from total risk retention to total insurance coverage.

3.2 Total or Almost Total Risk Retention

Self-insurance
As previously discussed, the choice of total risk retention means that the firm will take care of the possible liabilities that stem from environmental risks by making use of its own assets, or possibly borrowed assets. We are thus talking about some wholly financial treatment of the risk. In this respect, having no insurance may be a perfectly rational choice. This method

is often referred to as *self-insurance*, meaning that the firm supports the full costs that might be related to any environmental risk. The advantages of the method are found in the resulting savings in insurance costs, insurance-brokerage commissions, and other similar costs. Furthermore, the firm might be better aware of the technical details of its risks, while the insurer might not be fully informed and conscious about these risks; a lack of information reflected in high insurance costs, such that it might be less costly for the firm to take care of the risk internally. Self-insurance, however, is meaningful only if the firm builds up some financial reserves in order to cover the potential environmental liabilities. This is done through provisioning some suitable amounts in the firm's accounts that must correspond to available assets. The drawback of this procedure stems from the fiscal treatment of these provisions, which are not fiscally deductible in many countries, except perhaps for some activities such as mining. In the case of mining, provisions for rehabilitation of the site over its economic lifetime are submitted to the usual rules of asset depreciation and are tax-deductible. In that case, however, we are not facing a risk, but an expense that is certain and mandatory, due to regulations that impose restoration of the site after its economic life. Therefore, generally, self-insurance is fiscally more costly than direct insurance, since insurance premiums are generally tax-deductible. It amounts to building up a financial reserve taken from the available cash flows. This has the advantage of contributing to some kind of *income sustenance* for the company's shareholders, meaning that the dividends are thus kept more or less stable over time. In terms of physical pollution-prevention investments, as discussed in the previous chapter, self-insurance may provide a strong incentive for such investments, which might be tax-deductible through depreciation of environmental-protection equipment. One has to check, however, whether this investment provides a sufficient IRR compared to the investment into the financial reserve.

Financial reinsurance
Financial reinsurance is a different scheme, which also implies complete risk retention. It is not, actually, a true reinsurance scheme. It simply means that the firm negotiates with a bank a line of credit, available in the event of some environmental occurrence. Usually, the firm will pay some 'insurance

premiums' beforehand, in order to constitute some kind of financial reserves. Should an occurrence happen, it will obtain a credit that completes the financial reserves and it will reimburse this credit at a suitable rate of interest.

The value of risk retention

Complete risk retention, however, is interesting only if the firm has an effective control of its environmental risks, and if these are kept low enough. This is because the firm, in this case, is in the situation of either the insurer who is not reinsured, or the reinsurer: as shown on Figure 7.2, it saves the cost of the insurance premium after tax deduction, which is $P(1-\tau)$ if P

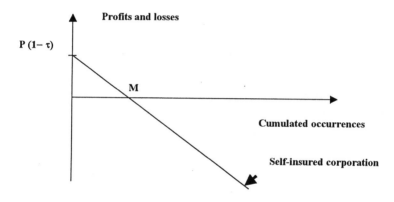

Figure 7.2 Profile for profits and losses against cumulated occurrences: the case of a self-insured corporation

stands for the premium, while τ stands for the rate of corporate tax, but otherwise risks are unlimited (or at least limited to the firm's equity). The situation here is similar to the situation of an insurer who is not reinsured, or to the situation of a reinsurer, as discussed above.

The management of environmental risk should, in that case, keep the physical risk as low as possible. Self-insurance is not, therefore, always an interesting solution. A more appealing solution, which generally involves less risk retention, is to establish, or to rent, a so-called *captive insurance company*.

3.3 Captive Insurance Companies

Characteristics of captives

A *captive insurance company*, usually called simply 'a captive' if no ambiguity is possible[5], may be defined as an insurance company that is entirely controlled by some parent company and that sells insurance services mainly or even exclusively to this parent company. In practice, the captive is wholly owned, or majority-owned (often at more than 90 per cent), by its parent company, but it should legally be a completely different and autonomous entity, with a separate management and administration board, being able to conduct business of its own. In this respect, one may distinguish between *pure captives*, which operate exclusively for their parent companies, and *broad captives*, which carry out significant insurance business with third parties independent from the parents.

Historically, as noted by Porat and Powers (1995), the first captives appeared after the end of the First World War and throughout the 1920s. In the United States, captives became an accepted alternative tool for corporate risk management in the 1960s and 1970s. This is because of failures in the markets for some new risks that appeared and developed at that time, such as medical malpractice, product-related risks, and, of course, environmental risks, with little or no insurance products available, or very expensive ones. Captives established in tax-free jurisdictions, such as the Bahamas or the Bermuda Islands, were also often used in the past as tax evasion vehicles in a way that will appear below.

However, a captive insurance company can be established without any intent of tax evasion. It may be an invaluable tool for managing environmental risks, as well as other major risks such as natural disasters, including, for instance, hurricanes or earthquakes. It works as follows. First, the captive is established and is provided an initial capital according to the regulations of the country in which it is incorporated.[6] It should have actual substance and be managed as an independent profitable company. Then, the parent company, and affiliated companies in the case of a large group, are charged insurance premiums by the captive just as in the case of an ordinary insurance company. The captive is free to calculate its insurance premiums for profitable operation. The premiums contribute to financial reserves that match the firm's environmental risks.

In the early 1980s, premiums paid to captives in the USA, European countries and elsewhere, were fiscally deductible, so that captives established in offshore tax-free or low-tax jurisdictions were used as vehicles for tax evasion, since they enabled some corporations to constitute corporate tax-free affiliated companies with the added benefits from fiscal deductibility. Nowadays, things have changed, because in the USA, the deductibility of premiums paid to captives was, in principle, disallowed, at least for pure captives; the US Tax Reform Act of 1984 provided that offshore captive insurance companies insuring US corporations were taxable as US companies. Similar tax legislation was passed in most European countries. A number of American states, such as Colorado, Georgia, Hawaii, Illinois, New York, Tennessee and Vermont (and also British Columbia in Canada), modified their legislation and made much easier the establishment of captives; the same is true of some European Union member countries, which are akin to tax havens: the Republic of Ireland and Luxembourg.[7] These are onshore jurisdictions in which *bona fide* captives, or captives established solely in order to take care of corporate risks, can operate either throughout the USA or Canada in the case of American jurisdictions, or throughout the European Union in the case of European jurisdictions, provided the company is ready to accept that premiums will *not* be deductible, as is now, in most circumstances, the case in the USA and in a number of European countries.[8]

In the USA, for instance, the legal doctrine under existing legislation and under the jurisprudence of US tax courts, is that insurance implies the existence of an insurable risk with (1) actual risk-shifting and risk distribution to another party, independent of the insured, and (2) operating on a competitive commercial basis (Porat and Powers, 1995). Under the existing US jurisprudence, on top of the above conditions, the existence of a significant market share concerning insurance business with third parties unrelated to the parents of the captive is crucial in granting tax deductibility for captive insurance premiums (in some cases a market share of more than 30 per cent appeared sufficient to uphold tax deductibility). In practice, the US tax authorities may permit tax deductibility provided the captive has an important ownership and an important insurance market share from outside its parent companies.

In some cases, if the captive is not authorized to operate in the country of the insured, its services have to be mediated through fronting. Fronting means that the insurance policy is negotiated with a so-called fronter, or fronting insurance company, which is authorized to operate in the country but retrocedes the risk to the captive, charging a commission for this service. Even deprived of most of its fiscal advantages, the captive is, as mentioned above, a very powerful tool for the management of environmental risks. This is because the captive has distinct advantages over other environmental risk-management techniques such as conventional insurance and self-insurance.

Captives compared to self-insurance and conventional insurance
With respect to self-insurance, the use of a captive insurance company offers distinct advantages. The captive is, from the legal point of view, an autonomous entity. From an economic point of view, it can be an autonomous profit centre aimed at distributing dividends to its parent company. This feature enables the management of the parent company to monitor the efficiency of its risk-management policy. It thus provides a stronger incentive than does self-insurance to achieve a better control over physical risks and, in particular, over environmental risks. The captive is thus comparable to a defeasance structure, or a structure to which bad debts (and the risks associated thereto) are transferred. Furthermore, at least in the case of large industrial groups, there is some pooling of the risks, because the captive insures several affiliated companies. This also provides the possibility of some scale effects, and hence smaller costs, due to the comparatively large turnover. In the case of large industrial groups, the captive will generally insure several types of risks, including environmental risks but also other uncorrelated risks; it may also provide[9] some personal insurance services to the parent group's employees and executives, the risks of which can be largely uncorrelated with other industrial risks. Therefore,

to some extent, risks are not correlated, which is one of the desirable features of conventional insurance, with the added benefit of possible scope effects (that is, cost reductions that stem from the fact that the captive is producing several products at the same time). Finally, contrary to self-insurance, the use of a captive provides a direct access to reinsurance, as well as a direct control of the negotiations with the reinsurer. As noticed by David and Barnaud (1999), the captive is, so to speak, 'a window on reinsurance'. This feature is obvious in the case of Swiss Re, one of the largest reinsurance companies (Case Study 7.2): captives are one of the key segments of Swiss Re's markets for reinsurance concerning environmental risks.

Thus, the use of a captive for reinsurance makes it possible to limit risks, whereas, as discussed previously, the risks in the case of self-insurance are generally unlimited (until bankruptcy), a situation which is, of course, rather undesirable.

With respect to conventional insurance, a captive also offers some definite advantages, including the fact that the company has direct control over its access to reinsurance, which is not the case if it uses traditional insurance services. An industrial group using a captive also benefits from the fact that moral hazard and adverse-selection problems are less present, since the captive is owned by the group. This implies smaller costs of monitoring than in the case of an external insurer. There also is an incentive to make the captive profitable through reducing physical risks through suitable investments and, in general, through suitable security management. Of course, even with conventional insurance systems, well-managed companies can avoid being pooled with moral hazard or adverse-selected companies. They can negotiate a smaller insurance premium if their risk is kept under control, but this is not always possible in the case of environmental risks, where traditional insurers will as a rule be reluctant to insure the risk altogether. The operation of a captive, which provides a strong incentive to control environmental risks, is thus a valuable alternative to this situation.

Conditions under which captives are valuable alternatives
The operation of a captive, however, is profitable only if the risks are kept under control and low enough, so that the cost of operating the captive is

smaller than the cost of insurance premiums that would be charged by conventional insurance companies, taking into account the fiscal situation. Further, the fact that captives are competing with traditional insurers should not be underestimated. As will be seen later, conventional insurance companies have also developed services adapted to environmental risks, in the form of insurance pools and finite coverage products, among others. It is therefore interesting to give some quantitative terms of comparison between conventional insurance and the operation of captives. Let P be the insurance premium (possibly including brokerage commissions and taxes) that could be charged for environmental risks to some corporation or industrial group. If τ is the rate of corporate tax, and if P is a deductible expense as is generally the case, the operation of the captive will save P $(1 - \tau)$. Let us now consider the net consolidated expenses, at the level of the industrial group concerned, due to the operation of the captive. It is clear that the premiums charged by the captive are *not* consolidated expenses; they must rather be considered for what they are, that is, investments which aim at building up suitable reserves in order to be able to face expenses due to occurrences. This is precisely the way they are considered by the tax legislation of a number of countries. Thus, the only expenses to be considered in the operation of the captive are the brokerage and fronting fees B (if any), the financial reinsurance premiums F, the reinsurance premiums proper R, and, finally, the operating costs of the captive C (including any taxes). We assume that these expenses are deductible. The savings S on fixed costs achieved through the operation of the captive are:

$$S = P (1 - \tau) - (B + F + R + C) (1 - \tau) \tag{7.1}$$

Finally, the graph of S against cumulated occurrences (Figure 7.3) shows the conditions of profitability of a captive with respect to conventional insurance. A necessary condition for profitability of the captive with respect to conventional insurance is that the savings on the fixed costs be positive:

$$S = P (1 - \tau) - (B + F + R + C) (1 - \tau) \geq 0 \tag{7.2}$$

Equation (7.2) gives an estimate of the opportunity benefit of operating a captive with respect to insuring with an ordinary insurance company. If it is positive, the operation of a captive will be profitable. Otherwise, operating a captive leads to an opportunity cost. We assume here that the insurance premium P charged by the captive would be the same in the case of an ordinary insurance company. Actually, the premium charged by an ordinary insurance company might be higher: this would enhance the interest of establishing a captive.

The break-even point corresponds, of course, to equality, and occurs for value M_0 of cumulated occurrences. Therefore, at least in our simple model, for the profitability of the operation of the captive, the cumulated occurrences V, or the risks, have to be kept small enough, under this value M_0, with a reasonable probability. If $M_0 \leq V \leq M$, there is a loss, but it is limited to a maximum value of L_0, due to the reinsurance. If $M_0 \leq V \leq M$, there is a loss, but it is limited to a maximum value of L_0, due to the reinsurance. We may conclude that the captive is an interesting tool if one is able to maintain a low risk, and it provides an incentive to do so.

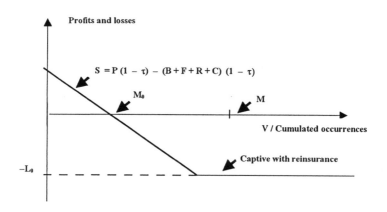

Figure 7.3 Profile for profits and losses against cumulated covered occurrences for the operation of a captive, as compared to conventional insurance, with reinsurance above some maximum value M for cumulated occurrences

If $M_0 \leq V \leq M$, there is a loss, but it is limited to a maximum value of L_0, due to the reinsurance. We may conclude that the captive is an interesting tool if one is able to maintain a low risk, and it provides an incentive to do so. This is valid, however, only after the captive has operated for some time, thus being provided with a sizeable amount of reserves that make it able to face some significant occurrences. Difficulties, however, do occur in the first years of operation of the captive, when it lacks financial reserves. It must then rely more on financial reinsurance and on reinsurance proper, and the reinsurance treaty must provide for this during these first years of operation.

3.4 Conventional Insurance and its Variants

Short of traditional insurance by a single insurance company, which has been discussed in the previous section, there are several variants of conventional insurance that may be applied to the management of environmental risks. These variants are adapted to the specific characteristics of environmental risks. Insurance is an innovative industry, and there are several answers to the problems caused by environmental risks.

Coinsurance or insurance pooling

The first variant is *coinsurance*, or insurance pooling. An insurance pool is an association of several insurance and reinsurance companies, among which the risk is spread. Usually, the pool is an association of companies, with each company having a definite share in the pool. Coinsurance is distinct from reinsurance, and the pool may reinsure above some maximum value for cumulated occurrences. In Europe, there are several country-specific environmental insurance pools, such as Assurpol in France, Pool Inquinamento in Italy, MAS Pool in the Netherlands, Danpool in Denmark, and PEC in Spain.

In France, Assurpol was established in 1989 as a joint venture between insurance companies (with 49 per cent of the capital), and reinsurance companies (with the remainder; that is, 51 per cent, of the capital); among the reinsurance participants, Swiss Re (see, for example, Case Study 7.2) holds a stake of 7.5 per cent of Assurpol. Practically, Assurpol works as follows. For smaller risks, the insurance policy is issued by one of the participant insurance companies, but the risks are receded to Assurpol; larger policies are issued by Assurpol itself. To manage the problems of moral hazard and adverse selection, before issuing the policy, Assurpol, or the participant company, conducts a preliminary environmental audit in order to assess the risks. Currently, Assurpol refuses to grant coverage in about 30 per cent of the cases. Furthermore, some risks are excluded; in particular, risks caused to the insured are not covered by Assurpol's standard policy. Finally, there is a ceiling on the guarantees, which is currently 200 million FRF (about 30.49 million €), as well as an excess threshold, in order to create some incentives for the insured companies to reduce both small risks and very large risks. Assurpol's success has been quite disappointing, because demand for the standard Assurpol contract is rather weak (the total premiums collected by Assurpol are currently 40 million FRF (about 6 million €) per year. Some industrial companies complain that Assurpol is in a monopoly situation, but there is effective competition with other European insurers. For instance, a large European chemical company discussed insuring its French subsidiary with Assurpol, but finally found a cheaper coverage with a foreign insurer. A number of observers, such as Kronenberg (1995), and David and Barnaud (1999) contend that the existing European insurance pools are not economically efficient, mainly due to the lack of demand for coverage.

In other countries, such as the United States and, to a lesser extent, the UK, a number of insurance companies have been able to propose several types of insurance policies covering environmental liabilities. Several prominent American companies offer Environmental Impairment Liability (AIL) coverage with several lines of products, including off-site and on-site pollution liability, contractors pollution liability, consultants professional liability, and combined liability products. Typical policies apply, with coverage limits up to several millions of US$ per loss, under a premium of at least US$ 10 000 for the lowest risks with a coverage of US$ 1 000 000 (1 per cent of maximum coverage) and a risk-retention threshold which is US$50 000. These products may concern both gradual exposures and sudden exposures. Premiums are calculated according to an estimate of the exposure, often resulting from a suitable environmental audit. In the USA, there is a significant demand for environmental coverage, which, in particular, is due to the enormous development of environmental litigation before courts. For this reason, the costs of coverage in the USA are quite expensive, at least by comparison with the costs observed for the available insurance products in Europe.

In the Netherlands, the average premium charged by the Dutch pool (MAS) is of the order of magnitude of US$ 2000; a figure which is considered very low by Kronenberg (1995), because it does not even cover the fixed costs of an environmental audit. However, it may be argued that the policies offered by MAS in the Netherlands provide only small coverage, and that most Dutch insurants requiring environmental coverage are small businesses and small farmers.

In the UK, individual insurance companies may insure environmental risks. The Association of British Insurers issued a guideline (ABI, 1998) in order to make available to British insurance companies the latest technical developments on environmental damage prevention, as well as benchmarks to assess environmental risks, and a standardized questionnaire to be able to complete risk information from prospective corporate policy holders. However, the ABI guideline recommends coverage for only sudden, accidental events. As noted below, this guideline was developed with the participation of Swiss Re (Case Study 7.2).

Mutual insurance companies
Another alternative to insurance coverage, which is akin to insurance pooling, is proposed by industrial *mutual insurance companies*, which are strong, in particular, in the United States. The first American factory mutual company, called the Manufacturers Mutual Fire Insurance Company, was established in 1835 by Zachariah Allen, a Rhode Island cotton-mill owner. There used to be up to 42 factory mutual companies, and these mutual companies addressed most of the problems of industrial insurance by imposing on insured companies risk-prevention techniques, with some previous audits or inspections, before granting a policy. Until recently, following a number of mergers, three of these mutual insurance companies remained, called Allendale Insurance, Arkwright and Protection Mutual,

these also holding as a joint venture the Factory Mutual System, with common research facilities involved in industrial risk-prevention. These three companies recently merged (1999) into FM Global (officially Factory Mutual Insurance Company). FM Global has assets in excess of US$6 billion, and is present in several countries, including the United States; Canada; Latin America; Western European countries such as Belgium, France, Germany and the UK; East Asia (China, Japan Korea and Singapore); and Australia. The main feature of FM Global is encouraging risk prevention, in particular through granting the Highly Protected Risk label to companies that meet high-quality norms in risk reduction. Although damages to property are the chief concern of FM Global, it has been concerned with environmental risks, especially since the revision of the US Clean Air Act in 1990.

New market trends are leaning towards risk retention, so that, significantly, FM Global is also present in the captive products market. It manages two captives established in the Bermuda Islands[10] (New Providence Mutual Ltd and New Providence Insurance Company Ltd). These are innovative concepts of joint-venture captives in which insurants may obtain some share of ownership (called a cell, which is akin to an independent limited liability company according to an Act of Parliament recently passed in Bermuda). Each cell is completely independent of other cells, and has a separate account that enables controlling the profitability of the insured's risk management; reinsurance of the cells is of course possible.

Other insurance pools concerned with environmental risks exist at the level of particular industries, such as Oil Insurance Ltd, which was founded in 1971, after the *Torrey Canyon* oil spill. Oil Insurance Ltd is an insurance pool owned by oil companies designed to take care of their risks, especially pollution risks on sea and land. The net assets of Oil Insurance Ltd are about US$1.2 billion. It provides coverage up to US$200 million, with a threshold of risk retention which is beween US$5 million and US$100 million, an option in the individual policies.

Finite insurance: hybrid products combining risk retention and insurance coverage

Besides insurance pools, there are other insurance products that combine risk retention and insurance coverage In particular, there are so-called *finite* insurance products.   These are but conventional insurance policies with upper limits in risk coverage offered by insurance companies external to the insured company. Finite insurance products are hybrid products, combining risk retention and insurance coverage. In a typical finite policy, coverage has an upper limit on both each occurrence and cumulated occurrences (say over five years). In typical cases, this upper limit might be US$20 million for cumulated occurrences, and US$10 million for each occurrence. Finite policies also provide incentives to risk reduction, and, in particular, premiums are increased if the cumulated occurrences are too high (typically, above a limit of US$5 million, the premium might increase by 25 per cent); conversely, the insured is entitled to some participation in the profits if the cumulated occurrences are low, which might, for instance, be 80 per cent of premiums, less cumulated occurrences, with an interest accrued on premiums. These features are just basic features, and finite products might involve more complex characteristics.

4. CONCLUSIONS

The above discussion leads us to several conclusive remarks.

A first point is that most instruments used in the management of environmental risks, whether they are captives, coinsurance, insurance pools, mutuals, or finite products, provide some kind of blend between risk retention and risk transfer. Of course, the optimal instrument should be found in each case. A second point is that conventional insurance products do not cover all needs in terms of environmental risk management. There even seems to be a trend towards more risk retention, due to the fact that traditional insurance products tend to be expensive, and, in some cases, are not adapted to cover environmental risks. Thus, the use of new risk-management instruments such as captive insurance companies is growing.

A third point is that environmental risks, including the risks from natural disasters, are closely linked, and correlated, to other risks, such as security risks. Furthermore, it should be clear that all the instruments are also used for the management of other risks, uncorrelated to environmental risks. This is an important point, because the existence of uncorrelated risks is beneficial to the efficiency of risk management as a whole, and to the efficiency of the management of each particular class of risks, including environmental risks.

Finally, all this concern about environmental risks is triggered by public concern and by more complete environmental protection regulations evolving in many countries. In cases where market products are not available, government programmes have also provided for funds that might support anti-pollution costs. An example is the 'superfund' established in the USA under CERCLA, which aims at supporting the costs of land clean-ups for sites where the owner is unknown, or unable to meet his or her liabilities. Other similar fund schemes exist in several other countries, including, for instance, European countries.

Other regulations, however, are not necessarily helpful for the management of environmental risks. There is a debate, for instance, about regulations concerning captive insurance companies, which (for instance, in the USA) have mainly been directed at fiscal evasion and at protecting insurance companies from systemic and large risks through prudential regulations.[11] However, it might also be argued that these regulations also hamper competition between insurance products and alternative products, and might hence impinge on the use of these alternative products for the management of environmental risks. However, in this area also, the present evolution is towards some deregulation of the establishment of captives.

CASE STUDIES

7.1 RENFLEX: Lessons from an Environmental Disaster

RENFLEX[12] used to be, and still is, a medium-sized company that, after a few years of difficulties, was in very good financial condition in 199*, just when the accident occurred. Founded in the early 1960s, it was established in the centre of a large European Union member country; it produced high-value-added chemicals on a small niche market, and was commercially very successful on export markets at that time, having just received an internationally celebrated award for some its nearly 900 products. Its brand new facilities were situated nearby a large river and, at that time, it employed 300 people.

The accident happened at the beginning of the 1990s, at about 3 a.m. An explosion, followed by a very strong fire, occurred. The fire brigade were obliged to make use of large quantities of foam and water in order to prevent nearby stocks of very dangerous products being caught by the fire and subsequently exploding. However, in the absence of any adequate security facilities, the waters were polluted by some chemicals caught in the fire and by some waste chemicals that were buried over the site. These reached the nearby river, leading to devastating pollution, destroying freshwater life (fish and other aquatic species) over a large area, as well as some birds and other ground animals that were involved in the ecological systems in that area. Furthermore, in the nearby city (more than 200 000 inhabitants) about 160 000 persons were deprived of drinkable water for several days. At the time when the fire started, about ten persons were present, including a foreman. Nobody knew the precise time when the fire started, nor its exact origin. A subsequent inquiry by official authorities led to a report in which it was assumed that an error in the mixture of chemicals in a reactor was a likely cause of the explosion. This official report also pointed out that at least two other less serious accidents had occurred over the previous ten years, and that the people present in the plant apparently had received no adequate security, emergency or fire training. The consequences of this accident were quite heavy for all of the firm's stakeholders. One of the workers present was seriously burnt; personal injuries were also sustained by members of the fire brigade, while others suffered from smoke inhalation. Damage to the environment concerned both the atmosphere and fresh-water nearby. A cloud composed of highly toxic chemical species, such as hydrogen cyanide and nitrogen oxides, was dispersed into the atmosphere, but the heaviest toll concerned the nearby river, where chemicals had devastating effects on most of the aquatic species. About 20 tonnes of dead fish were taken from the waters and buried. Since almost all aquatic species had been hit, it took a considerable time to restore all the ecological chains. The total costs – exclusive of compliance costs that were subsequently imposed on the firm by the authorities – amounted to €24.56 million, out of which €12.08 million represented damage to the firm's production facilities and buildings, as well as financial losses due to the fact that the plant was closed down for several months after the accident. The remainder of €12.48 million concerned damage to other stakeholders, including employees, the nearby local authorities, the community as a whole, and the environment, as well as to other private firms. However, RENFLEX's insurance policy only provided for a maximum coverage of €0.9 million, so that RENFLEX, as a result of this disaster, had to face enormous liabilities, much in excess of its insurance coverage. Moreover, the subsequent compliance and preventive costs (building a retention wall to prevent any waste waters from reaching the river, suitable security investments for the protection of personnel, and waste treatment facilities) amounted to about €500 000. It was very clear from the official and subsequent expertise reports that, had such an investment (representing only a comparatively small 3.2 per cent of the damages) been carried out beforehand as a preventive step, it would have been very effective in preventing most (if not all) of the damage that occurred.

The firm's image, as well as its financial situation, was severely damaged for more than four years as a result of this disaster. It was able to overcome the huge costs imposed by this accident, through its own funds, as well as through a bank loan. This, though, necessitated severe cuts in its expenses, personnel decreasing to some 240 persons over the next five years. A little less than ten years after the disaster, the firm invested some €15 million, including about €1 million for pollution prevention equipment that completed previous environmental protection investments. This new investment aimed at doubling its production, thus creating 90 new jobs.

In terms of risk-management arrangements, after the accident the firm established a captive in Ireland, with coverage for environmental liabilities up to €9 million, with reinsurance over €2 million. The reinsurance company conducted a very strict environmental audit before signing the reinsurance treaty with the captive, and its guarantee became effective only after completion of the suitable environmental protection investments amounting to €500 000 that occurred just after the accident; the reinsurance company also fostered some adequate training of the personnel immediately after the new facilities were available.

7.2 Swiss Re: A Reinsurance Company Concerned with the Environment

Introduction

Swiss Re, formerly Swiss Reinsurance Company[13], was established in 1863. It is one of the largest Swiss companies, quoted on the Swiss Stock Exchange (at Zürich and Geneva, in particular). It has affiliated companies in over 30 countries throughout the world and in all continents. It employed about 8,800 persons (5,700 in Europe) at the beginning of 1999. In early 1999, the shareholders' equity was about CHF17 billion at market values, its gross premiums turnover was CHF18 billion, and its net after-tax result in 1998 was CHF2.504 billion. As shown by its name, the company is involved in reinsurance and insurance products, concerning both life and non-life insurance, asset management, and other financial activities linked with its reinsurance activities. Taking into account environmental concerns is one of its key orientations, and the environment is integrated into its management both in terms of supplying environmentally oriented products, and in terms of taking into account the environment in all its operations. It established an environmental management system for ISO 14001 certification some time during the year 2000. Let us successively examine its environmentally oriented products, its investments, and the environmental management of its operations.

Environmentally oriented products

Concerning one of its main activities, which is of course reinsurance, Swiss Re offers reinsurance coverage oriented towards environmental protection and protection against natural catastrophes on all the segments of its markets: traditional insurance companies, captive insurance companies, and insurance pools. Underwriting of reinsurance is only provided after a careful audit of the environmental risks of its clients' policy-holders. This means imposing some prevention efforts and investment guidelines on insurance companies and insurance pools, and on large corporations that reinsure coverage granted through a captive. It also supports insurers and corporations in developing efficient prevention against environmental risks. In several European countries, Swiss Re has a sizeable stake in the capital of the existing environmental insurance pools, such as Assurpol in France (its participation being 7.5 per cent), Pool Inaquimento in Italy, MSV Pool in the Netherlands, and other similar pools in Denmark and Spain. In the UK, Swiss Re participated in a task group of the Association of British Insurers, contributing to establishing a guideline for issuing environmental risk-insurance policies, directed at British insurers. It also built engineering software tools for the assessment and benchmarking of environmental risks in various industries, including the oil and petrochemical industry.

Investments

In terms of investment, Swiss Re is managing a venture-capital portfolio of about CHF100 million, which is directed at young companies with promising financial prospects and good ecological performances and orientations. These investments mainly concern companies world wide involved in renewable energies, such as solar and wind energy. Specific methodologies have been developed to estimate sustainability criteria and outlooks. Swiss Re is also conducting research with some leading academic institutions (including the Wharton School at the University of Pennsylvania) in order to assess corporate environmental risks.

Environmental management of Swiss Re's operations

Last, but not least, Swiss Re has been concerned with its operational environmental management since the early 1990s, in terms of purchasing management of consumable office supplies and equipment. This concerns all its main locations, including Zürich (about 2 700 employees), New York (about 1 200 employees), London (about 700 employees) and Munich. Environmental management has become an important part of its logistics, including not only procurement but also business travel, and, in particular, aiming at reducing CO_2 emissions due to business travel.

Swiss Re established a number of environmental management indicators (Table 7.2) for its Zürich site, which it aims to improve in the future.

As mentioned previously, Swiss Re intends to obtain ISO 14001 certification by the end of the year 2000.

Finally, Swiss Re has numerous exchanges with suitable partners about environmental risks and natural disasters, concerning which it conducts studies and supports research.

Table 7.2 Environmental performance indicators for the Zürich facilities of Swiss Re

Indicators	Absolute	Relative
Electric energy consumption	20 173 MWh	7 455 kWh per employee
Heating energy consumption	11 070 MWh	85 kWh/m^2
Water consumption	89 893 m^3	1 331 per employee per day
Paper consumption	504 tonnes	186 kg per employee
Copying paper consumption	37 240 881 A4 sheets	55 A4 sheets per employee per day
Total amount of waste	938 tonnes	347 kg per employee
Total business travel	37 522 975 km	13 687 km per employee
Total CO$_2$ emissions	20 667 tonnes	7 638 kg per employee

Source:
Swiss Re Environmental Report (1998).

NOTES

1. We gratefully acknowledge the reviewing of this chapter by Ephraim Clark, Greg Hertzler, and John Quiggin. Any remaining errors or omissions are of course our sole responsibility.
2. This applies, in principle, to common property. However, whenever Hardin's parable of tragedy of the commons' (1968) is valid, the protection of common property will be less efficient than in the case of private property. This is true even under the legal principle of liability for damages to property. The validity of Hardin's parable, however, is restricted to societies where individualism prevails with little or no social control over 'free-riding' behaviour. Examples of collective property that is well kept are common in other cultures.
3. In many jurisdictions, however, all other insurance companies will cover the defaulting insurer's liabilities, at least up to a ceiling.

4. Up to its equity, as mentioned above in the case of ordinary insurance companies that are not reinsured.
5. In some jurisdictions, captives are not allowed to sell insurance services outside their parent group and affiliates, as this is considered as unfair competition to the country's traditional insurance companies.
6. In most countries, because of prudential regulations, a minimum capital is necessary to establish an insurance company.
7. In Ireland, captives established in Dublin's International Financial Services Centre (IFSC) support a taxation rate of only 10 per cent; in Luxembourg, income deductions for fluctuations of occurrences of up to 20 times the amount of premiums are allowed, so that captives are virtually tax-free.
8. Captives established in Ireland and Luxembourg may be liable to corporate tax in some other European countries as if the profits were obtained in these countries, which deprives them of any fiscal advantage.
9. Personally insuring the group's employees through captives may be restricted or prohibited in some jurisdictions.
10. As noticed previously, the Bermuda location is no more a tax-free location for American companies, but its advantages are that only minimal capital is required for the establishment of an insurance company, and that the regulatory constraints are also minimal, thus preventing delays for administrative approvals.
11. Involving, for instance, minimum equity or net worth constraints.
12. This is a real case; however, for confidentiality reasons, the name of the company and some features of the case have been either changed or hidden.
13. Suisse de Réassurance in French and Schweizer Rückversicherung in German.

REFERENCES

Association of British Insurers (ABI), Joint Pollution Working Group (1998), *Recommendations for the Underwriting of Pollution Risks*. London: ABI.
Calow, P. (ed.) (1998), *Handbook for Environmental Risk Assessment and Management*, Oxford: Blackwell.
David, L. and Barnaud, L. (1999), *Insuring what Risks? An Inquiry in Industry and with Insurers. Synthesis and Analysis*, Paris: Presses de l'Ecole des Mines de Paris, in French.
Freeman, P.K. and Kunreuther, H. (1997), *Managing Environmental Risk Through Insurance*, Boston: Kluwer.
Hardin, G. (1968), 'The tragedy of the commons', *Science*, **162**: 1243–8.
Kronenberg, W. III (1995), 'The Environmental Insurance Markets in the US and Western Europe: A US underwriter's observations', *The Geneva Papers on Risk and Insurance*, **20** (76) (July): 336–47.
Porat, M.M. and Powers, M.R. (1995), 'Captive insurance tax policy: resolving a global problem', *The Geneva Papers on Risk and Insurance*, **20** (75) (April): 197–229.
Ritchie, B. and Marshall, D. (1993), *Business Risk Management*, London: Chapman and Hall.

Swiss Re (2000), *Financial Reports* for various years, http://www.swissre.com.

Wilson, A.R. (1991), *Environmental Risk: Identification and Management*, Chelsea, MS: Lewis Publishers.

Zagalski, C.A. Jr. (1991), *Environmental Risk and Insurance*, Chelsea, MS: Lewis Publishers.

Zeckhauser, R. (1996), 'Insurance and catastrophes', *The Geneva Papers on Risk and Insurance*, **21** (78) (January): 3–21.

8. Environmental Management Systems: the ISO 14001 and EMAS International Standards

SUMMARY

Whereas the previous chapters were mostly concerned with specific management functions, Chapter 8 examines the all-encompassing and company-wide concept of the environmental management system (EMS). An EMS involves the highest management levels, and, inasmuch as the environmental quality of goods is closely related to the environmental performance of the firm, the EMS is of interest to many stakeholders. The chapter first provides historical perspective by relating how the ISO 14001 and EMAS group of norms emerged. They were an offshoot of the Total Quality Management movement, which had sprung up in reaction to Taylorism. After a brief discussion of the basic differences between ISO 14001 and EMAS, a detailed description of each is given, together with further possible extensions that have been suggested. Because ISO 14001 is genuinely international in scope, it is very open and flexible. This translates into a lack of any specific performance standards. Instead, given that different countries vary widely in their environmental regulations, the focus is on continual improvement from wherever the firm started. EMAS is narrower in scope, mainly limited to industrial sites in EU countries; but, being more demanding, it provides greater assurance to financial bodies (banks, insurers, investors). These differences carry forward to third-party certification, the benefits and costs of which are analysed. Finally, the value of ISO 14001 certification in the context of globalization is considered. It seems that the richest countries, and the largest firms with multinational activities, are mainly concerned. One may ask, is ISO 14001 certification a game for the rich? Things, however, are evolving quickly.

1. INTRODUCTION

In previous chapters, we discussed how the environment might be taken into account by various business functions, such as accounting and financial management (Chapters 4, 5 and 6) and risk management (Chapter 7). However, for various reasons, environmental management appears to be an all-embracing concern, which is therefore of interest not only to specialized management functions but also to the top management of a firm. Thus, the concept of an overall Environmental Management System (EMS) has become one of the key concepts of environmental management.

There are several reasons why environmental management has become an all-embracing concern. A main one is that the environmental quality of goods and services is a quality attribute, which is of increasing importance to consumers, including end-consumers and corporate consumers. Furthermore, inasmuch as the environmental qualities of goods are closely related to the environmental performance of the firm, they are of interest to most stakeholders and must, thus, be a concern of management globally, including Chief Executive Officers (CEOs). Finally, stakeholders might want evidence of the firm's commitment towards environmental protection. The firm's clients, shareholders, bank and insurance company, together with the environmental protection agencies of the country or countries in which it operates, are just some examples of stakeholders that might request some evidence of the firm's environmental performance. Such evidence can be obtained through third-party certification of the firm's EMS, a concept which recently emerged with international EMS standards such as the ISO 14001 standards and the EMAS European Union standards.

The present chapter thus mainly intends to discuss the international EMS standards that emerged recently, and especially the ISO 14001 and EMAS standards. It is organized as follows. After a historical survey concerning the emergence of the ISO 14000 and EMAS families of norms for environmental management, we shall discuss the contents of these norms, focusing on the international ISO 14001 norms, which lend themselves to third-party certification. We also discuss the importance of these norms in the management of the firm. These norms are useful in that they provide clear and standardized guidelines, which make it easier and less costly to set up and run an EMS. These norms are voluntary and international in essence, and provide one of the vectors of environmental performance in today's global economy.

2. THE EMERGENCE OF THE ISO 14000 AND EMAS FAMILIES OF ENVIRONMENTAL MANAGEMENT NORMS

Standardization and industrial standards have been an important feature of business management since the Industrial Revolution, and many large industrial corporations have used them since the middle of the nineteenth century. The very name of one of the most famous of these companies, Rockefeller's Standard Oil Company (founded in 1871), is a witness to this trend: as is well known, Standard Oil based its early reputation on supplying a constant and standardized quality of lighting oil. Standardization of product quality was something Fredrick Taylor insisted on in his *Scientific Management*, published in 1911, which was a pioneering work in industrial management, giving operational principles for the management of large industrial organizations. An important Taylorian principle, however, is that one of the sources of industrial competitiveness is to be found in *standardizing the qualities of the product*, these being defined as observable technical qualities. Clearly, this principle was hardly a novelty in Taylor's time, as many large corporations had already applied it. The same was true with the other basic management principle invoked by Taylor, which was that *productivity of labour* may be enhanced; in particular, through a rational industrial organization stressing *division of labour* rather than through other variables such as qualification and personnel training. Clearly, Taylor's insistence on division of labour was not something new when his *Scientific Management* was published in 1911: more than one century earlier, in 1774, Adam Smith in his *Wealth of Nations* had stressed the importance of division of labour as one of the sources of economic growth and wealth creation.

Natural resources played only a negligible role in Taylor's corporation and its management, inasmuch as they were often, implicitly rather than explicitly, considered as goods for which there was an almost unlimited supply at a very low price. As for the environment as such, it was (implicitly again) considered as a free good, supplying free services to production and to firms. In particular, the environment acts as a receptacle for undesirable by-products. These by-products could be gaseous, solid particles, liquid emissions or solid waste, which are diluted, transformed and in some cases even destroyed when the environment is an infinite receptacle; an implicit assumption that was made in the Taylorian corporation. Here, however, is the problem, because environmental services, once thought of implicitly as free, become more and more costly, often in an indirect manner, through regulations and through consumer concerns. Moreover, goods that were once thought of as free goods, such as water for industrial and agricultural production, have become costly goods. They have a price. They are no longer free goods.

Another feature of Taylor's management, which has changed rapidly since the early 1960s, is its conception of product or service quality. In Taylor's original approach, quality is a set of technical specifications, such as mechanical and physicochemical properties, which may be verified by the consumer, either directly or indirectly (through guarantee systems). More indirect qualities of a good, such as its environmental qualities, that are not directly accessible to consumers, were of less interest to Taylor's corporation. For Taylor and his followers, quality is a set of direct technical characteristics that are maintained at a satisfactory level through standardization of productions.

Historically, and more recently, there has been a strong shift against Taylorian conceptions, and this shift was especially oriented towards a new attitude to quality that may be traced back to the Second World War. A forerunner of this movement was Walter Shewart, who used to be a research physicist with AT&T-Bell Laboratories before the Second World War. During and immediately after the Second World War, Shewart's ideas were actually implemented in large American industrial corporations; first, for military equipment, and, at a later stage, for all other industries, including services. Shewart's ideas, as implemented in some large US industries, represented a break with Taylorian practices.

The latter, which were still in use in many US and European industries and activities well after 1945, involved scrapping or dumping defective products as refuse. This is a costly practice because defective products have been produced at a cost and cannot be sold. Dumping scrap products, however, amounts to using the environment as a free receptacle, thus creating pollution or nuisances. To address the problem of defects, Shewart, with a small think-tank created at Stanford University in California for training war-industries engineers and managers, was one of the first advocates of *total quality management*. By total quality management, we mean a total *ex ante*, often automatic or built-in the equipment control of the technical attributes of quality. On the other hand, Taylorian corporations, in order to foster simple and high-productivity tasks, often only practised an *ex post* control, which was but another specialised task within the framework of an extremely developed division of labour.

A student of Shewart at Stanford was W. Edwards Deming, who happened to be sent to Japan by the US Census Bureau in 1946 with a mission that was to contribute to the training of Japanese managers to new quality-management methods that had been developed in the USA. Japanese engineers and managers, and Japanese firms, were especially receptive to new ideas on quality, and a number of influential members of the Japanese Union of Scientists and Engineers (JUSE) themselves became pioneers of the new Total Quality concepts. The name of Kaoru Ishikawa remains prominent within this movement, that, in the 1950s and 1960s, was to take on enormous importance in Japanese industries, while European and American Corporations still stuck to Taylorian recipes and practices. Early in the 1950s and 1960s, Japanese firms implemented the new industrial management methods. Toyota was one of the first major firms to put these methods into practice, and that is why it has become customary to refer to them and their practical development as Toyotism, as opposed to Fordism. What is the essence of these new management methods, which are in many respects a break with Taylorian methods and techniques?

The basic idea about quality is that it is no more capable of *ex post* control as any other specialized task within the Taylorian division of labour, which is supposed to boost productivity to its highest level. In the Taylorian corporation, we typically have specialized persons, whose task is to control or inspect finished products and/or half-products, detecting any defects within these. The defective product is thus either reconditioned or scrapped, which, in the latter case, leads to environmental problems.

The new management approach, as applied first to Japanese industries and later to European and American corporations, is quite different. Here, the idea is to check for defects *ex ante*, avoiding or preventing defects rather than having to correct them or eliminate defective products *ex post*. Thus, there is a built-in control process that ideally should avoid any defects; hence the idea of Total Quality Management (TQM), or zero-defect management, which appeared in Japan during the 1960s, and later in the United States and elsewhere. In TQM firms, everybody is responsible for altogether *avoiding*, rather than eliminating defects; hence the idea (probably born in Japan) of *quality circles*. In these quality circles, members of personnel of a firm gather informally, and irrespective of their position in the hierarchy of the firm, to solve quality problems before they ever give rise to defects. The very idea of quality circles is completely at odds with the Taylorian organization of the firm, which rests on a vertical, quasi-military hierarchy in which communication between employees with different tasks is excluded.

By the early 1970s, American and European observers and managers began to worry about the loss of competitiveness of their corporations in comparison to their Japanese competitors. One of the reasons invoked to explain this situation was the implementation by Japanese firms of Total Quality Management systems, as opposed to their ongoing Taylorian practices. These concerns eventually lead to viewing the Japanese corporation as a model, to such an extent that it even became for some a sort of a mythical model. Recently, however, some weaknesses of Japanese firms showed up, especially with respect to their financial management. It remains true, however, that a number of principles concerning quality management have been put into practice by Japanese managers, and now also by managers throughout the world.

Since the 1960s, quality has broadened and extends now to symbolic qualities of products, as well as to quality attributes, which, while they are practically observable, cannot be verified or ascertained by consumers or firms' clients. Environmental qualities of goods are part of such attributes, also called *experience attributes* or *credence attributes*. Closely linked to

TQM is the problem of international norms for quality-management systems, which were addressed by the ISO 9000 norms for quality management at the end of the 1980s.

The ISO (International Standards Organization) was established in 1946, with its headquarters located at Geneva, Switzerland. At that time, its main objective was to issue worldwide technical and safety standards for various categories of products, including industrial products and, later, services, such as telecommunication services. By the end of the 1980s, the ISO became concerned with the introduction of Total Quality into management practices, this concern leading to the ISO 9000 series of standards for quality management. One may well argue that the ISO 9000 standards introduce TQM into management patterns, for they are concerned with a concept of quality that is much broader than mere technical specifications. This narrower quality concept based on technical specifications prevailed in the early days of ISO, in line with the Taylorian concept of standardization of industrial products.

General, complete and detailed environmental management guidelines were recently defined by the ISO. These guidelines are very helpful to firms wanting to enhance the environmental qualities of their goods.

The British Standard Institution (BSI) first introduced national standards concerning environmental management in the UK by defining the BS (British Standards) 7750 environmental management norms in 1992. The ISO 14001 international norms for environmental management were first introduced four years later, in 1996, along the lines of the ISO 9001 quality-management standards. These ISO 14001 standards closely followed the BS 7750 standards.

At the same time, the European Union developed another series of environmental management standards called the Eco-Management and Audit Scheme (EMAS) aimed at all the 15 European Union member countries (including the UK). The EMAS system closely followed the BS 7750 system, and is also quite close to the ISO 14001 standards.

However, the EMAS system differs from the ISO 14001 norms in several ways. First of all, there is a significant difference between the two families of standards. The ISO 14001 system represents a *group of norms* issued by an international body representing almost all countries of the world. The

EMAS system is a *regulation* issued by the European Union, which is a political body representing the 15 member states. Thus, the ISO 14001 norms are *universal* (or almost so) in their geographical covering; however, the EMAS standards, while primarily derived for EU member countries, are, in effect, international standards, because any firm from any country may endeavour to meet them. A more important limitation of the EMAS system is that it covers only industrial productions. By contrast, the ISO 14001 norms are universal in their activity scope, because any organization, whether producing material goods in agriculture or industry, or producing immaterial services, is eligible for ISO 14001 certification or registration. As we have seen, this is not true of the EMAS system. This limitation is an undesirable one, because we have seen several times in this book that many service organizations, such as banks, should be concerned, and indeed are concerned, with the environment.

The same is true of agricultural activities, which may, in many cases, have a strong and often undesirable impact on the environment, especially whenever intensive farming practices are being used. Another undesirable limitation of the EMAS system is that only sites (production units) are eligible for certification, whereas a whole firm may comply with the ISO 14001 environmental management norms. Thus, the prevailing group of norms of environmental management at the international level is the ISO 14001 system, which is more universal in its scope than the EMAS system, not to mention the fact that the EMAS system concerns only EU member countries. There remains the fact that EMAS norms are more complete in many respects. Thus, a site complying with the ISO 14001 environmental management norms will usually have to take significant steps to comply with the EMAS norms, but the converse is not generally true. We shall describe in detail the contents of the ISO 14000 family of environmental management standards later.

International standards are important from an economic standpoint, because their general implementation should ideally tend to eliminate hidden non-tariff barriers arising from specific national environmental standards, as well as unfair competitive advantages due to low environmental standards.

What we call the ISO 14000 group of norms was developed in 1996 and subsequent years. It is now almost complete and includes several aspects. First, it provides norms for EMSs, including the ISO 14001 norms, which, as mentioned above, are those that lend themselves to registration. Second, it provides norms for the environmental aspects of product quality that are not open to certification, and that concern ecolabelling and Life-cycle Assessment (LCA). These are the ISO 14020, 14021, 14024 and 14025 norms for ecolabelling, and ISO 14040, 14041, 14042 14043 and 14049 norms for Life-cycle Assessment. Thirdly, it provides tools for quantitative evaluation of environmental impacts, including environmental audits (ISO 14010, ISO 14011, ISO 14012 and ISO 14015 norms), environmental performance assessment (ISO 14031 and ISO TR 14032 norms).

Finally, the ISO 14050 norms constitute a standardized vocabulary. Figure 8.1 gives an overview of this categorization of the ISO 14000 group of norms for environmental management systems, product quality-oriented norms, norms for environmental management tools, and also norms for terms and definitions, providing a standardized vocabulary, while Box 8.1 gives the detail of such norms under the same categorization.

We are now going to describe in more detail the contents of the ISO 14000 group of norms, starting with the ISO 14001 EMS-related norms. These norms constitute one of the most important sub-groups within the ISO 14000 group of norms, because they are open to certification. We shall also discuss the EMAS European norms and the EMAS registration scheme, which is very similar to the ISO 14001 certification scheme, just as the EMAS norms are close to the ISO 14000 norms. These are also quite important given the position of the European Union in international trade.

The environmental auditing norms (ISO 14010, 14011, 14012 and 14015), and the environmental accounting aspects of LCA norms (ISO 14040, 14041, 14042, 14043 and 14049) were discussed briefly in Chapter 4 with the various quantitative concepts of environmental accounting. The norms of the ISO 14020 subgroup, concerned with environmental labelling, will be developed in the next chapter, in which the environmental quality of goods will be analysed under other angles.

Figure 8.1   The ISO 14000 norms: an overview

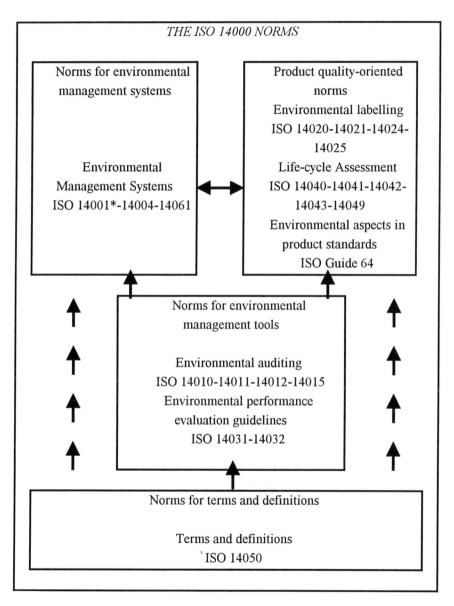

Box 8.1 The detail of the ISO 14000 norms

Norms for environmental management systems
ISO 14001: Environmental Management Systems – Specification with Guidance for Use (1996) ISO 14004: Environmental Management Systems – General Guidelines on Principles, Systems and Supporting Techniques (1996) ISO 14061: Information to Assist Forestry Organizations in the Use of ISO 14001 and ISO 14004 Environmental Management System Standards (1998)

Product quality - oriented norms
Environmental Labelling ISO 14020: Environmental Labels and Declarations – General Principles (2000) ISO 14021: Environmental Labels and Declarations – Self-declared Environmental Claims – Type II Environmental Labelling (1999) ISO 14024: Environmental Labels and Declarations – Type I Environmental Labelling – Principles and Procedures (1999) ISO/TR 14025: Environmental Labels and Declarations – Type III Environmental Declarations (2000) Life Cycle Assessment ISO 14040: Environmental Management – Life Cycle Assessment – Principles and framework (1997) ISO 14041: Environmental management – Life-cycle Assessment – Goal and Scope Definition and Inventory Analysis (1998) ISO 14042: Environmental management – Life-cycle Assessment: Life-cycle impact assessment (2000)

Box 8.1. (continued)

ISO 14043: Environmental Management – Life Cycle Assessment – Life Cycle Interpretation (2000)
ISO/TR 14049: Environmental Management – Life Cycle Assessment: Examples for the Application of the ISO 14041 to Goal and Scope Definition and Inventory Analysis (2000)
Environmental aspects in product standards
ISO Guide 64: Guide for the inclusion of environmental aspects in product standards [Formerly ISO 14060] (1997)

Norms for environmental management tools

Environmental auditing and related environmental investigations
ISO 14010: Guidelines for Environmental Auditing – General Principles (1996)
ISO 14011: Guidelines for environmental auditing: Audit procedures: Auditing of environmental management systems (1996)
ISO 14012: Guidelines for environmental auditing: Qualification criteria for environmental auditors (1996)
Environmental performance evaluation guidelines
ISO 14031: Environmental Management – Environmental Performance Evaluation – Guidelines (1999)
ISO/TR 14032 : Environmental Management – Examples of Environmental Performance Evaluation (1999)

Norms for terms and conditions

Terms and definitions
ISO 14050: Environmental Management – Vocabulary (1998)

We will also come back to the LCA concept in the next chapter, inasmuch as it is related to environmental quality, because the sound evaluation of environmental quality is valid only if it is carried out on the whole life cycle of the product and we will thus deal there with the LCA norms ISO 14040, 14041, 14042, 14043 and 14049. The environmental performance norms (ISO 14031 and 14032), which are especially useful in the application of the ISO 14001 norms, deserve some discussion, however, within this chapter.

3. THE ISO 14001 EMS NORMS

3.1 Overview

In this section, we intend to discuss the general philosophy of the ISO 14001 norms. We will also be concerned with their practical implementation, which is discussed in detail by Sheldon and Yoxon (1999). At the start of our presentation of the ISO 14001 EMS norms, it is useful to make it clear that *they are not norms of environmental performance*. They are rather standards for environmental management standards, committing the firm to *comply with the existing regulations*, irrespective of environmental performances beyond those imposed by such compliance. These norms may be certified through an audit by a third party, usually some specialized or consulting firm. One of the essential features of these norms is that they provide standards for the description and fulfilment of environmental objectives and targets, with further commitment to *continuous improvement* in environmental performances. However, provided compliance and continuous improvement standards are respected, the firm conforming to the ISO 14001 norms is free to set up the level of these objectives and targets. The quantitative levels of these objectives and targets are thus not provided for in the ISO 14001 norms. They are left to the individual firm setting up an EMS, provided they comply with the existing regulations. This scheme carries several implications. First of all, norms for environmental performance are manifold, as they vary from country to country and industry to industry according to the local environmental policies and the environmental regulations applying to specific industries.

EMS norms, as described by the ISO 14001 standards, are not norms of environmental performance. They are EMS norms, and they are universal. They may apply to any firm or organization, whatever its activities, nationality, or location of its facilities.

The ISO 14001 norms, which are open to certification, are based on a management principle that was initially applied to quality management and to ISO 9000 quality-management norms. This principle, as applied to quality management, is *continual improvement* of product quality. It is the cornerstone of modern quality management, which constitutes the basis of the ISO 9000 norms. More precisely, the continual improvement approach of the ISO 14001 norms rests on a variant of the so-called *Deming cycle*, or Deming's 'plan–do–check' cycle, also called 'Deming's wheel' by some authors. Deming's 'plan–do–check' cycle basically requires a planning stage, then an action stage, and then a checking stage, before coming back to the planning stage and carrying out a second Deming cycle, followed by successive cycles on a continuous-improvement basis. The somewhat more complex continual-improvement cycle of the ISO 14001 norms is composed of five steps: environmental policy; planning; implementation and operation; checking and corrective action; and, finally, management review (Figure 8.2). This aims at creating a self-sustaining virtuous circle, with continual improvement of the environmental performance of the firm. The idea is that, although there is no environmental performance norm or target supplied in the ISO 14001 norm, such a norm, if suitably implemented, is able to foster some kind of continuous-improvement cycle that will enable the firm to reach targets for high environmental performance.

We will discuss further the role and the interest of the ISO 14001 norms, and of ISO 14001 certification for the relationships of the firm with its various stakeholders. Before doing so, it is of course important to give some details about the ISO 14001 norms. The outline of ISO 14001 appears in Box 8.2. In this outline, while points 1, 2 and 3 describe preliminary concepts and definitions relating to the ISO 14001 norms, point 4 gives detailed specifications for the various steps of the continuous-improvement process.

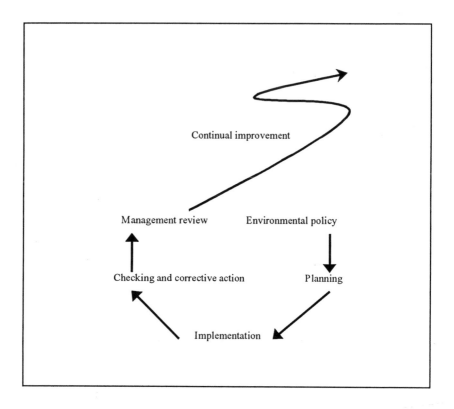

Figure 8.2   The continual improvement cycle of the ISO 14001 norms

As noted above, there are five essential steps that should be carried out for ISO 14001 certification: devising and stating an environmental policy for the organization; planning for environmental performance objectives; implementing an EMS; checking the results with appropriate corrective actions; and carrying out a management review. To these steps, that are clearly required for ISO 14001 certification, Sturm (2001) proposes the addition of two other steps: a preliminary environmental review, which should follow the establishment of a suitable environmental policy, and an environmental report after all other steps have been completed.

Box 8.2 Outline of the ISO 14001 norms

ISO 14001 norms (1996):

Environmental management systems – Specification with guidance for use

Introduction
1.   Scope
2.   Normative references
3.   Definitions
4.   Environmental management systems requirement
    4.1   General requirements
    4.2   Environmental policy
    4.3   Planning
       4.3.1 Environmental aspects
       4.3.2 Legal and other requirements
       4.3.3 Objectives and targets
       4.3.4 Environmental management programme
    4.4   Implementation and operation
       4.4.1 Structure and responsibility
       4.4.2 Training, awareness and competence
       4.4.3 Communication
       4.4.4 Environmental management systems documentation
       4.4.5 Document control
       4.4.6 Operation control
       4.4.7 Emergency preparedness and response
    4.5   Checking and corrective action
       4.5.1 Monitoring and measurement
       4.5.2 Nonconformance and corrective and preventive action
       4.5.3 Records
       4.5.4 Environmental management system audit
    4.6   Management review

Annexes
    Annex A Guidance on the use of specification
    Annex B Links between ISO 14001 and ISO 9001
    Annex C Bibliography

Note: These are extracts from BS EN ISO 14001 (1996), reproduced with the permission of BSI under licence number 2001SK/0133. Complete copies of the standard may be obtained from BSI Customer Services, 389 Chiswick High Road, London W4 4 AL, UK, or, in countries other than the UK, from the local national standard organization.

Although neither of these two steps is a requirement under ISO 14001 specifications, they are good practice, because some stakeholders might require them. Furthermore, an environmental report is compulsory under EMAS.

Our presentation of the ISO 14001 norms will stick to these five essential steps, mentioning in detail the additional steps that could be taken: environmental policy, planning, implementation and operation, checking and corrective action, and management review.

3.2 Step 1 (Point 4.1 of ISO 14001): The Firm's Environmental Policy

The definition of an environmental policy is the first and basic step, and the cornerstone of an EMS under the ISO 14001 norms. Working out an EMS system is a top-down approach, justified by the fact that commitment of the firm's top management is a prerequisite to any management pursuit. The ISO 14001 norms thus provide for *commitment of the firm's top management* towards some environmental policy objectives. This commitment will, of course, start with the approval of the company's Chief Executive Officer (CEO), and of other executives that stand at a responsible level. The process of establishing the environmental policy may be a trial-and-error process implying a progressive improvement of the policy formulation, converging towards a final formulation that will secure approval from the top management of the firm, and from its CEO. A draft environmental policy may be submitted to all these responsible persons, as well as to external consultants. At this stage, suggestions and remarks will be expressed, and they will be taken into account for a second draft, which will be submitted to the same process, resulting in successive drafts until a final version of the policy is approved by the firm's top management and CEO. The environmental policy resulting from that process will usually be described in some *environmental policy statement*, which will be a brief document, approved and formally endorsed by the company's CEO, with clear management objectives concerning the environment. These objectives should be appropriate and commensurate to the firm's situation, to its products or services, and to their environmental impacts. They must include *compliance with the environmental legislation and regulations applicable to the firm's facilities*, as well as to other environmental obligations and commitments accepted by the firm. An international group the facilities of which are located in several countries with different regulations has to define the contents of this compliance requirement, and several questions are to be addressed in this respect. Should it merely comply with the existing national environmental legislation and regulation in each country in which it operates, or should it go further than the existing national legislations and regulations? While a minimal compliance would require only compliance with the existing national environmental requirements at a given date, it may be good to take a proactive stance and to anticipate the future evolution of environmental requirements in each country. It may also be wise to avoid discrepancies in the standards applicable to various facilities located in different countries and to apply only the standards applicable in the country with the most stringent standards. This is, for instance, the approach taken by the Franco-Italian firm ST Microelectronics (as shown in the case study concerning ST Microelectronics at the end of this chapter).

Under ISO 14001, environmental policies also have to provide for *continual improvement* and for preventing, rather than repairing, environmental damages and impacts. This is indeed an essential (and mandatory) part of any environmental corporate policy under ISO 14001 norms. This means commitment towards continuously improving the environmental qualities of the firm's products, its environmental performance, as well as its environmental management system.

ISO 14001 does not explicitly require that the firm's environmental policy be described in a written document available to all stakeholders. The specifications, however, imply that the contents of the policy should be available, especially to employees and executives responsible for it, under the form of a written document or in written documents. These contents must therefore be described fully in adequate documents, implemented and maintained. The firm's environmental policy should be communicated to all the firm's employees. Finally, it should also be made available to the general public and to all other stakeholders.

In practice, many firms internally issue some detailed written documents concerning their environmental policy, which give a concise but accurate coverage of all aspects of environmental policies. It is clearly essential that these documents be supplied to all executives concerned with the environmental management of the firm. Shorter written environmental policy statements will usually be made available to all the firm's employees, and may be posted in suitable places throughout the firm's facilities. It is also good practice to make these available to all other stakeholders, and to the general public, so that an environmental policy statement will usually be included within the firm's environmental report.

However, while a written document that should publicly be disclosed is mandatory under the EMAS system, the requirements under ISO 14001 are less stringent; it must only be 'documented' and publicized under ISO 14001 norms. Another difference is that, under the EMAS norms, the environmental policy statement has to be formally certified by a third party, which in practice means that an environmental policy defined as a written statement summing up 'all the intentions and principles [of the firm] in relation to its overall environmental performance' (ISO 14001) is made available. Environmental policy statements are related to so-called quality charters developed in the context of quality management and within the framework of the ISO 9000 family of quality-management norms. As mentioned above, the ISO 9000 norms have provided a model along which the ISO 14000 family of EMS norms were developed. They are also related to environmental charters that will be discussed in Chapter 9. Provided they are suitably oriented, these environmental charters can be a component of environmental policy statements issued by individual firms under ISO 14001 norms. These environmental charters, or the environmental policy charters or statements are useful in that they sum up, in a concise and incisive manner, the main principles of the detailed environmental policy of the firm: no more and no less. In the context of ISO 14001 certification, they may appear in a document concerning the firm's environmental policy, which in turn may appear in a firm's environmental report.

Environmental policy charters state the main principles, objectives and aspects of an environmental policy. In this context, they are usually followed by some more detailed description of the firm's environmental corporate policy, which constitutes the firm's environmental policy statement, which itself is followed by the bulk of the firm's environmental report.

The guidelines of environmental policy of the Sony group in 1999, are, for instance, given below (Box 8.3); it is part of Sony's environmental report for 1998. The Sony group has been the first large industrial group to be certified under ISO 14001 norms, even before the ISO 14001 norms were officially published, since it complied with these norms at the end of 1995. This environmental policy guideline statement is indeed in line with the ISO 14001 certification, so that many of its aspects are consistent with the requirements of the ISO 14001 norms. It gives some ideas about the principles underlying Sony's environmental policy. More generally, it provides some ideas about the principles underlying the environmental policy of a firm that underwent ISO 14001 certification, as is the case of the Sony Group since 1995.

There are several key points here. The statement explicitly mentions compliance with existing legislations, regulations and agreements throughout the world (point 3), mentioning autonomous standards for 'even more effective environmental protection'. It also clearly refers to continual improvement in Points 2, 4 (in which it is mentioned that the Group will 'pursue improvements' of its environmental management) and 7. Points 9 and 10 address the internal and external communication and information requirements.

Finally, the first mandatory step in the implementation of an EMS is to define the details of an environmental policy adapted to the firm's needs, products and specific economic situation, providing in particular for compliance and continual improvement.

This policy has to be approved in its final details by the management of the firm at the top responsible levels (and in particular by the company's Chief Executive Officer (CEO), suitably documented, made known to the firm's personnel and executives, and made available to the other stakeholders in a appropriate form. This will be, for instance, a written statement which is part of the company's environmental report, expressing the CEO's commitment towards some basic principles that constitute the environmental policy of the company.

Box 8.3   Environmental policy statement of the Sony group (1999)

Sony group environmental policy guidelines

1. The Sony Group will form and maintain an organization that can promote a variety of environmental promotion activities.
2. The Group will establish technically and economically viable environmental objectives and constantly seek to enhance the quality of its conservation activities.
3. Group companies will observe all applicable laws, regulations and agreements related to the environment. Moreover, the Group will create autonomous standards for even more effective environmental protection.
4. The Group will pursue improvements in all areas of operations, including resource and energy conservation, recycling and the reduction of waste.
5. To the fullest extent possible, the Group will adopt alternative technologies and materials in place of environmentally harmful processes and materials, such as ozone-depleting substances, greenhouse gases and other pollutants. The Group will also collect and recycle such substances and take other steps to minimize their use.
6. The Group will make products and develop technologies that minimize environmental impact.
7. Through environmental audits, the Group will continually endeavour to update its environmental management capabilities.
8. The Group will contribute to society through community activities related to the environment.
9. Through education and internal communications, the Group will strive to install a better understanding of its environmental issues among all employees.
10. As required, Sony will publicly disclose information on its development of environmental technologies, materials and products as well as its environmental management activities.

3.3 Step 2 (Point 4.2 of ISO 14001): Planning the Environmental Policy

Assuming that the environmental policy has been defined, completed and approved by the top management of the firm, *planning* is the second essential step in implementing an EMS according to the ISO 14001 norms. This means that any firm or organization that is implementing the ISO 14001 norms should formulate a plan aimed at fulfilling the objectives of its environmental policy. This planning step starts by identifying the environmental aspects and impacts of the activities of the firm or organization. It has to identify environmental objectives and targets that are in line with the environmental policy, with the legal requirements and with performance criteria. Although this is a requirement only under the EMAS system and not under ISO 14001, it is advisable to conduct an initial environmental review before the planning step of Deming's cycle.

This initial environmental review is important in supplying the data on which the planning step will rely in building up some quantified objectives and targets, which are part of a continual improvement process. It may be used in order to assess to what extent the firm or organization complies to the requirements of ISO 14001 in the first place. If the firm does comply, the review will identify the areas in which continual improvement of the environmental performance may be sought and planned.

A prerequisite to any implementation of the planning step, which is part of the step under ISO 14001, is to evaluate the *environmental aspects* of the firm's activities, ideally using the results of a preliminary environmental review. This means that the environmental risk exposure due to all activities of the firm, and to all its productions and services, must be identified.

The planning step of the ISO 14001 norms also requires that the *specific legal and other requirements* applying to the environmental impacts of the firm's activities be clearly identified, as well as the degree of compliance with these requirements. At this stage, one may define some objectives and targets in terms of compliance. This requirement is obviously important, given that ISO 14001 implies commitment towards complying with these legal, regulatory and other requirements.

More generally, after completing these preliminary evaluations of the environmental aspects of the firm's activities, and of the legal and other requirements applying to it, one may define *objectives and targets* that should contribute to continual improvement of the firm's environmental performances. According to ISO 14001, *objectives* may be defined as *problems that are identified and have to be solved concerning some of the environmental impacts of the firm's activities*. These are stated as qualitative questions to be addressed, while *targets* are *quantitative goals* to be achieved by some specified deadline in order to solve the above problems or in order to contribute to their solution. For instance, an objective might be for a large industrial firm to 'minimize the emission of greenhouse gases in our European sites', while a target related to this objective might be 'on our European sites, to reduce by 30 per cent our net CO_2 emissions within a two-year period'. In setting up these objectives and targets, it is also worthwhile distinguishing between short-term tactical issues and long-term strategic issues. While the former might imply a time horizon of something like two years, the latter would typically imply a time horizon of five to ten years. Tactical issues, on the one hand, might be minor processes such as retrofitting and overhauling, implying maintenance efforts rather than large investments. On the other hand, strategic issues might involve taking advantage of a large investment for an altogether new facility or plant. Strategic issues might also take advantage of an investment for the complete renewal of existing facilities to improve significantly the environmental performance of these facilities or plants. For instance, a short-term tactical objective might be to 'achieve compliance within three years with the Dutch norms (assumed to be the most stringent) in terms of soil pollution on all our European sites'. A more long-term objective would be to 'achieve a performance of 20 per cent better than the Dutch norms in terms of soil pollution by the main organic pollutants, within seven years, on all our European sites'.

It is important to consider, when setting up such objectives and targets, the technological, financial and commercial constraints that they imply. The firm's objectives and targets, once determined, are then inserted into an environmental management programme. To implement these objectives and targets, whether in the short term or long term, one must determine, taking into account the financial and capital-budgeting possibilities of the firm, which objectives and targets come first and which ones should be delayed or even abandoned. This is a difficult task because this choice among the objectives and targets is a complex multicriteria choice. Furthermore, the environmental management programme is not isolated from the other programmes of the firm; it will be much more efficient if it is fully integrated within the firm's programmes (and in particular within the firm's investment programmes). This is because adequate resources and adequate support from the company's top management are essential in actually implementing the programmes. One may think that this implementation will be optimal if the environmental programmes are fully integrated into the firm's programmes and if the responsibilities for these programmes are clear and effective. The environmental programmes thus bridge the gap between the objectives and targets and their actual implementation, which is the next step of the ISO 14001 continual-improvement cycle.

3.4 Step 3 (Point 4.3 of ISO 14001): Implementation and Operation

Implementation and operation of the programmes comes next. As was already discussed, the actual implementation of the environmental programmes of the firm requires a definition of responsibilities, and, more precisely, under point 4.4.1 of ISO 14001, of *structures and responsibilities*, meaning, in particular, 'roles, responsibilities and authorities'. It also requires that the firm's management allow for the supply of resources that are essential to actual implementation, especially, human and capital resources. These are indispensable to ensure that the programmes in question are actually implemented and operated. In terms of responsibilities, managers will be appointed, who might or might not have other responsibilities, but who will be responsible for specific aspects of the implementation of environmental management. The appointment of these managers will ensure that the operation of the environmental management system complies with the ISO 14001 standards. These managers will also be responsible for 'reporting on the performance of the environmental management system to the top management'. The existence of clear-cut responsibilities at the senior management level is important in so-called compliance insurance schemes, whereby some of the stakeholders obtain some guarantee that there is indeed compliance; a matter that has strong implications in terms of environmental liabilities, in the United States and elsewhere.

The actual implementation and operation of the environmental management system under the ISO 14001 norms next requires the identification of training and qualification needs related to the operation of the environmental management system. This will ensure that the executives and employees of various functions will be aware of the various issues related to the implementation of the environmental management system of the firm, and will have the appropriate 'education, training, and/or experience'. Whenever and wherever necessary, firms should therefore identify the training needs for their employees, and have them properly trained. In the case of vacancies, they should also identify the qualifications and experience needed. This applies at all levels of responsibility, and for all functions related to the firm's environmental management.

Operating controls are also of paramount importance in the implementation and operation of any environmental management system. This means that adequate procedures are to be provided to avoid any departure from the environmental policy of the firm. This concerns all the steps of the life cycle of products, including supply, processes, contracting, and clients. In terms of procurement and supply, this means that the firm must request from its suppliers some specifications about the environmental performance of their products, and that procedures for the environmentally safe processing of these products must be issued. At the process level, if some reputable engineering firm supplies the process technology, it will supply a process book with detailed written procedures for the operation of this technology. Similar procedures are to be established for any internal processing technique, and they should include the operation of the facilities and equipment (for which written directives for use and maintenance should be given to the employees and/or contractors). Finally, this should extend to the firm's clients, which should be supplied products with procedures for use and maintenance avoiding any environmental problem or hazard.

In short, operational control essentially means establishing technical procedures directed at all parties involved at some stage of the life cycle of the products and technologies of the firm, and ensuring that they comply with the requirements imposed by the firm's environmental management system.

More generally, the implementation of the environmental management system requires, under ISO 14001, that some *documentation*, and some *document control*, must be provided for. It is important that internal records documents concerning the EMS are accessible, classified, maintained and updated, and new documents created if necessary. First, this ensures that all pertinent information concerning the EMS is accessible when requested throughout the organization and at all levels of responsibility. It also provides a basis for occasional auditing and reviewing of the EMS and its performance, especially when third-party auditing is carried out. In particular, in the process of ISO 14001 third-party certification, it provides useful and even indispensable information for the certifying or auditing firm.

A related issue is *internal communication*. An EMS should involve channels for communication between the various levels, functions, geographical sites and branches of the firm. All means of communication may be used, and ideally communication should lead to an exchange rather than a one-way flow of information. Any information concerning the EMS that is of general interest in the firm, such as environmental reports, environmental policies and changes in environmental policies, should be made available throughout the firm.

Finally, the implementation of the EMS requests *emergency preparedness and response*, meaning that prevention of accident and emergencies should be strongly emphasized in the first place, to reduce the risk of emergency. If, however, an emergency occurs, procedures that minimize the damages should be provided for. Alert exercises and emergency drills should, for instance, be organized to ensure that an adequate response to an emergency. The security officers, as well as employees generally, should receive adequate training in order to be able to respond satisfactorily to any incident or accident.

3.5 Step 4 (Point 4.4 of ISO 14001): Checking and Corrective Action

Checking and corrective action is the next step of our EMS continual-improvement cycle. It aims at detecting, through suitable auditing processes, any departure from the environmental policy of the firm, from its environmental plans in general, and from the objectives and targets, as well as any nonconformance to the operational control procedures, and taking corrective action if necessary.

It should be emphasized that the expression '*checking and corrective action*' has to be interpreted in a broad sense, meaning that this step of the continual-improvement cycle should rather involve a proactive attitude towards environmental risks. Therefore, *corrective action* in this extended sense is to be primarily interpreted as preventive actions aimed at avoiding falling short of the environmental objectives of the firm. It also means, of course, that appropriate corrective actions in the restricted sense of the term should be conducted if the environmental goals of the firm are not fulfilled, or if an environmental accident or incident occurs.

This step rests heavily on monitoring, measurement and auditing, ensuring that the actual environmental performance complies with the objectives and targets of the EMS. It enables evaluation of conformance and nonconformance, leading to corrective actions whenever necessary.

Measurement and evaluation provides basic information for the firm's management, which is indispensable for checking and corrective action. This is achieved through the implementation of an efficient environmental accounting system (as described in Chapter 3) oriented towards the objectives of the environmental policy. Rather than following up a large number of evaluations and ratios, this environmental accounting system should be aimed at supplying a comparatively small number of figures that correspond to environmental policy objectives. It should also supply, of course, any figures necessary to assess compliance with existing regulations.

As has just been discussed, one of the basic features of this checking and corrective action step of the ISO 14001 is to prevent any nonconformance, and, should it occur, to correct it. It will try to identify the reasons for any nonconformance, if observed, and then to take appropriate steps to correct for it, and to prevent it in the future. The environmental accounting system should also be suitably modified if it proves inadequate in preventing and monitoring any nonconformance. This accounting system is closely related to maintaining *records* of environmental performance and data. These records constitute, so to speak, the memory of the EMS. They should be kept and protected safely. In addition to being useful to the firm's management, they can also be used to answer any requests for information from the firm's stakeholders.

More generally, an *environmental management system audit* procedure should be established, with regular and periodic environmental audits, in order to assess compliance with the firm's EMS objectives and with the ISO 14001 norms.

3.6 Step 5 (Point 4.5 of ISO 14001): Management Review

Management review, the last step of our continual-improvement cycle, involves periodic review of the EMS for the information of the firm's top management. This review will supply the information necessary to modify and improve the firm's environmental policy and to make new environmental plans. More generally, it will start a new cycle of continual improvement.

This periodic management review will investigate the efficiency of the firm's EMS. It will use, for this purpose, conclusions drawn from the periodic EMS audits in order to assess compliance not only with the objectives of the EMS but also with new requests of stakeholders, as well as with technological change. These management reviews should also trigger continual improvement of the processes and of the products with respect to environmental concerns.

3.7 The Other Features of the ISO 14001 Standard

ISO 14001 and ISO 9001-9002-9003 standards
The ISO 14000 standards are very similar to the ISO 9000 standards for quality-management systems. This is, in particular, true of the ISO 14001 norms, and Annex B of the ISO 14001 specification gives the links between ISO 14001 and the corresponding ISO 9000 standards. However, there are

three corresponding specifications within the ISO 9000 series, which are the ISO 9001, ISO 9002 and ISO 9003 series. The ISO 9001 norms are the most complete norms, since they encompass quality management throughout a large part of the life-cycle of the product, including the product design, the production and the quality-control aspects of quality-management systems. The ISO 9002 norms only involve the production and the quality-control aspects of quality-management systems and, finally, the ISO 9003 norms are restricted to quality-control management. All three ISO 9001, ISO 9002 and ISO 9003 may be certified and correspond closely to the ISO 14001 norms, because they involve more or less the same steps, based on a continual-improvement process and on the Deming-cycle concept. However, the ISO 9001, 9002 and 9003 norms are mainly directed to *consumers or clients*, while the ISO 14001 norms are directed to *all stakeholders*. Thus, the orientation of the ISO 9001, 9002 and 9003 norms differs from the orientation of the ISO 14001 norms; it may be argued that ISO 9001, 9002 and 9003 are actually quality norms, while the ISO 14001 norms are EMS norms. It may of course be argued that they are in some way environmental quality norms, but, owing to the fact that they are not environmental performance norms, they may be only minimal environmental quality norms. In other words, they are one element, among others, of environmental quality, which has to be completed by some other elements, such as environmental performance norms, as assessed through the results of an LCA.

Despite these differences, the ISO 9001, 9002 and 9003 norms closely follow the Deming cycle, involving steps that are very similar to those of the ISO 14001 norms. It is therefore quite easy for firms that are already certified under, for instance, the ISO 9001 norms, to implement the ISO 14001 norms, as the EMS may quite readily be built up by using the already existing quality-management system.

Moreover, a growing trend is to integrate quality management with environmental management. An emerging concept is the concept of Total Quality Environmental Management (TQEM) (McInerney and White, 1997; Wever, 1996). The ISO 19011 norms, under preparation in early 2000, are a witness to this trend, as they will constitute a common standard for quality and environmental auditing.

Environmental performance evaluation in ISO 14001 EMSs: the ISO 14031-14032 standards

Other ISO standards which are very useful for the implementation of the ISO 14001 standard are the ISO 14031-14032 standards (ISO, 1999a, b) of Environmental Performance Evaluation (EPE). The ISO 14031 norms, in particular, describe themselves as guidelines for EPE. They rest on the fact that EPE is present at all the stages of the plan–do–check Deming's cycle which form the basis of the ISO 14001 system. One of the essential aspects of the planning stage of the ISO 14001 EMS is EPE planning. At the 'do stage' of the ISO 14001 EMS, one has to use EPE data and information (collecting, analysing and converting data, assessing information, and finally reporting and communicating information). At the 'check and act stage' of the ISO 14001 EMS, one has to carry out reviewing information from EPE data, and the cycle triggers further improvement of the firm's EPE. The ISO 14031 norms, which we will not describe here under their technical details, provide standards for the EPE and for their use within Deming's plan–do–check framework, especially as applied to the ISO 14001 standards. However, while ISO 14031 norms are especially useful as a complement to ISO 14001 norms, they can also be used independently. The ISO/TR 14032 document (ISO, 1999b) provides examples of application of the ISO 14031 EPE standards.

3.8 The EMAS Standards

As mentioned previously, the EMAS norms differ in some ways from the ISO 14001 norms. We already briefly mentioned some of the differences, but we explore these now in more detail.

As noted previously, the scope of the ISO 14001 norms is broader than that of EMAS. The EMAS scheme is restricted to individual sites, and only applies to a limited number of industrial activities. It is in principle geographically restricted to the EU and EEA[1] member countries, but sites outside Europe may seek to meet EMAS standards and obtain EMAS validation. Conversely, the ISO 14001 norms apply to all countries of the world, to whole firms as well as to sites and to all sorts of activities.

It is clear that the EMAS scheme is more demanding and comprehensive than the ISO 14001 scheme. One can say that EMAS certification involves reaching a certain level of environmental performance; from our above discussions, this is not the case of the ISO 14001 norms, so that some stakeholders, such as financial stakeholders, and insurers, prefer EMAS certification to ISO 14001 certification because it indicates a lower level of environmental risks.

Comparing the EMAS norms to those of ISO 14001 leads us to stress the following points :

- EMAS requires a *publicly available environmental statement*, verified by an independent auditor, and an annual statement, which is not a requirement under ISO 14001; EMAS requires a public environmental policy, while ISO 14001 only requires that the environmental policy be publicized.

- EMAS requires an *initial review*, which is only advised under ISO 14001.

- EMAS requires a *full inventory of environmental aspects* on a given site, while ISO 14001 requires the *identification of significant environmental aspects*.

- *Continual improvement* applies to the environmental performance under EMAS, and to the EMS under ISO 14001; environmental objectives should be timed under EMAS, while the EMS should be time-framed under ISO 14001.

- Under EMAS, a firm has to consider the *environmental performance of its contractors and suppliers*, which is not a requirement under ISO 14001.

- Under EMAS, *environmental audits* are to be conducted *every three years* at least, while only periodic audits are required under ISO 14001, with no specification of the periodicity. Quite logically, ISO 14001 audits are EMS audits, while EMAS audits are more performance oriented.

In short, one can say that there are two main differences between EMAS and ISO 14001 norms. The first is that the EMAS norms are more oriented towards environmental performance, while those of ISO 14001 are more EMS oriented, and rest on the Deming 'plan–do–check' cycle, which is less evident in the EMAS norms: EMAS is a *regulation* which is more prescriptive (and more demanding when applicable) than ISO 14001. A second difference is that EMAS requires a *comprehensive environmental statement* which has to be verified by an independent external auditor, together with a simplified annual environmental report: these are not requirements under ISO 14001. A recent *bridging document* between the EMAS and ISO 14001 schemes highlights these differences between the two schemes.

Finally, as far as *certification* is concerned, the EMAS scheme also differs from the ISO 14001 scheme. While self-certification is possible under ISO 14001 (giving to the various stakeholders a signal, which is dependable subject to the reputation and credibility of the firm – see Chapter 9), it is not possible under EMAS. EMAS certification (or rather *verification*, as will be shown later) is more complete and more demanding than ISO 14001 certification. Clearly, in both cases we have *third-party certification* carried out by *external environmental verifiers*. In the EMAS scheme, the term *verification* rather than certification is in use, because an essential part of certification is verification of the environmental statement and of the periodic environmental audits. Furthermore, for EU and EEA-located sites, EMAS verification carries *registration* by some official authority, often an Environmental Protection Agency or Ministry or its equivalent, on the basis of an accredited verifier's report. For sites located outside the EU or EEA, as already mentioned, third-party validation or approval may be sought but this does not carry registration. As far as accreditation of verifiers is concerned, the accreditation bodies for EMAS and ISO 14001 also differ.

Recently, however, the European Commission moved toward closer relationships between the two schemes, through giving the possibility to ISO 14001-certified organizations to have their sites certified under EMAS with only minimal supplementary requirements, mainly including the verification of an environmental statement.

Table 8.1 sums up our comparison between the two systems of standards.

Table 8.1 A comparison between ISO 14001 and EMAS

System element	ISO 14001	EMAS	Features under ISO 14001
Nature of system	ISO 14001	Council Regulation No. 1836/93 Of 29 June 1993	International standard for a voluntary norm
Environmental Management System	Point 4.0 and annex<A1	Annex I, Part B	May concern any organization or firm, in any country
Preparatory environmental review	Annex A.4.2.1	Article 3, paragraph B	Not mandatory
Environmental policy	Point 4.1	Annex I, part C Annex I, parts A and D	Implies commitment to compliance and continual improvement, and must be 'documented and publicly available'
Objectives and targets	Point 4.2	Annex I, part A 4.	ISO 14001 distinguishes between general objectives and quantitative targets
Implementation and operation	Point 4.3	Annex I, parts B4-B5 and D6-D7	–
Checking and corrective action	Point 4.4	Annex I, parts B5-B6 and D6-D7, and annex II	–

	Point 4.5	Annex I, part B1	
Management review			–
Environmental statement	Not mentioned in the ISO 14001 standards	Articles 4 and 5, and Annex V	Not a requirement inasmuch as not mentioned in the ISO 14001 standards
Certification/ registration	ISO 14010, 14011, 14012 and 14015 Norms	Annex III	Certification by accredited third-party; self-declaration possible
Contractors and suppliers	Not mentioned in the ISO 14001 standards	Annex I C	Not a requirement inasmuch as not mentioned in the ISO 14001 standards
Bridging problems	Not mentioned in the ISO 14001 standards	Article 12	EMAS-certified firms usually comply easily with the ISO 14001 norms

4. THE CERTIFICATION OF ENVIRONMENTAL MANAGEMENT
    SYSTEMS: ISO 14001 CERTIFICATION AND EMAS
    VERIFICATION

4.1 General Considerations

As mentioned previously, one of the essential features of the ISO 14001
norms is that they lend themselves to certification, which is an assessment
by an accredited third-party, usually a private firm or an individual, such as
an environmental consultant or auditor, that a firm or organization complies
with the ISO 14001 standards. The third party has to be independent of both
the firm seeking certification and its stakeholders.   It also has to be
accredited by a suitable accrediting body, which verifies that the certifying
organization and/or the auditor has suitable qualifications or experience.
These qualifications are defined under the ISO 14012 norms, which provide
qualification criteria for environmental auditors.

Third-party certification, however, is not necessary in implementing an
EMS under the ISO 14001 standards. Organizations that, for some reason,
do not wish to obtain ISO 14001 certification may meet the requirements of
the ISO 14001 standards and publicize this through self-declaration.
Although such a self-declaration is less credible for an interested
stakeholder, it might be useful, especially for SMEs for which certification is
a costly and complex procedure, and also as a first step in demonstrating
their interest for environmental protection for firms that want to obtain
certification at a later stage.

4.2 The Importance of ISO 14001 Certification and EMAS Verification and Registration

There are several reasons why a firm may be interested in seeking ISO
14001 certification, often at the request of some interested stakeholders. It is
clear that such certification is useful in demonstrating to interested
stakeholders a firm's concern with the environment: Although, as already
mentioned, ISO 14001 certification does not guarantee a high   level

of environmental performance, it is one element, among others, that is often considered by interested stakeholders as part of the environmental qualities of the firm's products and services. We outline below the advantages of certification in relation to the interests of various stakeholders.

- For *consumers and clients*, it may be regarded as a significant contribution to the firm's products or services, to be supplemented by other elements such as ecolabelling, thus giving the firm some competitive advantage.
- For *financial stakeholders, including shareholders, banks and lenders, and insurers*, it is a positive element in the assessment of corporate risks; it may thus lower the cost of capital, and the cost of insurance, for the firm.
- For *public environmental protection agencies*, it gives a reasonable guarantee of commitment towards compliance with the environmental regulation, thus making easier to obtain permits and authorizations.
- For firms which are in the position of being *contractors, subcontractors or suppliers* of other firms, it may be a prerequisite towards access to certain markets that it hopes to expand into.

As far as the management of the firm is concerned, the standardized guidelines of the ISO 14001 and EMAS norms are useful in making it easier, and thus less costly in terms of internal management resources, to implement environmental management systems. They also make it easier and less costly to transfer environmental management systems, and hence environmental quality norms, from a firm to its contractors, subcontractors and suppliers. However, ISO 14001 and EMAS certification imply fixed costs that might be considered as sunk costs, and that might be comparatively high. These may also be considered as investment costs, which have to be evaluated against the benefits they foster. As an order of magnitude, and depending upon the characteristics and the particular situation of the firm being certified, the fee of the certifying entity might be anything between US$10 000 and US$100 000; possibly even more. Other costs are due to the procedural character of implementing standardized EMS norms: many firms fear that the implementation of EMSs will generate 'red tape'. All these costs might be a problem for some firms, especially in the case of SMEs.

A further problem is that, as noted previously, certification under ISO 14001 or EMAS norms is by no means a guarantee of a high environmental performance or high environmental qualities of the firm's products. The virtuous circle that we invoked might, in some cases, not be triggered. In these cases, ISO 14001 or EMAS will not be of much interest, and might even prove counterproductive to the firm's interests.

However, in such cases, one might ask whether it is really the ISO 14001 or the EMAS schemes that are called into question, or rather their ineffective or inadequate application. The ISO 14001 norms are just tools for implementing an EMS. They are closely related to compliance with environmental regulation, a necessary condition for their applicability, but, in many cases, over-compliance rather than mere compliance best serves the interests of the firm. Firms that are ahead, or even far ahead, of existing regulations, avoid the risk of having hastily to comply with new regulation, often at a larger cost than if proactive action is taken. As noted by Brophy (1998), over-compliance demonstrates the commitment of firms to conform *on a voluntary basis* to strict environmental standards, thus removing some of the need for further regulation. A number of theoretical and empirical works have been interested in the economic principles underlying *voluntary compliance* (Arora and Gangopadhyay, 1995; Arora and Cason, 1996; Carraro and Lévêque, 1999; Clapp, 1998; Eden, 1996; Labatt and Maclaren, 1998). In many cases, and as noted above, international firms with facilities located in a number of countries throughout the world will conform to the strictest environmental regulations that apply to their facilities worldwide (see, for example, the case of ST Microelectronics which is discussed at the end of this chapter).

Finally, especially in the case of the ISO 14001 standards and because these norms are global, the interest of EMS norms has to be examined in the context of globalization. This issue is addressed in the next subsection.

4.3 The ISO 14001 Norms, and Globalization

The ISO 14001 standards are international standards that are recognized throughout the world. They are global tools, the advantages and shortcomings of which have been discussed in Sheldon (1997). Consequently, they have to be related to the globalization of markets. If, by globalization, we mean worldwide free-trade markets, and therefore worldwide flows of goods and capital, since the early 1990s, the evolution of the world economy has certainly been in the direction of globalization. In the context of globalization, norms that are issued by national public organizations become ineffective, such that voluntary norms like those defined under ISO 9000 and ISO 14000, take on an added significance as environmental tools. As shown by Gleckman and Krut (1997), the ISO 14001 scheme may lead to international trade standards that are operated without the participation of any national administration or international organization. These standards are not trade barriers, because they are voluntary, not mandatory. However, they may develop to reach the status of an almost universal private standard. This would be a management rather than technical standard, comparable to the technical hardware and software standards that prevail in the computer industry. The number of such ISO 14001 and EMAS certifications is growing at a fast pace, as shown in Table 8.2.

In this table, we can see that the number of ISO 14001 certifications varies dramatically from country to country. A number of questions stem from this unequal distribution. First of all, is ISO 14001 certification, and therefore environmental management, a 'game for the rich'? Clearly, the richest countries in the world, such as OECD member countries, do have the highest number of certified firms. Among OECD member countries, we note that countries where public opinion is strongly 'environmentally conscious' tend to have a higher number of certifications than other OECD countries, allowing for the size of their economy. Switzerland, and Scandinavian countries such as Denmark and Sweden, seem to fall into this category, inasmuch as they are ahead of OECD countries in terms of number of certifications related to their GDP.

This, however, is not the end of the story. Among other countries, so-called emerging countries, including emerging Asian countries such as Korea, Taiwan, Singapore, are characterized by a high number of certifications, usually with very high rates of growth, probably due to policies providing incentives to register.

All other countries with low or very low GDP per capita are characterized by very small numbers of certifications (less than ten). All this seems to indicate that ISO 14001 certifications mainly concern international or large firms that are involved in international trade and that operate either in rich or in emerging countries. Thus, it may be concluded that ISO 14001 certification is directly related to globalization and that the environmental management policies of small firms are less dependent on international EMS or environmental management standards than is the case for large organizations.

Table 8.2: Number of ISO 14001 certifications per country (March 2000)

Country	Number of ISO 14001 Certifications *	Rate of growth (%)**
Argentina	88	137.83
Australia	350	150.00
Austria	223	11.50
Barbados	3	0.00
Belgium	130	0.00
Brazil	146	124.60
Canada	272	202.20
Chile	5	0.00
China	85	209.50
Colombia	18	500.00
Costa Rica	3	50.00
Croatia	4	33.30
Czech Republic	54	170.00
Denmark	350	0.00
Egypt	46	206.70
Equador	1	?
Estonia	1	?
Finland	347	116.90

France	453	92.80
Germany	1 950	56.00
Greece	10	66.70
Guatemala	1	?
Honduras	1	?
Hong Kong	50	25.00
Hungary	106	241.90
Iceland	1	?
India	117	95.00
Indonesia	55	25.00
Iran	12	140.00
Ireland	95	15.90
Israel	25	92.30
Italy	246	123.60
Japan	3 318	115.20
Jordan	2	100.00
Lebanon	1	0.00
Liechtenstein	5	0.00
Lithuania	1	?
Luxembourg	6	0.00
Malaysia	155	93.80
Malta	1	0.00
Mauritius	2	0.00
Mexico	64	60.00
Morocco	4	33.30
New Zealand	35	25.00
Nigeria	1	?
Norway	129	115.00
Oman	2	100.00
Pakistan	2	0.00
Peru	6	500.00
Philippines	50	117.40
Poland	15	36.40
Portugal	15	87.50
Puerto Rico	1	?
Rumania	1	0.00
Russia	1	0.00
Saint Lucia	1	?
Saudi Arabia	1	0.00
Singapore	87	11.50
Slovak Republic	25	92.30
Slovenia	23	283.30

South Africa	72	140.00
South Korea	463	0.00
Spain	665	298.20
Sweden	1 025	98.60
Switzerland	508	51.20
Taiwan	652	54.10
Thailand	245	145.00
The Netherlands	605	68.10
Trinidad-Tobago	1	?
Tunisia	1	?
Turkey	50	11.10
United Arab Emirates	15	275.00
United Kingdom	1 014	26.75
Uruguay	8	700.00
USA	740	124.20
Venezuela	1	0.00
Vietnam	3	?
Zambia	1	?
Zimbabwe	2	?

Notes:
* March 2000
** Annual growth with respect to figure available in March 1999; ? indicates uncertain or non-significant figure (zero in March 1999).

Source: Institut fürWirtschaft und Ökologie, University of Saint Gallen (2000).

5. CONCLUSION

This chapter has given an analysis of the ISO 14001 and EMAS international standards for EMSs, both of which are liable to third-party certification. Their utility and effectiveness for environmental management has also been analysed. While the implementation of these standards does not necessarily amount to high levels of environmental performance, it does help firms to improve their environmental performance, and hence the environmental qualities of their products, and eventually to reach high environmental performances. Owing to the costs of certification, and due to their very international nature, these standards seem to address mainly, but not exclusively, the needs of large corporations that are involved in international trade.

EMS certification is, in this context, just one indicator, among others, of environmental quality attributes of products and services. It is clear that prospective consumers and clients have at their disposal more specific indicators of such environmental qualities, through ecolabelling and other channels of information. These are discussed in the following chapter.

CASE STUDY: ST MICROELECTRONICS – TQEM AND ISO 14001 CERTIFICATION FOR A WORLD LEADER IN MICROELECTRONICS

Introduction

In 1999, the Franco-Italian company ST Microelectronics was the eighth largest semiconductor company worldwide, with sales of US$ 5056 million and a corresponding net income before tax of US$ 707 million, also in 1999. Its 1998 revenue was the second highest revenue among the top ten international semiconductor companies. The company sells all sorts of semiconductors, microprocessors and computer memories and is a leader in some advanced electronic, telecommunication and computer technologies. It is quoted on the New York Stock Exchange, on the Paris Bourse and on the Milan Bourse. It has facilities all over the world, with its European headquarters being located in Turin and its Asia-Pacific headquarters in Singapore.

ST Microelectronics is also noted for its advanced environmental management, which is the object of the present case study. It has gone beyond mere compliance with existing regulations, instead taking a proactive attitude. One of its principles is to conform to 'the most stringent' environmental standards and even to better standards in those countries where the company operates. Furthermore, the company has defined long-term objectives for the 2000–2010 period, which aim not only at continuous improvement of its environmental performance but also at very ambitious absolute environmental performance objectives. One of the most important of these objectives is progressively, completely and ultimately to eliminate net CO_2 emissions and perfluorinated compounds (PFC), both of which contribute to the greenhouse effect. All this has been done through an EMS at the level of ST Microelectronics worldwide, which has been ISO 14001 certified and EMAS validated. More precisely, all the 17 sites of ST Microelectronics worldwide have been ISO 14001 certified. Furthermore, all its seven EU sites have been EMAS-registered and all of its 11 non-EU sites have, in addition, obtained EMAS validation (Table 8.3). The fact that ST Microelectronics complied with EMAS for all of its production units is indeed a significant token of ST Microelectronics' commitment towards the environment, because the EMAS scheme is, as noted previously, more demanding than the ISO 14001 scheme.

Table 8.3: Dates of ISO 14001 certification and EMAS registration or validation for the sites of ST Microelectronics worldwide

Sites	ISO 14001 Certification	EMAS registration or validation
Crolles (France)	1997	1996
Rennes (France)	1997	1996
Rousset (France)	1997	1996
Tours (France)	1997	1996
Agrate (Italy)	1997	1998
Catania (Italy)	1997	1997
Cornaredo (Italy)	1997	1998
Malta	1997	1995
Ain Sebaa (Morocco)	1997	1997
Bouskoura (Morocco)	1997	1997
Rancho Bernardo (USA)	1996	1995
Carollton (USA)	1996	1997
Phoenix (USA)	1997	1997
Singapore AMK	1996	1997
Singapore TP	1996	1996
Muar (Malaysia)	1996	1996
Shenzhen (China)	1997	1997

Source: ST Microelectronics Corporate Environmental Report (2000b)

We are therefore going to examine ST Microelectronics' EMS using the five steps of ISO 14001 continual-improvement cycle as a guideline.

The Environmental Management System of ST Microelectronics

The environmental management system (EMS) of ST Microelectronics can indeed be analysed in terms of the ISO 14001 continual-improvement cycle. On this basis, it first rests on an *environmental policy* that is clearly stated and is related to precise objectives that account for the *planning step* of the ISO 14001 cycle. This environmental policy (Box 8.4) as presented in ST Microelectronics' Corporate Environmental Report, is endorsed by the company's CEO in a text given at the beginning of the report; this indicates commitment from the firm's management. These objectives are detailed in a so-called 'environmental decalogue' added as an appendix. ST Microelectronics also relates its environmental management to its Total Quality Management (TQM) approach, and therefore presents its environmental management in terms of Total Quality Environmental Management (TQEM). This means that it considers environmental performance as a component of the quality attributes of its products and that its environmental management system is integrated into its quality-management system. The environmental policy of ST Microelectronics given in Box 8.4 also conforms to the so-called Business Charter for Sustainable Development issued by the International Chamber of Commerce (ICC) and by the World Business Council for Sustainable Development (WBCSD). This charter is discussed in Chapter 9. It has been approved and implemented by a large number of large firms (more than 400 according to Brophy, 1998) such as Shell, British Airways, General Motors, Ford and many others, including ST Microelectronics. However, as noted by Brophy (1998), the ICC/WBCSD environmental charter is less demanding in a number of areas than other management charters, such as the CERES Principles, also discussed in Chapter 9. It could even, in some cases, imply little or no tangible commitments in terms of environmental management. However, this is not the case here: ST Microelectronics is incorporating the ICC/WBCSD Charter for Sustainable Development within the framework of its own EMS.

This EMS system in the case of ST Microelectronics implies some tangible long-term environmental objectives and investments, under some long-term environmental planning scheme. These long-term objectives are, as already mentioned, detailed in the firm's so-called environmental decalogue (Box 8.5).

The *implementation and operation* step of ST Microelectronics' EMS is also detailed in its corporate environmental report. This step implies the definition of an organizational framework and of responsibilities. These are given in the report. The company has a corporate vice-president and director of Total Quality Environmental Management, and a TQEM director who is in charge of a TQEM organization. An environmental strategy and international quality programme (ES–IQP) organization headed by an ES–IQP director is one of the components of this TQEM organization. While its structures and responsibilities are defined, this ES–IQP organization appears to be in charge of implementation and operation of the EMS, including, in particular: operating control, documentation, internal environmental training, external and internal communication (through Internet and Intranet), are described in ST Microelectronics' corporate environmental report as being carried out under the ES–IQP organization. Results of the company's environmental management actions are reported in the environmental corporate report for energy management, water, paper and chemicals, and these results are compared with planning objectives and most of the time seem to be ahead of targets previously defined. Emergency response planning is reported in the application of the TQEM system as compared to the 156 ICC principles. This implies that *the checking and corrective and preventive action*, another of ISO 14001 steps, is present here. Environmental-data corporate reporting is provided for in the ES–IQP organization. According to ST Microelectronics Corporate Environmental Record, the ES–IQP 'conducts periodical audits, develops and proposes environmental rules and objectives'. Appropriate corrective actions for problems encountered on various European and other sites are also reported. A Corporate Environmental Steering Committee, which is directly chaired by the CEO, appears to carry out management review, which constitutes the last step of the ISO 14001 continual-improvement cycle.

Conclusion

As it stands, and as described within the company's Corporate Environmental Report, the environmental management achievements of ST Microelectronics worldwide appear to be quite impressive. This advanced environmental management system seems typical of high-technology companies. As a matter of fact, and as already mentioned, ST Microelectronics is part of the global Dow Jones Sustainable Group Index, one of the stock market indexes of ethical companies worldwide, which has been described in Chapter 5. As noted in that chapter, high-technology companies appear to be over-represented in ethical indexes such as the Domini and the indexes of the DJSGI family. This means that, on average, these high-technology companies tend to be more advanced than other companies in terms of ethical criteria, including environmental management criteria.

Box 8.4: The environmental policy statement of ST Microelectronics

---

CORPORATE ENVIRONMENTAL POLICY

Chapter 1 – PURPOSE/SCOPE
The purpose of this policy is to establish the major principles for improving the environmental performance and permitting ST to become one of the best industrial companies with regard to the environment, and to obtain recognition from governments and our stakeholders for our environmentally friendly operations.

Chapter 2 – ORGANIZATIONAL UNITS AFFECTED
This policy applies to all ST activities, mainly: Design, Manufacturing, Purchasing, Logistics, Sales and Marketing and Generic administrative activities (Legal, Human Resources, Accounting etc...).

Chapter 3 – POLICY STATEMENT
Environmental care is an integral part of ST existence. It is therefore always present in all Company activities through the following ST commitments:

Box 8.4 (continued)

ENVIRONMENTAL MISSION:
To eliminate or minimize the impact of our processes and products on the environment, maximizing the use of recyclable or reusable materials and adopting, as much as possible, renewable sources of energy, striving for a sustainable development.

ENVIRONMENTAL VISION:
Following our 'Environmental Decalogue' (see appendix 4) to be recognized by all our stakeholders as a leader in environmental care, by exceeding regulatory requirements in both degree and timing wherever possible; and as a reflection of this commitment, to acquire the 'Eco Management and Audit Scheme' (EMAS) validation, or equivalent, in all communities in which we operate.

ENVIRONMENTAL POLICY:
To aim, in addition to providing for compliance with all relevant regulatory requirements regarding the environment, at the reasonable continuous improvement of environmental performance with a view to reducing environmental impacts to levels not exceeding those corresponding to economically viable application of the best available technology (EMAS art. 3a).

▸ To take a proactive approach in our environmental activities, built on the TQM principles, being guided by the 16 principles of the ICC (International Chamber of Commerce) 'Business Charter for Sustainable Development'.
▸ To be a world leader on the basis of:
- Moral obligation towards the environment;
- Economic importance (to invest in environmental protection gives a significant strategic advantage over those companies who wait; the financial efforts will, to a large extent, be repaid if we are capable of designing and implementing processes that are pollution free and which also reduce the use of valuable material resources and energy. This means that investments for the environment must have priority.
- Human resources (to attract the best young people, and to motivate the Company's employees in the Challenge for a better quality of life).
▸ In addition to the local regulation, we will strive to adopt the most stringent ecological standards of any country in which we operate.
▸ To apply the most stringent regulations at least one year before their implementation deadlines.

Box 8.4 (continued)

Chapter 4 – GENERAL PRINCIPLES

▸ Total company environmental awareness is the base for meeting these goals.

▸ The 16 principles of the 'Business Charter for Sustainable Development' are the guideline for continuous improvement.

▸ The Council Regulation (EEC) 1836/93 of 29 June 1993 (Voluntary participation by companies in the industrial sector in a Community Eco-Management and Audit Scheme – EMAS) gives an excellent guideline for what we have to implement in our sites to manage the environmental issues (including the environmental audit activities/methodologies).

▸ The ISO 14000 series, in the emission phase, gives, at worldwide level, guidelines similar to EMAS.

▸ The TQM approach is the practical way of working and managing all the aspects of business to achieve the best results. In the environment world it is named TQEM (Total Quality Environmental Management).

▸ Our suppliers will be involved to adopt similar approaches in respecting the Environment.

Source: ST Microelectronics (2000b)

Box 8.5   *The environmental decalogue of ST Microelectronics*

Environmental decalogue

The 10 environmental commandments of ST Microelectronics
Our vision for environmental responsibility and sustainable development

At ST Microelectronics we believe firmly that it mandatory for a TQM driven corporation to be at the forefront of ecological commitment, not only for ethical and social reasons but also for financial return, and the ability to attract the most responsible and performant [highly achieving] *people. Our 'ecological vision' is to become a corporation that closely approaches environmental neutrality. To that end we will not only meet all environmental requirements in those communities in which we operate but, in addition, we will strive to comply to the following ten commandments:*

Box 8.5 (continued)

1. Regulations
‣ **1.1** Meet the most stringent environmental regulations of any country in which we operate, at all of our locations.
‣ **1.2** Comply with all international protocols at least one year ahead of international deadlines at all our locations.

2. Conservation
‣ **2.1** Energy – Reduce total energy consumption (Kwh Per k$*) by at least 5% per year, through process and facilities optimization, conservation and building design.
‣ **2.2** Water consumption - Continue to reduce water draw-down (cubic meters per k$*) by at least 5% per year, through conservation, process optimization and recycling.
‣ **2.3** Water recycling – Reach a minimum of 90% recycling ratio in two pilot sites by the end of 2005.
‣ **2.4** Trees – Reduce office and manufacturing paper consumption (kg per employee) by at least 10% per year, and use at least 95% recycled paper, or paper produced by environmentally certified forests.

3. Greenhouse Gas Emissions
‣ **3.1** CO_2 – Reduce total emissions due to our energy consumption (tonnes of carbon equivalent per M$*) by at least a factor of ten in 2010 vs. 1990, which is a goal five times better than the average of the industries meeting the Kyoto Protocol goal.
‣ **3.2** Renewable energies – Increase their utilization (wind, photovoltaic and thermal solar) so that they represent at least 5% of our total energy supplies by the end of 2010.

4. Pollution
‣ **4.1** Noise – Meet a 'noise-to-neighbours' target below 60db(A) at any point and at any time outside our property perimeter for all sites, or comply with the local regulation (wherever the most restrictive).
‣ **4.2** Contaminants – Handle, store and dispose of all potential contaminants and hazardous substances at all sites, in a manner to meet or exceed the strictest environmental standards of any community in which we operate.
‣ **4.3** ODS – Phase out all remaining class 1 ODS included also in close loops of small equipments before the end of 2001.

Box 8.5 (continued)

5. Chemicals
▸ **5.1.** Reduce the consumption of the six most relevant chemicals by at least 5% per tonne (tonnes per M$*), through process optimization and recycling (baseline 1998).

6. Waste
▸ **6.1** Landfill – Reduce the amount of landfilled waste below 5% of our total waste by 2005.

▸ **6.2** Re-use or recycle at least 80% of our manufacturing and packing waste below 5% of our total waste by the end of 1999, and 95% by the end of 2005.

▸ **6.3** Use the **ladder concept** as a guideline for all our actions in waste management.

7. Products and processes
▸ **7.1** Design products for decreased energy consumption and for enablement of more energy-efficient applications.

▸ **7.2** Contribute to global environmental control by establishing a database of Life-cycle Assessment of our products.

▸ **7.3** Systematically include the environmental impact study in our development process.

▸ **7.4** Publish and update information about the chemical content of our products.

8. Proactivity
▸ **8.1** Support local initiatives for sponsoring environmental projects at each site in which we operate.

▸ **8.2** Sponsor an annual Corporate Environmental Day, and encourage similar initiatives in each site.

▸ **8.3** Encourage our people to lead/participate in environmental committees, symposia, 'watch-dog' groups etc…

▸ **8.4** Include an 'Environmental Awareness' training course in the ST University curriculum and offer it to suppliers and customers.

▸ **8.5** Strongly encourage all suppliers and subcontractors to be EMAS validated or ISO 14001 certified, and assist them through training, support and auditing. At least 80% of our key suppliers should be certified by the end of 2001.

Box 8.5 (continued)

9. Measurement
▸ **9.1** Continuously monitor our progress, including periodic audits of all our sites worldwide.
▸ **9.2** Cooperate with international organizations to define and to implement eco-efficiency indicators.
▸ **9.3** Measure progress and achievements using 1994 as a baseline year (where applicable), and publish our results in our annual Corporate Environmental Report.

10. Certification
▸ **10.1** Maintain the ISO 14001 certification and EMAS validation of all our sites worldwide.
▸ **10.2** Certify new sites within 189 months of their operational start-up, including regional warehouses.

Source: ST Microelectronics (2000b).

NOTES

1. EEA stands for European Economic Area, which includes all the 15 EU member countries, as well as Iceland, Liechtenstein and Norway.

REFERENCES

Arora, S. and Cason, T.N. (1996), 'Why do firms volunteer to exceed environmental regulations?', *Land Economics*, **72** (4): 413–32.
Arora, S. and Gangopadhyay, S. (1995), 'Toward a theoretical model of voluntary overcompliance', *Journal of Economic Behavior and Organization*, **28**: 289–309.
Brophy, M. (1998), 'Environmental Guidelines and Charters', Chapter 6 in R. Welford (ed.), *Corporate Environmental Management. 1. Systems and Strategies*, 2nd edn., London: Earthscan Publications Ltd, 102–15.
Carraro, C. and F. Lévêque (1999), *Voluntary Approaches in Environmental Policy*, Amsterdam: Kluwer.
Clapp, J. (1998), 'The privatization of global environmental governance': ISO 14000 and self-regulation in environmental policy, *Global Governance*, **4**: 295–316.
Eden, S. (1996), 'The politics of packaging in the UK : Business, government and self-regulation in environmental policy', *Environmental Politics* **5 (4)**, 632-53.

Gleckman, H. and Krut, R. (1997), 'Neither International nor Standard: The Limits of ISO 14001 as an Instrument of Global Corporate Environmental Management', in C. Sheldon (ed.) *ISO 14001 and Beyond. Environmental Management Systems in the Real World*, Sheffield, UK: Greenleaf Publishing, Part 1, pp. 45-60.

International Standards Organization (ISO) (1996a), *ISO 14001. Environmental Management Systems – Specification with Guidance for Use*, Geneva: ISO.

International Standards Organization (ISO) (1996b), *ISO 14004. Environmental Management Systems – General Guidelines on Principles, Systems and Supporting Techniques*, Geneva: ISO.

International Standards Organization (ISO) (1999a), *ISO 14031. Environmental Management – Environmental Performance Evaluation – Guidelines*, Geneva: ISO.

International Standards Organization (ISO) (1999b), *ISO/TR 14032. Environmental Management – Examples of Environmental Performance Evaluation*, Geneva: ISO.

Labatt, S. and MacLaren, M.V. (1998), 'Voluntary corporate environmental initiatives: a typology and preliminary investigation', *Environment and Planning. C (Government and Policy)*, **16**: 191–209.

McInerney, F. and White, S. (1997), *The total quality corporation. How 10 major companies added to profits and cleaned up their environment in the 1990s*, New York: Truman Talley Books.

Rothery, B. (1995), *ISO 14000 and ISO 9000*, London: Gower.

Sheldon, C. (ed.) (1997), *ISO 14001 and Beyond. Environmental Management Systems in the Real World*, Sheffield, UK: Greenleaf Publishing.

Sheldon, C. and Yoxon, M. (1999), *Installing Environmental Management Systems. A Step-by-Step Guide*, London: Earthscan.

ST Microelectronics (2000a), *Financial Report 1999*, http://www.st.com.

ST Microelectronics (2000b), *Environmental Report 1999,* http://www.st.com.

Sturm, A. (with Upasena, S.) (2001), *ISO14001. Implementing an Environmental Management System*, Revised version 2.0.2., Basle, Switzerland: Ellipson Management Consultants, http://www.ellipson.com.

Taylor, F. (1911), *Scientific Management*, New York: Harper and Row.

Institut fürWirtschaft und Ökologie, University of Saint Gallen (2000), *Certificates worldwide (Data compiled by R. Peglau, Umweltbundesamt, Berlin)*, http://www.iwoe.unisg.ch.

Wever, G.H. (1996), *Strategic Environmental Management. Using TQEM and ISO 14000 for Competitive Advantage*, New York: Wiley.

9. Eco-marketing and the Environmental Quality of Goods[1]

SUMMARY

This chapter follows on from Chapter 8 by examining the firm's possibilities for communicating to its stakeholders not only its environmental management performance but also the environmental qualities of its products and services. This poses a signalling problem, which is particularly crucial in the case of so-called credence attributes of goods, of which environmental attributes are a special case. We first clarify the economics (that is, the value to the firm and to its stakeholders) of signalling the environmental quality of goods. We then look at the different marketing techniques the firm has at its disposal. There are three main categories: self-declared environmental claims and environmental advertising; third-party certification and ecolabelling; and an indirect technique known as organization marketing. The first category is the easiest and cheapest to implement but carries little credibility with consumers and thus little value for the firm. The second category involves, in particular, the international ISO standards, as well as other regional, national or private certification schemes. These usually carry high credibility. The last category includes so-called environmental charters and environmental reports, of which EMS certification is an aspect. The following section examines a key tool for eco-marketing: the use of life-cycle analysis (LCA), and how its use can be made to increase the credibility of environmental quality claims. The last section pays special attention to why there may be a demand for environmental quality of goods and services, to how important this demand is in reality, and to whether current trends should be considered as simple fads, or due to last and indeed to grow. The chapter ends with a case study, looking at Volvo's highly praised efforts in improving the environmental quality of its products.

1. INTRODUCTION

At least in countries where the protection of the environment is of interest, consumers and the public opinion are increasingly sensitive to what might be called the *environmental quality* of products or goods. These products might be material goods, which are tangible objects or intangible services. In all cases under discussion in this chapter, environmentally conscious consumers, whether individuals or corporations, are assumed to be sensitive to the environmental impacts of products.

There are so-called green or environment-friendly products that possess such environmental qualities. Many examples of such products may be given. Organic foods in the context of agricultural products, renewable and non-polluting energies such as solar energy, as well as intangible services that contribute indirectly to environmental protection such as 'green' investment funds and many other marketable goods, may be described as environment-friendly products.

The management of the environmental qualities of goods may be given several directions, in relation to the firm's stakeholders. If we stick to our definition, all aspects of environmental management, including the aspects we already discussed in Chapters 3, 4, 5 and 6, contribute to producing the environmental quality of products in a broad sense. In particular, we have been concerned with accounting, monitoring and reporting (Chapters 4 and 5), financing (Chapter 6), and insuring (Chapter 7). All these management actions contribute to the environmental quality of goods and services.

One of the key aspects of marketing[2] is communicating and publicizing the positive attributes of goods and services supplied by a corporation, so as to match customers' demands and expectations. This includes providing information to actual or potential clients on quality attributes and prices, and reciprocally obtaining information from clients about their demands and expectations. Marketing thus involves providing information about the 'quality mix' and the pricing of products, so as to meet consumers' or clients' demands in terms of quality and price.

Environmental quality attributes of goods are important for some segments of the market for both consumer products and industrial products. What one might call eco-marketing is an important and even fundamental aspect of environmental management. *Eco-marketing* may be defined as the branch of marketing that refers to consumers' sensitivity to the environmental quality attributes of goods. The various methods for signalling and advertising the environmental qualities of products are important aspects of managing their environmental qualities that have not hitherto been discussed. Because the market place is vital to the firm's activity, marketing is a key and strategic aspect of management. Effectively marketing one's products is the fundamental aim of the entrepreneur, without which he or she could not exist as such. It can be argued that all other aspects of corporate management provide only a means to this end. Financial and human resource management, for instance, however important they may be, are only means towards efficiently managing the capital resources that are needed to produce the firm's goods, and ultimately to sell them on the market place. If one talks about environmental management, one of its ultimate goals is to supply products on the market place that have suitable environmental quality attributes.

Since the topics discussed in this chapter are closely interrelated and that there tend to be multiple causality links, this chapter will be organized as follows.

First, we intend to discuss how consumers might be suitably and reliably informed about environmental qualities. More generally, one of the aims of this chapter is to present the channels whereby consumers or clients may be informed (and, if possible, reliably informed) about the environmental quality attributes of goods, which might be thought of as components of their overall quality attributes.

Second, we wish to discuss the techniques that enable us to assess the environmental qualities of goods, and, in particular, Life-cycle Assessments (LCA). We briefly mentioned LCAs in Chapter 4, but we did not discuss the use that can be made of them in terms of informing consumers and clients. The use of LCA as an eco-marketing tool stems from the fact that comparisons between the environmental characteristics of a good are only meaningful on a 'cradle to grave' basis. Many qualities of goods are thus at stake, pertaining to the more or less environment-friendly manner in which the good was produced, will be consumed and, finally, will be disposed of. In other terms, what is the product's impact on the environment throughout its life cycle.

Third, we will try to analyse the sources of consumer sensitivity to the environmental qualities of products, and to assess which segments of the market are likely to be affected by environmental quality attributes.

Of course, the problems related to the environmental qualities of goods do not concern only consumption goods but also industrial goods, the specific problems of which will also be discussed in various parts of this chapter.

2. SIGNALLING THE ENVIRONMENTAL QUALITY OF GOODS

2.1 The Problem of the Environmental Quality of Goods

The problem with environmental qualities of goods is that they are not immediately apparent to consumers. Nelson (1970, 1974) and Darbi and Karni (1973) developed a useful classification of the quality attributes of goods. They distinguish between *search goods*, *experience goods* and *credence goods*.

Search goods are goods with readily verifiable quality attributes, before or on purchasing the good (called *search* quality attributes, because they may be searched by consumers before buying the good),

Experience goods are goods with quality attributes that can be detected only upon using or consuming the good (called *experience* quality attributes, because they are revealed to consumers through experience).

Both these categories of goods are relatively easy to handle in terms of quality management. In such cases, consumers may directly or readily verify the quality that the manufacturer claims in its publicity or in its catalogue. Should these claims appear as unfounded or even false, consumers will be able to penalize the faulty firm through shifting suppliers, a real possibility provided that the market is competitive, or even through appropriate legal action if necessary. In the case of experience quality attributes, the supplier can offer a guarantee system to handle the difficulties that could occur after he or she has sold the product. Under a guarantee system, the product may, for instance, be refunded or replaced free of charge if it fails to satisfy the customer.

Credence goods constitute a third category. These are goods with non-verifiable quality attributes, whether upon purchasing the good or using it. Clearly, environmental quality attributes mostly fall into this category. Credence quality attributes, however, are more difficult to handle in terms of quality management. They rest on consumers' confidence in the firm's claims for quality, and these may not easily be verified, if they can be verified at all. Thus, there is a *signalling* problem in the case of credence quality attributes, and, in particular, in the case of the environmental qualities of goods. This problem can be solved in several ways. One is certification of the quality of the good by an independent organization (consulting firm, public or governmental service, and so forth) that is *credible* to the consumer. In general, signalling the environmental quality attributes of a good has to be done in such a manner that the client finds the information about these quality attributes reliable or credible.

By signalling environmental quality attributes to consumers, we therefore mean informing them, in a credible manner, about the environmental qualities of the goods or products the firm is selling. This is obviously in the interest of the firm, and reliable information is apt to give a firm a clear competitive edge with respect to its competitors. This is explainable because consumers will, all other things being equal, prefer a product which they are better informed about than a product for which they have less or less reliable information. A company that endeavours, through various direct and indirect means, to provide credible information to its clients will, all else being equal, have some kind of competitive advantage over its competitors.

Most of the environmental qualities of products are not readily verifiable by consumers. What, therefore, are the possibilities for a firm in providing reliable information to consumers? There are *direct* means, such as publicity, and other means of communication relating not only to customers but also to other stakeholders. These means require, of course, that the information supplied by the firm be sufficiently credible, or that the firm's reputation in this respect be positively established. Other means for signalling the quality of the firm's products are only indirect means, which imply certification by some reliable independent third party. All these signalling methods will be examined in the next sub-section, and analysed in more detail thereafter.

2.2 Environmental Labelling: Economic Principles

There are several ways of signalling the environmental quality attributes of goods. These may of course apply to search and experience attributes, whenever consumers are able to assess these quality attributes by themselves. However, as noted earlier, the environmental qualities of a good are mostly credence attributes, which are not readily observable by consumers. Some of the techniques of signalling we are going to discuss are more adapted to such credence attributes, and thus to the environmental quality of products. Among these techniques, there are *direct* and *indirect* techniques.

Direct environmental marketing techniques are techniques whereby clients, whether they are individual end-consumers or companies, are suitably and directly informed about the environmental quality attributes of products. These direct environmental marketing techniques are generally termed *environmental claims*, and they include environmental labelling – a particular case where clients are informed about quality attributes, environmental or otherwise. *Indirect environmental marketing* techniques provide background information that makes direct information more trustworthy.

From an economic point of view, both direct and indirect techniques (but especially direct techniques) can be analysed in terms of the competitive characteristics of markets. Markets are competitive only if all economic agents on the demand side are fully informed about the quality of the goods they intend to buy. This is especially true in the case of credence attributes, which do not permit verification by potential purchasers. Provided transparent information rules are established, markets for goods with credence attributes can be competitive. Such markets, in which sufficient information is available to buyers, have been termed *efficient* by Fama (1970, 1991), or *informationally efficient* in the case of asset markets.

Financial asset markets, such as stock markets, are markets where shares of companies, which are goods with typical credence attributes, are sold. Regulations impose that quoted companies disclose transparent, pertinent and comprehensive financial information, which enables potential buyers of their shares to be fully informed of their potential future profitability. These disclosure regulations, applied in most countries with efficient stock exchanges, provide for the publication of *third-party certification* of accounting documents that is carried out by independent auditors or audit firms.

The concept of *informationally efficient markets* is not restricted to asset or capital markets. It applies more or less to all sorts of markets with goods that have credence quality attributes, including environmental quality. An efficient market, most generally, is a market on which sellers cannot make unfair profits because they do not disclose the true quality of their goods. Rules that are very similar to the rules of disclosure imposed on regulated stock markets have to prevail in the case of the environmental quality of products if their markets are to be at all efficient.

This is why, in a number of countries, misleading advertising constitutes an offence, and of course this applies to deceptive environmental claims and labelling. In the United States, the Federal Trade Commission (FTC) is the authority that enforces legislative rules concerning misleading advertising and marketing practices. In the case of environmental claims that constitute direct signalling of the environmental quality of goods, the FTC has issued some guidelines about the application of general legal principles to these claims. These guidelines, although strictly speaking having no legal value, provide some detailed indications about what should reasonably be done in terms of environmental claims to comply with legal principles, and especially to avoid misleading advertising.

The economic principles underlying such guidelines and rules are clear; namely, that producers and marketers should not make unfair profits because of misleading environmental claims that overstate the environmental quality attributes of a product in relation to competing products that make no such or more honest claims. This is just a matter of providing conditions that contribute towards market efficiency in a sense that generalizes the concept of market efficiency introduced by Fama (1970, 1991) in the case of asset markets.

Rules and regulations concerning the environmental quality of goods are also related to the problems of international trade. There is indeed an international debate about environmental labelling and its relationships to free trade. Can the rules and regulations about environmental labelling, as practised in a number of countries worldwide, lead to non-tariff barriers for some products? The present international trade regime, as implemented by the World Trade Organization (WTO), prohibits, under the Agreement on Technical Barriers to Trade (TBT), discrimination and preferential treatment on the basis of technical regulations and standards issued by WTO member countries, but there is a debate among WTO member countries about the way in which the TBT Agreement applies to national ecolabelling schemes (Caldwell, 1996). Under this agreement, discrimination on the basis of Process and Production Methods (PPM) is prohibited. Clearly, environmental labelling is concerned with the PPMs of some products.

One of the answers to the questions raised is that, provided unlabelled products are not prohibited as such, and that the ecolabelling scheme is not in effect aiming at promoting a country's domestic products, a national ecolabelling scheme is likely not to be discriminatory. Distinctions based on PPMs can be considered as legitimate so long as they serve a public policy purpose, such as protecting human health, and do not discriminate on the basis of national origin of the product. This implies that access to environmental labelling of all types, and especially to national third-party certified ecolabelling, is not actually denied to foreign products.

As analysed by Dawkins (1996), ecolabelling seals or third-party certified ecolabelling is not in itself contrary to fair international trade rules, except if the certification process preferentially favours a country's industry, or if the certifying body is dominated by oligopoly interests and tends to exclude outsiders.

As far as the guidelines issued by the FTC in the United States and other similar guidelines are concerned, inasmuch as they are aimed mainly at enforcing the prohibition of misleading marketing and publicity, they do not constitute as such a TBT, even if they refer to technical characteristics of products.

Are such guidelines, provided and enforced by some kind of public authority such as the FTC in the United States, the only way of ensuring that the market is informationally efficient? There are also voluntary compliance rules that are issued by private bodies and by international organizations such as the ISO.

The ISO 14020 norms (ISO, 2000a) are an example of voluntary compliance rules, which provide for some general definitions and principles that apply to all types of environmental labelling. They lay down principles that apply to environmental labelling defined under the ISO 14020, 14021, 14024 and 14025 group of norms (ISO 1999a, b; 2000 a, b). As mentioned previously, these can be self-declarations (ISO Type II-labelling; the less stringent norm), LCA-based environmental declarations (ISO Type III-labelling), or third-party-awarded environmental labelling (ISO Type I-labelling; the most stringent norm, which applies only to the best products).

The general ISO 14020 norms define a number of basic principles that are common to all the above types of environmental labelling. According to these norms, environmental information has to be founded on significant bases and to be sincere.

As a first principle, environmental declarations and labelling must be exact, sincere, and open to verification. They must be pertinent, in line with real environmental problems, and they should not misinform consumers in any manner. A second principle is that procedures for environmental declarations and labelling should not lead to barriers in international trade. They should, furthermore, rest on detailed and exhaustive scientific procedures and methodologies that should back the environmental declarations and labelling, with exact and reproducible results. These methodologies must, whenever possible, take into account the whole life-cycle of the product.

Moreover, as mentioned in the previous chapter, and as detailed in Table 9.1, some of these techniques have been classified and standardized in a sub-group of the ISO 14000 family, which is the ISO 14020 sub-group. As seen in Table 9.1, there are three types of environmental labelling defined under the ISO 14020, 14021, 14024 and 14025 norms:

- *Type 1-labelling* corresponds to *third-party certified ecolabels* and is the most complete labelling scheme. It is standardized under the ISO 14024 norms. It implies third-party certification of the product on a voluntary compliance basis. It has to be based on an LCA, which passes some predetermined criteria of environmental quality, as examined by a third party under reliable and transparent conditions. It is signalled to the client by a suitable ecolabel.

- *Type II-labelling* is defined as encompassing *environmental claims and self-declarations*. It is standardized under the ISO 14021 norms that define the conditions under which such self- declarations can be made pertinent and sincere.

- *Type III-labelling* is defined as encompassing *environmental declarations*. It is standardized under the ISO 14025 norms, which are the most recent norms of the ISO 14020 sub-group. These norms define the conditions under which such self-declarations can be made pertinent and sincere.

Table 9.1 The main signalling techniques for the environmental quality attributes of products according to the ISO 14020 sub-group of norms

ISO 14020 norms	Contents
ISO 14020	General definitions and principles
	(All types of environmental labelling)
ISO 14021	Type II-environmental labelling
	(Self-declarations and environmental claims)
ISO 14024	Type I-environmental labelling
	(Third-party certified environmental labelling for the best products)
ISO 14025	Type III-environmental labelling
	(LCA-based environmental declarations)

Source: ISO 1999a, b; 2000a, b

The ISO 14020, 14021, 14024 and 14025 norms are but one example of the way in which environmental labelling can be standardized in order to ensure better and transparent information of consumers, to avoid deceiving them through misleading, insignificant or altogether false environmental claims and statements channelled through environmental labelling of goods. First, there are legally enforced rules in many countries that prohibit false advertising and tend to limit the deception of consumers through various claims on products, including of course environmental claims. Furthermore, a number of public and private bodies other than the ISO issue guidelines for environmental labelling in which principles of fair environmental advertising, labelling and information are developed.[3]

In addition to normalized environmental signalling techniques, there are other forms of direct environmental claims that are not normalized and are nonetheless significant. These include what one might call informal *eco-advertising* through usual advertising channels. Indirect techniques for signalling the environmental quality attributes of products can also be used. In particular, *organization marketing*, defined as general information on the environmental management of the firm, can be used as an indirect way of establishing and confirming the environmental reputation of the firm's products. Information through environmental reports, including information concerning the EMS of the firm, especially when certified (for instance, under ISO 14001 norms) can be used for organization marketing. Finally, *third-party eco-marketing* through independent third-party channels and the media is also important in informing the public (and, in particular, potential clients) of the environmental quality of products.

The signalling techniques or channels that will be discussed in the next section will therefore be: (1) self-declared environmental claims and other environmental declarations (for example, ISO Type II-labelling and ISO Type III-labelling); (2) third-party certified environmental labelling (for example, ISO Type I-labelling); (3) organization marketing and other indirect environmental marketing techniques.

3.   ENVIRONMENTAL MARKETING TECHNIQUES

3.1 Environmental Advertising, Self-declared Environmental Claims, and other Environmental Declarations

The problem of *eco-advertising* is that of communication with the firm's stakeholders in an authentic manner; that is, in such a manner that these stakeholders (in particular, clients, but also government agencies, lenders, shareholders and potential investors) and public opinion at large, believe and trust the statements and the information they are given. In a competitive situation, as mentioned above, the way communication about environmental matters is effected and its credibility are taken into account by potential consumers or clients as a criterion for choice. Of course, the situation may be different depending on whether one is dealing with experience attributes, which are experimentally verifiable by any technically equipped third party, or with credence or symbolic attributes, which are more difficult for independent observers to verify.

Through its usual advertising channels, an established firm may try to inform consumers of the environmental quality of its goods. There is clearly, in that case, a credibility problem: will consumers believe such information, as channelled by advertising? This is an issue related to the *reputation* of the firm. A firm like Volvo, which enjoys a long-term established reputation for the quality of its automobile products, will be trusted if it refers in its communication and advertisements to its achievements in promoting environmentally friendly products. Any false or dubious statement may endanger and even, in severe cases, ruin the firm's reputation. Any such false and deceptive statements, however, are generally ruled out by specific national legislation concerning fair competition and deceptive advertising claims. For example, in the United States, the Federal Trade Commission (FTC) guidelines about environmental claims first advise clear and precise claims, giving details about the actual quality attributes advertised. Do the ecological characteristics of the product concern only the package, or parts thereof, or its contents? What aspects of environmental impacts are reduced? Vague or ambiguous environmental statements such as 'Environment-friendly product' or 'Eco-safe product' without any other information or qualification are likely to constitute misleading advertising. Such vague statements may lead consumers to overestimate the environmental quality attributes of the product. Since they are not described in detail, they might in fact be lower than for other competing products that do not make environmental claims. In a country where the use of CFCs is prohibited because they have a negative impact on the ozone layer, a statement such as 'this product is without CFCs and is environment-friendly' concerning a shaving foam is misleading in that all shaving foams have to comply with the legal requirements. Such a statement overstates the environmental benefits of the product in relation to competing brands, because there are none.

The FTC also provides guidelines concerning the use of more specific or more particular environmental quality attributes, such as the biodegradability or recyclable nature of a product, or its ozone-friendly character.

However, there are also, as mentioned above, voluntary compliance schemes, such as self-declarations and environmental claims, as standardized under ISO 14021 norms (ISO, 1999a). Self-declarations and environmental claims are normalized as Type II-environmental labelling under these norms. They are just a particular case of environmental advertising and direct information of consumers under a voluntary compliance scheme. Such schemes constitute a formalized approach to environmental advertising, providing guarantees about its sincerity and its foundations. They also constitute international rules that are in line with most accepted national legislations concerning competition and misleading marketing.

In submitting to the ISO 14020 norms, they voluntarily comply with rules that ensure that self-declaration is pertinent and sincere. ISO 14021 further normalizes the use of certain terms related to environmental quality, called environmental claims, so that consumers get information that is clear, transparent and based on scientific methodology. Usual environmental claims, which in effect are environmental quality attributes, are defined, and the norms to which they are subject are detailed.

There are 17 such environmental claims, among which 12 are covered in more detail by the ISO 14021 norms and can be classified as follows:

1. Environmental quality attributes related to saving natural resources (reduced energy consumption, reduced resource use, reduced water consumption, recovered energy);
2. Environmental quality attributes related to minimization of the wastes produced by a good or through its disposal (compostable, degradable, waste reduction);

3. Environmental quality attributes related to the recyclable and the
    reusable character of the good (recyclable, recycled content, designed
    for disassembly, reusable and refillable, extended life product).

The definitions and characteristics of the norms for these various claims
are technical and often complex. They are outside the scope of this work,
and the details concerning them are given in the text of the ISO 14021
norms (ISO, 1999a). One of the most important of these attributes is
recyclable or *recycled content*. The ISO 14021 norms also recommend that
the Mobius loop seal on packages be the only mark used for information on
these attributes. The Mobius loop seal, which is also recommended by a
number of national environmental guidelines, is normalized as three twisted
clockwise-oriented arrows forming a circle. In the case of claims for recycled
material, a percentage within or near the circle may indicate the proportion
of recycled content of the product.

LCA-based self-declaration environmental claims constitute another
category of environmental labelling, which is intermediary between ISO
Type II-labelling and ISO Type I-labelling. They have recently been
normalized by the ISO under ISO 14025 standards (ISO, 2000b) and
constitute ISO Type III-labelling. These labelling norms are rather technical,
because they disclose details obtained from LCAs rather than just a
particular environmental quality attribute, such as recyclability. They are
thus adapted to technical products for industrial users rather than for end-
consumers.

3.2 Third-party Certified Environmental Labelling or Ecolabelling (ISO Type I-labelling)

Certifying the qualities of a firm's products can also be undertaken by
independent organizations, following a pre-established guideline set up by
independent authorities, public or private. These are an effective and direct
means of signalling the environmental qualities of a firm's product to the
public. This is called *environmental labelling* or *ecolabelling*. Ecolabels are
delivered or awarded by independent third parties to the *best* products from
an environmental point of view. They represent an effective and credible

means of communicating with consumers, being awarded following a certification process in which an independent organization assesses the environmental qualities of the firm's goods.

There are a number of *third-party environmental labelling* schemes, which have been developed as either publicly supported national or international schemes or as purely private schemes. One of the earliest schemes was the German *Blauer Engel* ('Blue Angel') scheme that was developed in Germany in 1978. There are numerous other national, regional or international ecolabel schemes that have developed since the end of the 1980s and the early 1990s. Examples of these ecolabelling schemes are given in Table 9.2.

Table 9.2   National and international ecolabelling schemes

Country	Name of ecolabel (date established)	Publicly sponsored or purely private scheme
Germany	Blue Angel (1978)	Publicly sponsored
Canada	Environmental choice (1988)	Publicly sponsored
Japan	Eco-Mark (1989)	Publicly sponsored
Nordic countries*	Nordic Swan (1989)	Publicly sponsored
United States	Green Seal (1990)	Purely private
France	NF-Environnement (1992)	Publicly sponsored
The Netherlands	Milieukeur (1992)	Publicly sponsored
European Union	EU Eco-label (1992)	Publicly sponsored
Spain	AENOR-Media Ambiente (1993)	Publicly sponsored

Note: * Denmark, Finland, Iceland, Norway, Sweden.

The German ecolabelling programme is the oldest, dating back to 1978, all other schemes having been established ten years later or more. It is effectively the prototype of all further third-party environmental labelling schemes, and, in particular, of the European ecolabel. It applies to end-consumer products as well as to industrial products. It is based on an evaluation of the performances of products through a Life-cycle Assessment with multiple criteria. A standard of 'best practice' is thus established for various categories of products, and the ecolabel is awarded to all products that meet these 'best practice' criteria. It gives the producer the right to mark its products with the 'Blue Angel' seal. A panel of independent experts, which includes scientific and academic experts, the industry, ecological associations and consumers' associations, carries out the evaluation. The 'Blue Angel' ecolabel is only awarded to products that have satisfactory environmental performances for all criteria.

Most other national or international third-party certified ecolabelling schemes are based on very similar principles. There are, however, national variations regarding (1) the scope of ecolabelling (does it concern only products for individual consumers, or does it extend to products for industrial end-users?); (2) the procedure in which the ecolabel is awarded; and (3) the involvement of public authorities in the programme. The most complete programmes are aimed at both individual and industrial consumers. This is the case with the German 'Blue Angel' scheme. It applies to products aimed at individual consumption, such as tissue-paper products, washing machines, dishwashers, laundry detergents, and many other products, but it also applies to products aimed at industrial consumption, such as certain building materials.

Although they do not substitute for the standards set by national and international ecolabelling schemes, the ISO 14024 norms (ISO, 1999b), concerning ISO Type I environmental labelling, give a useful characterization of what an ecolabelling programme should be. They are useful in providing guidelines to companies wishing to have their products certified under third-party-certified ecolabelling schemes. Practically, the ISO 14024 standards present themselves as the application of the ISO 14020 general guidelines to the particular case of ISO Type I environmental labelling. In particular, these norms are described as voluntary. Furthermore, just like the ISO 14001 EMS standards, they are also described as implying conformance to the existing environmental regulations. They insist that non-discriminatory access to the ecolabel for all products that meet its requirements has to be provided for: thus, the existence of national ecolabelling schemes will not be a TBT. The standards impose LCA-based evaluation of the environmental performance of the products. The enhanced environmental performances of the product should not be detrimental to its other quality attributes. The process for awarding an ecolabel should be transparent and be open to experts representing the various stakeholders.

The ISO 14024 standards are interesting in that, just as the other norms of the ISO 14020, 14021, 14024 and 14025 sub-group, they state commonly accepted international principles, especially those that conform to both national environmental legislation and international free trade agreements. These principles are more or less those that lie at the root of all ecolabelling schemes previously described.

There are a number of other ecolabelling schemes, including labelling for organic foods and for other agricultural, forestry and fishing products. As far as organic foods are concerned, technical standards have been established for public health reasons by regulation in the USA (US Organic Foods Products Act, 1990) and in the European Union (Regulation 2092/91, 1991). However, a number of private standards with adequate labelling exist in many countries (USA, European Union member countries, and Australia, among others). Table 9.3 gives some examples of these private labelling schemes for organic foods, and other agricultural, forestry and fish products.

Table 9.3   Ecolabels for organic foods and other agricultural, forestry and fish products

Country	Name of label	Products concerned
Australia	Biological Farmers of Australia	Mainly organic foods
Germany	Natürland	Mainly organic foods
Netherlands	Skal Eko-Label	Mainly organic foods
UK	Soil Association Organic Standard	Mainly organic foods
United States	California Certified Organic Farmers	Mainly organic foods
United States	Food Alliance	Mainly organic foods
United States	Forest Stewardship Council	Timber
United States	Salmon Safe	Wild Salmon (Oregon)

Markets for organic foods are among the most dynamic for 'green' products, because in all these countries, and in developed countries in general, public opinion is very concerned with the consequences of intensive agriculture.

3.3 Organization Marketing and Other Indirect Environmental Marketing Techniques

Background

There are a number of indirect ways in which a firm's stakeholders receive information that makes claims about the environmental performance of its products trustworthier. One of these is *organization marketing*. It is defined as publicizing the firm's EMS and its general environmental performances, especially if the EMS has been third-party certified, for example with ISO 14001 certification. The firm's adhesion to an external environmental charter, or code of environmental conduct, is also an indirect way of making credible the firm's commitment toward the environmental quality of its products. Finally, having independent third-party media inform consumers about the environmental achievements of the company is also an indirect way of publicizing the environmental quality of its products.

Environmental reports and EMS certification

Environmental reports and advertising about the firm's EMS, especially when it has been third-party certified under ISO 14001 or EMAS schemes, are an indirect way of publicizing the environmental quality of a firm's products. These constitute a communication channel of the firm with its shareholders, possibly extending to other stakeholders (in particular, the public at large and the firm's potential clients). Environmental reports, when they are trustworthy, will generally include some kind of environmental charter, which is very similar in spirit to so-called quality charters that are used to signal the general qualities of a product. They will also, more generally, include some detailed factual and quantitative information about the company's achievements and progress in its care for the environment.

In order to signal to various stakeholders, and, in particular, to its customers and clients, its environmental management efforts, a firm may seek to conform to the ISO 14001 (or EMAS) environmental management norms, or to specific parts thereof. This is a good and rather effective way of certifying to stakeholders of the firm the environmental qualities of goods. The ISO 14001 certification process (or the verification–registration process in the case of EMAS) is carried out by a third party. As mentioned several times in Chapter 8, the ISO 14001 norms are, on the face of it, management norms. However, at heart, they are norms of environmental quality; a point that numerous recent works, both applied and analytical, have stressed, insisting on the close link that exists between the ISO 14000 and 9000 standards. Just as the ISO 14001 are environmental management norms, the ISO 9001, 9002 and 9003 norms concern *quality management*, leading to quality as such, and to improved quality through the continuous-improvement process.

In particular, ISO 14001, to which we have devoted much of Chapter 8, is primarily a system of EM norms, which may, among other things, be used as a way of signalling the environmental quality of a firm's goods. Signalling certification of the firm's EMS under ISO 14001 standards may be used to inform the firm's clients and other stakeholders of the environmental quality of its products and services.

Environmental charters

Environmental charters (Brophy, 1998) are akin to quality charters that are used in the management of total quality. Companies also use them as a way of directing information to all stakeholders (in particular to clients, consumers of their products, and the public at large). As discussed in the previous chapter, these charters may be part of what the ISO 14001 standards require in terms of environmental policy statements, but they are usually distinct in both purpose and requirements.

Some environmental charters are general statements issued by international bodies such as the World Business Council for Sustainable Development. Individual companies may both adhere to these general principles and adapt them to their particular situation and products.

Generally speaking, there are at least four categories of environmental charters that may supply at least background information to the potential clients of a firm. Some charters are issued by (usually private) national or international organizations, which fall into two broad classes. The first is composed of confederations acting on a whole-industry basis and at either a national or regional-international level, such as the Confederation of British Industries (CBI) in the UK, and the Union of National Industry Confederations in Europe (UNICE), which acts at a regional-international level, in this case the European level. A second class of organizations represents particular industries or industrial branches, such as the chemical or oil industries, also at a national or regional-international level. All the organizations that fall into these first and second categories may logically be expected to express the views and the interests of the firms that they represent. Charters in a third category are issued by organizations that are more or less independent from particular business interests; these charters may be either endorsed or approved by individual firms. Finally, a fourth category of charters are those issued by individual corporations; usually large transnational corporations or groups.

The CERES principles, issued by CERES (Coalition for Environmentally Responsible Economies) (see Box 9.1), are an example of an environmental charter. This charter falls into the third category, inasmuch as CERES claims to be independent from particular business interests. It has been analysed as rather demanding and as fostering long-term sustainability goals and objectives (Brophy, 1998). A number of large corporations, mostly American, such as General Motors, have approved, and are apparently implementing, the principles underlying this charter.

Information through independent channels
In a democratic society with enough freedom of information, consumers may be informed by independent journalists or observers. These might be more or less credible, but if there is a competitive market for independent information, some credible information might emerge, establishing or ruining the reputation of a firm and its products. The environmental qualities of its products, as well as other qualities, would of course be included.

Box 9.1   An example of an environmental charter: the CERES principles

---

The CERES Principles

By adopting these Principles, we publicly affirm our belief that corporations have a responsibility for the environment, and must conduct all aspects of their business as responsible stewards of the environment by operating in a manner that protects the Earth. We believe that corporations must not compromise the ability of future generations to sustain themselves.

We will update our practices constantly in light of advances in technology and new understandings in health and environmental science. In collaboration with CERES, we will promote a dynamic process to ensure that the Principles are interpreted in a way that accommodates changing technologies and environmental realities. We intend to make consistent measurable progress in implementing these Principles and to apply them to all aspects of our operations throughout the world.

Protection of the Biosphere
We will reduce and make continual progress toward eliminating the release of any substance that may cause environmental damage to the air, water, or the earth or its inhabitants. We will safeguard our habitats affected by our operations and will protect open spaces and wilderness, while preserving biodiversity.

Sustainable Use of Natural Resources
We will make sustainable use of renewable natural resources, such as water, soils and forests. We will conserve non-renewable natural resources through efficient use and careful planning.

Reduction and Disposal of Wastes
We will reduce and where possible eliminate waste through source reduction and recycling. All waste will be handled and disposed of through safe and responsible methods.

Energy Conservation

We will conserve energy and improve the energy efficiency of our internal operations and of the goods and services we sell. We will make every effort to use environmentally safe and sustainable energy sources.

Risk Reduction

We will strive to minimize the environmental, health and safety risks to our employees and the communities in which we operate through safe technologies, facilities and operating procedures, and by being prepared for emergencies.

Safe Products and Services

We will reduce and where possible eliminate the use, manufacture or sale of products and services that cause environmental damage or health or safety hazards. We will inform our customers of the environmental impacts of our products and services and try to correct unsafe use.

4. LIFE-CYCLE ASSESSMENT (LCA) AND ITS IMPLICATIONS

4.1 From Cradle to Grave

As mentioned previously, evaluating the environmental quality of a product would be meaningless if it did not involve its whole life cycle. This includes the way in which raw materials, parts and other intermediary goods used in production have been obtained, the way in which the good itself is made, distributed, consumed and finally disposed of. One also allows for transport and logistics. Evaluating the environmental impacts of a product over all its life cycle constitutes, by definition, a Life-cycle Assessment (LCA).

An LCA, as summarily defined above, requires both highly technical skills and instrumentation. These technical details are outside the scope of this book; they have been described elsewhere (Curran, 1996; Frankl and Rubik, 1999; and, for simplified or so-called 'streamlined' LCAs: Weitz, Todd and Malkin, 1996; Graedel, 1998). In addition, a number of standards and guidelines have been published by various organizations. The Society for Environmental Toxicology and Chemistry (SETAC), the US Environmental Protection Agency (EPA), the European Commission (EC) and the International Standards Organization (ISO) have published guidelines and norms (Fava et al., 1992; Consoli et al., 1993; Fava et al., 1994; Barnthouse et al., 1997; Todd and Curran, 1999; US EPA, 1995; EC, 1997; ISO, 1997, 1998b, 2000c, d, e). The ISO has, in particular, issued the ISO 14040, 14041, 14042, 14043 and 14049 norms (that will be described for the sake of brevity as the ISO 14040 norms) which define standards applying to LCAs (ISO, 1997, 1998b, 2000c, d, e). These guidelines and norms are detailed in Table 9.4.

A summary description of the steps involved in an LCA will be useful here. Let us just say that an LCA involves several steps once the product to which it applies has been defined:

1. The *system* to which the LCA applies should be carefully defined. This implies an identification of the various parts of the life cycle of the products that are pertinent and that have significant impacts on the environment from various points of view. This step defines *the scope* (as defined by the ISO 14040 norms) of the study.
2. A *mass and energy balance,* which is in effect an ecobalance, has to be carried out. More generally, an *inventory* (as defined by the ISO 14040 norms), including not only mass and energy balances but also other impacts, such as the noise produced, has to be established for each of these parts of the life cycle, with mass and energy inputs and outputs. Among these outputs are the various pollutants, the impact of which have to be assessed.
3. Evaluating the *impacts* (as defined by the ISO 14040 norms) of the various parts of the life cycle on the environment is the next step.

Table 9.4   LCA technical references, guidelines and standards

Issuer	Reference	Contents
SETAC	Fava et al. (1992)	Conceptual framework
SETAC	Consoli et al. (1993)	Guidelines
SETAC	Fava et al. (1994)	Technical framework
SETAC	Barnthouse et al. (1997)	State of the art
SETAC	Todd and Curran (1999)	Survey concerning streamlined LCAs
US EPA	US EPA (1995)	Conceptual framework and survey of existing techniques
EC	EC (1997)	Guidelines
ISO	ISO 14040 ISO (1997)	Environmental management – Life-cycle Assessment – Principles and Framework.
ISO	ISO 14041 ISO (1998)	Environmental management – Life-cycle Assessment – Life-cycle Inventory Analysis.
ISO	ISO 14042 ISO (2000c)	Environmental management – Life-cycle Assessment – Impact Assessment
ISO	ISO 14043 ISO (2000d)	Environmental management – Life-cycle Assessment – Life-cycle Interpretation.
ISO	ISO 14049 ISO (2000e)	Environmental management – Life-cycle Assessment: Examples for the application of the ISO 14041

There usually are *several* impacts on the environment for each part of the life cycle, which are independent variables. Thus, after an LCA has been completed, one is usually left with an *impact evaluation matrix*, which is a double-entry table with columns corresponding to the various parts of the life cycles, and rows corresponding to the various impacts on the environment. Table 9.5 below, which is taken from European Union guidelines related to the EU ecolabel scheme (EC, 1997), gives a simplified but pertinent example of an impact evaluation matrix.

Clearly, more complex matrices can typically be encountered. For instance, air contamination can be broken down into several distinct atmospheric impacts, including those causing global warming through greenhouse gas emissions, acid rains, damage to the ozone layer, and several others (see Table 4.5 in Chapter 4). One should also include hazards due to toxic organic and inorganic pollutants, and solid particles and dusts (see Table 5.1 in Chapter 5).

Usually, as shown in Chapter 4, these impacts can be suitably and meaningfully aggregated along any row. The energy impacts, for example, can meaningfully be aggregated for all energy sources (coal, fuel-oil, natural gas, electricity); this is also true of greenhouse gases, because the effects of CO_2 and methane can, for instance, be aggregated.

Table 9.5   Example of an environmental impact evaluation matrix

Environmental fields	Product life-cycle				
	Pre-production	Produc-tion	Distribu-tion	Utiliza-tion	Disposal
Waste relevance					
Soil pollution and degradation					
Water contamination					
Air contamination					
Noise					
Consumption of energy					
Consumption of Natural resources					
Effects on ecosystems					

Source: European Commission (1997).

Once these individual effects have been aggregated along each row, the overall comparison and ranking of two brands or two different life cycles for the same product is clearly a multicriteria problem.

This implies defining the relative importance that the decision maker attributes to each of these impacts as a criterion for ranking these two brands. In the context of ecolabelling, which is a major application of LCAs, the decision whether or not to award the ecolabel is rather simple: one defines a profile for the best products from the environmental point of view, with a minimum value of the detrimental impact on the environment for each of the criteria defined above. Other more complex decisions, such as comparing various brands of some product on the basis of an LCA, are typical multicriteria decisions. They imply, for instance, valuation by weighting the different criteria (Welford, 1998), or a partial aggregation 'outranking' method, as developed by Roy (1996). An application of such ranking techniques is comparative publicity between various types or brands of the same product. Clearly, comparative publicity should not be manipulated to the point of becoming misleading, as stressed in the FTC guidelines for environmental claims. Taking into account the fact that comparing products is usually a multicriteria decision, this implies a very careful and transparent comparison scheme, which should if possible be validated by a panel of independent experts or by third-party audits.

4.2 Implications for the Environmental Aspects of Operations Management

The main application of LCAs is the evaluation of the environmental quality of products. This evaluation is important from several points of view. First, it supports environmental claims of all sorts, including self-declarations (ISO Type II-labelling), but also ISO Type-III labelling. It is of course useful in helping to meet the standards of a third-party certified ecolabelling scheme (ISO Type I-labelling). In all these situations, LCA is an invaluable tool, and an indispensable one in the case of ISO Type-I and Type-III labelling. This remains true in spite of the shortcomings of LCA described in Chapter 4.

Meeting environmental quality standards has, of course, implications in terms of operations management, as noted by A. and F. Hutchinson (1997). The main operations to be taken into account by an environmental quality-conscious company are production (including packaging) supply chain management, transport and distribution.

Production is an internal concern for the company, the environmental aspects of which may be analysed through an LCA. Production of a good, inasmuch as it is performed internally, is generally a multi-stage process that may suitably be analysed in terms of an LCA for its impact on the environment. This usually is private and confidential information, because it may reveal a competitive advantage or, on the other hand, some competitive disadvantages. This LCA may constitute the basis for a continual-improvement cycle, often within the framework of an ISO 14001-certified EMS. Within production operations, packaging is an important one given its environmental implications, and it should be carefully studied within the LCA analysis.

The *supply chain* is also an important aspect of operations management. It can be under the responsibility of a purchasing officer, a key function because of its implications in terms of cost controlling. The environmentally conscious company, especially if it operates an ISO 14001-certified EMS, has to select suppliers on the basis of their environmental performance. This can imply careful and detailed specifications that often require comparisons of Production and Process Methods (PPMs) on the basis of LCAs, and take into account or even impose on the supplier various norms and standards. These might typically be ISO 14001 EMS systems, or suitable environmental declarations, such as ISO Type I- or ISO Type III-labelling of products.

In terms of operations management, the *transport chain* also leads to environmental concerns, whether it concerns the supply side or the demand side. Modes of transport thus have to be analysed in terms of cost, but also in environmental terms by the environmentally conscious company.

Finally, *distribution* of the product to end-consumers will involve, if its environmental quality is at stake, suitable labelling, either through self-declared environmental claims or through ecolabels reflecting 'best product' from the point of view of environmental quality.

5. ECO-MARKETING AND THE DEMAND FOR ENVIRONMENTAL QUALITY

5.1 General Considerations

Comparatively little has been published on the marketing of 'green' or environment-friendly products and, more generally, on the demand for these products (see, however, concerning the situation in the UK, Blaza and Chambers, 1997; MORI, 1995, and National Consumer Council, 1996).

There are many markets for products and services with assessable environmental qualities. Furthermore, their environmental qualities are usually many, and often difficult to assess in a simple quantitative manner or through a single index. Even with powerful tools such as Life-cycle Assessment, which have been the object of international standardization (ISO 14040, 14041, 14042 and 14043), there are difficulties in reaching clear-cut conclusions (see also discussion in section 2.3 of Chapter 4). There are also, for a given product or family of products, numerous market segments, concerning different classes of consumers or clients, and markets in various places and countries. Furthermore, consumers and clients are often imperfectly informed, or even have no information at all, regarding the environmental qualities of the products they are interested in. It may be difficult to assess their demand for environmental quality even if all other problems concerning the analysis of these markets have been solved.

The marketing of products with environmental qualities is often a difficult task. It naturally depends on the firm's efforts and those of other stakeholders to publicize the relevant qualities through various channels that will be described in the next section. However, basic features of the analysis of such markets, which are useful at least as guidelines, may be developed. Various classifications for known environmental qualities enable us to define variables that influence the demand for product qualities and may be studied. Classifications in terms of the nature of the product, consumers' income in a given geographical area, and to end-consumers as opposed to corporate clients, are amongst the most useful for this purpose.

5.2 Investigating the Demand for Environmental Quality

As already noted, the characteristics of demand for environmental quality are not fully known. However, some basic principles and quantitative benchmarks can be given, for use by environmentally conscious managers.

Regarding the attitude of consumers with respect to the environmental quality of goods, several questions may be formulated. In what countries are consumers sensitive to the environmental quality of goods? Provided there are segments of end-consumer markets that are sensitive in some countries, are they ready to pay a premium for better environmental quality?

Although (as already emphasized) ISO 14001 certifications are *not* directly certifications of quality, we believe they are an indirect token of the environmental quality of a firm's products. We saw in Chapter 8 that a number of ISO 14001-certified firms follows some distinguishable patterns. In particular, developed countries – that is, the richest countries – are overwhelmingly over-represented in the number of ISO 14001 certifications. Even within these countries, unequal patterns persist. Countries that happen to be the most affluent – such as Switzerland, the Scandinavian countries, the Netherlands, Germany and Japan – appear to dominate in terms of the number of certifications. It is likely that public opinion in all these countries is particularly sensitive to environmental concerns. Firms from Asian countries with a comparatively high number of certifications, such as Japan, South Korea and Singapore, are interested in gaining comparative advantages on export markets, but it is also clear that, for cultural or perhaps historical reasons, public opinion there is again very sensitive to environmental problems. Other rich countries, in which 'green' consumer attitudes are perhaps less prevalent, are nonetheless very important in terms of their demand for environmental quality because of the sheer size of their markets. This, of course, is the case with the United States, and increasingly so with the EU single market. It is thus likely that, in all rich countries, consumers are to some extent sensitive to the environmental quality of consumer goods. This means that firms in countries that show sensitivity to the environment through ISO 14001 certification will also be sensitive to the environmental quality of the industrial products that they purchase, be they wholesale or intermediary. Such conclusions confirm those of a theoretical model by Auriol, Lesourd and Schilizzi (1998). Their model indicates that the demand for certified quality is, in general, positively correlated to income, the wealthiest consumers being the most quality-concerned. This is especially true of the certification of credence goods and of third-party-certified environmental quality.

Within rich countries, what are the segments of consumer markets that are most concerned with the environmental quality of the products? Whether we rely on theory or common sense, we could expect consumers in the upper-income brackets to be the most sensitive to environmental quality. Empirically, one could rely on surveys. In the UK, a 1995 survey (MORI, 1995) indicated that a broad majority of people surveyed were sensitive to the environment, perhaps something like 70 per cent, while 49 per cent had bought products with recycled packaging and 53 per cent products made of recycled material. However, most apparently were not ready to pay a premium. A majority of these consumers were most likely to prefer products with specific environmental quality attributes, provided they were not dearer than others. Only a minority (23 per cent) was ready to avoid products supplied by companies with a poor environmental record. It is likely that this minority alone would have accepted paying a premium for environmental quality. In the United States, the picture looks very similar. Ottman (1998, 1999) asserts that most American consumers are sceptical about environmental claims by firms, but that in the case of clearly authentic environmental quality, many consumers (probably in the upper-income bracket) will accept paying at least a slight premium for environmental quality. Ottman's study implies that consumers with an income above US$ 30 000 will be most likely to pay for such a premium. The study mentions markets in the United States that are booming, such as markets for organic foods.

6. CONCLUSION

Eco-marketing is probably one of the most interesting issues related to environmental management, because it is linked to fundamental issues at the beginning of a new millennium. First, environmental quality is related to credence quality attributes, for which the average consumer has to rely on information supplied by experts; hence the importance of third-party certification through ecolabelling schemes. A second point is that any meaningful evaluation of environmental quality has to be LCA-based. This means that concerns for environmental quality will usually spread from a company to its suppliers and throughout the supply chain, as well as to the transport chain and its clients, who are the ultimate driving force behind any movement toward environmental quality. Or are they? Direct and indirect evidence still indicates that consumer sensitiveness is restricted to wealthy countries, and, among these, to those with highly sensitive public opinion. Apparently, many and even most consumers are not ready to pay anything but a small premium for environmental quality. Yet it seems that products with clearly identified environmental quality attributes, such as products with ecolabels and organic foods, are experiencing strong demand.

CASE STUDY: VOLVO – ENVIRONMENTAL QUALITY AND ENVIRONMENTAL MANAGEMENT

Introduction

The Volvo Group, since it sold its car division to Ford, is one of the world leaders in the production of trucks, buses, construction equipment, marine and industrial engines, and aircraft-engine components and services. As of 31 December 1999, its balance sheet total was SEK (Swedish Kroner) 195.6 billion (US$ 23.64 billion) with a shareholders' equity amounting to SEK 97.7 billion (US$ 11.80 billion). In 1999, its net sales amounted to SEK 125.019 billion (US$ 15.11 billion) with an operating income (excluding the proceeds from the sale of its car division[4]) of SEK 6.554 billion (US$ 0.792 billion), and a net income of SEK 8.437 billion (US$1.02 billion). This means an operating income-based return on equity (ROE) of 10.1 per cent. Its operating cash flow has been SEK 9.673 billion in 1999. Table 9.6 gives the evolution of these financial data since 1997, corrected for comparability in terms of incomes (excluding the consequences of the divestment of the car section). The Volvo share is quoted on the Stockholm, Brussels, Frankfurt, London and Tokyo stock exchanges and on the NASDAQ in New York. At the end of 1999, the Volvo Group employed 53 470 people, including 24 840 in Sweden. The Volvo Group consists of six business units: Volvo Truck Corporation, Volvo Bus Corporation, Volvo Construction Equipment, Volvo Penta Corporation (marine engines), Volvo Aero Corporation and Volvo Transport. It is also involved in all sales financing services. The Volvo Group is a global company. It has production subsidiaries all over the world and on five continents, in Europe (Sweden, Belgium, Denmark, Finland, Germany, Poland, UK), in North America (United States, Mexico), in South America (Brazil, Colombia, Peru), in Africa (Morocco, South Africa), in Asia (China, India, Iran, Malaysia), and in Australia (Queensland). It also has commercial subsidiaries in many other countries.

Table 9.6: The evolution of Volvo's financial data (1997–1999)

Financial data	1997	1998	1999
Total of assets (SEK billion)	164.820	205.745	164.815
Total of assets (US$ billion)	21.600	25.820	23.640
Shareholders' equity (SEK billion)	97.692	69.375	61.951
Shareholders' equity (US$ billion)	11.810	8.710	8.120
Sales* (SEK billion)	125.019	114.854	92.212
Sales* (US$ billion)	15.109	14.415	12.087
Operating Income* (SEK billion)	6.554	3.552	3.908
Operating Income * (US$ billion)	0.792	0.446	0.512
Net Income * (SEK billion)	5.527	8.437	10.481
Net Income * (US$ billion)	0.668	1.059	1.374
Return on Equity (ROE) (%)	6.710	5.120	6.310
Operating margin (%)	5.240	3.090	4.230

Note: *Comparable data, excluding car sales

Volvo's Environmental Management

The Volvo Group has established a long-standing reputation for the *quality* of its products, including (until 1998) cars, trucks, buses, construction equipment, marine and industrial (especially diesel) engines, and aircraft products. It is also renowned for its commitment toward *safety*, whether it concerns cars (until 1998), trucks or other vehicles. A third more recent commitment (but a firmly established one) is toward the *environment*. Thus, the core values of Volvo's corporate culture are *quality, safety* and *environment*, and this is strongly emphasized in Volvo's environmental reports, published annually. Volvo's corporate culture, especially the importance of the environment, has not changed since the sale of its car division. Furthermore, significant environmental information, including the Volvo group's eco-balance, is given in the company's annual financial reports.

Volvo is very concerned with the environmental impact of its operations, and publishes environmental accounts that show a continuous decrease in the environmental impacts of its production sites (Table 9.7).

Table 9.7   Environmental   performance   of   Volvo's   production   units worldwide

Absolute values / net sales	1996	1997	1998	1999
Energy consumption	20.0	16.6	14.7	14.5
Water consumption	70.3	64.1	49.0	53.8
NO_x emissions	3.8	3.5	2.9	2.7
Solvent emissions	18.2	14.4	8.8	10.7
Sulphur dioxide emissions*	149.0	98.0	6.0	77.0
Hazardous wastes*	156,060.0	182,293.0	207,539.0	125,019.0

Note: *Absolute figures in tonnes.

One can say that Volvo's environmental management is strongly oriented toward the environmental quality of its products, and especially in reducing their environmental impacts over their whole life cycle: during their production, use and disposal.

Volvo has been concerned for a long time with the environmental performance of its cars (De Sèze, 1993). It invented the catalytic exhaust in 1974, and the catalytic converter in 1976 (with the German automobile equipment company Bosch). It also dramatically improved the efficiency of its car gasoline and diesel engines, as well as their environmental performances. Volvo cars have been designed as completely recyclable. Their environmental impacts have been minimized on a life-cycle basis. The company also devised a filter reducing by 80 per cent the emission of solid particles by diesel engines.

This orientation toward the environmental quality of its products still applies to the new scope of Volvo's products after the company sold its car division to Ford. Volvo has constantly lowered the environmental impacts of its truck and other diesel engines, including emissions of solid particles. Volvo trucks have lower fuel consumption than other models, and the latest Volvo truck diesel engine, the D12C (introduced in 1999) has a specific consumption which is 5 per cent lower than its predecessors. Volvo is also supplying new Volvo 7000, Volvo 5000 and BL7 city buses with fuel consumption lowered by 10 per cent and emissions likewise. Furthermore, natural-gas trucks and buses with much lower emissions have been introduced. Volvo is testing new filters that will further reduce emissions for both trucks and buses. Regarding construction equipment, Volvo is developing new models in which fuel consumption and noise levels will be dramatically reduced. Volvo Penta, which is Volvo's marine subsidiary, is manufacturing new engines, such as the TAMD74L, which consumes 8 per cent less fuel than older models. Volvo is also manufacturing diesel locomotives for rail propulsion, with improved exhaust emissions.

The management of the environmental quality of Volvo's products is in line with Volvo's EM systems. Volvo is gradually establishing EM systems for all its production units complying with ISO 14001 and/or EMAS norms. On 31 December 1999, 24 of Volvo's production units (out of a total of 63) were ISO 14001-certified and/or EMAS-verified. Volvo is gradually aiming at ISO 14001 certification and/or EMAS registration of all its production sites, and at ISO 14001 certification or EMAS verification for all its suppliers by the end of year 2001. It conducts periodic environmental audits on all its sites and Life-cycle Assessments for all its products.

In terms of corporate organization, Volvo's executive committee is in charge of the group's environmental management. It has established a Group Environmental Council which is in charge of studying all related technical and strategic problems, in three areas: product development, production, marketing and communication. There is one environmental coordinator for the group, and an environmental manager for each of the six corporations.

Finally, the Volvo group has, since 1996, carefully trained all its employees through a thorough environmental training programme.

Conclusion

As mentioned above, the environmental quality of Volvo products may be identified with the core values of the group: quality, safety and environment. It is related to the group's other core values, and especially to the long-standing tradition of overall quality of its products. The divestment of Volvo's car division should not affect this orientation, and the environmental quality of Volvo's commercial vehicles, industrial engines and equipment remains as strong and strategic an orientation as ever. The orientation towards the environmental performance and qualities of Volvo's products is closely related to the group's EM system, which will gradually be ISO 14001-certified and/or EMAS-verified. Volvo is, very logically, imposing similar environmental constraints implying ISO 14001-certification and/or EMAS-verification to all its suppliers.

NOTES

1. We gratefully acknowledge the reviewing of this chapter by David Webb. Of course, any remaining errors or omissions are our sole responsibility.
2. Traditionally, marketing is presented under the headings of the four P's: product, price, promotion and place. Here we shall be concerned as much with 'promotion', as with the other three aspects. 'Product' will refer to environmental attributes and 'price' to development costs and such like (We thank David Webb for attracting our attention to this point.)
3. Note that there are here two non-exclusive motivations behind these principles and guidelines. One is ethical (fairness), the other aims at market efficiency, in Fama's sense.
4. These amounted to SEK26.695 billion (US$3.226 billion).

REFERENCES

Auriol, E., Lesourd, J.B. and Schilizzi, S. (1998), *Quality Signalling through Certification. Application to the Environmental Quality of Goods.* Communication, Conference of the Association Française de Sciences Economiques, Toulouse, May.

Barnthouse, L., Fava, J., Humphreys, K., Hunt, R., Laibson, L., Noesen, S., Norris, G., Owens, J., Todd, J., Vigon, B., Weitz K. and Young, J. (1997), *Life-Cycle Assessment: The State of the Art* (2nd ed.), Pensacola, FL: SETAC.

Blaza, A. and Chambers, N. (1997), 'Environmental Management Standards: Who Cares?' Chapter 11 in C. Sheldon (ed.), *ISO 14001 and Beyond. Environmental Management Systems in the Real World*, Sheffield: Greenleaf Publishing, pp. 197-210.

Brophy, M. (1998), 'Environmental Guidelines and Charters', Chapter 6 in R. Welford (ed.), *Corporate Environmental Management. 1. Systems and Strategies*, 2nd ed., London: Earthscan, pp. 102–15.

Caldwell, D.J. (1996), *Environmental Labeling in the Trade and Environment Context*, Washington DC: Trade and Development Centre.

Consoli, F., Allen, D., Boustead, I., Fava, J., Franklin, W., Jensen, A.A., de Oude, N., Parrish, R., Perriman, R., Postlethwaite, D., Quay, B., Séguin, J. and Vigon, B. (eds) (1993), *Guidelines for Life-Cycle Assessment: A 'Code of Practice'*. Pensacola, FL: SETAC.

Curran, M.-A. (1996), *Environmental Life-Cycle Assessment*, New York: McGraw-Hill.

Darbi, M.R. and Karni E. (1973), 'Free competition and the optimal amount of fraud', *Journal of Law and Economics*, **16**: 67–88.

Dawkins, K. (1996), 'Ecolabelling: Consumers' rights-to-know or restrictive business practice?', Minneapolis, MN: Institute for Agriculture and Trade Policy.

De Sèze, A.-D. (1993), 'Volvo: Un industriel fier de son bilan', in M. Beaud, C. Beaud and M.L. Bouguerra (1993), *L'état de l'environnement*, Paris: La Découverte, pp. 400-401, in French.

European Commission (1997), *Guidelines for the Application of Life Cycle Assessment in the EU Ecolabel Award Scheme*, Brussels: European Commission.

Fama, E. (1970), 'Efficient capital markets: A review of theory and empirical work', *Journal of Finance*, **25**: 383–417.

Fama, E. (1991), 'Efficient capital markets, II', *Journal of Finance*, **46**: 1575–617.

Fava, J. A., Consoli, F., Denison, R., Dickson, K., Mohin, T. and Vigon, B. (1992), *A Conceptual Framework for Life-Cycle Assessment*, Pensacola, FL: SETAC.

Fava, J.A., Denison, R., Jones, B., Curran, M.A., Vigon, B., Selke S. and Barnum, J. (1994), *A Technical Framework for Life-Cycle Impact Assessment*, Pensacola, FL: SETAC.

Frankl, P. and Rubik, F. (1999), *Life Cycle Assessment in Industry and Business: Adoption Patterns, Applications and Implications*, Heidelberg: Springer Verlag.

Graedel, T.E. (1998), *Streamlined Life-Cycle Assessment*, Upper Saddle River, NJ: Prentice Hall.

Hutchinson, A. and Hutchinson, F. (1997), *Environmental Business Management. Sustainable Development in the New Millenium*, London: McGraw-Hill, pp. 141–78.

Ippolito, P.M. and Mathios, A.D. (1990), 'Information, advertising, and health choices', *Rand Journal of Economics*, **21**: 659–80.

International Standards Organization (ISO) (1997), 'ISO 14040. Environmental Management – Life Cycle Assessment – Principles and Framework', Geneva: ISO.

International Standards Organization (ISO) (1998), 'ISO 14041. Environmental Management – Life Cycle Assessment – Goal and Scope Definition and Inventory Analysis', Geneva: ISO.

International Standards Organization (ISO) (1999a), 'ISO 14021. Environmental Labels and Declarations – Self-declared Environmental Claims – Type II Environmental Labelling', Geneva: ISO.

International Standards Organization (ISO) (1999b), 'ISO 14024. Environmental Labels and Declarations – Type I Environmental Labelling – Principles and Procedures', Geneva: ISO.

International Standards Organization (ISO) (2000a), 'ISO 14020. Environmental Labels and Declarations – General Principles', Geneva: ISO.

International Standards Organization (ISO) (2000b), 'ISO/TR 14025. Environmental Labels and Declarations – Type III Environmental Declarations', Geneva: ISO.

International Standards Organization (ISO) (2000c), 'ISO 14042. Environmental Management – Life Cycle Impact Assessment', Geneva: ISO.

International Standards Organization (ISO) (2000d), 'ISO 14043. Environmental Management – Life Cycle Assessment – Life Cycle Interpretation', Geneva: ISO.

International Standards Organization (ISO) (2000e), 'ISO/TR 14049. Environmental Management – Life Cycle Assessment – Examples Application of the ISO 14041 to Goal and Scope Definition and Inventory Analysis', Geneva: ISO.

MORI (1995), 'Business and the Environment: British Green Consumers (MORI Survey of UK General Public)', London: MORI (September).

National Consumer Council (1996), 'Green Claims: A Consumer Investigation into Marketing Claims and the Environment', London: National Consumer Council, (March).

Nelson, P. (1970), 'Information and consumer behavior', *Journal of Political Economy*, **78**: 311–29.

Nelson, P. (1974), 'Advertising as information', *Journal of Political Economy*, **81**: 729–54.

Ottman, J. (1998), *Green Marketing: Opportunity for Innovation*, Lincolnwood, Ill: NTC Business Books.

Ottman, J. (1999), *Will the Consumer Pay a Premium for Green?*, New York: Ottman Inc.

Roy, B. (1996), *Multicriteria Methodology for Decision Aiding*, Dordrecht: Kluwer.

Todd, J.A. and Curran, M.A. (1999), 'Streamlined Life-Cycle Assessment: A Final Report from the SETAC North America Streamlined LCA Workgroup', Pensacola, FL: SETAC.

US Environmental Protection Agency (USEPA) (1995), 'Life-Cycle Impact Assessment: A Conceptual Framework, Key Issues, and Summary of Existing Methods', Research Triangle Park NC: Office of Air Quality Planning and Standards. EPA/530/R-95/011.

Weitz, K.A., Todd, J.A. and Malkin, M.D. (1996), 'Streamlining life cycle assessment: consideration and a report on the state of practice', *International Journal of Life Cycle Assessment*, **1** (2): 79–84.

Welford, R. (1998), 'Life Cycle Assessment', Chapter 8 in R. Welford (ed.), *Corporate Environmental Management. 1. Systems and Strategies*, (2nd ed.), London: Earthscan, pp. 138–47.

10. Conclusions

SUMMARY

A tension exists between the growing need to include environmental concerns into standard business practices, as per the book's title, and the inherent limitations of such a process. These limitations show up through the wide variation across countries rich and poor, and across businesses large and small. The factors explaining these variations underscore the costs and benefits of environmental management. These have gradually become visible through a number of key processes, summarized below. We will then bring together, as per the first part of the book's sub-title, the new directions in environmental management identified throughout the book, hinting as we go at an emerging field not covered in previous chapters: the supply of environmental services and the production of environmental technologies. The next section addresses the second part of the book's sub-title, by summarizing the economic insights that have been gained into business practices in relation to the environment and why they are important. One conclusion cannot be sufficiently emphasized: the growing need to link the environmental and financial management of the firm by utilizing the tools of financial economics in both, based on future-oriented time and risk-dependent decisions. The crowning achievement should be the quantification of potential environmental liabilities and their inclusion into standard business accounting. The final section addresses a question that readers may have asked from the very beginning of the book: environmental management or sustainable development? Although we leave readers free to interpret our book as they see fit, we propose our own interpretation and show how, to a large extent, we have addressed, by way of four mechanisms, some of the key issues of sustainable development.

1. WHAT TAKE-HOME MESSAGE?

Modern works of art tend to avoid any clear message, preferring to let consumers derive one of their own. Although it might be seen as modern, this book is not a work of art! It does have a message, hopefully a clear one.

As the title of the book suggested, environment 'in' corporate management conveys the idea that 'environmental management' (EM) is not yet universally accepted or integrated into standard business practice, unlike financial management. No one would think of saying 'finance in corporate management'; 'financial management' is a universally accepted concept and practice. Yet, as this book has endeavoured to show, things are moving quickly and, as we begin the new millennium, we can safely say that EM is heading towards widespread acceptance and implementation, even if it is still in its early stages. However, one may also ask whether it will ever reach as universal a level of implementation as financial management. Explaining this trend, and its inherent limitations, has been the key purpose of this book. It is worth summarizing both sides of the equation underlying this tension.

EM is spreading, but it is spreading unequally across firms and across countries. Clearly, large corporations and wealthier countries are concerned first and foremost. Is this because EM is primarily a 'game for the rich'? Our answer is, yes and no. Larger firms and wealthier communities are now subject to stronger feedback mechanisms that tend to 'internalize' the social consequences of environmental impacts. This is clearly the case with firms quoted on the stock market where shareholders are 'democratically distributed'. There, financial markets are most active, and investors, lenders and insurers have the means of exerting increasing influence on corporate management. Not surprisingly, the areas of environmental and financial management are increasingly overlapping every day. Additionally, in wealthier communities, the range of products on offer in the market is greater, and consumers have more purchasing (that is, negotiating) power and can therefore also exert increasing influence on corporate management. To do so, quoting Hirschman, they can use 'exit, voice or loyalty'.[1] Last, but not least, government agencies have more resources and are less prone to corruption; regulation and enforcement of standards is more effective.

Clearly, this is less true of poorer countries, or countries where less development means less market diversity and less exposure to financial markets. Underlying all this lurks a common driving force: the strength of democracy. EM is an heir to democracy. Even today, Russia and other former Soviet-influenced countries rank bottom on ISO 14001 certification.

To some extent, the same may be said of small and medium-sized enterprises (SMEs), and of firms not quoted on the stock market. Their greater number compared to large firms also means that their clientele is more fragmented and less likely to co-ordinate their action against any one of them. On the other hand, unless they occupy a narrow niche, SMEs are more 'substitutable', having more competitors.

As a result, and for the reasons given above, previously hidden costs and benefits have come to the surface more quickly and more thoroughly in wealthier countries and for larger firms, especially those quoted on the stock market. In other words, for them, the benefits of EM have been greater. Let us summarize why.

- Firstly, the sheer growth in physical environmental impacts: resource depletion, habitat destruction, air and water pollution, species extinctions and large-scale catastrophes have increased dramatically in the latter half of the twentieth century. In spite of concurrent technological 'miracles' and increased material wealth, people's quality of life and physical and mental health have been directly affected.

- Secondly, huge technical improvements have been made in the last 30 years or so, greatly reducing the costs of EM. This is particularly true of environmental monitoring, accounting, analysis and reporting, but also of the efficiency of risk-management tools, whether financial or, through new insurance schemes, physical. National and international regulation and standard setting, in particular the ISO 14001 international norms and rules for eco-signalling (labelling and advertising), have further contributed in reducing the transaction costs of EM for all stakeholders.

- Thirdly, the development of information technologies has allowed ever-increased efficiency in communication and information processing, allowing the media and watchdog organizations to instantly alert huge numbers of people worldwide to a company's doings. Not only has the 'delay in discovery' of some wrongdoing been shortened, reducing the cumulative profits therefrom, but the sheer scale of the consequences have grown manifold, the more so for larger multinational corporations.

One may summarize the factors that have contributed towards reducing the costs of EM and those that have contributed towards increasing its benefits. The former include new technologies for pollution abatement and for monitoring, analysing, and communicating environmental data; increased awareness by managers and employees; new financial and insurance instruments; newly adapted management structures (EMSs), and the development of both national and international norms and standards. These help reduce transaction costs. The factors having contributed towards increasing the corporate benefits of EM include the development of increased legal liabilities, both current and contingent on future events; extended and more stringent government regulations; awareness by consumers, watchdog organizations and investors of the environmental impacts of firms, themselves a by-product of the increase in actual impacts; the appearance of environment-oriented investment portfolios and stock-market indices; modern IT communication systems; the spillover effects, especially for large corporations, from one activity branch to another; and the increasing importance of intangibles in giving the firm a competitive edge.

As for the processes that have actually contributed to revealing previously hidden costs and benefits, we may summarize them as follows:

1. The appearance of environmentally concerned consumers, investors and citizens, and their empowerment to buy or boycott goods and services, to stock-pick company shares, and to use their voting power and other means of political pressure.

2. The translation of these trends into new regulations and market incentives to produce environmental quality goods and services, and, in particular, corporate environmental reports.

3. In order to inform these reports, need for environmental accounting and its integration to the financial accounting framework, itself evolving under the pressure of financial economics.

There is a clear, though complex, causal chain from the first to the last of these trends, made possible by a subtle interplay of democratic, market and community mechanisms.

Compared to larger firms, SMEs will not experience to the same degree the scale and scope effects in EM-cost reduction or benefits increase; their usually tighter or more unstable or less predictable financial situations will not give EM as high a priority; and this will correlate to a different 'company culture', usually (but not always) exhibiting shorter planning horizons; regarding contingent liabilities, SMEs in many countries can more easily disappear and be reborn under new names. Firms not quoted on the stock market, which comprise most SMEs, will not be subject to shareholders' influence or to investors' pressure; in addition, the range of financial instruments to which they have access is smaller, reducing the opportunity costs of not implementing EM. Finally, countries with less-efficient financial markets and smaller or less-diverse commodity markets will similarly provide less room for consumer, investor and, more generally, stakeholder influence on firms. Poorer countries also stand to have less-efficient law-enforcement systems, meaning that liabilities, especially if corruption is rife, are less likely to be counted as costs by companies. All these factors reduce the attractiveness and the incentives for including EM into standard business practices. To some extent, these are the same factors that combine to sustain environmental degradation, be it deforestation, pollution, or resource depletion.

If firms in less-developed countries, which tend to be SMEs, are to follow the EM practices introduced by large corporations, coordinated international action will need to be relied on. EM may then appear under the same light as rainforest preservation: inasmuch as the environmental impacts of firms in these countries create concern in other, richer, countries, EM may be viewed as a public good worthy of targeted institutional arrangements, such as debt-for-EM swaps, whether at the firm or at government levels. Of course, this holds for SMEs in more developed countries too. By contrast, some SMEs may implement the most efficient EM systems, especially if their business is high-tech and strongly oriented towards the future.

The net result of the spread of EM across the business spectrum is likely to accentuate the difference in economic value between heavily polluting and lightly polluting industries, and tend to drive the first out of the market at a quicker pace than if EM was not included in business practices. This may provide a way for less-developed countries to short-circuit the polluting development path adopted by currently more-developed countries. Positive externalities in the form of new technologies and production methods, developed by large corporations in richer countries, should facilitate this process. Currently, for instance, Western technology is helping Chinese industry, if not to avoid dirty coal at least to burn it more cleanly and reduce atmospheric pollutants. The spread of EM could also accentuate differences in economic value between technologies and favour, for instance, renewable or cleaner energies and recycled materials. The switch from coal and oil to natural gas in Australia and elsewhere was partly motivated by cleaner energy considerations.

2. WHAT NEW DIRECTIONS IN ENVIRONMENTAL MANAGEMENT?

In the course of this book, we identified a number of new directions in EM. Following the chapter order, we may summarize current and future developments as follows. Trends tending to reveal otherwise hidden environmental costs and benefits, through both institutional and technical means, should accelerate as an initially spontaneous process becomes self-conscious and directed. The ethical responsibilities of firms are being defined in an increasing number of countries, allowing stakeholders to hold them accountable to greater effect. This materializes through company statements of commitment regarding EM; and the specification of clear management responsibilities within the firm, important for obtaining certification of an EMS. Most importantly perhaps, environmental accounting systems are being developed to achieve integration of the ecological and financial aspects of EM; this will facilitate monitoring and analysis, performance assessment, comparisons and communication with stakeholders. A crucial aspect will be the quantification and inclusion of contingent environmental liabilities in the core financial report, an achievement that the current crisis in financial accounting will make easier. Just as financial reporting improvements corrected many of the deficiencies existing prior to the 1929 stock-market collapse, we may hope that current environmental reporting improvements will, by allowing more efficient stakeholder involvement, counter widespread environmental damages. The development of financial instruments, in particular regarding environmentally induced financial risks, should help 'internalize' these risks by creating costs for firms; for instance, by having to pay higher risk premiums. This supposes that banks, and other investors, are sensitive to environmentally induced liabilities of firms. Government legislation can influence such 'sensitivity', but, ultimately, it is the general public, as consumers and voters, at least in democracies, that will create the drive and the incentive. These developments are further facilitated by the appearance of new risk-management instruments that give firms greater flexibility in combining risk-retention and risk-transfer (or insurance) strategies. Last, but not least, the production of international norms and standards will not only clarify stakeholder expectations but reduce EM-implementation costs, whether it be for the firm's internal EMS or for the environmental quality of its goods and services. Standards will also allow firms to better capture (or internalize) the benefits of their efforts. As a side benefit, we believe that environment-related standards will influence financial standards.

One important aspect not covered in this book, though lightly touched upon in the last chapter, is the rise of a new field of business activity, the supply of environmental services and the production of environmental technologies. That is, a field of activities where environmental impacts are no longer a characteristic of the goods and services produced, but constitute the goods and services themselves. This is an emerging field, but a fast growing one. It includes solar-powered technologies, waste-recycling systems, pollution-abatement equipment, ecological monitoring systems, resource rehabilitation projects, environmental training and expertise, and so on. As environmental damages become more widespread, the profitability of such activities is bound to rise, attracting yet more companies. This leads us to the next point.

3. WHAT ECONOMIC INSIGHTS, AND WHY?

One of the claims of this book, signalled in its sub-title, is that it promised to provide 'economic insights'. What are they, and why bother? The literature on environmental management and its related aspects of accounting, finance, risk management, product quality and standard setting, is simply colossal. Thousands of books and tens of thousands of articles have been published. However, most if not all of them focus on technical and legal aspects; and they do so by asking two types of questions: (1) 'How should it correctly be done?' and (2) 'Why should it be done?' The first question leads to practical, professional-oriented material, with references to current or developing legislation, business practices and professional standards. 'Do it right' seems to be the main goal. The second question leads to a 'softer' kind of literature, focusing on moralistic discourse ('do the right thing: care for the environment, it's your responsibility'), or highlighting the benefits of EM ('you can care for the environment and still make, even increase, profits'), depending on whether a duty-based or a utilitarian ethic is referred to and relied on. What does the economic point of view add to the picture?

The answer follows directly from the definition of an economic viewpoint. At bottom, it is a view that tries to balance benefits and costs in relation to a recognized population of stakeholders. In this case, we adopted the micro-economic perspective of the firm, focusing on the benefits and costs to the firm. This may be interpreted as excluding anyone outside the firm, but such an interpretation would be misled. The combination of economics and stakeholder analysis, with a particular emphasis on corporate shareholder value, focuses on how external stakeholders, both direct and indirect, can have a strong influence on the firm's performance and, therefore, decisions (see Tables 2.1a, b in Chapter 2). That is, a change in stakeholders' costs and benefits, whether monetary or not, is likely, sooner or later, to translate into a change in the firm's financial performance and shareholder value. The sensitivity of the latter to the former (theoretically measurable as the ratio of the relative percentage variations) is of course the crucial thing: the greater the ratio, or the greater the sensitivity, the stronger the dependence of corporate profits on public well-being. This sensitivity depends directly on the legal system that defines and prices the firm's liabilities (through fines, compensation schemes, and so on), and on the degree of democracy of the political system that empowers stakeholders, such as consumers and communities, to exert effective pressure.

The economic question reads: 'What is the value of EM to the firm?' Furthermore, when is it valuable and when is it not, and what are the factors affecting this value? The big picture has just been provided above (section 1), but we also wished to highlight what questions firm managers need to ask themselves when considering the type and extent of EM for their firm. The concept of optimal involvement was common to every chapter (though worded differently each time: optimal monitoring effort, optimal disclosure, optimal risk exposure, and so forth). There are both benefits and costs to the firm of 'managing' or 'caring for' the environment. To be sure, the costs of EM have been falling and its benefits have been rising, and this trend is even likely to increase in the future; but costs of EM will not fall to zero, and some 'EM restraint' will always be optimal. In particular, firms, whether we like it or not, will always be willing to take certain risks with the environment, even if this also means taking risks with their financial liabilities.[2] Secondly, different firms and firms in different countries, with different social, political and legal features, will experience different costs and different benefits. For some, it is likely that zero EM involvement will remain optimal.

There will be readers who will perhaps be shocked by such a statement, as many are when they hear the phrase 'optimal rate of species extinction'. Surely, the only acceptable extinction rate is zero! However, as Chapter 3 asked, what happens when others do not hold the same beliefs as you do? Use of force (for example, prohibition) is an option, but usually an expensive and ineffective one. The economic approach to the problem is to say, do not tell firms what their optimal involvement in EM should be; rather, see how you can shift their optimum in the desired way. An optimum reflects the actual cost benefit structure of a business. You do not change it with a magical wand. Instead, carefully negotiated changes in laws, regulations, fiscal and other incentives are far more likely to serve the environment. Also, institutional creativeness and incentives for R&D investments can provide a greater number of options and increased flexibility for corporate decision making. This will allow shifts in optimal solutions to be more fluid and less costly. Society gets what it pays for. Of course, macroeconomic issues of employment, growth and international competitiveness also matter, but they are not necessarily a hindrance – a topic worthy of discussion but outside the scope of this book.

The previous paragraph highlighted the 'comparative statics' of increased EM, but the dynamics are even more important. Given the rising importance of financial instruments in business management, and the pending revolution in financial accounting[3], EM forces firms, and should also force the regulator, to be more forward-looking and to consider the two most important decision factors: time and uncertainty. The timing of expected costs and benefits and their degree of uncertainty must be considered if EM is to be of most value to firms, and also to society. According to H. Kierkegaard (1997), current accounting methods do not provide such information. As a result, contingent environmental liabilities continue to generate costs hidden both to the firm and to society. They are thus undervalued, and excessive risks are taken with the environment. When this happens, not only does the environment suffer unduly but many of the firm's stakeholders also get angry, and in the end the firm's regret is greater than if it had factored in those liabilities properly. This leads us to our last point: sustainable development.

4. ENVIRONMENTAL MANAGEMENT, OR SUSTAINABLE DEVELOPMENT?

The reader will have noticed that never, in this book, did we use the expression 'sustainable development' (SD). Yet the authors are well versed in the corresponding issues.[4] Some will consider that this is what we were talking about all the time, whereas others will consider we skipped the issue altogether. We may legitimately ask: is EM a goal in itself, or is it just a stepping-stone to SD?

Firstly, as suggested by the title in note 4, SD supposes that 'sustainability' has been defined clearly, after which, 'sustainable growth' will need to be defined; only then can we define SD. Clearly, we did not think it worth our while. The examination of a number of corporate environmental reports only confirms our impression that SD is a declaration of intent, a kind of moral commitment, perhaps a rallying motto for employees, or, sometimes, just a marketing or publicity device, geared towards reassuring a certain category of stakeholders. Nowhere did we see any operational definition of what SD means, how it is to be measured, and how it is to be applied in decision making. It is more like a philosophical framework that signals to stakeholders: 'We are mindful of three things, economic performance, environmental protection and social justice'. In the case study of Chapter 3, the investment fund 'Ethos' used exactly such criteria to discriminate among financially viable firms. If this is all that SD means, then this book might appear to have focused on one of the three dimensions of SD: environmental care. Such a view, however, assumes independence of the three dimensions when in fact they are potentially interdependent. The answer to the question 'EM or SD?' will depend on it.

Clearly, this book is about investigating the links between economic (indeed financial) performance and environmental impacts, thus encompassing at least two of the dimensions of SD. We saw the links can sometimes be positive, sometimes negative, but the links were investigated. Through stakeholder analysis, and the importance of future liabilities, the links between economic performance and social impacts were also investigated. Indeed, the links between the social and the environmental dimensions, through stakeholder involvement for the environment, were shown to generate the feedback effects linking economic performance to environmental care by the firm. This book can be seen to have dealt with all three dimensions of SD, a conclusion totally at odds with the one in the preceding paragraph. We leave the reader free to choose his or her preferred interpretation, though we obviously would like to defend this last one. Nevertheless, it may be thought, EM is not SD. If this is so, what more would be needed to achieve SD on top of EM?

Luckily, we do not believe we need a precise definition of SD; suffice it to acknowledge the mutual interactions between its three dimensions and extend them to their dynamics. That is, economic growth (increased market share, net capitalization, and so on) cannot be allowed to happen at the expense of (uncompensated) environmental degradation and social externalities (health, job security, discrimination, inequality, and such like). Even from this perspective, this book suggests four strategies by which firms may gradually be enticed to jointly account for the three dimensions of SD and improve them over time:

1. harness the market mechanism (for goods and services) and make it work efficiently;
2. harness financial markets and make them work efficiently;
3. harness risk-management tools and make them work efficiently.

The fourth strategy is subservient to these three:

4. generate and use an efficient information system for ecological and environmentally induced financial impacts.

The first two conditions are not an apology for any kind of *laissez-faire* liberalism. Some *laissez-faire* liberals can demonstrate ignorance of economics and of the conditions under which markets can function efficiently. These conditions are hard to achieve; and they are impossible to achieve without strong, but appropriate, government regulation. However, government has its own shortcomings, and in the rapidly expanding field of environmental economics, it is now widely recognized that markets fail as often as governments, and vice versa. The solution lies in designing 'appropriate', tailor-made institutional mechanisms so that market failure and government failure can, if not neutralize each other, at least mitigate their respective weaknesses.[5] Efficiency in this context is meant to mean economic efficiency, where resources are used at their maximum social value. As previously stated, democracy appears as a necessary precondition for such efficiency to materialize. The third condition refers both to institutional devices, like the hybrid insurance mechanisms of Chapter 7, and to risk management techniques, such as those based on dynamic stochastic models of future events. Efficiency here refers to risk minimization. As for the fourth condition, it refers to monitoring, accounting and reporting systems that generate, with minimal delay[6], all the relevant information for environmental decision making. If these four conditions could be met, the three aspects of SD should be fully catered for.

Of course, they cannot be perfectly so; but then, in an imperfect world, continuous improvements should be good enough.

NOTES

1. In his book *Exit, Voice and Loyalty*, A.O. Hirschman (1970, Cambridge, Mass: Harvard University Press) refers to the ability of consumers to defect from a firm's products and prefer that of a competitor, or substitute products (exit), their ability to protest and, for instance, boycott a firm's products (voice), or their ability to bend the firm's business practices by offering conditional 'loyalty' and remain the firm's clients and customers even through hard times; that is, all else approximately equal, to prefer this firm to its competitors. In short, Hirschman refers to the dynamics of consumer pressure.

2. This is one reason why it is absolutely essential that the modern techniques of stochastic dynamic forecasting be put to use, and all contingent liabilities, even if they might seem unlikely to materialize, be included in core financial statements. This requires both legislative and political courage and technical effort, but, given modern technology, is now easily within reach. We believe it would be one of the most important factors in internalizing environmental externalities created by business activities.

3. H. Kierkegaard, *Improving Accounting Reliability: Solvency, Insolvency and Future Cash Flows*, 1997, Quorum Books, (initial title, translated from Danish: *Dynamic Accounting*, 1989).

4. See, for example, D. Pannell and S. Schilizzi (1999): 'Sustainable agriculture: a question of ecology, economics, ethics or expedience?' *Journal of Sustainable Agriculture*, 13 (4): 57–66.

5. Another rapidly growing field in economics is that of 'incentive-mechanism design', the theoretical underpinnings of which lie in dynamic game theory. We believe IMD will be a key element of efficient policy design in the future, wherever private and public interests need to be coordinated.

6. Kierkegaard (see note 3) proposes an accounting system that could ideally provide such information in real time; that is, as events happen, as liabilities are created, and so on. Efficiency, here, refers to relevance and minimum time delay.

REFERENCES

Hirschman, A.O. (1970), *Exit, Voice and Loyalty*, Cambridge, MA: Harvard University Press.

Kierkegaard, H. (1987), *Improving Accounting Reliability: Solvency, Insolvency and Future Cash Flows*, Quorum Books, initial title (translated from Danish) *Dynamic Accounting*, 1989.

Pannell, D. and Schilizzi, S. (1999), 'Sustainable agriculture: a question of ecology, economics, ethics or expedience?' *Journal of Sustainable Agriculture*, 13 (4): 57–66.

Index

ABI *see* Association of British Insurers
absentee ownership 6
accountability relationships 99–100
accountables 100
accountants
    accountability relationship 99–100
    environmental reporting 157–9
accountees
    accountability relationship 99
    appearance of new 100–3, 159–60
accounting *see* corporate environmental
    accounting
Accounting Standards boards 158
accountors 99
Acid Rain Program 27–8
act-utilitarianism 54
activities, ecological impacts of
    116–20
activity-based accounting 105
adverse selection 254, 257–8
advertising
    EMSs 355
    environmental 348–50
    misleading 344
AES Corporation 68
agency theory, accountability 100
agents, accountors 100
aggregation
    ecological accounting 118–20
    social preference ordering 52
Agreement on Technical Barriers to
    Trade (TBT) 345
Air Quality Management Districts
    (AQMD) 28–9
Alcoa 38, 135, 140, 141
Allowance Tracking System 28
anthropocentrism 50–1
AQMD *see* Air Quality Management
    Districts

Arrow, Kenneth 52
Asian countries, certification 324, 366
assessability, information 165, 166
asset markets, financial 343–4
Association of British Insurers (ABI)
    275
Association of Certified Chartered
    Accountants (ACCA) 170, 171–4
Assurpol 273–4
asymmetric information, environmental
    reporting 154, 156
atmospheric emissions, environmental
    accounting 137–8
ATOFINA 31
attitudes, ethical 71–2
auditing
    corporate benefits of 184–6
    ISO 14000 norms 297
audits 159
Avebe Chemicals 81
awards, environmental reports 170,
    171–5

Bail Dulra Teoranta 242
balance sheets, environmental
    accounting 104, 108
banking activities, environment 229–32
Barclays Bank plc 244–7
Barclays' Environmental Risk
    Management Unit 245
Beech Nut Nutrition Corporation 68
benefit curves, demand and supply of
    information 155–6
benefits
    auditing and certification 184–6
    environmental accounting 96–7
    environmental investments 217–18
    environmentally related 110, 113
    reducing environmental impacts 20

see also hidden benefits; positive
    externalities
biblical heritage 48
Blue Angel scheme 352-3
bonds, ratings of 207
BP-Amoco Group 31
British Standards Institution (BSI) 292
broad captives 267
business, environmental ethics 44-84
Business Charter for Sustainable
    Development 329

capital costs, managing environmental
    risks 35
capital depreciation, accounting 223-6
capital goods 201
captive insurance companies 34, 221
    characteristics 267-9
    compared to self-insurance and
        conventional insurance 269-70
    as valuable alternatives 270-3
catastrophes, environmental 250-1
categorical imperative, deontologism 53
causality, environmental damage 255
CERCLA 56, 109, 258, 259, 278
CERES principles 357, 358-9
certainty equivalent 205
certification
    corporate benefits of 184-6
    EMAS system 317
    EMSs 320-6
    ST Microelectronics 327-36
Clear Air Act (US) 27
Coase, R. 255
coinsurance 273-5
colonialism, business ethics 47
communication
    eco-advertising 348-9
    EMSs 311
comparability, information quality
    166-7
compensation, externalities as demand
    for 152-3
competence, information quality 166
completeness, information quality 166
compliance, environmental norms 322
compliance insurance schemes 310
Comprehensive Environmental
    Response, Compensation and
    Liability Act *see* CERCLA

Confederation of Business Industries
    (CBI) 357
conflicts of interest 7-8
consumer sovereignty 51-2
consumers
    advantages of certification 321
    disclosure rate 164
    environmental concerns 36-7
    environmental quality, goods 339,
        366-7
consumption goods 201
contingent liabilities 128
continual improvement cycle 299, 300,
    303, 329
continuity, information quality 166
conventional insurance
    and its variants 273-7
    versus captives 269-70
core values
    corporate environmental ethics 66-7
    Volvo 370
corporate culture 66-7
    Volvo 370
corporate environmental accounting 2
    accountees, appearance of new 100-3
    benefits and costs 96-7
    case studies 134-42
        energy consumption 135-7
        atmospheric emissions 137-8
        water use and materials 139-40
        costs, risks and financial aspects,
            EM 141
    conclusions 133-4
    crisis of traditional accounting 97-100
    definition, scope and purpose 95-6
    eco-financial integration 123-6
    ecological accounting 114-22
    environmentally related financial
        impacts 106-13
    future of 126-32
        strategic accounting 130-2
        using shareholder and stakeholder
            value concepts 129-30
        valuing environmental liabilities
            126-8
    stewardship function 156-7
    summary 94
    three stages of 103-6
corporate environmental ethics
    case study, ethical investments 77-84

conclusion 76-7
economics 56-63
ethical values, stakeholders 64-5
firms' core values 66-7
globalization and cross-cultural issues
    65-6
implementing 67-73
    compliance or proactive initiative
        70-2
    ethical dilemmas 68-70
    values, hierarchy and initiative
        72-3
investments 73-6
perception of 38
corporate environmental reporting
accountants, demand and supply
    relationship 157-9
accountees, appearance of new
    159-60
auditing, benefits of 184-6
case studies
    Wirralie Gold Mine Pty Ltd 188-9
    WMC Ltd 190-4
    WMC/Volvo comparison 194-5
certification, benefits of 184-6
conclusion 186-7
demand and supply 151
disclosure
    determinants of 162-3
    globalization 164-5
    information entitlements and rights
        161-2
    optimal disclosure 163-4
    role of government authorities 164
    value of information 160-1
economic rationale for 154-7
externalities as a source of demand
    152-4
information quality
    defined 165-7
    optimal, not maximum 167-8
summary 150
towards a common framework 176-84
see also environmental reports
corporate finance, EM 199-247
case studies
    Barclays Bank plc 244-7
    Triodos bank 241-3
conclusion 240
environment in 200-1

investment appraisal and project
    management 201-13
investment projects 213-28
stock markets and financial activities
    229-39
summary 199
corporate governance, conflicts in
    56-63
corporate loans 229-32
corporate management, environment in
    1-13
corrective action, EMSs 312-13
cost curves, demand and supply of
    information 155-6
costs
    environmental accounting 96-7
    environmental impacts 19-20
    environmental investments
        allocating 107-8
        reductions and increases 218-19
    information disclosure 160-1
    reduction, through EM 23, 32, 35,
        378-9
    see also environmental costs; indirect
        costs
covariance, between risks 253-4
credence attributes 291
credence goods 342
credibility 185
Crédit Suisse 34, 105, 174-5, 239, 244,
    246, 247
cultural issues, environmental ethics
    65-6

declining-balance method 225
deep ecology movement 50
demand, for environmental quality
    365-7
demand and supply, environmental
    reporting 151, 155-6
    accountants as instrumental
        stakeholders 157-9
Deming, W. Edwards 290
Deming cycle 299
deontologism *see* duty-based ethics
depreciation, accounting for 223-6
Deutsche Bank 239, 244, 247
direct environmental costs 110
direct environmental marketing 343
direct stakeholders 21-2

disasters, environmental 34, 117–18, 250–1
disclosure *see* corporate environmental reporting
disclosure rules, accounting profession 98–9
distribution, LCA 364
division of labour 288, 290
document control, EMSs 311
Domini 400 Social Index 234, 235–6, 238
Domini Social Equity Fund 234, 235, 236–7, 238
Dow Jones Sustainability Group Index (DJSGI) 237–8
Dreyfus Premier Third Century Fund 234, 237
Dupont 135, 137, 138
duty-based ethics 51, 53–4, 77

EAP *see* Environmental Accounting Programme
earthquakes 250–1
eco-advertising 348–50
eco-balances 105
    ecological impacts of activities 116–20
    energy accounting 114–16
eco-dumping 66
eco-efficiency indicators 123–4, 177
eco-financial integration 123–6
Eco-Management and Audit Scheme (EMAS) 292–3
    comparison with ISO 14001 315–19
    environmental policy statements 304
    importance of verification and registration 320–2
eco-marketing
    case study, environmental quality and management 368–72
    conclusion 367–8
    environmental quality
        demand for 365–7
        signalling 341–8
    introduction 339–41
    labelling *see* environmental labelling
    Life Cycle Assessment 359–63
    summary 338
    techniques
        advertising 348–50

environmental claims 350–1
organization marketing 355–9
self-declarations 350
third-party certified labelling 351–5
ecocentrism 50–1
ecolabels 351–5
ecological accounting 112–13, 114–22
ecological function efficiency 124
ecological payback period 124
ecological product efficiency 124
ecological rate of return 124
economic risk 252
economic value added 124, 182–3
economics
    corporate environmental ethics 56–63
    corporate environmental reporting 154–7
    disclosure 160–5
    environmental management 4, 383–5
    information quality 165–8
Economics of Welfare, The 20
ecosystem integrity, environmental ethics 50
EDF *see* Environmental Defence Fund
EEI *see* expected environmental impact
efficiency, ecological 123–4
EIA *see* environmental impact added
EM *see* environmental management
EMAS *see* Eco-Management and Audit Scheme
emergency preparedness and response 311
Emission Reduction Credits (ERCs) 29, 30
emission trading
    international 31–2
    United States 27–30
emissions, environmental accounting 137–8
EMSs *see* environmental management systems
end of pipe investments 214
energy accounting 112–13, 114–16, 117
energy consumption, environmental accounting 135–7
energy management 32–3
energy producers, environmental reporting 178
entrepreneurs, ethical 73

environment
  banking activities 229-32
  in corporate finance 200-1
  in corporate management 1-13
  financial intermediaries 229
  and firms 17-23
  investments and stock markets 232-9
Environmental Accounting Programme
    (EAP) 126
environmental accounts 107
environmental charters 304, 356-7
environmental claims 350-1
environmental concerns
  consumers 36-7
  ethical 48-51
  social stratification 47
environmental costs 110-12, 113
  environmental reports 141
environmental decalogue 329, 333-6
Environmental Defence Fund (EDF) 31
environmental ethics
  foundations of 51-5
  historical overview 46-8
  social expectations 55-6
  two basic concerns for 48-51
  see also corporate environmental
      ethics
environmental impact added 123, 124
environmental impact agent 182-3
environmental impact points 119-20,
    125
environmental impacts
  in accounting 105, 128
  perception of 18-19
Environmental Impairment Liability
    274-5
environmental investments 73-6
  allocating financial costs 107-8
  appraisal
    and eco-financial integration 124-6
    and project management 201-13
  case study, Ethos 77-84
  general considerations 213-17
  practical assessment 226-8
  stock markets 232-9
  Swiss Re 282
  value drivers of 217-26
environmental labelling
  economic principles 343-8
  ISO 14000 norms 296-7

  third party certified 351-5
environmental liabilities
  in accounting 104, 108-9, 111
  growing importance of 134
  shareholder value 129
  valuing 126-8
environmental management
  an emerging field 3-5
  benefits to stakeholders 15-41
  corporate finance *see* corporate
      finance
  economic insights 383-5
  environmental quality, case study
      368-71
  new directions in 381-2
  stakeholder approach 5-9
  or sustainable development 385-8
  Swiss Re 282
  universal acceptance and
      implementation 377-81
environmental management systems
    (EMSs)
  advertising 355
  case study 327-36
  certification
    general considerations 320
    ISO 14001 and EMAS 320-2
    ISO 14001 and globalization 323-6
  conclusion 326-7
  emergence of norms and standards
      288-98
  firms with 40
  introduction 287-8
  ISO 14001 norms 298-319
  shareholder value 35
  summary 286
  WMC Ltd 191
environmental performance
  environmental quality, goods 287
  evaluation 312-13, 315
  increasing economic and 58
  objectives and targets 308-9
  pressure to improve 169
  Volvo production units 370
environmental performance indicators
    123-4
  Swiss Re 283
environmental policies
  Barclays Bank 246
  checking and corrective action 312-13

defining 302-6
implementation and operation 309-11
management reviews 313
planning 307-9
ST Microelectronics 329
environmental policy statements
EMAS system 304
environmental objectives 302-3
ST Microelectronics 331-3
environmental protection agencies,
advantages of certification 321
Environmental Protection Agency (EPA)
27, 28, 360
environmental quality
demand for 365-7
and environmental management, case
study 368-72
of goods 291
consumer sensitivity to 339, 366-7
environmental performance 287
signalling 341-8
Environmental Reporting Awards
Scheme (ERAS) 170, 171-4
environmental reports
costs, risks and financial aspects of
EM 141
evaluating 170-5
information quality 167
organization marketing 355-6
use of 168-70
environmental resources, directly
managing 26-33
environmental risks
Barclays' lending practice 245
characteristics of 255-9
environmental reports 141
loans 230-1, 231-2
managing 34-6
insurance *see* insurance
introduction 250-2
summary 249
reduction, environmental investments
219-23
environmental services, supply of 382
environmental strategy and international
quality programme (ES-IQP) 330
environmental technologies, production
of 382
environmentally sensitive information,
withholding 163-4

EPA *see* Environmental Protection
Agency
equity concern, environmental ethics
49-50
equity residual method 212
ERCs *see* Emission Reduction Credits
ERR *see* ecological rate of return
ethical dilemmas 68-70
ethical entrepreneur 73
ethical incentives 61-2
ethical investment funds 75, 233-9
ethics of economics 60-3
see also environmental ethics
Ethos 75, 77-84, 386
EVA *see* economic value added
evaluation
environmental performance 312-13,
315
environmental quality of products 363
environmental reports 170-5
exhortation, disclosure 164
expected environmental impact (EEI)
182
experience attributes 291
experience goods 341-2
external stakeholders 21-2
externalities 20-1
environmental reporting 152-4
sites of economic activity 251
Exxon Valdez 152, 256

FASB *see* Financial Accounting
Standards Board
Federal SO_2 Allowance Trading
Programme 27-8
Federal Trade Commission (US) 344,
349, 350
feedback channels, industry 187
financial accounting 103, 108
Financial Accounting Standards Board
(FASB) 101, 158
financial community, insurance products
34-5
financial intermediaries 229
financial reinsurance 265-6
finite insurance 277
firms
advantages of certification 321
EM, less developed countries 380-1
with EMSs 40

and the environment 17–23
environmental policies *see*
    environmental policies
indirect costs and benefits, EM 36–9
managing environmental risks 34–6
stakeholder categories 26
stakeholder relationships 24–5
see also corporate environmental
    accounting; corporate
    environmental ethics; corporate
    environmental reporting; larger
    firms; managerial firm; small
    and medium-sized enterprises
fixed capital, environmental
    management 35
flow-efficiency indicators 123–4
FM Global 276
free cash flows 202
free rider emissions 29
freedom of choice, ethical standards 63
Friedman, Milton 97, 99
Friends Provident Stewardship 234, 238
full-cost accounting (FCA) 112
functional aggregation 119

game theory, economics and ethics 63
German Blauer Engel 352–3
global accounting services 100
globalization
    corporate environmental ethics 65–6
    and disclosure 164–5
    and ISO 14001 norms 323–6
going concern hypothesis 127–8
government
    environmental reporting 164
    influence on planning horizons 65
green unit trusts 234
greenhouse gas accounting 119
guidelines, LCA 361

hidden benefits, environmental
    management 37–8, 379–80
high technology firms, ethical
    investments 238–9
honesty, information quality 166
hotels, energy accounting 115
hypothetical imperative, deontologism
    53

identity crisis, accounting 98

impact evaluation matrix 361–2
improvements, environmental
    performance 169
incentives
    disclosure 164
    ethical 61–2
    to decrease risk 257
indexes, ethical investments 235–6,
    237–8
indirect benefits, EM 37–9
indirect costs, EM 36–7
indirect environmental marketing 343
industrial activity, environmental
    impacts 18–19
industrial ecology model 176–8
Industrial Products Inc. 58
Industrial Revolution, business ethics 48
industry 'feedback channels' 187
information
    disclosure
        costs of 160–1
        determinants of 162–3
    provision, costs and benefits 155–6
    quality
        defined 165–7
        optimal not maximum 167–8
    stakeholders' entitlements and rights
        to 161–2
    value of 160–1
    withholding environmentally sensitive
        163–4
information technology, accounting 100
information-overload strategy 168
informationally efficient markets 343–4
INFORMS 170
initial environmental reviews 307
instrumental stakeholders, accountants
    157–9
insurance, and environmental risks 34
    background 252–3
    captive insurance companies 267–73
    case studies
        RENFLEX disaster 278–80
        Swiss Re 281–3
    characteristics of environmental risks
        255–9
    conclusions 277–8
    conditions of insurability 253–5
    conventional insurance 273–7
    financial community 34–5

limitations for management 259–62
range of instruments 262–4
total risk retention 264–7
insurance pooling 34, 273–5, 282
internal audits 185
internal rate of return (IRR) 201,
 208–11, 215, 216–17, 220
internalization, ethical standards 61–2,
 63
international standards 292, 293, 323
International Standards Organization *see*
 ISO
intertemporal externalities
 environmental reporting 153–4
 equity concern 50
investments *see* environmental
 investments
IRR *see* internal rate of return
ISO 122, 186, 292, 360
ISO 9000 norms 292
ISO 9001 norms 314
ISO 9002 norms 314
ISO 9003 norms 314
ISO 14000 norms 56, 294, 295–7
ISO 14001 norms 292
 certification 320–2, 366
 comparison with EMAS 315–19
 environmental performance evaluation
  315
 environmental policies
  checking and corrective action
   312–13
  defining 302–6
  implementation and operation
   309–11
  management review 313
  planning 307–9
 globalization 323–6
 ISO 9001–9002–9003 standards
  313–14
 overview 298–302
 ST Microelectronics 327–36
ISO 14020 norms 346, 350
ISO 14021 norms 350–1
ISO 14024 norms 353, 354
ISO 14031–14032 standards 315
ISO 14050 norms 294
ISO 19011 norms 314

Johnson & Johnson 69

joint and several liability 258
junk bonds 207

Kantism 53, 59
Kwinana Industrial Region 62
Kyoto agreement 31

labelling
 genetically modified foods 185
 see also environmental labelling
larger firms, EM 377–8
LCA *see* life-cycle assessment
Le Monde 122
less developed countries, EM in 380–1
lexicographic preferences 52
liability
 environmental risks 255, 258–9
 see also environmental liabilities
liability insurance 255
life-cycle assessment 104
 accounting 121–2
 eco-marketing 340
 from cradle to grave 359–63
 implications for operations
  management 363–4
Lisbon earthquake 250–1
loans, corporate 229–32

3M-3E programme 33
management reviews, EMSs 313
managerial firm, concept of 6–7
manipulation, information quality 167–8
Manufacturers Mutual Fire Insurance
 Company 275
marketable emission permits 27–30, 183
marketing
 environmental reports 170
 see also eco-marketing
Marshall, Alfred 20
Marx, Karl 60
Master Environmental Account (MEA)
 178–84
materials depletion, environmental
 accounting 139–40
MEA *see* Master Environmental
 Account
measurement
 environmental accounting 133
 environmental costs 20
 environmental performance 312–13

Migros 106, 136, 139, 140
Mill, John Stuart 60
mine-site rehabilitation 61, 74, 104, 177
Minnesota Mining and Manufacturing 33
misleading advertising 344
Mobius loop seal 351
money-market funds 233
Monte-Carlo technique 219
moral dimensions, economics 60-1
moral hazard 254, 257
mutual funds 233
mutual insurance companies 275-6

negative externalities 21
    environmental reporting 152
net present value (NPV) 201, 202-8,
    215-17, 219-20
New Environmental Business Ethics
    62-3
nitrogen oxides, emission permits 27, 29
non-economic values, environmental
    assets 50
Normandy Ltd 188
NPV *see* net present value

objectives
    environmental performance 308-9
    environmental policy statements
        302-3
OECD countries, certification 323
Oil Insurance Ltd 276
Ontario Hydro 112
operational control, EMSs 310-11
operations management, LCA 363-4
optimal disclosure 163-4, 186-8
Organic Food Products Act (US) 354
Organic Milk Suppliers Cooperative 242
organization marketing 348, 355-9
over-compliance, environmental norms
    322
ozone depletion potential 119

P2 investments 214-15, 217-19, 220,
    227-8
Pacioli, Luca 98
Pax World Fund 234
payout time (POT) techniques 201, 211
pension funds 233
perception, of firms' ethics 38
Pigou, Arthur 20

plan-do-check cycle 299
planning horizons, government's
    influence on 65
pollutants, ecological accounting 119,
    120
pollution
    awareness of problem 19, 47
    emission trading 27-30
    externalities 21
positive externalities 20-1
    environmental management 38
    environmental reporting 152
precautionary principle 54, 55
precision, information quality 166
prices, ERCs 30
principals, accountees 100
Principles of Economics 20
private information, environmental
    reporting 156
probabilistic studies, risks 256-7
Process and Production Methods (PPMs)
    345
process retrofitting investments 215
production, LCA 364
productivity of labour 288
products
    assessment of ecological qualities
        103-4
    ecological impacts of 121
profits, expressing 201-2
Protestant ethic 48
public, disclosure rate 164
public externalities, environmental
    reporting 153-4
public good, corporate environmental
    management 76-7
pure captives 267
put option 259-60

quality
    emergence of standards 288-98
    see also Air Quality Management
        Districts; environmental quality;
        information quality; Total
        Quality Environment
        Management
quality management methods 290
Quebec Hydro 178

rating agencies 207

reality, accounting systems 101–2
RECLAIM Trading Credits (RTCs) 29
recyclable content 351
recycling, environmental accounting
    139–40
Regional Clean Air Incentives Market 29
regulations
    disclosure 164
    environmental accounting 142
    environmental quality, goods 344–5
    insurance 278
reinsurance 251, 265–6, 281–3
reliability, information quality 166
religions, pre-Christian, business ethics
    48
religious-based values, environmental
    assets 52
RENFLEX disaster 256, 278–80
reporting *see* corporate environmental
    reporting
reputation, of firms 349
reputation risk 221
resources *see* environmental resources
responsibility
    environmental 101
    environmental damage 255
    environmental impacts 19
    retroactive 56
responsibility without fault 56
retroactive liability 56, 118, 258
rights, to information 161–2
risk premium 205–6
risk retention, total 264–7
riskless interest rate 205–6
risks *see* environmental risks
Rousseau, Jean-Jacques 250–1
RTCs *see* RECLAIM Trading Credits
rule-utilitarianism 54–5

Saint Exupéry 49
San Francisco earthquake 251
Scientific Management 288
scope, information quality 165
search goods 341
segregation, of risks 254, 257–8
self insurance 264–5
    versus captives 269–70
self-declarations 350
SETAC *see* Society for Environmental
    Toxicology and Chemistry

shareholder value 6, 35, 129–30, 187
shareholders' opportunity cost of capital
    (SOCC) 206, 212, 213
Shell
    core values and corporate culture 67
    environmental accounting 118, 135,
        137, 139, 140, 141
    ethical incentives 61–2
Shewart, Walter 289–90
Shipdrove Organic Farm 242
SIPs *see* State Implementation Plans
small and medium-sized enterprises
    environmental management 378,
        380–1
    environmental reporting 187
Smith, Adam 6–7, 52, 60, 288
social accountability, corporations 97, 99
social ethics, internalization of 61–2
social expectations, environmental ethics
    55–6, 76
social preferences, utilitarian ethics 52
social stratification, environmental
    concerns 47
Society for Environmental Toxicology
    and Chemistry (SETAC) 359–60
solvency, environmental liabilities 128
Sony group 305, 306
South Coast Air Quality Management
    District 29
species extinction 18–19
spectrum of ethicality 69
ST Microelectronics 303, 327–9
    environmental decalogue 333–6
    environmental management system
        329–30
    environmental policy statement 331–3
stakeholder approach, environmental
    management 5–9
stakeholder value, in accounting 129–30
stakeholders
    access to environmental reports 169
    accountability relationship 101
    accountants as instrumental 157–9
    advantages of certification 320–1
    audits 159
    determinants of information disclosure
        162–3
    ethical and unethical actions with
        68–70
    ethical values 64–5

evidence of commitment to environmental performance 287
external 21-2
firm's categories 26
firm's relationships 24-5
information entitlements and rights 161-2
interaction with firms 17-18
standard accounting, versus strategic accounting 131, 132
Standard Oil 288
standardization
business management 288
LCA 122
Standardized Eco-efficiency Indicators 177
standards
environmental reports 170
LCA 361
see also ISO
State Implementation Plans (SIPs) 27
state monopolies, information qualities 167
stewardship function, environmental reporting 156-7
stock market 232-9
straight-line method 224-5
strategic accounting 130-2
strategic information, rights to 161
strategic issues, environmental performance 308
strict liability 258
sub-matrices, MEA 179
sulphur dioxide, emission trading 27-8, 29
sum-of-the-years' digits method 225
Summa de Arithmetica, Geometria, Proportioni e Proportionalità 98
superfund 259, 278
supply chain, LCA 364
sustainable development 385-8
ST Microelectronics vision 333-6
Swiss Re
environmental accounting 106, 136-7, 138, 140
environmental management concerns 35, 239
insurance, environmental risks 273-4, 281-3
synergic strategic planning 214

tactical issues, environmental performance 308
targets, environmental performance 308-9
Tax Reform Act 1984 (US) 268
Taylor, Frederick 288-9
technologies, environmental risks 257
Theory of Moral Sentiments, The 60
third party certified labelling 345, 346-7, 351-5
third party eco-marketing 348
tort liability 254
total quality, concept 290
Total Quality Environmental Management (TQEM) 314
ST Microelectronics 327-36
Total Quality Management (TQM) 291-2
total risk retention 264-7
tradable emission permits 27-30, 183
trade standards, international 323
trading and profit and loss accounts 104, 108
traditional accounting, crisis of 97-100
training, EMSs 310
transparency, information quality 166
transport chain, LCA 364
Triodos Bank 241-3
Triodos Greenfund 243
two-stage value systems 54-5
Tylenol 69
Type I-labelling 345, 346-7, 351-5
Type II-labelling 347, 350
Type III-labelling 347

UCITS (Undertakings for Collective Investments in Transferable Securities) 233
uncorrelated risks 253-4
Underground Storage Tanks (USTs) 259
Union Bank of Switzerland (UBS) 105, 244, 247
Union of National Industry Confederations in Europe (UNIC) 357
unit trusts 233
United States, emission trading system 27-30
universalism 53
utilitarian ethics 51-3

utilitarianism 51, 59, 77

valuation gap, companies 126-7
value drivers, environmental investments
    217-26
values
    environmental assets 50, 52
    firms' ethical 72-3
    stakeholders' ethical 64-5
    see also stakeholder value
variance reduction 253
Veblen, Thorstein 6
verification, EMAS system 317
virtue ethics 58-9
voluntary compliance, environmental
    norms 322, 346
Volvo 368-9
    environmental accounting 105, 106,
        136, 137, 138, 139, 141
    environmental management 369-72
    environmental reporting, comparison
        with WMC 194-5
    reputation 349

waste disposal, duty-based ethics 53-4
waste generation, environmental
    accounting 139-40
water use, environmental accounting
    139
Wealth of Nations 6-7, 60, 288
wealthier communities, EM 377-8
Weber, Max 48
weighted average cost of capital
    (WACC) 208, 212, 213
welfare, environmental impacts 49
welfare theory 52
Wind Fund 243
window dressing, accounting 98
Wirralie Gold Mine Pty Lt 135, 188-9
WMC Ltd
    environmental accounting 104, 105,
        135-6, 139, 140, 141, 142
    environmental reporting 190-5
World Business Council for Sustainable
    Development 329, 356-7

X-efficiency of firms 123